SAS BAND OF BROTHERS

ALSO BY DAMIEN LEWIS

World War Two:

War Dog
Judy: A Dog in a Million
Churchill's Secret Warriors
The Nazi Hunters
Hunting Hitler's Nukes
SAS Ghost Patrol
Smoky the Brave
SAS Italian Job
SAS Great Escapes
SAS Shadow Raiders

Modern Day Elite Forces:

Operation Certain Death
Bloody Heroes
Cobra 405
Zero Six Bravo
Operation Relentless

Co-authored by Damien Lewis:

Sergeant Rex
It's All About Treo
Fire Strike 7/9
A Dog Called Hope
Operation Mayhem
X Platoon
Homeland

Damien Lewis

SAS

BAND OF BROTHERS

THE LAST STAND OF THE SAS AND THEIR HUNT FOR THE NAZI KILLERS

Quercus

First published in Great Britain in 2020 by Quercus.
This paperback edition published in 2021 by

Quercus Editions Ltd
Carmelite House
50 Victoria Embankment
London EC4Y 0DZ

An Hachette UK company

Copyright © Omega Ventures 2020

The moral right of Damien Lewis to
be identified as the author of this work has been
asserted in accordance with the Copyright,
Designs and Patents Act, 1988.

All rights reserved. No part of this publication
may be reproduced or transmitted in any form
or by any means, electronic or mechanical,
including photocopy, recording, or any
information storage and retrieval system,
without permission in writing from the publisher.

A CIP catalogue record for this book is available
from the British Library
MMP ISBN 978 1 78747 525 0
Ebook ISBN 978 1 78747 526 7

Every effort has been made to contact copyright holders.
However, the publishers will be glad to rectify in future
editions any inadvertent omissions brought to their attention.

Quercus Editions Ltd hereby exclude all liability to the extent
permitted by law for any errors or omissions in this book and for any loss,
damage or expense (whether direct or indirect) suffered by a
third party relying on any information contained in this book.

PICTURE CREDITS

1, 6, 16 – Imperial War Museum/Public Domain: 2 – Public Domain: 3, 28, 34 – Mayne family
private collection: 4, 5, 8, 10, 11, 18, 20 – Dumfries Museum: 7 – Paradata/Airborne Assault Museum:
9 – National Army Museum/Public Domain: 12, 22, 26 – Sean Garstin: 13 – © Collection Adrien
et Antoinette Wiehe, Source – Lieutenant John H. Wiehe (1916–1965) – Album Illustré – STREAK
DESIGNS Ltd & CORÉTRA Ltd (2016): 14 – Alamy: 15, 25 – German Federal Archive/Public
Domain: 17, 19 – USAAF Archives/Public Domain: 21, 27 – Air Commando/Serge Vaculik: 23 – Getty
Images: 24 – Bundesarchiv, Bild 101III-Alber-096-11/Alber, Kurt/CC-BY-SA 3.0: 29, 36, 37 – National
Archives: 30, 38 – Courtesy of the family of Eric 'Bill' Barkworth: 31, 33, 39 – Phil Rhodes:
32 – Simon Kinder: 35, 40 – Chris Drakes: 41 – James Irvine

10 9 8 7 6 5 4 3 2

Typeset by CC Book Production Ltd
Printed and bound in Great Britain by Clays Ltd, Elcograf S.p.A.

MIX
Paper from
responsible sources
FSC® C104740

Papers used by Quercus Editions Ltd are from well-managed forests and other responsible sources.

For Captain Patrick Garstin, MC and the men
of the SABU-70 patrol – those who made it home again
and those who did not.

And for all those drawn into the Nacht und Nebel –
the night and fog.

The hero is commonly the simplest and obscurest of men.

Henry David Thoreau

Contents

Route flown by Stirling–
SABU-70 Mission No.2

SCOTLAND

Glasgow •
• Edinburgh

Kintyre •
• Darvel
(SAS Headquarters)

N

0   100 miles

0   200 km

ENGLAND

IRELAND

WALES

NETHERLANDS

Gloucestershire
RAF Fairford •

London ◼

Ford Airfield •

BELGIUM

English Channel

Normandy

Paris ◼

La Ferté-Alais
(Drop zone)

F R A N C E

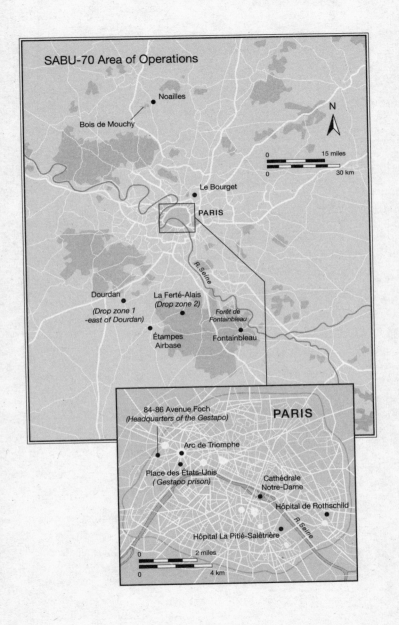

SABU-70 Area of Operations

Noailles

Bois de Mouchy

N

0   15 miles
0   30 km

Le Bourget

PARIS

R. Seine

Dourdan

(Drop zone 1
-east of Dourdan)

La Ferté-Alais
(Drop zone 2)

Forêt de
Fontainbleau

Étampes
Airbase

Fontainbleau

84-86 Avenue Foch
(Headquarters of the Gestapo)

PARIS

Arc de Triomphe

Place des États-Unis
(Gestapo prison)

Cathédrale
Notre-Dame

Hôpital de Rothschild

Hôpital La Pitié-Salêtrière

R. Seine

0   2 miles
0   4 km

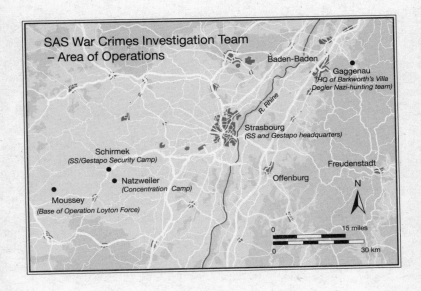

SAS War Crimes Investigation Team
– Area of Operations

Baden-Baden

Gaggenau
*(HQ of Barkworth's Villa
Degler Nazi-hunting team)*

R. Rhine

Strasbourg
(SS and Gestapo headquarters)

Schirmek
(SS/Gestapo Security Camp)

Natzweiler
(Concentration Camp)

Freudenstadt

Offenburg

N

Moussey
(Base of Operation Loyton Force)

0   15 miles

0   30 km

Author's Note

There are sadly few survivors from the Second World War operations depicted in these pages. Throughout the period of researching and writing this book I have sought to be in contact with as many as possible, plus surviving family members of those who have passed away. If there are further witnesses to the stories told here who are inclined to come forward, please do get in touch, as I will endeavour to include further recollections of the operations portrayed in this book in future editions.

The time spent by Allied servicemen and women as Special Service volunteers was often traumatic and wreathed in layers of secrecy, and many chose to take their stories to their graves. Memories tend to differ and apparently none more so than those concerning operations behind enemy lines. The written accounts that do exist tend to differ in their detail and timescale, and locations and chronologies are sometimes contradictory. Nevertheless, I have endeavoured to provide an accurate sense of place, timescale and narrative to the story as depicted in these pages.

Where various accounts of a mission appear to be particularly confused, the methodology I have used to reconstruct where, when and how events took place is the 'most likely' scenario. If two or more testimonies or sources point to a particular time or place or sequence of events, I have opted to use that account as most likely.

The above notwithstanding, any mistakes herein are entirely of my own making, and I would be happy to correct any in future editions. Likewise, while I have attempted to locate the copyright holders of the photos, sketches and other images and material used in this book, this has not always been straightforward or easy. Again, I would be happy to correct any mistakes in future editions.

Some of those individuals who took part in Operation Toby 3 may also have been part of the previous SABU-70 mission, at Dourdan and Étampes. In spite of exhaustive researches, I have been unable to verify the exact make-up of SAS Captain Garstin's stick – his patrol – during that first mission, other than those names that I have mentioned in the text. If any reader is able to shed clarity on this point, please do get in touch.

Curiously, I can find no official report or war diary entry dealing with SABU-70's first mission. Not all small-scale raids were documented, of course, and most if not all of the men on that mission were subsequently captured or killed or forced to go on the run. There are several first-hand accounts of the mission, including ones written by Vaculik, Wiehe and Jones, the key survivors. Those accounts corroborate each other on many levels. Still, I would be keen to learn more about SABU-70's first mission.

Chapter 1

Barely a week after the D-Day landings the shadowed form of the Short Stirling heavy bomber clawed into the unseasonable June skies, getting airborne under cover of darkness. Hunched over the controls in the dimly lit cockpit of this often underrated yet peculiarly graceful warplane was the pilot for tonight, Flight Sergeant Sutherland, a man who would go on to win a Distinguished Flying Cross (DFC) before the year was out, during the ill-fated airborne missions over Arnhem, on Operation Market Garden.

Sutherland and his crew were on no bombing mission this 13 June night. The first four-engine 'heavy' to see service with the RAF, the Stirling had been deemed largely obsolete by 1942, as the Avro Lancaster came into service. But this iconic warplane had gone on to acquire a second lease of life, as the foremost aircraft delivering SAS raiding parties, plus agents of the SOE – the Special Operations Executive, more commonly known as Churchill's Ministry for Ungentlemanly Warfare – deep into enemy-occupied lands.

Tonight's was a hybrid mission born of those two outfits: it was very much an SAS undertaking, but one orchestrated by the SOE, who had arranged both the drop-zone and the reception party that should be waiting on the ground.

As a lone aircraft flying low at night across hundreds of miles of hostile airspace to an – at best – uncertain rendezvous, the

Stirling had proven a remarkably tough and reliable workhorse, one able to take considerable punishment. Despite her size and weight, the aircraft had also shown herself to be surprisingly nimble and manoeuvrable when forced to shake off the Luftwaffe night-fighters, or evade the enemy's deadly radar-directed search-lights and flak. Considering the Stirling's sheer dimensions – at just short of 70 feet from nose to tail, she was a good 16 feet longer than the Lancaster, and stood higher off the ground – this was no mean achievement for such an imposing warplane.

As with all aircrew of 190 Squadron – one of the few RAF units dedicated to special forces operations – Sutherland and his fellows knew precious little about tonight's mission or the brave men they were flying into war. Codenamed 'SABU-70' – SABU being this unit's radio call-sign, and very likely an abbreviation for the SAS catchphrase 'Safe All Business As Usual' – this was the first 'stick' (patrol) of several that would follow. With each, the aircrew would know only the bare bones of the operation: timings, destination and the criteria upon which to determine if the drop should go ahead or not.

Aircrew logbooks generally recorded scant details for such 'Sunflower' flights, as the RAF codenamed these top-secret missions. Pilots were deliberately kept in the dark, for obvious reasons. If a Stirling were to be shot down and its crew captured, the enemy had ways of forcing even the toughest to talk. Any knowledge aircrew might possess of an SAS patrol's intentions could prove fatal, and what a man didn't know he couldn't tell. On the rare occasions when pilots such as Sutherland did learn more – a mission objective; the specific target details – it meant that someone had been talking out of turn. And in the summer of '44, careless talk really did cost lives.

As the Stirling swooped across the Sussex coastline, powering on towards the cliffs of France, Sutherland took the aircraft down to just a few hundred feet above sea level, the warplane's elusive silhouette flitting across the ink-black seas. During an English summer sunset can be as late as 9.30 p.m., and normally the light lingers long in the skies. The June '44 weather had proven storm-lashed and overcast, but it was still well after last light by the time Sutherland got airborne. All being well, his human cargo would be plunging into the war-torn skies in the early hours of the morrow – 14 June 1944.

There was little doubt that they would jump – every man jack of them, and no matter what the conditions might be like over the drop-zone. While they might know precious little about tonight's mission, Sutherland and his men had few illusions as to the calibre of those riding in the Stirling's hold. One glance at their distinctive berets, mysterious winged-dagger cap badges and the medal flashes many wore on their uniforms testified to the single-minded determination and courage – not to mention the long years at war – of the SAS raiding party.

All the 190 Squadron aircrews shared that same appreciation. 'These special troops are the most decorated men I have ever seen,' one pilot would remark, 'especially the officers – quite a number have the DSO and bar. There is quite a collection of "vets" in the mess these days.'

The Stirling powered onwards through the darkness, speeding SABU-70's commander, Captain Patrick Bannister Garstin, MC, and the eleven men under his command to war, the sonorous thunder of the warplane's four Bristol Hercules powerplants rever-berating through the hold, providing a steady soundtrack to the coming mission. The fact that there were *four* engines – capable of propelling the aircraft through the skies at some 270 mph – was, of course, a distinct bonus: it meant they could afford to lose one at least to enemy action, and the Stirling should still remain airworthy. Compared to what had gone before, that was a real blessing.

Prior to the Stirling making an appearance, such missions had mostly been flown by the twin-engine Armstrong Whitworth Whitley, a medium bomber more affectionately known as 'the Flying Barn Door'. Compared to the Whitley, the Stirling was almost luxurious. There were seats ranged in rows down either side, offering space for twenty-plus paratroopers – more than enough for Garstin and his men. By contrast, in the Whitley they'd been forced to squat on the icy metal of the fuselage, legs concertinaed against the far side. Fitted with seats, weapons racks and stowage bays for packs and personal gear, the Stirling felt positively made for airborne operations.

But the very best thing was the Stirling's exit point, known to all as 'the trap'. In the Whitley, the dorsal (ventral) gun turret had been replaced by a narrow steel tube not dissimilar to a dustbin. Through that horribly constricting orifice each parachutist had had to drop vertically, arms tight by his sides, risking smashing his forehead against the far side – known fatalistically as the 'Whitley kiss' or 'ringing the bell'. By contrast, the Stirling's trap – which resembled a large bathtub sunk into the floor where the bomb-bay used to be – was a positively cavernous aperture through which to jump.

As the Stirling thundered across the night-dark waters of the Channel, the interior grew positively chilly, and Captain Garstin and his men drew their distinctive jump-smocks closer, to ward off the icy cold. Somewhere there would be the rum-jar to warm bellies and stiffen spirits. It was Lieutenant John H. Wiehe's job to remember the all-important rum, and he was usually a stickler for such things. Garstin's second-in-command, Wiehe had spent four long years at war, during which time he'd soldiered his way across half the world, earning the nickname 'Lt Rex' in the process, for few could pronounce his surname properly.

One of two French-speakers on Garstin's team, Wiehe would have a crucial role on the coming mission. Hailing from Mauritius, the tropical paradise islands set in the midst of the Indian Ocean, Wiehe's family had Danish heritage – hence the surname – plus French and British colonial roots, leaving him fluent in both languages. When his Danish forebears had journeyed to Mauritius to set up home, they'd established vast sugarcane plantations, building up a considerable family fortune and founding the Labourdonnais estate, the centrepiece of which was a beautiful, colonnaded colonial-style mansion.

Mauritius had been a British colony since 1810, and come war's outbreak, Wiehe – not yet twenty-four years of age – had answered Churchill's call to arms, sailing via South Africa, arriving in Egypt on 7 January 1941, whereupon he'd signed up with the Royal Engineers and trained in the hazardous duties of bomb disposal. His war journal would record his tumultuous North African experiences: while 'bullets, bombs and shells cause death . . . or mutilate bodies . . . it doesn't take as much to mutilate minds.'

From there, via an extraordinarily tortuous route, Wiehe had made it into the SAS, and he could have wished for no better commander than Captain Pat Garstin to lead him and the others into war. Around 6 feet 2 in height, athletic of build, with swept-back, somewhat unruly dark brown hair, Garstin had a rare intensity to his coal-black gaze and striking good looks. He also had a singularly impressive combat record, plus he was possessed of more reasons than most to hunger to take the fight to the enemy.

Born in Bombay in July 1919, Garstin hailed from a long-lived military and ecclesiastical tradition. The family was descended from 'the ancient house of Garston . . . Lords of the Manor of Walton in the 13th Century', Walton then being a parish in the northeast of England. After emigrating to Ireland, the Garstins settled in County Meath, to the north of Dublin, though Patrick Garstin's father, Richard Hart Garstin, was born in Randalstown, in County Antrim. Having joined the Royal Indian Marines, Richard Hart Garstin fought in the First World War, before serving in the Royal Indian Navy during the inter-war years, during which time his son, Patrick, was born.

Richard Garstin had already won a Croix de Guerre – a French decoration for acts of heroism – in the First World War, and the entire Garstin family had been heavily involved from the earliest months of the Second. While Patrick Garstin had earned his Military Cross in spring 1940, serving with the British Expeditionary Force in Belgium, he also had two younger brothers serving in the military, and his father would go on to be awarded the CBE in August 1941, for his role in a top-secret naval operation.

That mission, Operation Countenance, was the joint Anglo-Russian seizure of Iran. A senior naval officer commanding the seaborne side of Countenance, Richard Garstin had led the assault from the waters of the Persian Gulf, striking in a swift and surprise attack. Iran was taken within days, securing her precious oilfields from Nazi Germany's predations. But a year later, Richard Garstin was lost to enemy action in horrifying circumstances.

It was October 1942, and while serving as the Vice Commodore of Ocean Convoys he had been sailing from West Africa to Britain aboard the SS *Stentor*, a merchant ship carrying a cargo of palm oil. For seven days and seven nights the forty-strong convoy was stalked by German U-boats. When U509 unleashed her torpedoes on the lead vessel, the *Stentor*, one struck on the starboard side, the massive explosion throwing up the palm oil in a horrific, fiery conflagration, rendering the entire ship and surrounding water a mass of boiling flame.

Those who could dived into the sea to save themselves. The lucky ones were hauled onto one of the escorts, the Royal Navy corvette HMS *Woodruff*. But amongst the 200-odd survivors – many of whom were terribly burned – Vice Commodore Garstin was nowhere to be found. Badly injured in the blast, he had gone down with the ship, as did both the *Stentor*'s captain and the ship's surgeon, William Chisholm. Chisholm had remained at Garstin's side to the very last, tending to his wounds, even at the risk of his own life. He would be awarded the Albert Medal posthumously.

Having lost his father so tragically, Captain Patrick Garstin was even more determined to play his part in the war. He was twenty-four years of age in the summer of 1944, and his and his wife's first child, named Patrick after his father, would very likely have his first birthday while his father was away on operations. Regardless, Captain Garstin was heading deep into enemy-occupied France with fiery havoc and mayhem in mind.

Tellingly, Captain Garstin had had to fight every inch of the way to be allowed a frontline role. Having enlisted in the Royal

Ulster Rifles (RUR) in July 1939, Garstin had first seen action in May 1940, in the battle for the medieval city of Louvain in Belgium. As Major General Bernard Montgomery had positioned his forces along the city's main railway line, Garstin – then only twenty-one, and known to all as 'Pat' – had found himself leading the defence of the city's main railway station, holding the entrance hall and Platforms 1 and 2, plus the subways.

At dusk on 14 May the Germans had attacked. For many of the defenders, this was their first experience of being on the wrong end of the fearsome MG 34 machine gun – the 'Spandau' as it would become known – a weapon with so rapid a rate of fire that the human ear was unable to distinguish between each gunshot, earning it the nickname 'Hitler's buzzsaw'. By dawn on the 15th, German forces had succeeded in penetrating the rail yard, and had taken up firing positions amongst the shattered remains of the rolling stock, but still Garstin and his platoon held firm.

Dashing from subway to subway, his small force kept popping up all over the station to unleash bursts of fire, giving the impression they were far greater in number than they really were. As bullets tore apart the glass roof above them, Garstin led from the front, repeatedly driving back the enemy, which led to headlines in the British press – 'The Battle Now Raging on Platform 1'. Up and down the railway track troops had fought with incredible bravery, often to the last round, and the battle for Louvain would earn for the Durham Light Infantry the first Victoria Cross of the ground war.

By the time Montgomery ordered a withdrawal to new defensive lines, Garstin was among several men to be decorated in the field, earning a Military Cross for the heroic stand. Full of fighting spirit, but hugely outnumbered and outgunned, British forces executed a fighting withdrawal to Dunkirk. There, during nine incredible days, 338,226 men were taken off the beaches and spirited back to Britain. But the losses were staggering. Almost 70,000 were listed as killed in action, missing or prisoners of war. Along with the hundreds of tanks and field guns left behind, 288 ships had been sunk and 372 aircraft lost to enemy action.

In Britain, the government propaganda machine cranked out the message that Dunkirk was somehow a heroic victory. Heroic it certainly had been, but it was no victory, as Winston Churchill was at pains to point out. On 4 June 1940, even as the Dunkirk evacuation came to an end, Churchill delivered a rousing speech to Parliament, lauding the rescuing of so many, 'out of the jaws of death and shame'. But he added a stinging note of caution: 'We must be very careful not to assign to this deliverance the attributes of a victory. Wars are not won by evacuation.'

As for Captain Garstin, it was all but a miracle that he had made it off the Dunkirk beaches at all. Already suffering partial deafness due to a grenade blast at Louvain, he was wounded by shrapnel while awaiting pick-up by the minesweeper, HMS *Skipjack*. Worse still, as the heavily laden warship had pulled away from the gently shelving shoreline, she was struck by a series of bombs and rapidly sank, most aboard being killed.

Garstin, though injured, managed to slip away from the sinking ship and to struggle back to land. He finally made it to Britain aboard another vessel, and by September of that year he felt recovered enough from his injuries to travel from his home in Canterbury to Buckingham Palace, to receive his Military Cross. Three months later, he found himself in East Africa attached to the 1st Battalion, the Northern Rhodesia Regiment, a unit raised in what was then Rhodesia (present-day Zimbabwe) whose ranks combined black and white soldiers under the motto *Diversi Genere Fide Pares* – Different in Race, Equal in Fidelity.

Barely weeks into that posting Garstin was admitted to a local hospital suffering from acute appendicitis. Given two months' sick leave, he instead chose to return to his unit, whereupon he was promoted to lieutenant and became embroiled in the fierce fighting of the East African campaign. Though heavily outnumbered, a mixed force raised from Britain, South Africa, India and across the African continent defeated the Italian East African Command, which combined units of the *Regio Esercito* (Royal Army), *Regia Aeronautica* (Royal Airforce) and *Regia Nautica* (Royal Navy), plus some 250,000 soldiers of the *Regio Corpo Truppe Coloniali* (Royal Corps of Colonial Troops).

This little-known campaign represented the first significant Allied victory of the war, but throughout the fighting – which in the remote African bush often assumed a guerrilla-like intensity, with wild skirmishing and hit-and-run attacks – Garstin was dogged by ill health. By June 1941, the abdominal pains were back to plague him. A medical board dispatched him to Britain, ominously for 'treatment and final disposal'.

Garstin, however, was having none of it. Deftly sidestepping that 'final disposal' order, he instead volunteered for airborne operations, earning his parachutist's wings by March the following year. Abdominal surgery and several months of convalescence followed, after which he married Susan Nicola Beresford-Jones in the autumn of 1942, before embarking for North Africa, where he was to serve with the Long Range Desert Group (LRDG), the intelligence-gathering and raiding force that pre-dated the SAS. Raids on German airfields and transport followed, before

Garstin suffered two further hospitalisations, first in Tunisia and then in Algeria.

Once again he was returned to Britain, so his injuries could be treated and to convalesce. Instead, and demonstrating a truly indomitable spirit, on 15 February 1944 Garstin volunteered for 1 SAS, a unit commanded by a fellow Irishman of towering repute, Lieutenant Colonel Robert Blair 'Paddy' Mayne. Of course, it was no exaggeration to say that Pat Garstin shouldn't have been in any position to put himself forward for special service duties: in truth, he should have been invalided out of the military some three years earlier. It was the mark of the man that he volunteered, regardless of the dangers that were to come.

Equally, it was no secret that Mayne – already the recipient of two Distinguished Service Orders (DSO and bar), plus a Mention in Dispatches – cast a favourable eye on any Irishmen applying for the ranks, regardless of whether they hailed from north or south of the border. Indeed, during the earliest days of the SAS it had been Lieutenant Eoin (pronounced 'Ian') McGonigal, a southern Irishman and a Catholic, who had argued most persuasively that there was room for a man like Mayne in the fledgling Special Air Service.

Forging a friendship long before the war, via Eoin's brother Ambrose, and at Queen's University, Belfast, McGonigal and Mayne had shared a passion for rugby, Mayne going on to play for both Ireland and the British Lions prior to the war. When hostilities were declared, McGonigal and Mayne had been the first two officers from an Irish regiment to join No. 11 Commando, in 1940, seeing fierce and bloody action in Syria in June 1941. Over the years they had truly become inseparable, until McGonigal was killed during a disastrous parachute jump over Libya, on one of the fledgling SAS's first ever missions.

Mayne was said to have been shattered by the loss of McGonigal, a man who, like himself – and Pat Garstin – had enlisted first in the Royal Ulster Rifles. Bearing in mind Garstin's distinguished war record, not to mention his experience of guerrilla-style warfare and his dogged refusal to let injury stand in his way, his application to join the SAS was welcomed by Mayne, especially since he was desperately short of experienced officers, after nearly three years of the SAS being at war.

Following a relentless series of North African and Italian missions, plus raiding operations that had spanned the length and breadth of the Mediterranean, the SAS had been pulled back to the UK for a period of recuperation and expansion, in preparation for the hardest battles of all – the D-Day landings and the liberation of Nazi-occupied Europe. A unit that had originated in North Africa in the summer of 1941 with seventy-odd recruits – 'the originals' – was to be grown into four regiments, composed of some 2,500 troops.

In theory two of those regiments – 1 and 2 SAS – were made up of the British contingent, but in reality the SAS had returned from the long months overseas with just about every conceivable nationality within its ranks. Basically, anyone possessed of the right qualities and who hungered to take the fight to the enemy had been welcome. Mayne's command, 1 SAS, was described as some kind of piratical 'foreign legion', boasting scores of Irishmen, a good dose of Russians, one or two Americans and even a smattering of Germans within its ranks. Upon their return to the UK, many of Mayne's men proved to have no record of ever having served within the British Army at all.

Two French regiments – 3 and 4 SAS – plus a Belgian parachute company were also being raised, while F Squadron of the GHQ Liaison Regiment – specialist signallers, better known as 'the Phantoms' – were being attached, to make up the shortfall in radio operators.

Widely experienced in behind-the-lines raiding and sabotage, most of the SAS old hands hadn't seen Britain for years and were little accustomed to the rigours of regimental soldiering – drill, spit and polish and the adherence to rigid military convention – which did little to win them any easy friends within the top brass. Mayne, 1 SAS's commanding officer, was foremost amongst them. All too often portrayed as a psychopathic Irishman with a famously volcanic temper, especially when he'd been drinking, Mayne was in truth far from that. Recruited into the SAS by its founder, David Stirling, Mayne had reputedly destroyed a hundred aircraft during SAS raiding operations, immobilising one by ripping out the control panels 'with his bare hands, when he had run out of bombs'. At times executing more than a dozen raids per week, Mayne was said on one occasion to have calmly approached 'a German officer's mess and "liquidated" it', thus fuelling his reputation as a cold, calculating killer.

Certainly, the citations for Mayne's decorations reflected an utterly driven personality, a man who led from the front. In February 1942, his first DSO recorded: 'this officer was instrumental ... in destroying, with a small party of men, many aeroplanes, a bomb dump and a petrol dump. He led this raid in person and himself destroyed and killed many of the enemy.' Mayne's citation for his second DSO, for the October 1943 Sicily landings, stressed his 'courage, determination and superb leadership . . . He personally led his men from the landing craft in the face of heavy machine gun fire.'

With David Stirling's capture by Erwin Rommel's forces, in January 1943, Mayne had taken over command of 1 SAS, shaping and nurturing the unit through to its return to the UK. During that time he'd proved himself to be of a paradoxically shy and retiring nature, a soldier-poet who cared passionately for those under his command. Since its publication in 1944, Mayne had carried on his person a poetry anthology entitled *Other Men's Flowers*, compiled by Field Marshal Lord Wavell, formerly Commander-in-Chief Middle East, whose remit had included the North African campaign.

'He wasn't the hard-drinking, fearless, mad Irishman of popular myth,' Mike Sadler, one of the SAS originals, would remark of Mayne. 'He was intelligent, sensitive and warm underneath.' A former Irish and British Lions rugby international and the Irish Universities heavyweight boxing champion, Mayne would fight doggedly to safeguard the unique ethos and *esprit de corps* of 'his' regiment. That was not to be diluted in any way, which seemed to threaten to be the case, as the SAS contemplated D-Day operations.

Formerly a freewheeling outfit answerable largely to itself, the SAS had been shoehorned into 1 Airborne Corps upon its return to Britain. Brigadier Roderick McLeod, formerly of the Royal Artillery, was placed in overall command of the SAS. As McLeod himself was the first to admit, he was a peculiar choice for such a role. His military career had hitherto consisted mostly of 'hunting, polo, pigsticking . . . followed by staff college', and his initial view of the men who had fallen under his command was of a band of 'colourful and curiously dressed ruffians'.

While the placing of the SAS under 1 Airborne was viewed as being an 'entirely unnecessary evil', McLeod would prove to have a surprisingly appropriate light touch. Not so higher command, which seemed determined to drag the SAS, kicking and screaming, into line. Amongst other unwelcome developments, the men were ordered to replace their distinctive beige-coloured beret with the standard red version worn by 'all' airborne troops.

Typically, Mayne's quiet resistance took the form of continuing to wear his battle-worn sandy version, and few were the men who would argue to his face that he should do otherwise. As Mayne's prescription for his ideal SAS recruit would reveal, much of his fearsome martial spirit sprung from the need to stand tall amongst his fellows, and to stand firm by their sides. It was camaraderie, and his devotion to his brother raiders, that drove Mayne on.

'I have a mental blueprint of the ideal SAS man,' he would declare. 'No one fits it exactly, but when I look at a man and listen to him, he must come close.' That blueprint included: stamina, both mental and physical; intellect and cunning; the ability to operate as a team; a certain versatility and self-confidence, without ever being brash or arrogant; iron-willed self-reliance; and an indomitable spirit.

For Mayne, these things were key, and over the long years that he'd spent at war Captain Patrick Garstin had more than proven to possess these qualities. Indeed, tonight's mission – SABU-70's top-secret tasking – would call for such attributes in abundance, and it was one in which Mayne had played a pivotal role.

Parachuting into occupied France in support of Operation Overlord – the codename for the D-Day landings – would call for very different skills and tactics than driving columns of jeeps

15

through the empty deserts of North Africa, to strike at targets many hundreds of miles behind enemy lines. Dropping into France – densely inhabited, heavily garrisoned by the enemy and with a population reeling from the long years of occupation – would prove a whole different ball game, each mission presenting a wholly new and challenging set of circumstances on the ground.

As Mayne had advocated, when planning the coming operations, flexibility and adapting to fast-changing situations would be key. 'Ultimate leadership will be assumed by the person on the spot with the greatest determination and ability', he wrote, in a top-secret strategy document. 'SAS parties must not be put under command of any person outside the SAS, and Resistance Groups must be told that SAS parties are their own masters.'

For a man often accused of having psychopathic tendencies, Mayne wrote with surprising compassion regarding the treatment of enemy captives. 'Before they surrender, the Germans must be subject to every known trick, stratagem and explosive which will kill, threaten, frighten or unsettle them: but they must know that they will be safe and unharmed if they surrender.' Resistance groups were to be left in no doubt that 'instructions given by any SAS Commander as to the treatment of German prisoners must be implicitly obeyed'.

Captain Garstin and his eleven men aboard that Stirling would be amongst the first to put Mayne's edicts to the test. For tonight's mission they were charged with parachuting into the heart of France, to block German heavy reinforcements from reaching the D-Day beachheads, which would have calamitous consequences for Operation Overlord. Dropping some 200 miles behind the Normandy beaches, they would blow up railway lines, rolling stock and road transports, halting the German military in its tracks.

Their orders – classified top secret – were to cut 'the main lines in the area PARIS–ORLÉANS and keep these cut for as long as possible'. Specifically, they were to cut 'the EAST and SOUTH railways,' thus blocking the advance of German armoured units – chiefly 9 SS Panzer Division *Hohenstaufen*, 10 SS Panzer Division *Frundsberg* and 2 SS Panzer Division *Das Reich*. In doing so, they were to employ tried and tested SAS tactics: 'sabotage, disruption of communications, individual guerrilla action, etc., all designed to harass the enemy'.

Garstin's stick was slated to be one of the first to drop, but scores of similar teams were to follow, spreading chaos across the length and breadth of France. Without such disruption, planners for Operation Overlord feared that it would take a matter of days for the Panzer divisions to reach the Normandy beaches. If they did, some 150,000 Allied troops risked being driven back into the sea. At all costs the German heavy armour had to be stopped.

Small-scale hit-and-run operations such as Garstin and his men were now embarked upon were classic SAS taskings, yet it was only down to the dogged determination of Mayne and his fellow commanders that the SAS were going to be used in this way. Since their return to the UK, high command had failed utterly to grasp the unique nature and strategic value of such specialist forces. Indeed, initial plans drafted in support of Overlord had amounted to little more than a suicide mission.

On 29 March orders had been issued that the SAS would drop en masse on D-Day minus 1 – i.e. on 5 June – just a few miles to the rear of the landing beaches. There they would take up static positions to block any German forces from getting to the beaches. SAS commanders were aghast. They were never conceived of as a large-scale infantry fighting force; their skill was to wage war far behind the lines, in small, fast-moving bands executing shoot-n-scoot attacks, adhering to the tried and tested adage: 'He who shoots and runs away, lives to shoot another day.'

Indeed, in David Stirling's original conception the ideal SAS operational unit would be no more than four, so as 'to extract the very maximum out of surprise and guile'. Operating in four-man units, 'it was psychologically easier to make them all interdependent, so we had four pairs of ears that were listening and four pairs of eyes that were looking'. That way, an eighty-strong force could hit twenty targets in one fell swoop, before melting away into the night, which should ensure a string of successes.

Stirling, who famously described higher command as being 'layer upon layer of fossilised shit', averred that he sought recruits who were not inclined to say '"yes, sir" without thinking. Each one of them had to be an individual.' He was single-minded in his conviction that 'it was no good putting us under any orthodox . . . headquarters department . . . we had to have a special status of our own.'

With David Stirling's capture, his equally capable brother, Bill, had taken over 2 SAS command. 'Colonel Bill', as he was known, had been aghast at their 29 March 'suicide' orders. Deploying in such concentrated numbers in such a narrow, restricted area, the SAS would be tied down and cut to pieces. It would be a criminal waste of this highly trained specialist force. In order to underline his objections to what he rightly viewed as a senseless loss of life, Bill Stirling either resigned in protest, or was dismissed before he could resign.

In the wake of his departure, unrest seethed, as did dissension in the ranks. A string of senior SAS officers queued up to follow Colonel Bill's example and to fall on their swords. But thankfully, his sacrifice was not to be in vain. On 17 May high command cancelled their 29 March orders, accepting that a means needed to be found to use the SAS as they should be – crying havoc and letting slip the dogs of war far behind enemy lines.

In seeing good sense prevail, the SAS were fortunate to have backing from the very top. For months Winston Churchill had been agitating for the arming of resistance armies across occupied Europe. A die-hard advocate of special forces operations and guerrilla warfare, in the spring of 1944 he'd ordered arms drops to the French Resistance to be substantially increased. He'd cabled US president Roosevelt, urging him to help raise resistance armies across France 'à la Tito' – a reference to Yugoslavia's wartime guerrilla leader.

When the Stirlings of 190 Squadron – and its sister unit, 620 Squadron – weren't flying parachutists into France, their holds were stuffed full of containers of arms and explosives, to be dropped into French hands. That way, when the first SAS units plummeted into hostile airspace, they would have heavily armed Resistance parties awaiting them on the ground. All being well, it was just such a force of men-at-arms that would receive the SABU-70 raiders, on a night-dark field lying a few dozen miles to the south of Paris.

The Stirling was scheduled to be airborne for three hours before she reached the drop-zone (DZ). For some in Garstin's stick, this was their first foray behind the lines, and their nervous energy was plain to see. This called for the rum-jar, to provide 'a little Dutch courage'. But as Wiehe searched in his pack, the hapless lieutenant realised that amidst all the dash of their departure, he'd forgotten this most important accoutrement of waging war. He'd left it, full of rum and ready to go, in the mess. As the men threw angry looks in his direction, Wiehe – on his first ever SAS operation – felt mortified.

With no rum, the old hands started to sing, to lift their spirits. Captain Garstin had split his SABU-70 stick into two sections, each of six men. One was commanded by himself, with Corporal Serge Vaculik – a Free French SAS man – as his second-in-command, while the other had Lieutenant Wiehe in charge, with a Brit, Corporal Jones, under him. That way, each stick had a fluent French-speaker within its ranks, which gave it the greatest chance of being able to operate as David Stirling had originally intended – as a small-scale and independent unit, hitting targets by stealth and surprise.

Smoking was banned on the Stirling, but each man had his pockets crammed full of cigarettes. Every now and then a figure rose from his seat to stretch stiffened limbs, but weighed down under their bulky jump packs, plus the flight bags that were strapped to their legs, it was hard to do anything more than shuffle a few steps. Nervous individuals checked their watches: it was well past midnight. They knew it wasn't long before they'd be over the French cliffs. What they wouldn't give for a shot of that missing rum.

For some rueing the loss of the rum-jar, this was just one more mission after so many. With his shock of unruly red hair, his powerful physique and squat, boxer's nose, Corporal Thomas Jones had been with the SAS ever since the unit's formation in North Africa. A former miner hailing from the gritty streets of Wigan, the twenty-eight-year-old prided himself on being a fine footballer and an equally capable street brawler when the need arose. With his blue eyes and freckled face, Jones was a rough diamond type, and he would find himself busted back to the rank of 'trooper' more than once during the war.

On one occasion Jones would be in London on leave when an emergency order went out for all SAS troops to return to base. Stuck for transport, Jones grabbed the nearest thing 'available' – a US military policeman's (MP) jeep parked on the Tottenham Court Road – and crammed it full of his mates. On the wild drive that followed Jones figured it was only right to 'thank the Yanks for the loan of it. It's just as well to be polite.' They used the jeep's radio to call the MP's headquarters. 'Sorry, old man, but we've had to borrow Charlie for a while,' they announced. Charlie was the jeep's call-sign.

When Jones and his comrades reached SAS headquarters, there were twenty assorted cars and trucks – all purloined – lined up at the gates. Colonel Mayne greeted the sight with a fleeting smile. His only comment was to remark upon how 'they'll have me on the carpet' for 'all those cars outside'. The alacrity with which his men had returned, and the resourcefulness they had shown in finding transport by any means, proved how his regiment's *esprit de corps* remained undimmed.

Corporal Jones was known universally as 'Ginger', and most were ignorant of his real name – Thomas. He was even listed as 'Ginger Jones' on official SAS reports. Quick-witted and with a fast animal intellect, he was blessed with a typical British soldier's sense of humour. 'The wife says she's going to make a man out of me or die in the attempt,' he would remark, of his impending marriage. 'I've already ordered the flowers' – the flowers for the funeral.

Jones, who loved his drink, was just the sort to kick up a stink

21

about the missing rum-jar. But he'd formed a special bond with Lieutenant Wiehe, for whom he served as section corporal, a bond that was as strong as it was perhaps surprising. Though Wiehe appreciated how 'Ginger was a real SAS "type"', the two shared a camaraderie that was greater than the gulf in their backgrounds. As was so often the case in the SAS, to-the-manor-born public-school types would find themselves serving with those brought up on the toughest streets, yet the two rubbed along perfectly side by side.

In light of that, 'Ginger' was less inclined to fret over Wiehe's rare moment of forgetfulness. But perhaps the loss of the rum-jar was a bad omen for the coming mission.

As the Stirling powered onwards towards the French cliffs, trouble would not be long in coming.

Chapter 2

With the evocative sound of bursts of song echoing back and forth across the Stirling's shadowed hold, a figure enquired of the flight's dispatcher – the member of the aircrew whose role it was to oversee the jump – if he might borrow his intercom, via which to communicate with the pilot in the cockpit.

'Hello, Skipper, where are we now?' he asked.

Chatting away, he learned that the hitherto overcast sky 'was pretty clear now', and that the Stirling was making fine progress towards landfall over France. Handing back the intercom, he settled back with his thoughts. A clear sky – it was, of course, a double-edged sword. It should make it far easier to find the drop-zone, but it would also make it considerably easier for the enemy to see and to target the warplane. For Corporal Serge Vaculik, this promised to be one momentous jump, and he had more reasons than most to be both fearful and exultant at the same time.

Czech by birth, but French by adopted nationality – Vaculik had moved to France with his family as a child – he was about to parachute back into his homeland, as part of the Allied forces charged with liberating it from Nazi Germany's iron grip. That, for sure, was an exhilarating proposition. But on the flipside, the last time Vaculik had crossed swords with the enemy, he'd been part of a vanquished army that had awaited salvation at Dunkirk, and unlike Garstin, he'd failed to make it off those war-torn beaches.

As with the SAS captain, Vaculik had given his all to prevent the Nazi blitzkrieg from steamrollering across Belgium, when he was serving as a member of the French armed forces. But at Dunkirk he'd found himself in a rescue boat packed with would-be evacuees, which had capsized on a freak wave. Though half-drowned, somehow he'd made it back to shore, struggling through a sea churned white with explosions, onto a beach strewn with the 'dead and dying'. Fighting for his life, as flight after flight of Stuka dive-bombers screamed overhead, Vaculik had been knocked unconscious.

Wounded and floundering in a 'black emptiness', he had come to, only to realise that he had been taken prisoner along with thousands of other Frenchmen and Brits. Marched eastwards in a massive column of captives, Vaculik had risked a daring getaway by jumping into a river at night, before reaching the border with Germany, after which he figured any chance of escape was lost. Having been swept downstream and clambered ashore, Vaculik had embarked upon an epic journey, at first disguised as a tramp and even hitching lifts on German Army trucks to speed his way.

During an incredible six-month odyssey he had crossed half of western Europe, being variously shot at by border guards, hunted by the Gestapo through the streets of supposedly neutral Spain, locked in a Spanish military dungeon, and beaten and placed before firing squads. Over that time he was forced to jump from the roofs of speeding trains, to fight and kill a feral dog, to endure weeks locked in a Portuguese prison, and to brave being lost at sea in terrible storms, before finally reaching British shores in December 1940 . . . only to be arrested as a suspected German spy.

During one of his many incarcerations, Vaculik had met an Austrian count and fellow prisoner, who had given him a letter to carry to his sister, who lived in London. Having arrived in Britain with that letter – written in German – in his pocket, Vaculik had faced interrogation by Scotland Yard detectives about his alleged Germanic connections. He would spend forty-three days locked in a Pentonville prison cell.

'Do you know we could shoot you as a spy?' they'd warned him. 'If that Austrian isn't still in prison, it will be the worse for you.'

Luckily, 'that Austrian' – a fervent anti-Nazi – was able to vouch for Vaculik from his Portuguese jail cell. Released from prison, Vaculik had duly volunteered for the Free French parachutists and in due course he'd earned his jump wings. He'd been recruited into 1 SAS prior to the D-Day landings, being one of those desperately needed individuals in precious short supply right then – a combat-experienced, jump-trained, fluent French-speaker who also spoke excellent English.

Arguably, there was no one amongst the twelve aboard that Stirling who had suffered as much, or endured such a perilous or testing journey to make it to this moment, not even Lieutenant Wiehe or Captain Garstin. Vaculik couldn't wait to get his boots onto French soil again and to take the fight to the reviled – and much-feared – enemy.

For four long years his family had been mired deep in the conflict. His parents, living in a small village in Brittany, had been forced to endure the German occupation without either of their sons to hand. While Vaculik was variously fighting, evading capture or training to return to France, at age seventeen his younger brother, Antoine, had signed up with the Resistance.

As the Stirling thundered ever onwards, Vaculik thrilled to the idea that all being well, he might shortly be 'fighting side by side with' Antoine.

But hardly had he entertained such thoughts than the night sky to either side of the speeding aircraft was torn apart by the sudden roar of explosions. It could only signify one thing: they were over the French cliffs, and the German shore batteries had opened up on the British warplane. Each time a lone aircraft packed full of parachutists headed into Nazi-occupied Europe, it was forced to run the gauntlet, the German military having ringed the coastline with searchlights, flak nests and radar posts. Few amongst the SAS party had expected to get through without taking fire.

But right now on the beaches below hundreds of thousands of men-at-arms were locked in a herculean struggle to the death, and tonight's aerial onslaught had a special savagery to it. Vaculik had been on his feet stretching his legs, and he found himself flung from side to side, as the pilot executed a series of evasive manoeuvres, trying to steer the massive warplane along a path that avoided the worst of the flak. But all across the aircraft's front the heavens seemed awash with a seething mass of fire, each burst appearing to grope closer and closer, each blast seeming to shake the Stirling ever more powerfully, as if she had been swept up in some giant's angry grasp.

It can only have been seconds after the first opening salvoes, although it felt far longer, when the very worst happened and a deafening roar seemed to tear apart the parachutists' eardrums, a sudden rent being torn in the floor at their feet, shards of blasted metal and wood flying in all directions. As the twelve men gazed in abject fear, staring out through that jagged hole into the howling darkness, Vaculik was amongst the first to utter a cry of alarm.

'Jerry's got us! We're going to break our—'

His words were lost in the howl of straining engines and the thunderous on-rush of air, as the stricken Stirling began a nose-dive towards earth. Pitched forward by the sudden lurch, figures grabbed at the ropes lashed to the Stirling's sides, in an effort to prevent themselves from being thrown in a heap against the forward bulkhead. Even as the dive steepened, the concentration of enemy fire seemed to worsen, as if the pilot was flying down the enemy's very gun-barrels, the screaming of the Bristol Hercules powerplants growing ever more intense.

Pitched almost on the vertical, Vaculik feared they were done for. There would be no time to jump before machine and men ploughed into the unforgiving earth. Matters only worsened when the night sky to one side of the stricken warplane erupted in a blinding flash of fire and light. In an instant, the terrified men realised what had happened: one of their four engines had been hit and had burst into flame, the fiery conflagration licking past and almost through the jagged hole at their feet.

Convinced that they were done for, Vaculik waited for the 'final crash and death in this burning coffin of a plane'. But somehow, miraculously, the moment of impact never came. Instead, by superhuman effort Sutherland managed to nurse the Stirling back under control, and at what had to be treetop height he levelled out their flight, after which the Stirling began to claw her way skywards again, even as further bursts of enemy fire tore after the fleeing warplane.

It was the turn of Garstin and his men to marvel at the sheer courage and steely nerve of the Stirling's aircrew. Even before they'd gained altitude figures dashed aft, to battle with the flames. Fire extinguishers were wrenched off their mounts, and when those were exhausted the SAS men were prevailed upon to hand over their water bottles, to help douse the fires. The aircrew proved to be 'supremely self-confident and cool-headed', Vaculik observed. Their key priority had been to save the aircraft and the parachutists entrusted to their charge. 'Their own safety didn't matter.'

But the drama was far from over. Once the fire was deemed to have been suppressed enough to risk a bailout, Garstin and his men were ordered to go.

'Get to the trap, boys!' the dispatcher cried. 'Be ready to jump!'

No one was about to argue. As every man had had drummed into him during training, it was 100 per cent the pilot's decision when and where they should, or shouldn't jump. They were still a good 150 miles short of their DZ, but if the pilot said leap, they were going through the trap like a dose of salts. Everything else – location, onward route, missing kit, etc. – they could deal with once they were safely down.

As one, Garstin and his men levered themselves to their feet, reached upwards with free hands and clipped their static lines to the steel cable running along the roof of the Stirling. Like that, each line would go taut just seconds after jumping, ripping the parachute out of its pack to catch the air, even as the figure beneath it plummeted earthwards. None of their containers were likely to be coming with them – they were packed full of explosives, weaponry, ammo and assorted supplies – but this was an emergency, and far better that than to go down like a fiery comet hell-bent on death and ruin.

For what felt like an age the twin lines of men stood there, ready to shuffle forward and leap through the trap. But eventually, a figure appeared from the cockpit. It was the Stirling's co-pilot.

Seemingly utterly unruffled, he gestured at the dispatcher and cried: 'It's all right, Jim. They needn't jump! We'll get the old bus through.'

By 'the old bus' he meant, of course, the Stirling. It turned out that by one of those incredible occurrences that only ever seemed to happen during wartime, the fire had gone out by itself and before it had reached the aircraft's fuel tanks. So, instead of leaping through the trap into territory unknown, the twelve men turned back to their seats, using their jackets and pullovers to douse what remained of the flames inside the fuselage.

The note of the Stirling's engines had changed markedly now. Three laboured mightily to do what four had before, meaning their airspeed was considerably reduced, and while the Stirling might not be on fire any more, there was still a hole rent in her floor which let the night wind whistle in most disconcertingly. As the aircrew darted back and forth, faces blackened by soot, Garstin and his men caught an utterly fabulous sight up front: Sutherland had turned in his seat and with a wide grin on his face was yelling something at them. At first they couldn't catch the words above all the noise. But eventually they made out the gist: 'Everyone okay?'

As one, the twelve men raised their hands and gave the thumbs up. It was bitterly cold in the rear of the warplane, and their reduced speed and manoeuvrability had to make them a sitting duck for any enemy night-fighters that might be prowling the skies, yet Sutherland made it clear that he was pressing on with the mission. That took nerves of steel. It had to demand their ultimate respect. If the pilot and his crew could brave this out, so too could those twelve SAS men perched in that freezing hold.

All knew how vital was this mission. They were slated to drop near the town of Brétigny-sur-Orge, lying some 20 miles south of Paris, where a group of the Paris district Resistance would be waiting, showing the pre-arranged recognition signal. Once on the ground, they were to combine forces and blow up trains steaming through the area, and to wreak havoc upon nearby fuel and ammo dumps. That done, they were to be pulled out by an RAF aircraft that would land for the purpose of bringing them home, and at a destination as yet to be confirmed.

They weren't about to give up on all that now. After all, during long months of training these men had been forged as one in fire and steel, which meant they could go through the likes of what had just happened and take it all in their stride. They could almost lose their lives, their kit, their drop-zone and their comrades on the ground, and still hunger to take the fight to the enemy. That was exactly the spirit the SAS training regime was designed to inculcate in each and every recruit: that no matter what obstacles were thrown in their way, the mission was still doable.

From the very outset, SAS training had stressed endurance, independence and the need to do and to think the utterly unexpected; to take everything and anything in one's stride. The earliest recruits had hailed from all walks of life – from lawyers, merchant bankers and landed gentry to firemen, poachers, chip-shop owners and dockers. Over and above a certain level of physical robustness, the SAS's founder David Stirling had stressed the need for psychological strength – self-discipline, imagination, intelligence.

Initially, Stirling and his small band of originals had had no base from which to operate. Someone had asked the obvious question – where was their camp? 'Well, that's the first job,' Stirling had replied; 'You steal one.' That evening the men had headed down to a nearby military camp, 'where we stole tents, we stole everything . . . we stole a piano', Stirling recalled. 'By the next morning we had . . . probably the best camp in the area.'

The strategic value of that first lesson – stealing a camp – wasn't lost on anyone. From then on, recruits had to beg, borrow and pilfer wherever possible, for those would become vital skills when operating behind enemy lines. Recruits were given a list of things they had to purloin: 'a lady's bicycle . . . a cockerel, a hen, a bit of a car or a bus – anything', Jim Almonds, another of the originals, recalled. The focus on thievery played a two-fold role. It was also designed to 'find out what sort of people we were and what we were capable of'.

Encouraging individuality and initiative was key. So too was promoting the concept of merit-above-rank. Officers and men were subjected to exactly the same rigours in training, so that if only one individual reached the target he should still be capable of executing the mission, regardless of rank. The need to get along was paramount, especially when living together in small units for months on end, far behind enemy lines. The aim was to meld individuality and initiative with teamwork as never before.

Despite recent efforts to overhaul the SAS – to drag it into line – the peculiar rigours of the training regime remained largely unchanged. Captain Garstin and his men had enjoyed their own distinctive baptism of fire, starting off in the wild terrain around the Scottish town of Darvel in East Ayrshire, known locally as the *Lang Toon* – the Long Town – and the SAS's base upon their return to the UK. There Colonel Mayne had proceeded to set them his incredible, one-and-only, around-Britain challenge.

From their Darvel camp – set in a pair of disused lace-mills, and surrounded by the rugged Cunninghame Hills – they were to make their way to leafy Chelmsford, lying just to the east of London, a journey of around 400 miles. It would prove to be a good deal longer the way that Mayne prescribed it: en route, they were to sign in at various hotels, post offices and town hall registers, starting first with Glasgow, some 30 miles to the *north* of Darvel, and all without being caught.

A hunter force of police, assisted by the Home Guard, would be on their tail, alerted to their likely route. To make matters worse, all they had to complete the journey were the clothes they stood up in, a few bottles of vitamin pills, a handful each of Benzedrine tablets – known colloquially as 'bennies', and a powerful amphetamine – their personal weapons, and that was it. No food, no money, no rail tickets. Nothing. The around-Britain challenge was to be completed in competition with several other similarly charged SAS parties. And so the race was on.

For Garstin and his men their odyssey began in a bus, with hail thudding like gunshots against the windows. Of course, the conductor wanted their fares, but they had no way of paying. They met his demands with a menacing silence – glowering eyes under red berets, Colt pistols strapped to their sides. They dismounted before the scheduled stop – no one was about to argue – and melted into a remote patch of woodland. While Rex Wiehe and Ginger Jones, the inseparables, went on patrol, Lance Corporal Howard Lutton, another Irishman and something of a restless soul, kindled a roaring fire, while Captain Garstin produced a goose – recently purloined – from his backpack.

Lutton was something of a poacher by choice, and only a soldier by necessity. Born in Lurgan, Northern Ireland, in January 1919, he'd falsified his age so he could sign up a year early with the Royal Ulster Rifles. He'd gone on to serve in Palestine and India prior to the war, but had found home duties irksome, spending time in detention due to his high-spirited ways. Having volunteered for airborne duties, he'd found his calling, being judged a 'good average performer' and to have 'worked hard' when training for 1 SAS in April '44.

Once he'd rigged up a spit, Lutton soon had the goose roasting nicely, and the forest was thick with the mouth-watering aroma. By the time a squad of the local constabulary had put in an appearance, the fugitives were ready to jump them, whipping off their red berets and whipping out their weapons, which were jabbed into the captives' ribs. Ginger Jones, who had a long-lived dislike of 'coppers', kept cursing in the makeshift German he'd learned during long years at war, telling the 'prisoners' they were about to be shot.

They in turn complained that they were out after poultry-rustlers and had come to investigate the smoke. Having spied the roasting goose, they declared that Garstin and his party were under arrest. One of Garstin's men, Tom 'Paddy' Barker – another Irishman – was almost as large and fearsome as Lieutenant Colonel Mayne, who at 6 feet 2 towered over most. Three years back Paddy Barker, then working as a grocer's assistant and known to all locally by the nickname 'Tot', had signed up with the Royal Inniskilling Fusiliers, before volunteering for the SAS at age twenty.

Barker – an 'average all round performer, always cheerful', according to his parachute training records – tended to swear all day and drink all night, and as a result he – like Jones – had seen the inside of many a police cell. At his and Jones's hands, the captured 'coppers' ended up lashed to some nearby trees, so the wanted men could enjoy their meal in peace, the roast goose being washed down with a 'borrowed' bottle of whisky.

Leaving the policemen tied up, the party of desperadoes set off into the night. A bridleway led to the police car, a glorious Humber with eight seats. All piled inside, and with twelve gallons of fuel in the tank they set off, intent on completing a good chunk of their journey in style. With Ginger Jones at the wheel they sped past several police and Home Guard checkpoints, returning salutes, and with no one seeming to realise that the 'enemy' was 'passing under their noses'. Upon arrival at Glasgow, a phalanx of men in uniform piled out of 'their' police car and marched into the central post office to sign the register, and who was there that might venture to object?

Next, south to Kilmarnock, where their signatures were expected in the guestbook of the Bull Hotel. The hostelry's main entrance proved to be menaced by an alert policeman, but Howard Lutton knew of a back entrance. Once they'd stolen inside, a friendly barmaid agreed to purloin the register, so they could sign in the privacy of the back bar, whereupon she proceeded to serve them with a round of beer, for good measure.

South of Kilmarnock, the Humber finally ran dry. Not to be delayed, Garstin's desperadoes hijacked a bus, leaving the driver yelling angry threats about police cells and more. After a night laid up in the vehicle, they reached the outskirts of Carlisle – just short of 100 miles into their journey – but were forced to abandon their transport, which was all out of fuel. Shortly they came upon an army truck with a burst tyre. A Free French parachutist was cursing away, as he tried to change the wheel.

Garstin and his men gathered, apparently innocently offering help, not a man amongst them letting slip that he spoke any French. As they went about changing the wheel, the Free French parachutist kept making wisecracks in French, all at Garstin and his men's expense. When the work was done and the truck ready, Vaculik turned on the man and announced in fluent French: 'Thank you for all your politeness. Now you're going to get a good hiding.'

The terrified Frenchman was grabbed, bound and flung into a ditch. All that Garstin and his men really wanted was the truck, and the supplies of beer, bread and tins of Spam that it carried. Having got underway, and polishing off a good proportion of the food and drink en route, they made their way into Carlisle, whereupon the town hall register was duly signed without the slightest hint of any trouble.

Having reckoned they must have shaken off any pursuers, Garstin and his men trucked the hundred-odd miles south to York, whereupon they figured it was time for a little luxury. One man checked into a hotel, taking just the one room – a large suite complete with two beds and a magnificent bathroom. Then, one by one, they smuggled themselves inside, whereupon they spent a glorious night sharing the beds and even with two in the bathtub.

At the crack of dawn they filtered out again, washed, shaven and well slept, leaving the bill unpaid. Not far from the hotel they spied a double-decker bus, the driver and conductor sitting outside enjoying an early-morning cup of tea. Garstin eyed his men. The bus was perfect, especially as there were only one or two housewives with shopping bags waiting patiently inside. The fugitives filed casually aboard, before Ginger Jones slid into the driver's seat and they were off.

The driver must have raised the alarm, for shortly a policeman stepped into the road and held up a hand to stop them. Jones's only response was to gun the engine, driving straight at the 'copper', forcing the poor man to jump for his life. Figuring 'things were getting hot', Garstin and his party decided to separate for the next stage of their journey, fixing a spot in a wood just outside Sheffield as that evening's rendezvous.

Hitchhiking the seventy-odd miles south, one of the fugitives managed to cadge a lift in a police car, manned by those who were charged with apprehending 'a group of bandits in uniform' who'd stolen a bus. The police didn't think to suspect the lone hitchhiker, beyond taking a perfunctory glance at his papers. By the time all had gathered in the Sheffield woods, a purloined duck and a chicken were roasting over a fire, and only Paddy Barker, the giant Irishman, was missing.

No one was particularly worried. Barker was known to be able to look after himself. The Robin Hood warriors were tucking into their meal when a strange cry rang out through the dark woods. 'Git up there! Gee up, old hoss.' Sure enough it was Barker, riding a farmer's nag laden down with a sackful of bottled beer. A contented night was had by all, but shortly after dawn the men awoke to the sound of the horse's worried neighs. Fortunately they'd tethered her in a patch of nearby pasture and her early warning cries would serve to prevent their capture.

Melting into the trees, Garstin and his men watched as a party of the Home Guard marched into their camp – sleeping bags just vacated, fire still warm. 'Might be Germans about,' one declared, worriedly. 'Better get in touch with HQ.' A figure hurried off, but he was shortly rugby tackled by Barker, after which the others were surrounded by armed and dangerous men, who tied them up before breaking camp and setting off into the trees.

It was early by the time Garstin and his men made it to Sheffield, where the post office register had to be signed. In a nearby cafe they were served tea, as they waited for the post office to open. A group of RAF men were also in the cafe, and their gleaming car was parked right outside. Garstin eyed the vehicle and the RAF party, before announcing quietly: 'Let's hope they don't head off too soon.'

At nine o'clock on the dot they filed into the post office and signed the register, before stealing the car, complete with a resident airman fast asleep in the back. By the time he'd woken up to his predicament, Garstin and his band were well on their way. The car ran out of fuel after about a hundred miles, after which they tied up their hapless passenger, and via a lift first on a Churchill tank, and then on a furniture lorry, they made their triumphant way into Chelmsford . . . journey's end.

As a bonus, they were the first of the SAS bands to make it. But if they'd been expecting any kind of a prize – they'd been hoping for at least a few days' leave – they were to be sorely disappointed. Orders awaited, complete with rail warrants to speed them back to their Darvel base. Upon their return, they were warned to prepare for departure. Their entire SAS regiment was being dispatched to southern England, to a secret base from where they would be deploying into Nazi-occupied Europe.

With any number of around-Britain challenges underway at any one time, Mayne was accustomed to irate military police turning up on his doorstep. A highly decorated lieutenant colonel in what remained a mysterious and little-known regiment – there had been little, if any, publicity concerning the exploits of the SAS – Mayne was resolute in defence of his men, no matter what they might have been up to. Raiding Kilmarnock police station;

robbing a Home Guard's armoury; hijacking a steam train – for Mayne, all was fair in love and war. He had become a dab hand at tearing up all sorts of charge sheets.

With suitably irreverent grit, SAS commanders had taken to giving their missions the most inventive of codenames: Operations Squatter and Bigamy in North Africa, and Narcissus and Candytuft for Mediterranean missions. Likewise, Captain Garstin and his men were part of a squadron-strength deployment codenamed Operation Cain, as in the biblical son of Adam and Eve who, in a fit of jealousy, had murdered his brother, Abel, and been condemned by God to wander as an outcast for eternity. In similar spirit, there was a standing joke that the codename SABU had been adopted from Sabu Dastagir, the Indian actor who had played one of the lead characters in the 1937 movie *Elephant Boy*, and Mowgli in the 1942 film *Jungle Book*.

There was also an Operation Abel, for good measure, and that codename would last the full course. But once in the field, early messages sent by Morse code would end up transposing 'Cain' into 'Gain' and vice versa, with Gain soon being adopted as the mission's official codename. 'Operation CAIN should read Operation GAIN,' a top-secret order would determine.

Yet given SABU-70's dark fortunes tonight, 'Cain' might prove infinitely more appropriate.

Chapter 3

'Okay, boys, twenty minutes to the jump,' the dispatcher announced, as the war-wounded Stirling limped towards the drop-zone. *At last.* The dispatcher had to laugh at the eagerness with which Captain Garstin and his men clambered to their feet. No disrespect to the RAF crew, but it was high time that they were shot of that warplane and got their feet on solid ground.

In a flurry of movement the men made their final preparations, fastening the straps of their leg-bags tighter and forming up in the order in which they were to jump. The tough canvas leg-bags were stuffed full of the heaviest kit, and each would be lowered via a drawstring release system on 25 feet of rope, just before the parachutist touched down. That way the bag made contact first, warning the jumper how close he was to landfall and also taking its own weight, so saving his legs from the worst of the impact.

As figures jostled closer together, the dispatcher hinged back the thick plywood covers that closed the Stirling's trap. That done, he stepped down into the 'bathtub', keeping his feet balanced on the rims to either side, while he unfastened a pair of wingnuts that held the bottom of the 'bath' closed. Once they were free, it was pretty much wind pressure alone that swung open the floor of the 'bath', at which stage it was locked into position via the wingnuts.

One RAF dispatcher, Sergeant John Lunt, spoke of clambering

down into the trap to unfasten it in this perilous way, after which a paratrooper riding on the Stirling had remarked to him, in amazement: 'I wouldn't want your job for all the tea in China.' Lunt was thinking to himself, wryly: 'Well, I wouldn't want your job dropping behind enemy lines!'

Either way, the route was now free for Garstin and his men to jump through what was essentially the Stirling's bomb-bay, into the thin and raging blue. Of course, there were now two sources of icy blast tearing into the aircraft's hold – the open trap, plus the ragged hole torn in the Stirling's floor. The jumpers waited in position, silent, tense, expectant. Nervously, each checked the line of the man in front, ensuring it was firmly hooked up to the steel cable running the length of the hold, while the dispatcher walked along the columns of men, doing a final inspection.

Each SAS man wore a pair of rubber-soled boots – ideal for silent, stealthy operations – plus a Dennison smock, which came with a special strip of material that fastened between the legs, to prevent it from catching the air and billowing out during the descent. Bespoke, dome-shaped paratroopers' helmets had replaced the wide-rimmed British Army 'tin hats' of earlier years, and secreted somewhere on their person each man had his SAS beret – the red version, for that was one battle the top brass had largely won. Utterly distinctive and iconic, the red beret was perfect for frontline combat operations, but with its high visibility it was hardly ideal for heading deep behind enemy lines.

Apparently satisfied, the dispatcher returned to his place beside the howling maw of the trap. As figures gazed down into the empty blackness, several sets of hands were seen to be shaking. With some, it was the effects of the adrenaline buzzing through their veins. With others, it was the surge of raw animal fright that came with making the jump. One of those fear-stricken individuals was Vaculik, who kept repeating to himself over and over again that 'of course' his parachute would open. *Of course. Of course. Of course.*

But it was Lieutenant Rex – Wiehe – who had the greatest reason to dread the coming drop. Fearing he would miss out on frontline operations, in December 1942 Wiehe had volunteered for parachute duties. At first his regiment had refused to let him go, but his stubborn determination had won through. Yet when finally posted to his new unit, the 4th Parachute Brigade, then based at Moascar, in Egypt, his new commander, a Major Hardiman, promptly told Wiehe that the long months he'd spent at war were no proper qualification for an airborne unit, and he'd best return to where he'd come from.

The junior officers were far more encouraging, counselling Wiehe to ignore Hardiman, who was known as something of a blow-hard. Doggedly he persevered and he duly earned his wings, though he was to see one man drop to his death, another smash his collarbone and a third break his knee during training. Worse still, in June 1943, shortly after spending his third birthday at war – he'd just turned twenty-seven – Wiehe managed to injure his leg during training, not long before his unit was slated to drop into Italy, at the spearhead of the Allied landings.

Wiehe was sent before the squadron medic, who declared that his career as a parachutist was over. Seeing the abject distress on the young soldier's features, the doctor added, apologetically, 'I'm awfully sorry, but I'm afraid I can't help it.' Stunned at his run of ill luck, Wiehe contemplated spending the rest of the war as a 'pen-pusher'. Thankfully, by now Major Hardiman had warmed to his new recruit, and he offered to retain Wiehe as a 'non-jumping member'. Better still, he would fly into Italy aboard the gliders, bringing in the squadron's vehicles. That Wiehe proceeded to do, and in many ways the glider-borne landings proved as hazardous as the parachute insertions.

Upon his unit's return to the UK, in January 1944, Wiehe remained remarkably upbeat, again seizing the chance to volunteer for hazardous duties. Using the argument that he was a rare and valuable thing right then – an airborne soldier fluent in both French and English – he volunteered 'for any special position where my knowledge of French could be useful'. Interviewed by Colonel Mayne, Wiehe was accepted into the SAS on a two-week trial.

Having somehow managed to bury the fact of his being ruled unfit for parachute duties, he was dispatched to Ringway aerodrome, near Manchester, for parachute refresher training. At both the tethered balloon and the Whitley's narrow jump-tube, Wiehe found himself frozen with fear. It was summer 1943 when he'd been declared unfit for parachuting, and why should he be any more capable now? But by sheer force of will alone – a 'desperate appeal' to reason – he'd steeled himself to complete the necessary jumps, after which he was posted on probation to the SAS, in Scotland.

Ever since sailing to war, Wiehe had kept a diary, noting down key events, plus his hopes and fears. 'Training continues, intensifies,' he'd noted of the punishing regime he was subjected to in February '44 in the hills around Darvel. 'I fear for my foot and my knees, which are not too strong . . . Shall I be amongst those troops amongst the first to land in Europe? That is my wish.' Despite his worst fears, Wiehe passed the test and by March he was deemed a fully fledged member of the SAS.

On 4 June he penned a letter to his mother in Mauritius, giving his address as '1st SAS Regt, APO, England' (APO – Army Post Office). In it he wrote of the dangers he would shortly face, urging his mother to 'reassure' and 'encourage' his fiancée, Eda. Childhood sweethearts, he and Eda had grown up together on Mauritius and had long been expected to wed. He would shortly deploy to 'the European continent', Wiehe wrote, something that 'I would not have dared speak about . . . but the colonel told me yesterday it was allowed.' By 'the colonel', he meant of course Mayne.

He'd warned his mother that she should 'not be alarmed if after this letter you remain long without news from me . . . You won't even hear about my regiment in the news releases and I can't tell you what our role is. If our mission proves difficult to fulfil, still I leave full of confidence: I will be back soon.' He signed off, 'I kiss you very tenderly. Your son who loves you.'

Twenty-four hours after he'd penned those words, the D-Day landings had started, Wiehe noting in his diary how 'the great invasion of Europe began . . . Until dawn I was chatting with a friend, speculating as to the date of this great event, when a moment later the radio announced: "Allied forces have landed on the continent of Europe." There on the Normandy coast men, tanks, cannons are landing . . . from countless boats.'

Despite injury and ill fortune, Wiehe had stayed the course. And now here he was, moments away from playing his part in cementing the D-Day landings, and no matter that his legs might feel like the proverbial jelly. Whenever he was poised to jump, he was 'filled with an apprehension and anguish that was difficult to master. I am afraid, simply afraid,' he noted. But the worse thing was the agonising wait at the Stirling's trap, which seemed never ending.

For a good five minutes the warplane circled the Brétigny-sur-Orge drop-zone, but not a sniff of a recognition light or signal fire was there to be seen. All that showed below were the darker outlines of woodland, plus the lighter, blocky patches of cornfields. As the aircraft droned around and around, Garstin and his men were very much on edge. Vaculik found himself biting his lips and repeatedly pulling on his static line, just as some kind of a distraction.

Finally, the dispatcher stepped back from the trap, in response to some message from the cockpit, and he levered the aperture closed. As there was not the slightest sign of any reception party below, the jump had been cancelled. The decision was met with roars of indignation from the waiting men, plus strings of curses. Paddy Barker even threatened to 'throw out' the dispatcher, if he insisted on preventing them from going.

'Shut your big traps and listen up,' the man retorted. Sutherland had decided to head for the back-up DZ, which was but a few minutes' flight away. If Garstin and his men could only 'keep quiet and be patient', they should get a second chance at making the drop.

Grudgingly they agreed to do as exhorted. As all knew only too well, if there was no sign of any friendly reception party that normally signified some kind of enemy interference on the ground, which could spell bad news for any orbiting warplane. If anything, Sutherland had tarried too long and he had every right to move on.

'Our briefing for such an occurrence was not to linger,' Flight Sergeant David Evans, a highly experienced Stirling pilot, recalled of one such mission, but 'in our eagerness to supply our French allies we kept circling, hoping to see fire lit . . . Suddenly, when we were at about 2,000 feet, all hell broke loose: we were enveloped in light as tracer bullets came up at us from all directions.' Diving to treetop height, the Stirling had got away unscathed, but all knew the risks of hanging around for too long.

Shortly Sutherland put his war-ravaged aircraft into a second holding pattern, over the back-up DZ. While the trap remained closed for now, Garstin and his men could follow the fortunes of the search via the expression on the dispatcher's face, as he scrutinised the terrain below through one of the aircraft's porthole-like windows. A thick frown creased his brows. It didn't exactly look promising.

Sutherland kept at it for a good quarter of an hour, which was absolutely pushing the luck of all aboard that aircraft. As the minutes ticked by, the SAS men's rage at being barred from making the jump gave way to an overriding sense of frustration and impotency. Something dire must have happened to their comrades-in-arms on the ground, for there was not a sign of them.

Eventually, Sutherland gave the word that all dreaded. 'Sorry, boys, not a signal to be seen.' They were to return to base forthwith. But there was worse to come. 'We're losing speed and we're losing petrol. In fact, I don't even know if we've got enough to make it.'

Ginger Jones, who'd been chewing on some tobacco, spluttered in shock, almost swallowing the wad whole. Even the normally voluble Paddy Barker seemed lost for words. From the bitter disappointment of not being able to jump, this had now become a matter of raw survival. Figures unhooked their static lines, before slumping back onto their seats. Some bunched up their parachute packs to form makeshift pillows, falling into a wearied sleep. The on-again-off-again ebb and flow of the tension had proven exhausting.

But they would not be at rest for long.

Even as Sutherland nursed the Stirling northwards, setting a course for their airbase lying far to the west of London, sleeping men were jerked awake by the sudden blasts of enemy gunfire. Passing back across the French coast could prove equally as hazardous as any outward journey. For long minutes, the slow-flying Stirling was menaced by explosions, as she shuddered and lurched through the firestorm. It sounded as if some vengeful giant was 'throwing stones at us by the handful', Vaculik recalled. They appeared to be through the worst when a second engine began to cough and falter. By the time it eventually died, the Stirling was out over the dark expanse of the sea.

Deprived now of two of her four engines, the warplane slowed markedly and, ominously, the men in the hold could feel her losing altitude. It was obvious what now threatened: they were in danger of ditching in the drink. All along the hold, nervous figures fiddled with their inflatable life vests, checking that the compressed air cylinder was properly attached and that the tube to the vest hadn't perished.

From the cockpit Sutherland started yelling out a string of orders, as he struggled to keep the 25-tonne warplane airborne. By way of response, the dispatcher reached for the heavy plywood covers, seeking once again to hinge them back from the trap. What did Sutherland now intend? Were all about to be ordered to bail out over the Channel? Garstin and his men hurried to help, laying shoulders to the task of flinging the covers aside. That done, the dispatcher gave his orders: every item that wasn't bolted down was to be jettisoned into the sea, bar the men riding aboard that warplane.

First went the heavy cylindrical steel containers packed with the precious kit with which the men of SABU-70 had intended to wreak havoc deep behind enemy lines. Explosives, weaponry, ammunition, ration packs – one by one, the heavy containers were manhandled to the trap and sent tumbling darkly towards the sea far below. Once all had been ditched, the men's kit bags were hurled seawards. Out went the two pairs of underwear, the two shirts, the sleeping bag, map case, webbing belt, pistol, water bottle, compass and torch that each carried. Maps, bundles of cash, escape and evasion kits, wireless codebooks and decoding sheets – all was hurled towards the dark swell. Anything and everything had to go, in a desperate effort to keep the Stirling airborne.

As Vaculik dumped his shaving kit into the void, he grumbled: 'There goes my new safety razor!' Beside him, Captain Garstin – phlegmatic and unshakeable as ever – gave a wry grin. 'The mermaids will use it on any visitors.' It was a darkly humorous remark. No one aboard that aircraft fancied having a shave from one of those sirens of the deep, even if it was with Vaculik's safety razor.

As the men had been hurling out the excess weight, the Stirling's flight mechanic was struggling to get the recently failed engine operational again. Somehow he succeeded in achieving the seemingly impossible: all of a sudden, it coughed out a great gout of smoke and sparked back into improbable life. Garstin and his men felt their hearts lift. With three engines powering them onwards once more, Sutherland was able to claw back some precious height, bringing the Stirling up to some 5,000 feet.

But no sooner had he done so than the same engine coughed again and gave up the ghost for good. Deprived of its power, the Stirling almost stalled, and Sutherland had to place her into a steep dive, in order to increase airspeed and to gain control once more. This had become a rollercoaster ride to either death or salvation, and none aboard that warplane could predict how it might end. Only one thing was for certain: two Bristol Hercules powerplants were not enough to keep them airborne for long.

Fear roiled in the guts of the SABU-70 raiders now. The Stirling had lost so much height they were too low to jump. There wasn't even the space in which a parachute might open. Ghostly, pencil thin, gleaming silvery-blue in the moonlight, the white cliffs of Sussex hove into view, seemingly horribly distant. Still Sutherland nursed the ailing warplane onwards. Seeming to defy gravity itself, moment by moment the giant aircraft crept ever closer to making some kind of landfall.

'It'll be a belly landing!' cried the dispatcher. 'Roll into a ball, hands behind your necks.' The Stirling's landing gear must have been hit, for there was zero sign of any response from it. 'A crash-landing's the only way. It's all right. Don't get the wind up.'

The twelve men did as ordered, taking up crash positions. But no matter how the dispatcher might try to soothe frayed nerves, several amongst them were absolutely petrified. Vaculik felt convinced they were done for. 'I could already see my charred corpse in the blackened debris . . . But there was nothing to be done, just nothing.'

Oddly, Vaculik felt like laughing, even as they swept towards the towering cliffs. It was so ironic: he had survived Dunkirk, repeated captures and escapes, an epic sea voyage to Britain, and now being shot up by flak, only to die in a crash-landing on supposedly friendly soil. Without really realising it, he started to chortle. It must have sounded hideously ghoulish, for Ginger Jones turned a furious gaze upon him. During the long months of training, especially on their around-Britain challenge, the two men had become the best of friends, but there was little sign of that now.

'Shut up, you – or I'll push your face in!' Jones growled.

That was a threat not to be taken lightly. Although Vaculik was an inch or two taller than Jones, there was little doubt who would win in an all-out brawl. The Frenchman had once seen Jones take on Paddy Barker. The two had been engaged in a furious drink-fuelled argument when Jones had dropped Barker with a single right to the heart. But before Vaculik could so much as respond, there was an almighty crash and the jarring shock of impact, as the belly of the Stirling made contact with the ground and she began to plough forward at 100 knots airspeed, throwing up a cloud of dirt, grass and debris in her path.

A storm of stones, rocks and heavy clods of earth tore through the opening in the belly of the fuselage, a choking cloud of dust billowing inside. Unidentified projectiles smashed into the para-chutists' helmets, as 25 tonnes of careering warplane tore across the earth. Finally, after a deafening splintering and buckling of the fuselage, the wrecked aircraft came to a juddering halt, and all was enveloped in a ringing silence.

A few seconds later a surprisingly clear and steady voice rang out through the thick fog of dust and debris. 'You okay, boys?'

It was Sutherland, and he was crawling back along the fuselage towards his passengers. Gradually a degree of order was restored, and the men could be seen gingerly testing limbs to see if any-thing was broken. As the first individuals realised they were still miraculously in one piece, hands fumbled instinctively for packets of cigarettes, to calm frayed nerves.

'Idiots!' yelled the dispatcher. 'You want us all to go up in smoke? No matches, whatever you do.'

He was right. Already the air inside the fuselage was thick with the smell of petrol. At least one of the Stirling's four tanks must have ruptured during the crash-landing, and was gushing out fuel. Before any more could be said on the matter, there was a series of loud bashes from the exterior of the warplane, as if someone was knocking to be allowed entry.

A door opened and a bulky figure poked a head inside. He was kitted out in all the gear of a military firefighter, though the first man to venture inside was actually a medic. More followed, quickly manhandling the stunned passengers from the wrecked aircraft into the darkness outside. One look showed that Sutherland had somehow managed to get them down on a proper working airfield. Parked to one side was an RAF ambulance and a fire engine, ready for the worst of all eventualities.

Either a miracle worker or an utter prodigy of the air, Sutherland had succeeded in nursing the Stirling all the way to Ford Airfield, set some 2 miles back from the Sussex cliffs at Littlehampton, and an operational base for a squadron of De Havilland Mosquito warplanes. Amazingly, not a man amongst the SABU-70 party nor the Stirling's aircrew had suffered anything more than scratches, bruises and sprains during the crash-landing.

Plagued more by the fright of their lives, both SAS and aircrew were hurried into the Ford Airfield canteen, to 'drown our sorrows and celebrate our escape'. In no time a team of bustling WAAFs – the female auxiliaries of the RAF – had rustled up a breakfast fit for a king, including fried eggs and heaps of bacon. The RAF Ford squadron leader joined them, complete with a magnificent handlebar moustache and the cocker spaniel that served as their mascot. Though the crash-landing had ploughed up a good stretch of the airstrip, and left a deal of clearing-up work to be done, no one seemed to mind. All were simply over-joyed that every man had been brought back alive.

Later that day a Stirling landed to collect the SABU-70 stick and to whisk them back to Fairfield Camp in rural Gloucestershire, otherwise known as 'the Cage'. This was a top-secret and intensively patrolled base set under canvas and surrounded by barbed-wire, in which SAS and SOE parties would be incarcerated immediately prior to departure into enemy-occupied Europe. Adjacent lay the airbase of RAF Fairford, from where the fleets of Stirlings set forth for occupied France.

No one was allowed out of the Cage, unless he was flying into enemy territory, or for some reason had had his mission cancelled. No one was allowed to pass from camp to airfield without express permission: the passageway between was permanently patrolled by the Red Caps – the military police. The idea behind the rigorous strictures was to ensure that no snippet of intelligence might inadvertently leak to the enemy, due to a careless word uttered in a pub, or when saying goodbyes to loved ones.

For Garstin and his men, their return to Fairfield would be something of a bittersweet homecoming. They'd already been listed as missing in action, so their reappearance was something akin to coming back from the dead. But that wasn't so unusual: some SAS parties would be dispatched and returned half a dozen times, before finally getting to jump. Other Stirlings would be lost, one going down in the Channel without trace, and with all crew and passengers. Likewise, the SABU-70 stick – plus Sutherland and his crew – had narrowly escaped ending up in a dark and watery grave.

But there was no time to dwell upon any of that now. As Lieutenant Colonel Mayne made clear, Garstin and his men were to turn right around, once a Stirling could be made available, and were to fly back to France to complete their mission. There was one other factor that might delay their departure. The weather that mid-June was proving horribly temperamental and theirs was not the only stick that hadn't made it. Of the six that had set out that night, four had been forced to return, SABU-70 amongst them.

Airborne forces HQ was reporting 'weather conditions which could scarcely have been worse', with little sign of them stabilising anytime soon. They were also warning that 'there is a considerable strain on the personnel concerned if, owing to the weather, operations have to be cancelled several nights running, or if unsuccessful sorties are flown'. Add to that almost getting shot down and nearly ditching at sea, followed by a dramatic crash-landing, and the stress and strain was gargantuan, by anyone's reckoning.

Garstin and his men had maybe forty-eight hours in which to ready all the kit that had been lost at sea, and to prepare themselves to return. They'd best get cracking. But first, some amongst them were hell-bent upon their own tried and tested form of stress therapy. When Vaculik searched out Ginger Jones and Paddy Barker, they were nowhere to be found. Eventually he tracked them down to the Cage canteen manager's tent, where they were halfway through quietly sinking a barrel of beer.

'They had many ranks, but only one religion, and that was good strong drink,' Vaculik recalled of the men with whom he served, 'and it was with them that I first really learned to drink. In this respect they took after the colonel, who could give a good account of himself.' By 'the colonel' Vaculik meant Mayne, a man he viewed with the zeal almost of a disciple.

'Colonel M [Mayne] . . . saw to it that no weaklings got into his ranks. At the age of twenty-eight he already had the past of a hero, and the king had decorated him more than once. He took risks as another man went out for a cup of tea, and it was not long before he had communicated his dash and intrepidity to all of us and we swore by him. For my part, I was very proud to belong to a corps which had sown terror for months behind Rommel's lines, not to mention the Italian lines.'

Regarding the SAS's propensity for 'good strong drink', the same could be said for the 190 and 460 Squadron aircrews, in the airbase next door. There the parties were legendary. While the loss rate amongst the airmen of 38 Group – the RAF parent unit – was a fraction of that suffered by RAF Bomber Command, every mission proved challenging and hazardous in the extreme, and alcohol was the drug of choice to dull shattered nerves.

'Did I say clear the deck? Well! It's been cleared!' remarked one of the American airmen who flew with 38 Group. There were dozens of such American and Canadian flyers, for signing up with the RAF had been one of the few ways of getting into the fight, before America formally declared war on Germany. 'I've never been so drunk in all my days. Pint after pint . . . all night long. I ended up throwing pints of beer on the mess floor. When that got too tame, buckets were used! My shattered nerves – what a night!'

But despite the drinking and the inclement weather, some flights were still getting through. A handful of SAS sticks had made it onto the ground, and some had already sent back their first reports via radio. From those, Mayne and others in command concluded that there was everything to play for in the war-torn fields of France. The activities of the Resistance, in particular, were looking extremely promising, if only the RAF could ferry in enough men and supplies.

If 'adequately supported', the Resistance could furnish 'great assistance . . . to Overlord', a 'Progress Report on SAS Operations' declared that month, stressing the 'vital necessity of supplying resistance immediately with arms and equipment'. Certain areas, with the 'support of uniformed troops and arms, could very soon be taken over and freed . . . from any sort of enemy control'. The handful of SAS parties already in the field were already sending back 'useful intelligence . . . about enemy movements', plus 'information about enemy dumps, airfields, etc.'. Good communications had been established, and 'messages had been coming through regularly'.

Marked *top secret*, the report also bore the mysterious stamp of 'BIGOT'. This was supposedly an acronym dreamed up by Winston Churchill, which stood for 'British Invasion of German Occupied Territories'. In theory, there was no higher security classification, for 'the Bigots', as they were known, were privy to aspects of the Overlord plan, one of the most closely guarded secrets of the war. As Churchill had famously averred, the location and timing of the D-Day landings must be hidden from the enemy at all costs: it was a truth that had to be protected by a 'bodyguard of lies'.

To check if someone was on the BIGOT List – those privy to such ultra-sensitive intelligence – the question was supposed to be asked: 'Are you a Bigot?' Anyone with the appropriate security clearance was expected to reply, 'Yes, I'm a Bigot, by Neptune,' Neptune being a none-too-subtle inference to the coming amphibious landings. The BIGOT List was rigidly enforced. Supposedly, King George VI was turned away from the intelligence centre of a US warship, because nobody had realised that 'he was a Bigot'.

Of course, intelligence would be vital to securing the D-Day beachheads, and to winning the savage battles that followed. Fortunately, Mayne had just received a choice piece of intel about why his SABU-70 raiders had been turned back from their mission, and from none other than Special Operations Executive. SOE was a clandestine organisation known as 'the fourth armed service', after the army, navy and air force. Churchill had called upon SOE to 'set the lands of enemy-occupied Europe ablaze', and SOE agents had long been on the ground in France complete with radio sets. Not only were they organising SAS reception parties, they were also sending back reports on any problems.

Garstin and his men were called away from variously packing their kit, grabbing some rest or sinking copious quantities of beer. Mayne, never one to shy away from a good round of drinks, allowed the same amongst his men, but only as long as they remained operationally capable. Over long years, Jones and Barker had proven themselves suitably ready for war, no matter what intoxicating liquors they might have imbibed.

Mayne proceeded to explain why no reception party had been awaiting the SABU-70 raiders on either DZ. Apparently the terrain had been closely watched by the Gestapo – more formally, the *Geheime Staatspolizei* – the secret police force of Nazi Germany and the SS. It had been the Gestapo's unwelcome presence that had prevented the forces of the Paris Resistance from keeping the planned rendezvous.

Mayne had thought of a solution to this problem, which was as simple as it was stark. Garstin and his men were going to jump 'blind', without bothering with the niceties of any reception party.

Desperate times called for desperate measures: they were to carry out their mission 'at whatever cost'.

Chapter 4

On the afternoon of 16 June – the eve of their departure – the twelve men gathered for the all-important intelligence briefing, otherwise known as the 'griff', one of the most vital final stages of any such mission. On one wall of the ops tent was taped a massive map of the target area to the south of Paris, along with various operational instructions, while scattered across desks were envelopes stuffed full of reconnaissance photos. In addition to Garstin and his men, Mayne was present, though his would be a largely silent, watchful – almost fatherly – presence.

The figure who had taken central stage in the SAS's intelligence set-up was Major Eric 'Bill' Barkworth, a tall, steely individual, whose reputation almost rivalled that of Mayne. Barkworth was a man of iron will, unbreakable spirit and with a single-minded bent that could border on the eccentric. Intensely loyal and open-minded, Barkworth didn't give a damn about stuffy tradition or the dumb privilege of rank. Charming and cultured and blessed with a brilliant mind, he was to prove something of a thorn in the establishment's side, and quietly would enjoy being so.

Above everything, Barkworth cared for the fortunes and the preparedness of the men in his charge, especially when he was speeding them into hostile lands on the strength of intelligence gathered at his own hand. Blessed with an incisive mind, the SAS major tended not to suffer fools, and once met was never to be forgotten. When Barkworth was serving in No. 8 Commando, prior to joining the SAS, none other than Evelyn Waugh, the acclaimed novelist, had warned: 'Beware of Barkworth: he will lash you with his tongue.'

Hailing from Sidmouth in Devon, Barkworth had enlisted first with the Somerset Light Infantry, earning the nickname 'Bill' from an American acquaintance, and was unfailingly courteous – until he was crossed. Barkworth's irrepressible spirit shone through early in the war when, serving in North Africa, he'd had his appendix removed. Recuperating in hospital, he'd felt the need to 'walk about a bit'. The fearsome matron had scolded him, warning that she did not want to even see his feet touch the floor. By way of response, Barkworth had marched determinedly back and forth upon his bed.

From No. 8 Commando, he'd been recruited into a little-known outfit, the No. 101 Specialist Wireless Section. A mobile radio interception unit based in North Africa, the 101 was tasked to pluck from the ether the Afrika Corps' radio communications. The fact that Barkworth was fluent in seven languages, including German, made him a huge asset, not to mention his innate aptitude for such work. On 10 November 1941 he received a telegram from HQ, conveying heartfelt congratulations for his invaluable work 'breaking the German map reference code system. The additional information that will be obtainable through interception will be of the greatest value.' In layman's terms, breaking that code would enable the tracing of enemy aircraft, armour, troop convoys and shipping, and the planning of stealthy sorties against such targets.

From there, Barkworth had taken his radio-intercept skills into the SAS, when founding its pioneering intelligence arm.

In due course he'd detected enemy signals of profound importance. Listening in on a German military broadcast, in Italy, Barkworth had his second-in-command, Sergeant Fred 'Dusty' Rhodes, scribble down an urgent note of 'what he'd just picked up off the radio'. Of stunning import, it concerned what appeared to be an order emanating from the very highest levels, decreeing that Allied parachutists captured behind the lines were to be shot, without trial and without mercy.

Barkworth reckoned that he had caught the name of the directive – *das Kommandobefehl*, the Commando Order – and he passed on all that he had heard to Colonel Bill Stirling. But no one could quite be certain if all of this was true. The essence of the order was just so outrageous. It constituted a blatant and direct breach of the laws of war, which stipulate that soldiers taken captive in uniform should be afforded the protections of bona fide POWs. No one could quite believe that such a murderous directive might exist, and emanating from the highest levels of German command.

Then had come the escape of SAS Lieutenant James Quentin Hughes. In January 1944, Hughes had parachuted into Italy on Operation Pomegranate, tasked with blowing up an airbase. But from the outset, his six-man patrol was hunted by the enemy, and only he and one other made it to the target. Regardless, they decided to attack anyway. Under cover of darkness they placed charges on the target aircraft, but the last went off prematurely, the resulting explosion killing Hughes's comrade outright.

Hughes himself was badly wounded in the blast, which left him half-blinded, and he was taken captive by the enemy. While being treated at a German military hospital, he was visited by a Gestapo officer, who warned him, ominously, that he 'was not considered a prisoner of war'. Hitler had issued a 'Commando Order', the Gestapo man continued, under which all Allied saboteurs were to be executed. He warned Hughes to talk, or else.

Of course, Hughes had never heard of any such 'Commando Order'. Even so, with the help of a German medical doctor he managed to finagle his way onto a hospital train bound for a POW camp, before the Gestapo could liquidate him. En route Hughes flung himself off, after which he proceeded to execute an epic escape through the Italian mountains, reaching Allied lines in south-central Italy in May 1944. From there he returned to Britain, where he was awarded a Military Cross and bar, for the initial raid and the incredible escape that had followed.

Like all escapees, Hughes was debriefed in detail, but his reports of the Commando Order were dismissed as being nothing more than a cunning interrogation technique, designed to force captives to talk. Then Hughes had got to speak to Barkworth. In a report entitled 'Special Air Service Operations: Pomegranate' Hughes laid out in great detail his experiences at the hands of the Gestapo, who had sought to seize him so that he might be executed.

'As authority for this,' Hughes noted, 'they quoted an order alleged to have been issued by the Führer's HQ, in October 1942, which stated that all saboteurs, whether wearing uniform or civilian clothes, would be shot.' Repeatedly, the Gestapo had demanded that Hughes be 'handed over for execution'. It was only due to the help of his German military physician, plus Lieutenant Gerhard Schacht, a sympathetic German parachute officer, that Hughes had been able to slip the Gestapo's clutches.

Barkworth little doubted the veracity of Hughes's report. It chimed almost exactly with what he had detected, from the earlier radio intercepts in Italy. The question was, what to do about it? While they lacked an actual copy of the *Kommandobefehl* it seemed hard, if not impossible, to brief the men of the SAS in any detail. Still, they feared the effects of the order would prove dire on the ground in France. To counter that, they stressed how SAS raiding parties, even when working hand in hand with the Resistance, should take every precaution to be clearly identifiable as members of the British armed forces.

They would deploy in full uniform and wear service identity tags. In some cases, admittedly, these might be somewhat falsified. For example, Corporal Serge Vaculik carried dog tags and papers identifying him as the French Canadian 'Jean Dupontel'. This was because, by an unfortunate quirk of fate, since the French government had signed an armistice with the Germans, any Frenchman fighting on the side of the Allies was actually in breach of the rules of war – hence Vaculik needing a suitable cover. But in the main, identity tags and papers would be 100 per cent genuine.

If captured, any SAS man was to stress to his captors that he should be afforded the full protections of the Geneva Convention. It was an internationally accepted right for any nation to deploy its armed forces into any part of enemy territory. Indeed, the German high command had itself issued an edict in 1941, ruling that behind-the-lines operations by their parachute forces were perfectly legal. It was only when the British raids had begun to bite hard that they appeared to have changed their minds.

By the time of the D-Day landings, Barkworth – and Mayne – had decided that those deploying into enemy-occupied Europe should be made aware of 'Hitler's shoot-to-kill policy', at least in its bare-bones detail. Men were told to expect no mercy, and consequently to avoid at all costs being taken alive. If any man was to be captured, he was advised to warn his captors that if anything untoward happened, the SAS would investigate, hunting down the perpetrators of any such crimes.

Barkworth was a hard taskmaster, expecting of his subordinates a similar work rate to his own. In the run-up to the D-Day landings, the amount of intelligence required to underpin operations proved colossal, especially with the scope of deployments planned. The pace proved extremely stressful for those in his team. One man who seemed to thrive under such pressure was Barkworth's doughty second-in-command, Dusty Rhodes.

Together, the two men formed a somewhat unlikely yet unbreakable team. One, Barkworth, was the well-educated, deeply intellectual scion of a wealthy Devonshire family. The other, Rhodes, was the son of a gardener from Barnsley who'd gone into the family profession prior to the war. Nevertheless, amongst the many qualities they shared was an innate propensity for bluff and cunning. Barkworth eschewed all violence towards captives, including physical torture. Guile and psychological trickery, however, remained very much in play.

In Italy, a pair of German captives had been brought in, one an officer, the other a corporal. The former proved unwilling to talk. A simple ruse changed his mind. His comrade was marched outside, after which the SAS man holding him let out a long burst from his Sten gun, before returning and snapping off a salute, announcing that the job was done. In truth, the German corporal had been locked in a neighbouring hut. But upon witnessing the charade, the officer collapsed to his knees begging for his life. An otherwise brave man crushed by the power of his own imagination, he was ready to talk.

The legacy of Barkworth and Rhodes would be long-lived, echoing through the years with the SAS. It would also end up having a very powerful and personal resonance for Captain Garstin and all eleven of his SABU-70 raiders. But first, those twelve men needed to get their feet on the ground in France.

At their intelligence briefing on 16 June, they pored over maps of the area from which they had been forced to turn back. To the west lay the town of Dourdan, with its nearby railway line. Where the rail tracks snaked through thick woodland, disappearing at one stage into a tunnel, was the site of the planned attack. Intelligence reports suggested a large ammo dump was hidden in the woods, adjacent to the rail line. Garstin's mission was to hit both simultaneously – derailing a train travelling north from Orléans loaded with war materiel, and blowing the ammo dump sky high.

Orléans lay around 100 miles to the south of Paris, and the rail line was known to also carry passenger trains. Garstin was cautioned to ensure they hit the correct one, or hundreds of innocent civilians might die. It was up to him to secure intel locally in order to select the right target. How they were going to do so when dropping in blind was anyone's guess, but at least Garstin was blessed with having two French-speakers on his team.

Not only that, but by a stroke of good fortune Lieutenant Wiehe had relatives living in the area, or at least close enough that they might be of some assistance. With Mauritius being a former French colony, the links with the 'old country' remained strong. He had an aunt, Fanny Harel, living in a chateau in La Guette, a hamlet situated a few dozen miles to the east of the DZ. If push came to shove, Wiehe might call upon her for a place of hiding or to help gather intelligence.

Garstin and his men were warned about enemy forces stationed in the area – namely some SS units, an infantry battalion and a squadron of German tanks headquartered at Fontainebleau, a town lying to the south of their area of operations. And with that, the intelligence briefing was done. In dribs and drabs the men wandered outside. By rights, they were only a couple of hours away from getting airborne once more.

Vaculik turned to Paddy Barker. 'Sounds like a tough job,' he ventured.

'Could be. But by the grace of God we'll get through.'

'What about a pint?' Vaculik suggested. There was just enough time for one for the road.

'Never heard a better idea,' Barker enthused.

Not surprisingly, Ginger Jones was of a similar mind. Together they headed for the Cage's canteen, where all minds turned towards France

'How long since you've seen your mother and father?' Jones asked.

'Six years,' Vaculik replied, 'and I've never had a word, apart from the one Red Cross message . . .' He fished in his pocket and pulled out a scrap of worn and crumpled paper, one that went with him everywhere.

Jones stared at it blankly. 'Can't read your lingo.'

'Just says they're well and they'd like to hear from me,' Vaculik explained. 'Not much in six years.'

The conversation was cut short by a yell from the entranceway. 'CO wants you!'

At that the men drained their pints and hurried over to Colonel Mayne's tent. At their appearance, the SAS commander got to his feet and reached out to shake the first man by the hand. Despite his reputation as a hard, toughened killer, Mayne looked visibly moved. His handshake was firm but emotional. Though he himself was only twenty-eight years old, the men of SABU-70 were mostly a whole lot younger; some were barely out of school uniform.

This made it all the more surprising that between them they shared such widespread and varied battle experience. The SAS commander didn't doubt their resolve – each man was determined to take the fight to the enemy no matter what might transpire on the ground. But equally, Mayne didn't doubt that some at least would not be coming home.

Having bade their farewells, the men dashed to grab their personal gear and weapons, before jumping into the jeeps that would ferry them to the airfield. En route, they paused to collect their parachutes. A pretty young WAAF was handing them out, and almost without thinking Vaculik – known to be something of a ladies' man – turned on the charm.

'Why don't you come with us, love? Pleasant journey. Not too tiring. Foreign travel broadens the mind.'

The WAAF, a blonde, smiled. 'I wouldn't mind, especially with a Frenchy – to show me around, of course . . . But there you are, I'm stuck here.'

'Get on with it,' the others chided. 'Plenty of time for that when we're back, Casanova!'

Vaculik lingered for a few seconds more, long-enough to get the girl's name. 'As lovely as you are,' he announced, gallantly. 'So long, Mary.'

Minutes later, twelve figures were lining up beside the massive bulk of the Stirling, which, with its 6 foot-high wheels and 100-foot wingspan dwarfed them. For their previous flight, Garstin had had to draw straws with the other SAS commanders, for there weren't enough airframes to ferry all the parties into war. On 10 June they had gathered to do so, Garstin getting lucky and drawing lot number four of six. Tonight there would be no such uncertainties. And something else was markedly different about this departure.

Last time around, Garstin and his men hadn't taken off from RAF Fairford at all.

In its 12 June Operational Instruction No. 22, the SAS had ordered that 'Parties for DZ R.7603 will be . . . flown from TEMPSFORD for a reception committee with lights and EUREKA.' DZ R.7603 was Garstin and his men's destination, and RAF Tempsford was where the sneaky-beaky flights of the SOE were dispatched. Its existence was one of the best-kept secrets of the war.

Garstin and his men had taken off from RAF Tempsford, a 'ghost airfield' situated in rural Bedfordshire, and accessed via a side road marked 'Closed to the public'. Better known as 'Gibraltar Farm', during daylight RAF Tempsford had all the appearance of being nothing more than a ramshackle farmstead. But come nightfall, Churchill's secret aerodrome was revealed, as seemingly run-down farmhouses, barns and shacks transformed themselves ingeniously into hangars, storerooms and control towers.

RAF Tempsford was the nerve centre for the resistance armies being raised across Europe, at Churchill's urging. It boasted a direct and secure communications link to SOE headquarters in London, and from Tempsford weaponry, explosives, ammunition and radio sets were dispatched into Nazi-occupied Europe, along with the SOE agents charged with raising merry hell deep inside enemy lands.

As for 'EUREKA', the Rebecca-Eureka transponding radar was a homing system designed to navigate an aircraft directly to its target. It consisted of an airborne receiver – the Rebecca unit – fitted into the aircraft, which detected a ground-based radio signal emanating from the Eureka. The Rebecca calculated the range and position of the Eureka, from the timings and direction of the return signal, so as to steer the pilot directly to the drop-zone.

But tonight, at Mayne's urging, Garstin and his men were dropping blind, and that meant they would have no reception party, no beacons to guide them in and no need to head out from Churchill's ghost airfield. Still, more than any of the Cain/Gain missions, theirs had the hand of SOE stamped indelibly upon it. There was something about their targets that had caught SOE's attention, making their mission a true SAS–SOE hybrid, as future developments would powerfully demonstrate. But for now they were heading out from RAF Fairford, the base adjacent to the Cage.

The Stirling pilot shook hands with all in turn. 'So, you're the live cargo. Right-ho, lads, we'll get you there.'

They'd better do. No one fancied a second dose of false starts and on-off bailouts, let alone another crash-landing. As they went to climb up the steps leading through the Stirling's side door, a voice cried out a last-minute caution. 'What about the rum?' It was Ginger Jones, and he had suddenly remembered the calamity over the rum-jar last time around.

'It's all right,' Wiehe answered, 'I've got—'

His last words were lost in the roar of the first of the Stirling's four engines firing into life. The dozen men filed aboard, taking up their allotted positions – facing each other, backs to the fuselage, knees almost touching. Vaculik found himself sandwiched between Jones on the one side and Wiehe on the other. With a shake and a roar the Stirling got airborne, clawing into the skies above Fairford, the red and green navigation lights rising ever higher, until they were swallowed into the darkness.

The conversation amongst the raiders turned towards the inevitable – women. The chat went back and forth, alternately lifting up then denigrating the fairer sex, before Jones, typically, got the last word.

'Give me a pint of beer any day, and you can keep your women,' he grumbled. 'They cause nothing but trouble.'

At that point a voice interrupted, crying out above the deafening beat of the engines: 'Check your watches!' The dispatcher paused for a good few seconds, giving each man the time to get eyes on his timepiece. 'Okay, it's eight o'clock dead,' he announced, once all were ready.

'They've given me a dud,' exclaimed Jones, as he studied his watch-face disgustedly. 'It's over half an hour slow already, the dirty dogs.'

'Never mind,' said Wiehe, with a wink, 'you probably won't get time to use it.' The intimation was clear: you'll be too busy blowing up the enemy.

'I'll exchange it with a German's,' Jones growled.

To left and right the men chuckled. Jones's irreverent ways proved unfailingly contagious and served to lift the spirits. Most of the raiders wore military-issue watches, although the better-off amongst the SABU-70 party – Wiehe included – were wearing privately purchased ones. For sure, they'd want a quality timepiece that would last the course, for right now they were deploying for some considerable time, as the SAS's Operational Instruction No. 22 made clear.

'All parties will drop . . . containers loaded with food, ammo and explosives. The containers will be hidden upon arrival and will provide a reserve which will enable party to carry out operations for some time.' Weeks were envisaged, not days. 'After carrying out the first missions, each party will return to a temporary base formed in consultation with Resistance Groups, pick up fresh supplies and repeat the attacks.'

The warplane swung southeast, setting a course for France, and all lights were extinguished. Just one bare bulb illuminated the hold, with blackout curtains shielding the porthole like windows, the better to hide the Stirling from any watching eyes – a shadow, flitting across the darkened heavens. The men covered their faces with camouflage veils and tried to catch some sleep. If they could only get their feet onto the ground, their next proper rest was very likely a good few days, maybe even weeks, away.

Some time later, the dispatcher shook them awake. They were twenty-five minutes from the DZ, and somehow they'd sneaked across the French cliffs seemingly undetected. As figures shuffled towards the trap, checking the chin-straps of their helmets were tightly fastened and dragging their bulging leg-bags after them, Garstin gave a few final instructions.

They were dropping blind, he reminded his men, so they were to take cover and await his call. 'As soon as you land, stay where you are and listen hard. Then, when you see my signal, gather around . . . I shall give three flashes. Above all, don't shoot unless it's absolutely necessary.'

The eleven raiders held their commander in high esteem. Captain Garstin was phlegmatic, seemingly unflappable and a born leader of men. His long experience rivalled that of even Ginger Jones, not forgetting the Military Cross that he had won in the fevered battles before Dunkirk. His was a timely reminder, especially as SAS orders were to 'avoid a pitched battle at all costs' and to concentrate on their speciality of 'all-out guerrilla warfare'.

From where he was practically dangling out of the aircraft's bomb-bay, the dispatcher yelled for all to get ready: 'Five minutes to go.'

He signalled for the men to shuffle closer, as he moved to one side of the trap, making space for the raiders to file past and jump. Then: 'One minute to go. Action station number one.'

Seemingly even as he'd said it, the red jump-light flashed on, and an instant later it switched to green. Before any of the men had time to indulge in second thoughts, the dispatcher banged the first in line on the back, yelling 'Go!' One after the other the figures stepped past the crouching dispatcher, who gave each a slap and a Go!, before they plunged through the trap and were swallowed into the dark and howling void.

It took barely a second for each man to make the jump, plummeting through the Stirling's slipstream and dropping like stones. Within moments their chutes bloomed silver above them, catching the air with a sharp snap, swinging back and forth like pendulums. Ghostly apparitions, twelve figures dangled from domed stretches of quilted silk, laced in tight formation across the moonlit sky. It looked to have been a perfect jump, to follow a perfect flight. What a contrast to what had gone before.

Now, to discover what might await them on the ground.

Chapter 5

A tall, lean figure stood resolute at the DZ, his form silhouetted against the wide sweep of the night sky. Just as they'd intended, they'd come down in the middle of a cornfield that rolled towards the dark horizon on either side. The Stirling had executed a second pass over the DZ, dropping their all-important reserves – containers stuffed full of kit. As the thunder of its engines faded to a whisper, all settled into stillness and silence. Just the faintest breath of wind stirred the corn, which rippled like the surface of a calm, moonlit sea.

Satisfied that they were alone and unobserved, Garstin fished out his torch from his jump-smock and gave the signal – three brief flashes of light. To left and right figures rose to their feet, emerging from their places of hiding and dragging their chutes and kit behind, as they converged upon their commander's position. One of the first was Vaculik, who looked visibly elated – tearful, almost – to be back upon his native French soil.

'You all right, old man?' Garstin whispered, as the Frenchman joined him.

Vaculik smiled, his features lit with emotion. 'Couldn't be better.'

To the north there was a distant rumble like thunder, which reverberated across the heavens. Intermittent flashes rent the sky. It looked as if anti-aircraft fire had broken out over Paris, which had to mean that Allied bombers were hitting some of the factories and military targets on the outskirts of the city. For Vaculik, who'd lived in Paris as a student, it was a poignant reminder of why they had come – to help drive the invader from this land.

Four years earlier almost to the day, the French government – her forces comprehensively defeated, Paris lying in enemy hands – had signed an armistice with Nazi Germany. It had split the country into two halves. The north and larger segment was governed by the forces of Hitler's Reich, the south by the French Vichy state, named after the city from which it ruled. It was a day of infamy, but tonight was likewise a perfect riposte to the long years of ignominy and shame.

When all twelve were present and correct – no injuries suffered in the drop – Garstin decided it was time for a quick booster, for a long night's work lay ahead. 'What about a swig, Rex? I hope there's some rum left to celebrate our landing?'

'There is,' Lieutenant Wiehe – Rex – replied. 'I haven't let Ginger drink it all.'

True to type, Jones had made sure to get his hands on the rum-jar, while most had been sleeping. But there was a good deal remaining, and in reverential silence the precious tipple was passed around.

'Right, let's get on with the job!' Garstin announced, once thirsts had been properly slaked.

Wiehe and Paddy Barker were dispatched to a grove of nearby trees, to seek out a hiding place, somewhere both chutes and containers could be buried. Under normal circumstances, the French Resistance would be on hand to help carry and conceal such kit, but having jumped blind they'd have to manage by themselves. At the same time they'd have to ensure that they'd found a good place to lie low, by daybreak. It was well past midnight, which meant they'd have to get cracking.

'Jean, you and Ginger go find the containers,' Garstin announced. As 'Jean Dupontel' was Vaculik's cover name, it was how all would refer to him in the field. Garstin dispatched the others to form a perimeter guard, ordering them to raise a warning at the slightest hint of trouble. 'I'll stay here, so you'll be able to find me more easily.'

Sunrise was around six o'clock, with first light due a good deal earlier. A frenetic few hours ensued, as the containers were located, dragged into the depths of the woods and buried. By daybreak, apart from the odd flattened patch of corn, there was little visible sign that a dozen SAS men had dropped out of the sky, complete with all the supplies necessary for waging war. Garstin and his raiders were in position over 150 miles behind the frontline – the D-Day beachheads – and had set up camp deep in a patch of forest. It had taken a herculean effort to get here, but at last they were primed to go.

There was German armour and heavy reinforcements to be stopped. It only stood to find out when and where the first such trainload was due, and then they would be in business. Inevitably, that task would fall to Vaculik, the only native French-speaker amongst them. As tired men settled down to rest, Garstin ordered Vaculik to strike out on foot towards Dourdan, to see if he could gather useful intelligence on their intended targets.

With a thick greatcoat slung over his uniform – brought for the very purpose of disguise – and with his beret tucked deep in a trouser pocket, there was nothing to distinguish Vaculik from any other Frenchman who might be out and about at such an hour, at least at first glance. But his distinctive British uniform, plus the Colt .45 pistol he had secreted in the voluminous folds of the greatcoat, would be sure giveaways, if he were to be stopped and searched.

The thing that struck Vaculik as he emerged from the cover of the woodland was how calm and peaceful everything seemed here in the heart of war-torn France. It was still early, and apart from the cocks crowing and the odd dog barking, there was little to break the silence as he set off along a network of small roads. From the map, he'd figured it would take him a good two hours to reach Dourdan, if he had to walk the entire way, as opposed to hitching a lift on a passing farmer's cart.

As he stepped out, Vaculik reflected upon how dearly he loved his adopted country, the son of Czech immigrants as he was. Earlier, he'd paused to grasp a handful of soil, realising then how much he'd longed to free France – and all of Europe – from the dark yoke of Nazi oppression. Yet the feeling of elation was tempered by the knowledge of the responsibility that he shouldered: the entire fortunes of the SABU-70 raiders might turn on how he comported himself over the next few hours.

Having little idea exactly how he might go about gathering the intelligence they needed, he reached the outskirts of Dourdan. To either side sparse French farmsteads gave way to tree-lined avenues and rows of ancient townhouses. Dourdan dates back to pre-Roman times, and is steeped in the history of resisting invaders. Perhaps that boded well for Vaculik's mission. More or less immediately he spied a cafe, and something about it struck him as inviting. Deciding to follow his instinct, he plucked up courage and pushed at the door.

With a squeak of hinges it swung open. Vaculik found himself the only customer in a typical French cafe. From behind the counter the proprietor studied him. He clearly wasn't expecting any strangers at such an hour. Taking a seat at the bar, Vaculik ordered a cognac. It was something to settle the nerves – and in any case, French workmen habitually took a brandy with their early-morning coffee. Making small talk and ordering a second shot, Vaculik tried to gauge the calibre – and crucially the likely loyalties – of the man behind the bar. He had an honest, intelligent-looking face, but who knew? He could be in league with the enemy for all Vaculik could tell.

To chance his luck with the first person he met was some gamble, especially as the lives of eleven men – plus his own – might depend on its outcome, and few amongst them were under any illusions as to what would happen if they were caught. Of course there were Frenchmen who were risking their all to help liberate their country – hundreds and thousands of them. But equally there were the perfidious and the self-serving, ready to denounce anyone to further their own ends. Which might the cafe owner be?

Spurred by the fiery liquor, Vaculik ventured a first question, the response to which would very likely give him the answer. 'Tell me, whereabouts is the railway station around here?' He was about to add that he was after a timetable, but the cafe owner cut him off.

'It's at the end of the road to the right,' the man explained, sharply. He fixed Vaculik with a piercing look. Then, in an intense whisper: 'You're English, aren't you?'

For a moment, Vaculik was lost for words. Admittedly, he'd been away from France for well over three years, speaking mostly English, but how could the cafe owner know? He returned an equally searching look, wondering if he really could put his trust in this man. But the longer he delayed, the more difficult – almost impossible – it would be to deny it. A man with no connection to Britain would instantly have said so. Vaculik had singularly failed to speak up. What now?

Throwing caution to the wind – after all, something, some sixth sense, had driven him in here – he reached into his pocket and pulled out his red beret, opening it so the cap-badge was plain to see. Upon spying the iconic headwear, the triumphant smile that lit up the cafe owner's face was something that Vaculik would 'never forget'.

'So, you're here at last,' he declared, delightedly, as he motioned Vaculik to follow him into the back room. 'We've been expecting you for some time.' They entered the kitchen, whereupon the cafe owner cried out: 'Marie! Marie! Ham and eggs for this gen-tleman!'

Soon a sumptuous feast was set before Vaculik, while the cafe owner gave a hurried explanation of his links to the Resistance. They had been expecting British parachutists for several days, but for one reason or another – Gestapo surveillance, the weather – the drops kept getting cancelled. For his part, Vaculik explained that ideally, he'd like to speak to the town's stationmaster, if he was the sort who might be inclined to help.

'Nothing easier,' the cafe owner replied, effusively. 'He happens to be one of ours and he drops in every morning for a drink, so all you've got to do is wait.'

For an instant it struck Vaculik that this was all proving a little too easy. Perhaps all was not as it seemed. He lit a cigarette, and fingered the cold steel of the Colt that he had stuffed deep in his greatcoat. If the cafe owner was planning to sell him out, at least he wasn't completely defenceless. Vaculik had barely had time to finish his smoke when the cafe owner slipped away. Moments later the kitchen door opened again, and he was back with a second figure. This man, he announced, was the stationmaster himself.

The three had a round of conspiratorial cognacs, clicking glasses in a silent toast. Then the new arrival got straight to it. 'You want to know the timetable for the Boche trains,' he ventured. The term 'Boche' was an insulting one used for the enemy, meaning 'cabbage-heads' or 'thick-heads'.

'I do,' Vaculik confirmed, 'and the exact number of carriages.' In fact, he wanted to know every possible detail, including – crucially – what the trains might be carrying.

The stationmaster promised Vaculik he'd have the information by midday, when the Germans would send through details. While the war materiel travelling by rail was wholly German, the train drivers and the network staff were still mostly French. If Vaculik waited at the cafe, the stationmaster would return, just as soon as he had the required information. They shook hands warmly, after which the stationmaster left with a creak of the noisy hinges. A drop of oil on those wouldn't go amiss, Vaculik mused.

He killed time with the cafe owner, talking about the German sentries posted along the rail line and the patrols they tended to mount hereabouts. Vaculik made sure to commit all to memory, for this was priceless intelligence. But around eleven o'clock he heard the cafe door swung open as if 'by someone who owned the place', hinges squealing in protest. It was too early for the stationmaster, and he detected that a group of voluble Germans had crowded inside and were ordering drinks at the bar.

Vaculik figured there was nothing for it but to remain where he was, in the comparative safety of the kitchen. Surely there was no reason for any German to venture back here, not unless someone had ratted on his presence. The minutes crawled by, as he kept one nervous hand on his concealed Colt. Then, without warning, the kitchen door was pushed open and a German soldier appeared, framed in the doorway.

Vaculik tried not to stiffen when the soldier's eyes fell – unsurprisingly – on the stranger in the kitchen, draped as he was in a heavy greatcoat. One wrong move now and Vaculik didn't doubt he was done for. From all the noise they were making, he figured an entire German patrol had crowded into the cafe, and he wasn't about to eliminate them all with his Colt .45 pistol, which chambered just eight rounds.

It seemed a long time before the soldier finally spoke. 'You French?' he demanded, revealing right away his suspicions.

'Of course,' Vaculik countered, forcing himself to look the man straight in the eye and adopting what he hoped was a relaxed, convivial air.

'What are you doing here?' the soldier asked, giving voice to the obvious next question.

Fortunately, Vaculik had his answer at the ready. 'I've been ill, and I've come here to spend a few days in the country with my cousin.' He was sick, hence the thick coat.

The German eyed him, sceptically. 'Oh, I see,' he murmured. He didn't sound entirely convinced. 'It's just that I like talking French,' he added, as if to put Vaculik at his ease. He turned back to the doorway, gazing out into the cafe, as if undecided.

Vaculik steeled himself to flee. It was the SAS's credo: *He who shoots and runs away, lives to shoot another day.* Well, Vaculik might get off the first shot, to nail his inquisitor, but after that he'd have to make a mad dash out the back of the kitchen, for the cafe was sure to have a rear entrance. Even if he made it, he'd have an entire German patrol on his heels, and by the way they were acting these guys seemed to be regulars at the cafe, and Vaculik had to presume they knew the lie of the town.

As the figure hovered at the doorway, Vaculik felt his feet go cold as ice. They were thrust tight together far under the table, in an effort to hide his army footwear. He reproached himself for being such a damn fool, and for placing all his confidence in his very basic disguise and in the cafe owner; for not having asked to hide himself away, while he awaited the stationmaster's return; for risking everything on this one wild card.

From the far side of the doorway he heard the scrape of chairs, as people got to their feet. Now was the moment of truth. Voices called in German to their comrade, who still seemed frozen at the kitchen doorway. Finally, he turned back to Vaculik, and with what appeared to be a friendly wink he bade his farewell. Moments later, all twelve of them filed out of the bar.

Vaculik didn't know what to think. All he was sure of was that he wanted a stiff brandy to calm his nerves. The minutes dragged by, before finally the stationmaster put in an appearance. In hurried tones he gave Vaculik the lowdown. A train was expected around 1.30 a.m. the following night, one that would be packed full of munitions and fuel. It was scheduled to stop at Dourdan to take on water, before steaming towards the Normandy beaches, where its cargo was urgently needed to spur the German counter-offensive.

It seemed like the perfect target. 'Any other trains at around that time?' Vaculik queried.

'None. The last passenger train is at eight o'clock, and the first after that is at six in the morning. There's no danger of making any mistake.'

The risks of hitting a train crammed full of French civilians were minimal. Lastly, Vaculik asked about guards and watchmen. There were sentries posted at either end of the tunnel, their intended ambush point. As to the wood itself – the supposed location of the ammo dump – the stationmaster knew nothing about that. Vaculik had just about everything he needed, and it was time to cut and run. He thanked his helpers, but the stationmaster insisted that he guide Vaculik out of Dourdan via the back way.

They left by the cafe's rear entrance, after which he threaded his way expertly along a series of narrow alleyways and lanes, until open country beckoned. There the two men shook hands, the stationmaster wishing Vaculik good luck. As if in afterthought, Vaculik asked him one final thing: might he find a way to warn the train's driver and guard, especially if they were good loyal Frenchmen? Might there be a way to save their lives, without forewarning the enemy?

The stationmaster agreed to do what he could, after which Vaculik set off, taking a series of paths that wound through forests and fields and across streams. Now and again he opted to hide himself, as people wandered past, but mostly it was an uneventful if hot and tiring journey. Late that afternoon, he paused for a break in the shade of a wood, stooping to mop his brow. By his reckoning, it couldn't be far now.

All of a sudden a voice hissed out of the shadows to his rear: 'Hands up!'

'Pack it up,' Vaculik countered, recovering as best he could from his initial fright. He'd recognise the tones of Ginger Jones anywhere.

'We'd given you up for lost,' Jones announced, with a grin. 'What's the news? Any good?'

Vaculik assured Jones he'd got what was needed, after which Jones led him a few hundred yards into the depths of the woods, to where the raiders had set up camp. Sensing he had good news, Captain Garstin greeted Vaculik enthusiastically, shaking hands and slapping him on the back. There were cries of 'Good old Frenchy!' all around. Beams of sunlight pierced the shadows and birds chirped happily. Though fatigued, Vaculik felt elated. He'd done it. He'd pulled off his mission, even if mostly by good fortune and chance.

He proceeded to brief his fellows on what he had discovered. It was a bonanza of intelligence, that was for sure, but one vital piece was missing. They still knew nothing about the ammo dump in the woods. They needed to determine its exact location, the strength of any guard, sentry shifts, the amount of ammunition stored there and how best to blow it up. Ideally, they'd need to gather all that information tonight, if they were to be ready to strike by tomorrow evening.

Garstin figured four men should be enough to execute such a close target reconnaissance. Typical of a man who led from the front, the SAS captain would command the recce party, together with Paddy Barker and Ginger Jones. Vaculik would also have to go, as their native French-speaker, leaving Lieutenant Wiehe, who also spoke fluent French, in command of the rear party. They'd set out at ten o'clock that evening, as the summer light faded into darkness, which left Vaculik just a few hours in which to try to grab some kip.

Having gobbled up a tinful of Spam, washed down with a hot mug of tea, Vaculik pulled a pair of old socks over his muddy boots, crawled into his sleeping bag and fell instantly asleep, with Colt and grenade at his side just in case of any surprises. The trick with the socks was one learned during SAS training: it enabled you to emerge from your sleeping bag fully clothed and booted, and with grenade and pistol to hand, so you could move immediately and run and fight if needed.

At ten o'clock sharp the four men set out in single file, with Garstin in the lead. Minutes earlier, Vaculik had been woken by Paddy Barker, thrusting a steaming mug of tea into his hands. He'd just had time to gulp it down before the off. The moon was bright, despite a high veil of thin, wispy clouds, and it provided more than enough illumination by which to see and to navigate. Moving on a compass bearing, they marched across open country, through woods and along twisting bridlepaths.

Now and again a figure took a nip from a hip flask, passing it back and forth, and Jones and Vaculik chewed on wads of tobacco, to help keep alert. For three hours they pushed ahead into broken, difficult countryside, legs tiring at the pace demanded by Captain Garstin, until finally they emerged from a patch of woodland and stumbled upon the rail tracks, the pair of iron lines glinting beguilingly in the moonlight. Finally, they had eyes on the very thing they had come here to blow up, along with the locomotives that steamed back and forth.

But Jones for one seemed singularly unimpressed. 'I thought they said this was a mechanised war,' he grumbled. 'My poor feet are giving me real gyp.'

Garstin glanced at Jones, shaking his head in mock despair. 'Shut up moaning,' he chided, gently.

'The British soldier must grouse,' Jones countered, stubbornly. 'It relieves his ruddy feelings. What I'd give for a pint right now!'

Vaculik offered Jones his hip flask. It wasn't exactly beer, but it was half-full of whisky and Jones was welcome to a swig. Typically, the former miner from Wigan almost drained it dry.

'My God, what a swallow!' Vaculik complained, as he held the flask to his ear and shook it. 'You've practically emptied it!'

Before Jones could think of a suitable retort, Garstin announced that it was time to get down to business. The rails marked the dividing of the ways. One party, formed of himself and Paddy Barker, would execute a reconnaissance moving east, searching for the ammo dump, while Jones and Vaculik would head in the opposite direction.

'Once done, return to the camp direct,' Garstin instructed. 'Don't wait around for either party, don't shoot unless absolutely necessary and move like snakes.'

With his simple set of instructions given, the two parties shook hands and went their separate ways. It was now that the months spent amidst the rugged hills and dales around Darvel would truly come into their own, the countless nights spent prowling through darkened forests – or camping in rain-soaked woodlands – more than proving their worth.

Lieutenant Wiehe had written of such things in his war diary – of 'forty-three hours without sleep', of running for mile after mile 'in pouring rain and through swamps, risking getting stuck at every step'. He'd described an exercise on Kintyre – a peninsula on the rugged, storm-blasted west coast of Scotland – 'two days and three nights of walking, attacking, and practising all we will have to do' as the rain lashed down. But equally, he'd noted how 'at the farms where we stop we are the object of almost embarrassing hospitality: eggs, milk, butter . . . the benevolence of the locals is really charming.'

Now, the SABU-70 raiders would reap the benefits of such rigours many times over. For a short while Jones and Vaculik followed a path that ran alongside the rail tracks, pausing every now and again to wait and to listen. The cloud cover was heavier now, the moon obscured for long periods during which the night grew as still and dark as the grave. Windless and deathly quiet, it felt oppressive somehow, the air thick with some unseen but predatory menace. Now and again they lost their way, before finding it again, until finally, without warning, Vaculik dropped to the ground like a stone.

Jones followed suit, realising as he did just what had spooked his comrade. Somewhere nearby someone was stamping his feet, and whistling to himself under his breath. The tune was instantly recognisable: it was 'Lili Marlene', a German love song that had proven surprisingly popular with Allied troops as well. But neither man doubted that it could be anything other than a German soldier whistling that song, right here and now.

Raising their heads a fraction, the two SAS men spied the source of the noise: a sentry was positioned just a few paces along the railway embankment. It was a miracle that neither Jones nor Vaculik had been spotted. It was also testament to the stealth with which their training, plus their rubber-soled boots, enabled them to move through the dark. Further along the track, they could also make out the yawning black void of what had to be the entrance to the tunnel. This was it: their planned ambush point.

But however much Jones and Vaculik might appreciate the song, neither wanted to risk moving from their place of hiding, and as the minutes ticked by the cold from the gravel embankment seeped deeper into flesh and bone. Both men racked their brains for some means to slip past, but short of knifing the sentry, how were they to do so? If they killed him, his body would be discovered, which was sure to blow their mission wide open. They would have to stay put and gamble that eventually the sentry would move on.

More to the point, they'd have to hope that no train came steaming down the tracks to crush them where they lay.

Chapter 6

The minutes ticked by. Eventually a second set of boots was audible, this time tramping up the tracks from the direction of the tunnel. The inbound figure exchanged greetings with the sentry – '*Gute Nacht*' – before the latter slung his rifle over his shoulder and, still whistling 'Lili Marlene', prepared to depart. It was the changing of the guard, and the two watchers figured that this momentary distraction offered them the chance to sneak away.

Keeping on their bellies, they broke cover and crawled a short distance, before halting to watch and observe. It was one o'clock dead, so clearly they switched guards on the turn of the hour. After a few words, the 'Lili Marlene' whistler wandered off towards a patch of nearby forest, and Vaculik and Jones decided to follow. With any luck, he should lead them to the sentries' quarters.

With the two SAS men moving 'as silently as Red Indians on the war-path,' they reached a hut set in a clearing in the trees. The lone sentry slipped inside, but hardly a chink of light was visible, apart from what had been let out by the momentary opening and closing of the door.

'Stay here and give cover,' Vaculik whispered to Jones. He was going forward, to try to get a peek inside. That way they might gauge how many enemy soldiers there were in total.

Vaculik crept ahead. If he were captured, there was little

chance his French might save him now. He reached the wall of the hut, and risked a peep through a small window, spying a dozen figures ranged around the room. Some were asleep, others were playing cards, and several bottles of empty wine lay upon the table. It struck Vaculik how easy it would be to lob a grenade through the window, to shower the occupants with lethal shrapnel. But of course they had much bigger fish to fry.

Silently, he stole back to where he'd left Jones and reported what he'd seen. They decided it was time to split up. They still needed to find the ammo dump, which by rights should be situated in the woodland somewhere thereabouts. Two could search faster than one, and they agreed to rendezvous at this spot in an hour. Time was running out, and they had little margin for error if they were to make it back to their camp come daybreak.

They scurried off in opposite directions, moving towards the black wall of trees. Alone, the silence proved ever more intimidating, but each man pushed onwards into the forest's dark embrace. It made sense for the ammo dump to be nearby, for the trees would hide it from any marauding warplanes, and for sure, by the summer of '44, the Allies had mastery of the skies.

It wasn't long before both men stumbled upon a series of massive, shapeless heaps, roped over with tarpaulins. When they lifted the first corners, huge stacks of landmines, bombs and 88mm shells were revealed. Those 88s were the ammo not only for the German's superlative anti-tank guns but also for the *Tiger II* tank, a 70-tonne behemoth only recently introduced into service, plus the *Elefant* and the *Jagpander* heavy tank destroyers, all of which boasted an 88mm main gun. Those shells had been piled up here so locomotives could haul them north towards the Normandy beaches.

The oddest thing was that there didn't seem to be a single guard placed upon the heaps of munitions. Vaculik had counted ten giant piles, Jones eight. But upon reflection, maybe it did make some kind of sense to leave them unguarded? The raiders were 150 miles behind enemy lines, and what German soldier in their right mind would expect Allied troops to be wandering about here, in the depths of night, with havoc and mayhem in mind? Which meant that this was a target going begging.

'Eight whacking great dumps of bombs and not a sentry anywhere,' Jones whispered, once they were back together. 'Can't make it out.'

Vaculik concurred. He couldn't fathom it either. 'Never mind,' he added. 'Let's get cracking, or it'll be light before we can get away.'

With that, they set off on a compass bearing heading due east, hoping to navigate back to their camp by the most direct route, even though both men felt plagued by fatigue. Barely a word was said between them as they pushed on, but gradually the luminous dial of their compass grew less and less bright, as the sky above them lightened, presaging dawn. Sweat-soaked, munching chocolate for energy, they sensed all around them the land was coming to life. It would be a disaster to be seen now, after all the night's achievements.

Finally Vaculik and Jones stumbled into the woodland where they had their camp. As far as they could tell, they hadn't been spotted. Everyone was there, barring Captain Garstin and Paddy Barker. Their absence was worrying, especially as it was broad daylight by now. It wasn't quite so dire for Vaculik, or even Wiehe, to be out and about amongst the locals – at least they could speak French. But neither Garstin nor Barker could manage more than a few words. After chain smoking cigarettes in an effort to calm their nerves, Vaculik and Jones gave into the inevitable, crawled into their doss-bags and were shortly fast asleep.

The two missing men finally reached the camp around midday, having had something of a misadventure. En route, Garstin had been set upon by a German shepherd belonging to a local farmstead. He'd had no choice but to kill the dog with his Fairbairn–Sykes fighting knife, the iconic blade issued to all Commandos and special forces. With its 7-inch tapered blade and its two razor-sharp edges, heavy handle to give grip in the wet, plus cross-guard to prevent slippage when driving the blade in, it was designed to slip between an enemy's ribs or to thrust down through his clavicle.

Sadly, Garstin had had no option but to use it on the dog, in an effort to silence him and to get them back to their base undetected. Three years earlier, Vaculik had faced a similar dilemma, when escaping from the clutches of the *Carabineros*, the armed, quasi-military police force in Spain. Having faked a stomach upset, he'd managed to crawl out of a toilet's rear window and slip away. But as he'd headed into the mountains, a large dog had set upon him. Though he had hated having to do it, it was either 'kill or be killed, a struggle to the death without mercy'. Such were the dark and fearsome necessities of war.

After the night's activities, Garstin and Barker were 'just about all in' and they craved sleep. But first the SAS captain wanted to learn how Vaculik and Jones had got on. On hearing of their adventures, he figured that all was set for tonight's attack. Between them, they had garnered every snippet of intel they might possibly need. There were two sentries set on the rail track but none on the ammo dumps, of that they were certain. Garstin announced that he'd issue his orders that evening, after all had got some rest.

There was also the small matter of making up the explosive packages they would need for the night's attack. Vaculik and Jones would need eighteen separate charges, for the ammo dumps they'd found, and as Garstin and Barker had discovered twenty-five heaps during their recce, that made forty-three in all. Garstin decided they'd knock-up forty-five one-pound charges, so 'two for luck', plus another four for the railway itself.

Those charges placed on the ammo dump would need delay-action fuses, so that Garstin and his men could set them, then move to their ambush positions on the rail line, the ammo dump only being blown after they were long gone. They figured that four-hour delays should allow for any eventualities. While some crawled into sleeping bags and settled down to sleep, others began working on the explosives.

With typical British ingenuity the boffins at SOE had developed any number of specialist charges, disguised as everyday items. The so-called 'tyre-bursters', for laying on roads used by enemy convoys, had to look as realistic as possible. Explosives had been developed that resembled lumps of rock, and even dog or horse muck. But the most bizarre invention of all was the infamous exploding rat, about which the SOE instruction manual was very particular.

'A rat is skinned, the skin being sewn up and filled with PE to assume the shape of a dead rat. A standard No. 8 primer is set in the PE.' PE stands for plastic explosive, and the classic means of deploying the rat was to hide it in the coal scuttle of a locomotive. In due course the rat would be shovelled into the furnace, along with the coal, at which point it would detonate, perforating the steam boiler, which would trigger a devastating secondary explosion.

As Garstin and his men would be striking by stealth, no such items of subterfuge were necessary, barring one particularly ingenious SOE invention. Experience in North Africa, Italy and elsewhere had taught the SAS there was little point in simply blowing up rail tracks. The locomotive driver would likely spot the break in the rails and bring his train to an emergency halt, so defeating the object of the exercise. The damaged tracks could be lifted out and a new section dropped into place. It might delay the train for a few hours, that was all.

The answer the SOE had come up with was the 'fog signal'. Already a century-old design, the fog signal was a tried and tested piece of technology used on the railways to warn a train driver if a stop signal might be obscured by fog. It consisted of a small metal bowl and a pressure plate, which clamped to the rail. The bowl was full of black powder and detonators, and whenever the fog came down the signalman would attach fog signals to the rails ahead of the stop sign. As the locomotive went over them, they would detonate, the sharp crack warning the train driver to slow down.

The SOE's version of the fog signal was a cunning adaptation. A snout was added to the bowl, attached to a length of detonation cord. Hot gases produced by the explosion gushed out of the snout, triggering the detonation cord, which was connected in turn to a charge placed further ahead on the rails. The fog signal would detonate, triggering the explosion up ahead of the speeding train, and giving the driver no time to slow down. His locomotive would plough into the section of wrecked track at high speed, causing a catastrophic derailment.

'It was found that about 16–20 ft of cordtex from the fog signal to the charge was almost certain to derail the train,' an SAS report concluded (cordtex is another term for detonation cord). And that was exactly what Garstin and his men intended to do tonight.

In the evening, they gathered for the final briefing. 'We leave here at nine o'clock,' Captain Garstin began, portentously. 'At midnight we should be planting the first charges. If all goes well, an hour should be enough for the job.' By one o'clock in the morning, all forty-five charges should have been set on the ammo dump. 'Then, we deal with the sentries at the time the relief takes place. Ten minutes for that, and for setting up the Bren guns on the embankment. Open fire on the Jerries, then beat a retreat in groups.'

Garstin had split his force into four parties, each with a specific objective. Once the train had been hit, they were to make themselves scarce, moving back to a woodland rendezvous.

'Does everyone know exactly what he's got to do?' Garstin demanded, his eyes scanning the figures ranged before him. Eleven men nodded their assent.

'Okay, sir.'

'Everything's in order.'

'We ought to have some fun.'

At nine o'clock the parties set out, trying to stick to the trees and the deepest shadows. At that time it was still light, and farmers could be seen working in their fields. Occasionally a German military convoy rumbled past on a not-too-distant road. Wearing their jump-smocks, and with their red berets removed, the raiders had to hope that at a casual glance they'd be mistaken for a German foot patrol. By 11.50 p.m. all had converged on the rendezvous point, and they gathered for a few final words.

'Above all, silence,' Garstin stressed, as he reminded all of their roles. 'Silence and a cool head. We'll meet again here in an hour.'

That agreed, Garstin dispatched Jones to execute a quick recce of the ammo dumps, to check that nothing significant had changed. The eleven men waited in a tense and expectant silence, as Jones flitted off into the gloom. Minutes later he was back, with news that all was as it should be.

'The Jerries are all safely in their little hut, playing cards and drinking – lucky devils,' he reported, wistfully.

'We'll soon see about that, Ginger,' Captain Garstin replied, evenly. 'Now, let's get going.'

Upon Garstin's word, the SAS raiders slipped noiselessly into the trees. Vaculik, Jones and Barker – the three musketeers – formed one party. They picked their way through the forest towards where they knew the ammo dump had to lie. Now and again they paused to listen, checking for any sign of the enemy. To left and right the occasional rustle of leaves betrayed where the other parties were stealing towards their targets, but other than that all they could hear was the sound of their own hearts, pounding in their ears.

Though the night was noticeably chilly, each of the raiders was sweating. Vaculik made it to the first of the heaps, the one nearest to the guard hut. Kneeling down, he lifted one corner of the black sheeting, hardly daring to believe that it could all be this easy. Vital supplies for the enemy's Normandy offensive were within their reach, utterly unguarded. As he peeled the thick tarpaulin back further, it crackled alarmingly, the noise sounding like gunshots, loud in the silence. For a moment he froze, convinced the guards must have heard, but there was no answering cry of alarm from the hut.

Sweating profusely, he used his sleeve to wipe the drops from his brow, before biting down hard on the delayed-action timer. Each of their 'timer pencil' fuses consisted of a brass tube, topped by a copper cap – the thing Vaculik had just flattened with his teeth. Crushing that served to release acid into the tube, which ate away at its internal components, chiefly a steel wire that held a firing pin at the ready. When the wire was eaten through, the spring-loaded firing pin would shoot down the tube, striking a percussion cap and so detonating the charge. Differing combinations of acid strength and thickness of wire gave the timer pencils their varying durations.

If they'd got their sums right, these timer pencils should take four hours to go off. Fuse set, Vaculik thrust the charge deep into the heap of munitions, as far as he could reach. That way, it should detonate in the heart of the pile, triggering scores of secondary explosions. His first charge sorted, instinctively Vaculik made the sign of the cross. He wouldn't like to be in that guard hut when this little lot went off. In fact, he wouldn't particularly want to be within half a mile of the place when the explosions were triggered.

As Vaculik crawled towards the next dark pile, he reflected that to left and right other figures were engaged in similar stealthy work – placing delayed-action charges on the enemy's ammo dumps. He felt suddenly elated. 'They were all fine fellows,' he reflected, though of course 'a mistake on someone's part could blow us all to smithereens'. All it would take was for one of the charges to have been made up with a ten-minute delay, as opposed to a four-hour one, and they'd all be toast.

Just as he'd indulged such thoughts, the door to the guard hut swung open and a figure stepped out. As the German soldier strode purposefully towards Vaculik's place of hiding, he tried to flatten himself further into the vegetation and the gloom. He could hear the sentry's individual breaths as he drew ever closer. What the devil could have happened? What had aroused his suspicions, Vaculik wondered?

The German stopped. Vaculik felt as if his 'heart stood still'. But then there was the distinctive sound of a man relieving himself in the bush, and all Vaculik's fears subsided. They were replaced by a flash of rage. What a swine, he told himself. Was that the best place the man could find? Spurred by his anger, Vaculik crept around the other dumps, placing all of his charges with a grim determination. On the way back to the rendezvous point, he ran into a shadowy figure. It was Paddy Barker.

'How did it go?' Vaculik whispered.

'Couldn't have been better,' Barker replied, in his distinctive Irish tones, 'except I wanted to sneeze all the time. I must have got a cold, or hay fever or something.'

'Let's hope our luck holds. It seems almost too good to be true. We're a bit behind schedule though.'

'Half an hour before the sentry's relieved,' Barker pointed out, reassuringly. 'Plenty of time.'

An indistinct gleam of light drew them back to the rendezvous. It turned out to be one of the men studying his compass. He got a rocket for his pains: the faint light could have been spotted by the enemy. With all present and correct, the twelve raiders made their way towards the railway line, heading for the point where the tracks were swallowed up by the tunnel. Now for the bloodiest of tonight's work – taking out the sentries, without which it would be impossible to get to work on the rails.

Vaculik and Jones had been ordered to deal with one sentry,

Wiehe the other. Stealth and silence were all now. The guards would have to be killed without a sound, and that meant using the knife. Over the years the men of the SAS had learned just how hard it was to dispatch a man with a blade. It was a deeply personal, up-close, bloody way of killing, and could often prove somewhat hit and miss. It was far easier to shoot an adversary in the head with a pistol. But with silence being at a premium, that left only the knife.

Jones and Vaculik had talked through how they would do this. They'd set upon a ruse. Jones – something of a bold and brazen figure by nature – would step out into full view and throw out a challenge. With the sentry distracted, Vaculik would spring from behind, sinking his Fairbairn–Sykes blade down through the man's neck, at the clavicle. If executed correctly, it was a move that should prove quick and lethal, but also extremely bloody.

Vaculik didn't much relish the thought of having to 'strike a man down like a beast', even if he were the enemy. For his part, Wiehe had set upon a similar plan, recruiting one man to play the role of the distracting party while the other wielded the blade. Plan set, the four men settled down in the thickest shadows near the tunnel entrance to wait.

As the minutes ticked by, Vaculik's guts felt knotted up with anxiety and tension. He reflected upon how he was about to 'stain his hands with another man's blood'. It was one thing shooting a man at a distance, quite another to slide in the blade at close quarters, and to feel the victim's life blood ebb away. War, he figured, could be 'a rotten thing'.

His thoughts were dragged back to the present by a heavy tread moving along the tracks. It was one o'clock sharp and the Germans were nothing if not punctual. The changing of the guard was underway. Clodhopping boots thumped along from sleeper to sleeper, and then the watchers could hear the grounding of rifle butts, as a few words were exchanged in German. They gave the outgoing sentry a few minutes to get away, before they figured it was time.

'Off you go, Ginger,' Vaculik whispered. 'Good luck!'

On the far side of the track, they knew that Wiehe and his partner would be doing very much the same.

Loosening his knife in its sheath, Vaculik stole down the embankment. Up ahead his prey was whistling, keeping his back to Vaculik as he stomped his feet to keep warm. Reaching the bottom of the embankment, Vaculik stole into the tunnel entrance, hiding himself where it was darkest. He saw the sentry turn and start to move his way, little suspecting that 'death was waiting for him under the grim arch'.

Bang on cue the figure of Jones stepped out behind the man, crying out, 'Hey, Jerry!'

By way of response, the guard swung around and raised his rifle, uncertainly. Before he'd brought it to his shoulder, Vaculik was upon him, springing like a cat, his left hand snaking around the man's mouth to silence him, his right driving the dagger downwards at his neck, right to the hilt, just as they'd been taught during training. As Vaculik held him in a vice-like grip, an acrid salty tang filled his nostrils, and moments later he felt the man's life drifting away. He lowered the body, until the sentry lay in a lifeless bundle at his feet.

Killing done, Vaculik paused to wipe his bloodied blade on the dead man's uniform. 'Sooner him than me,' he told himself, darkly.

Figures swarmed onto the unguarded tracks now, explosives in hand. Each rail was fitted with a pair of 3-pound charges, each of which was linked by detonation cord to a fog signal. Each of the fog signals was clamped on top of the rails, so the locomotive's wheels would crush them, triggering the explosions.

'That's it,' remarked Garstin, as he double-checked the charges. 'The Brens are in position. Let's go join the others.'

The ambush had been set to one side of the embankment, where the grass was long and provided perfect cover. All being well, the train loaded with war materiel would come steaming out of the tunnel, trigger the charges and get thrown from the rails pretty much opposite where the Bren guns had been situated. While the Bren light machine gun might have had half the rate of fire of the German's MG 42 – introduced in 1942 as the replacement for the MG 34 – it was still the most accurate such weapon of the war. It was also foolproof, being capable of withstanding huge mistreatment and misuse. Soldiers swore by the weapon, as did Resistance forces and guerrilla armies alike.

The twelve raiders settled down in position. Grenades were readied in the grass, close to hand. It was all about timing now. If the train were significantly delayed, and if the sentry shift changed, Vaculik and Wiehe's bloody handiwork would be discovered, and all would have been for naught. What Garstin and his men were banking upon was archetypal Teutonic efficiency – that despite the Allied air raids that had swept across occupied France, the enemy would stick rigidly to their timetables.

The minutes ticked by. Edgy figures kept checking watches, or fiddling nervously with grenades, rearranging them in rows, or sliding magazines into and out of weapons. Finally, just the faintest hint of a rumble could be heard far to the south. Was that the train? Surely, it had to be. It was just before 2 a.m., which made it bang on schedule. Fingers curled tighter around triggers. Apart from the Brens, most of the raiders were carrying either Sten guns or the US M1 Carbine, a semi-automatic rifle packing a fifteen-round magazine.

The faint rumble grew to a throatier roar. Excitement spiked as the rails below started to ping and vibrate with the onrushing momentum of the approaching rail wagons, packed full of their heavy cargo. The distinctive chuffing of the locomotive became audible, plus the rattling of the individual carriages. Soon a long plume of black smoke became visible, tracking the locomotive's progress as it steamed towards the tunnel, the odd burst of cinders sparking the night air a ghostly orange.

The locomotive was swallowed into the tunnel entrance, the noise changing dramatically as it tore onwards, a few seconds later bursting out into full view. Almost instantly, there was a sharp crack and a blinding flash as the charges went off, and the locomotive seemed to be thrown into the air as the blasted rails disintegrated and buckled before it. Still the head of the train was driven onwards, ploughing up the embankment with a deafening shriek of tortured metal and gushing steam, as clouds of rocks and shattered sleepers were thrown in all directions.

Finally the engine ran out of momentum and toppled over onto one side, after which the carriages behind it buckled and telescoped into each other, in a deafening cacophony of ripping, tearing, crashing mayhem. As the entire length of the train came to a twisted halt, a petrol tanker to the rear of the locomotive burst asunder, showering the wreckage with fuel. There was a momentary silence, before the cries of the wounded and the roars of alarm cut the air, German soldiers trying to leap for safety.

'Open fire! Grenades!' Garstin yelled.

Swathes of Bren fire tore into the wreckage, followed by a volley of grenades. Almost instantaneously the first lick of hungry flame erupted, as the blasts ignited the spilt fuel. Within seconds the train was burning ferociously, trapped figures being incinerated in the flames and 'shrieking like all the devils in hell'. Here and there groups of enemy soldiers tried to muster some form of resistance, but the Brens tore into them, scything them down. A second and a third petrol tanker detonated now, as from end to end the train was engulfed in fiery ruin.

Waves of heat pulsed over the embankment, being so strong as to singe the saboteurs' eyebrows. Where the raging fire was at its most intense, it ignited the loads of ammunition the train was carrying, small arms rounds flying off in all directions, lacing the sky with smoky trails like some kind of demented firework display. The whistle of exploding rounds was so deafening that the figures on the embankment found themselves ducking instinctively, as bullets ripped and snarled through the air all around.

But a different sound also became audible now. Bursts of aimed fire stabbed out from the nearest patch of woodland. Whether it was from enemy soldiers who had managed to evacuate the train, or the local guard force, no one could be certain, but either way the enemy were fighting back.

'They're getting a line on us!' warned Jones, as bullets tore into the embankment.

By way of answer, he lobbed one of the few remaining grenades in the direction of the enemy fire. The explosion was followed by a sudden shriek of agony. Then, grabbing one of the Brens and firing from the hip, he raked the woodland with short, aimed bursts. It was clear that the balance of the battle was shifting now. There were twelve SAS raiders, and the train would have been carrying many more soldiers than that, not to mention the force of guards stationed nearby. It was time to split.

'Get out now!' Garstin yelled an order. 'Every man for himself!'

Figures broke cover, dashing down the rail tracks, leaving the burning wreckage and fiery confusion behind them. At the rear of the raiders, Jones stood resolute, Bren at the hip, ripping out bursts of suppressing fire. If any of the enemy were minded to give chase, he was determined to frustrate them. When finally the raiders paused to take stock, all had got away. Only Jones appeared injured, for one arm was stained with blood. Fortunately the bullet had only nicked him, but he'd been lucky.

Indeed, they'd all had been very fortunate to have Jones in their party, a long-experienced SAS man and a born warrior. As Vaculik readily admitted, it was 'thanks to him that we all got away'.

But only so far. From the maps, Captain Garstin had identified a wide swathe of woodland as the point where they would go to ground, but it was many hours' march away. It was 2.30 a.m. by now, the train ambush having taken no more than ten minutes to execute, though it had felt like a lifetime. They had three hours maximum before it started to get light, and many miles on foot to cover. And shortly there would be forty-five further blasts, as the ammo dumps blew sky high.

'Get a move on, lads!' Garstin exhorted. 'Those dumps are due to blow in an hour and a half.' By rights, every German soldier and his dog would be out searching for them by then.

They would need to set a relentless pace, if they were to evade the hunters.

Chapter 7

Relieved of the weight of the charges they'd been carrying, the raiders' packs were mercifully lightened, and they pressed on at a good pace, while behind them the heavens blazed a fiery orange. Every now and again an angry stab of flame erupted skywards, as fire spread further through the wreckage of the train, detonating a fuel tank or a cargo of explosives, each blast rolling across the heavens like a peal of ghoulish thunder.

Of course, these twelve men were fugitives now. Deep behind enemy lines and with no armed Resistance band with which to lie low, they felt very much the hunted. There would be no welcoming farmsteads at which to take refuge; no church to provide cloistered sanctuary; no remote manor house at which to go to ground. They were alone and they expected to be ruthlessly sought by an enemy hell-bent on vengeance.

'We were anxious to put as much distance between us and our pursuers – because, of course, we should be pursued . . . before the hunt started up in real earnest,' remarked Vaculik. Already their sense of elation and triumph was tempered with a dark uncertainty. 'We moved quickly, a line of silent, shadowy figures.'

Avoiding all major roads and well-used tracks, they cut across country, fording rivers, executing the kind of forced march that would have made Paddy Mayne proud during their Darvel training. But very quickly they were soaked to the skin, their heavy uniforms weighing them down, their boots squelching dispiritingly. Waves of fatigue washed over the twelve men, but still they forced themselves to go on, and with one aim in mind: to put enough distance between themselves and the fiery mayhem they had wrought that no enemy would be able to trace them.

'Our lives depended on the successful outcome of this flight under the stars,' Vaculik recalled, '. . . and none of us hung back.'

Typically, some gave vent to their feelings. Paddy Barker and Jones cursed as they marched. After Jones's heroic stand with the Bren, he'd earned the right to swear like any trooper. Vaculik joined them in the cussing, as a tree-root caught his boot and almost sent him flying. No man wanted to take a fall, for they were doubtful whether they'd have the energy to clamber to their feet again.

'Nearly four o'clock,' Garstin sent the word down the column of men. 'Don't let up now, boys.'

It was a timely reminder. Moments later a massive blast erupted far to their rear, the ground at their feet reverberating with its force, a huge mushroom cloud of smoke fisting high into the sky, streaked with gouts of fire and flying debris. As the raiders paused to watch the cataclysmic effects of their handiwork, a second and third ammo dump went up, each exploding with an almighty roar, which even at the distance of several miles sounded deafening.

The horizon to the west seemed awash with angry flame, and the raiders could only imagine what it must have been like to be anywhere near such blasts. No one in the vicinity could have survived such savage devastation. 'They were my enemies,' Vaculik remarked, of those figures that he'd spied through the window of the guard hut, 'but I couldn't help feeling sorry for them.' Even in the midst of war, human compassion and kindness somehow endured.

There was no time to stand and admire their handiwork, or to indulge any fleeting sense of regret. They had 6 miles still to cover before they should reach the woodland and barely an hour of darkness remained. Tireless as ever, Garstin urged them on. They passed a farm, early wisps of smoke curling from the chimney, cows grazing peacefully near at hand. Wistfully, the raiders remembered similar scenes during their training, when Scottish crofters had pressed fresh milk and eggs and butter into their hands. There was no chance of that now.

They struggled onwards, reaching a ploughed field and tripping over deep furrows. Only willpower kept them going. It was at moments like this that the men fell back on the lessons learned during training, each digging deep to find hidden reserves. Swimming icy Scottish lochs in the depths of winter, followed by a forced march for hours in soaking, freezing clothing, prepared a man for the very worst. So too did the long survival exercises amongst the snows of Ben Nevis, armed with only vitamin tablets, Benzedrine and initiative, all washed down with a mug of tea brewed from melted snow.

At such moments morale tended to plummet to zero, but over time it forged 'Commando soldiers capable of withstanding the utmost privations', Vaculik recalled. Of course, they'd also had to learn all the skills of behind-the-line operations, being taught jiu-jitsu – a Japanese martial art for close-quarter combat – knife work, rapid fire with all kinds of weapons, plus sabotage work, blowing up walls, trees, railway lines and road vehicles. In the Battle Course training, they'd had to conquer a series of seemingly insurmountable obstacles, including high stone walls, fierce mountain streams and ditches filled with the most unspeakable gunk imaginable.

They'd learned to lie across barbed wire while their comrades tramped over them, as a means to surmount such obstacles, all the while with their instructors unleashing a constant stream of live fire just above their heads. Real mines were detonated in close proximity as the sodden, exhausted trainees dashed past. Such realism came with its costs: the instructors reckoned upon a significant attrition rate – men lost to bullets or shrapnel, or other injuries – but the results were said to justify the means.

Here, on their desperate race to escape their hunters, the SABU-70 raiders were putting that to the ultimate test. The sun blinked above the eastern horizon, its blaze revealing a pall of black smoke lying thick over the distant battleground. The line of dark trees – sanctuary – was still a good way away, and here and there people were out and about, tending to their fields. Thankfully, no one seemed to pay the column of soldiers much heed, no doubt taking them to be German troops intent on executing their orders.

Step by step the forest drew closer, but a final obstacle lay in the fugitives' path: a main road. Every now and again trucks carrying grey-uniformed troops could be seen hurrying along it – doubtless the hunters, never imagining that the hunted might be so close. Having mastered their Battle Course training, they should be able to conquer this final impediment, despite their exhaustion. One last burst of defiance; one final jolt of energy fuelling shattered bodies, and they should be in amongst the trees.

When finally there was a break in the traffic, Garstin ordered his men to break cover and to dash across. All twelve made it, apparently without being spotted. Having struck deep into the woodland, they flung themselves down on a mossy bank, utterly exhausted. Fortunately, Paddy Barker still had the energy – and foresight – to get a brew going. Shortly, he was able to hand around a mug brimful of tea heavily laced with sugar. It proved hugely invigorating.

With all feeling a little refreshed, Garstin set a two-hour watch rotation. The plan was to move off again that evening, pushing deeper into the woods and further away from the scene of their sabotage. With no Resistance comrades to hand, and precious little explosives remaining, the SAS captain didn't doubt that they would need to be pulled out. With the hue and cry up, it was best to disappear as soon as humanly possible. The only issue was how, when and where to get the RAF to land – that was, if the plan remained in place to pull Garstin and his team out in such a daring manner.

Though rarely used in wartime, the concept of flying in to pluck small teams from out of enemy territory wasn't quite so groundbreaking as it might at first seem. For three years the SOE had been using the Westland Lysander – a light aircraft with exceptional short take-off and landing capabilities – to ferry in and to collect its agents from remote fields prepared by the Resistance. Named after a mythical Spartan leader of the same name, the Lysander had proven excellent at landing on a sixpence, and at hedge-hopping and steeple-dodging thereafter, to shake off enemy fighter planes.

Taking that concept a little further, SOE, working hand in hand with the RAF, had set up a special training school where SAS, Commandos and the like could be trained in the 'selection, preparation and operation of clandestine airstrips'. Before patrols were dispatched into the field, SOE would advise them on the best possible stretch of terrain to be checked out and prepared as a makeshift landing ground.

From RAF Blakehill Farm – just a short hop from Fairford – 233 Squadron were operating the recently introduced Douglas C-47 Dakota (or 'Skytrain' in US parlance), a twin-engine transport aircraft perfect for such daredevil operations. Though originally designed and built as a commercial airliner, the C-47 was of rugged construction and its durability was legendary. 233 Squadron had played a key role towing gliders and dropping parachutists, to support the D-Day landings. But they also flew clandestine missions on behalf of SAS and SOE, most usually hopping over to Fairford to pick up their charges, before dropping them on a remote field somewhere in occupied Europe.

The C-47 had proved rugged, versatile and ideal for putting down on rough and ready airstrips, hewn out of a French or a Norwegian farmer's field. In one instance, an entire SAS squadron – almost a hundred men-at-arms – would be pulled out of one such strip deep in rural France. But all of that lay some time in the future. If successful, Garstin's would be one of the first ever units to be extracted in such a way.

Understandably, he and his men were a little apprehensive of being used as the guinea pigs, especially as the failure of such a pick-up would likely have dire consequences. Lieutenant Wiehe was in charge of SABU-70's signals, and he'd managed to make contact with the UK, to assess the chances of the pick-up going ahead. The reply he'd received had proven unexpected in the extreme.

During the Second World War radio was the only viable means to make rapid contact from the field. For the SAS, the nerve centre of such communications was at Moor Park, Kilbirnie, some 30 miles to the northwest of Darvel. There a series of BBC transmitters, linked up to 'Jedburgh' radios – specialist elite forces wireless sets, known as 'Jed sets' – was able to transmit signals across hundreds of miles deep into occupied Europe. Once in the field, stick commanders used their portable Jed sets to receive and send such messages, each having a unique SABU call-sign via which to do so – Lieutenant Wiehe's being 'SABU-70' of course.

While one team at Moor Park manned an emergency frequency 24/7, in case any party in the field needed urgent help, units were supposed to restrict their signals to a once-daily comms window. Such restrictions meant that sending long messages – enciphered and via Morse code – was impossible. Communications were limited to the briefest of missives regarding air operations (most often, radioing in target coordinates), intelligence of immediate interest or urgent orders. As a result, once a patrol had parachuted behind the lines, it was largely self-governing. Little might be known of its movements, and little control could be exerted over it in the field.

There was another, compelling reason to ensure that communications were kept short and sweet. Knowing such teams were deploying to wreak havoc and mayhem, the Germans were hell-bent on finding them, and radio detection was one of the best means of doing so. Just as soon as a patrol risked coming up on the air, codebreakers from German intelligence might be handed intercepts to decrypt and decipher, plus the enemy's direction-finding units might be dispatched in their mobile tracing vans, in an effort to locate the source of the signals.

Morse code is a universal language – a series of dots and

dashes that represent the individual letters of the alphabet, plus numbers. As with any radio signal, intercepting a message sent in Morse code couldn't be prevented. Once it was plucked from the ether the codebreaking began, and the senders of the message became the hunted. Predictably the Germans had a highly efficient direction-finding unit within the signals intelligence division of their army, with a well-defined system for going about its work.

First, powerful transmitters picked up the clandestine signal, narrowing its location to a town, city or rural district. Then the mobile detecting vans trawled the area, trying to pick up further signals and pinpointing the exact source of the transmission. Once that was done, the location was raided in an effort to seize the radio set plus operator(s). The Germans sought to capture the top-secret codebooks, along with the sets, which made it a great deal easier to break future transmissions. Hence the need to keep any such communications to an absolute minimum, or to risk being caught.

Lieutenant Wiehe had received his own brief burst of dots and dashes, winging through the ether from Moor Park. When he'd decoded the short message, its content had proven extraordinary. Not only was the RAF fully intending to drop in and pluck them to safety, but they planned to do so from an *enemy* airfield. For the Mauritian lieutenant, this was some kind of news to have to deliver to his commander, a decorated SAS captain with long experience at the sharp end of operations.

When Garstin asked Wiehe if there was 'any news from London' and if the RAF pick-up was still to be expected, and if so when, Lieutenant Wiehe decided to give it to him straight.

'In three days' time exactly, at Étampes,' he replied. 'They've had the nerve to choose a Jerry airfield. We can only try it. What do you think, sir?'

As Garstin well knew from their briefings, there was an important German airbase situated at nearby Étampes. Having seized France in its lightning summer 1940 offensive, Nazi Germany had proceeded to build a series of airfields all along the Channel coast, from which to launch its air offensive against Britain. By late 1940, there were 700 such landing grounds across France. But by late 1942 those along the Channel coast were being pulled out of service, for fear of the Allies launching airborne operations – glider or parachute landings – onto those airstrips, as part of their invasion plans.

By the summer of 1943, only 100 airfields were in regular use across France, and the Luftwaffe had pulled back to those set a good distance from the coast. Étampes was one of these. In fact, there were three airbases at Étampes, forming a complex set within a 4-mile radius. Étampes-Bellevue was an emergency landing ground, which meant there was little there to see. Étampes-l'Humery was simply a dummy airfield, designed to draw Allied attacks away from the real airbase, which was Étampes-Mondésir.

Étampes-Mondésir was the real McCoy. It came complete with four large hangars, plus workshops, barracks, storage bays and thirty-one reinforced aircraft shelters. Fifteen separate flak positions ringed the airbase, which also boasted radar stations, a demolitions detachment, signals staff, air raid detachments, and refuelling and ambulance units. Most intriguingly, Étampes-Mondésir also housed *Feindgerät Untersuchungsstelle 6* – 'Enemy Equipment Examination Station 6' – a place where captured Allied war materiel could be taken apart, studied, replicated and ultimately defeated.

In recent months, US bombing raids had had a massive impact over France, and Étampes had played a key role in trying to assess what specific pieces of technology the Americans might have brought to the party. In particular, the Norden bombsight – which used an analogue computer calculating ground speed and direction, combined with an autopilot system to achieve unprecedented accuracy – was something the Germans were desperate to get their hands on. Development of the Norden was on a scale comparable to the Manhattan Project – the building of the atom bomb – and it had been granted a similar level of secrecy. If a Norden could be salvaged from a downed Allied bomber, *Feindgerät Untersuchungsstelle* 6 was just the kind of place to study, examine and master it.

There was also a battle-hardened Luftwaffe squadron based at Étampes-Mondésir. *Kampfgeschwader* 51 (KG 51 – Battle Wing 51) 'Edelweiss' was named after a white flower found high in the Alps that was known as a symbol of beauty and purity. Having fought in the Battle of Britain and the Blitz, KG 51 had been posted to the Eastern Front, before being pulled back west to counter the D-Day landings. Commanded by *Oberstleutnant* Wolf-Dietrich Meister, KG 51's most recent successes had been against the March '44 Nuremberg raid, during which RAF Bomber Command had lost more than 100 aircraft, accounting for 545 aircrew.

The Nuremberg raid constituted Bomber Command's worst night of losses in the entire war. In repelling the fleets of Allied bombers, *Oberstleutnant* Meister had executed a daring sortie deep into British airspace, piloting a twin-engine Junkers Ju 88, one of the most versatile combat aircraft of the war. At 4.30 a.m. he'd spotted a Lancaster bomber over Cambridgeshire. The aircrew, believing they were home and dry, had switched on their navigation lights. Meister put two long bursts of cannon fire into the Lancaster from dead astern, forcing it to crash-land at Wickenby airfield, where it collided with another bomber. Miraculously the aircrew survived.

Unsurprisingly, Meister and his Battle Wing were held in high esteem by German command, and KG 51 had recently received perhaps its greatest accolade of the war: it had been one of the first Luftwaffe units to receive the Messerschmitt ME 262 *Sturmvogel* – Stormbird – the world's first ever jet-powered fighter plane to enter active service. Boasting a top speed of some 560 mph, it was faster and more heavily armed than any Allied fighter, and was one of Hitler's so-called *Wunderwaffen* – supposedly revolutionary superweapons that would enable Nazi Germany to turn the tide of the war.

That, in a nutshell, was the airbase from which Garstin and his men had been ordered to expect a pick-up by RAF aircraft. Typically, after the long war that he had fought, Garstin didn't seem to turn a hair at the prospect. His main concern appeared to be whether he and his men could manage to hide from the enemy for long enough to make the rendezvous with whatever RAF crew was daring enough to fly in to collect them.

The Dourdan railway and ammo dump had been hit early on the morning of Wednesday 21 June: the pick-up was set for midnight, two days hence – so Friday 23 June. Two days to avoid capture. 'I think they're leaving it a little late,' Garstin told Wiehe. 'We'll be lucky if we don't get bagged before then. Still, it can't be helped, I suppose.' And with that, the matter was settled. If the RAF were up for it, so were the SAS: the pick-up would go ahead as planned.

Still, Garstin felt a recce of Étampes airbase might just be in order, to see what they were up against.

Chapter 8

As Garstin and his men had trekked deeper into the wild wood to the west of Étampes town, they'd discovered wide stretches of ancient, tangled forest – perfect for hiding out. But over a long and fretful night, the hunted found they had time on their hands. Perhaps too much time. Too long to dwell on their thoughts. Too many false alerts and alarms. Too long straining eyes and ears in an effort to detect pursuers amongst the maze of trees. Too long with the mind playing tricks.

'The woods seemed full of strange and louder-than-life noises,' Vaculik recalled. 'The sudden cracking of a branch or the rustling of foliage sounded tremendous. I almost thought I could hear a leaf fall.' Hour by hour, they'd felt their spirits darkening.

Despite his Canadian cover name, Vaculik – 'Jean Dupontel' – was a Frenchman, of course, and he had the most to fear if he was taken alive. For days now, he'd felt as if he'd not known 'a moment's relaxation when body and soul were at rest . . . Always at my shoulder was the thought of death and the dread of being captured . . . All life consisted of . . . the edge of the wood, a longed-for radio call and the danger of more shootings.'

All the better, then, that they had received a much-needed morale boost. It was the morning of their second day in hiding when London had called. Not via their Jed set, of course. For a good-news message such as this, headquarters wouldn't risk communicating via a means that might be traced. Instead, the SAS had developed an ingenious back-up system for the very simplest of communications, one that was believed to be foolproof in terms of tracking or interference.

Captain Garstin had been the first to detect it, as he tuned into the BBC, using a set of headphones to ensure no noise could leak into the surrounding woodland. Bizarrely, it was the distinctive, singsong opening lines of a French nursery rhyme that had drawn his attention, inserted into the normal running order of programming.

> *Sur Le Pont D'Avignon,*
> *L'on y danse, l'on y danse . . .*

On the bridge of Avignon,
They are dancing, they are dancing . . .
In Avignon, an ancient town in the south of France, there existed a thirteenth-century bridge that was the inspiration for the ditty. Indeed, the dance was supposed to be performed on or under the bridge itself. But for whatever reason – sheer bedevilment; a classic dose of British eccentricity; to better thumb one's nose at the enemy – those opening lines were played over the BBC in order to alert SAS parties scattered across France, and their Resistance brethren, to listen out for a message.

There was the briefest of pauses after the nursery rhyme lines had faded out, before the clear voice of the BBC announcer came on air: 'Hello SABU-70. Hello SABU-70.' For several days now, Garstin had been hoping to hear something like this – a message specific to their call-sign. Now, at last, it was happening.

'Hello SABU-70, this is London. Good work and thanks. Good work and thanks.'

Glowing with excitement, Garstin passed the headphones around to those who were awake, as the message was repeated several times over. The meaning was clear. The RAF must have got a reconnaissance aircraft over the Dourdan area, to check the damage they had wrought. Only if they had definitive evidence would they send such a clear message of congratulations. London was calling to let them know what a fine job they had done. It was only the briefest of missives, but it served to lift everyone's mood.

The twelve gathered in a circle with a newfound sense of purpose. None had doubted that their mission had been successful, but it was quite another thing having London say so. The woodland covered hundreds of acres, and they'd chosen a perfect spot as a hideout, where a clear stream tumbled through. One or two figures bent over the cool flow, using razor blades to shave, after which they wiped themselves clean with an old handkerchief. Others checked and cleaned their weapons and recharged magazines.

Jones and Vaculik declared they'd had enough of living on meat cubes and dry biscuits, the staples of their rations. They were intent on executing a covert scavenging operation. Their maps revealed a farm a few hundred yards away, on the fringes of the forest. They'd try for that. They set forth, and en route encountered not a soul, apart from one young boy who fled in terror at the very sight of the Robin Hood warriors.

The farmer seemed somewhat less perturbed at their unexpected appearance. Vaculik soon learned why: he had mistaken them for Germans. With a little gentle probing, Vaculik discovered what lay behind the man's misapprehension. The previous night, a force of enemy troops had searched the area in strength, including the farmstead. They hadn't let on exactly what or whom they were looking for, but Vaculik and Jones could hazard a guess. Clearly, they would need to be 'more cautious than ever' now.

Using the French francs provided as part of their kit, Vaculik purchased a brace of chickens and two dozen eggs. It made sense to leave the farmer with the impression that they were German soldiers, for obvious reasons. Vaculik figured that with his shock of red hair and stocky physique, Jones could just about pass as a Boche. As for Vaculik himself, with his dark hair and dark eyes, plus his height, he could just as easily be German as French.

With the deal done, the two men headed back to camp where they delivered the fresh provisions plus their news. Upon learning of the enemy search party, Garstin decided to stiffen their watch. Although they had put a good many miles between themselves and the site of their Dourdan sabotage, clearly the hunt was still on. And while they might be ensconced deep within the woods, Garstin made certain that they should keep the smoke from any cooking fires to an absolute minimum.

A day earlier, Howard Lutton – soldier by trade, poacher by nature – had rushed out of the forest excitedly. 'Plenty of rabbits around!' he'd declared. 'Traces everywhere. Rabbit pie on the menu in no time!'

'For crying out loud,' Jones had grumbled. 'Anybody'd think you'd bagged Hitler!'

Well, in scavenging those chickens and eggs, he and Vaculik had done something close to capturing the Führer, or so at least it seemed to those twelve men in their deep forest hideaway. It was a long wait, but when finally the meal was ready, they filed up one by one to receive their portion reverentially. Thankfully,

Wiehe had managed to husband a little of their precious rum. It was issued with the meal, a shot in a mug of steaming tea for each of Garstin's men. It proved sparse, basic fare, but rarely had they enjoyed a meal more.

The sun went down, shadows lengthening amongst the trees. It was time to undertake the recce of Étampes airfield. Garstin wanted to know the location of strong points and any weaknesses, plus where the guard posts were situated. That way, they could better plan how to steal onto the airstrip, to catch their RAF taxi service home. It made sense for Vaculik to undertake the recce, and he was free to choose who to take with him. Unsurprisingly, he picked Jones and Barker – the three musketeers once more.

Though the Irishman and the man from Wigan groused a great deal – as was their wont – in truth they were pleased to have something to get their teeth into. The three men slipped through the darkening woodland, pushing east towards the aerodrome. Situated some 6 miles to the south of Étampes town, the airbase lay in flat, open countryside, with a railway line cutting past its western perimeter. This was a different set of tracks from the ones the SABU-70 raiders had sabotaged, but as with all such routes hereabouts, the rails headed north to Paris and beyond.

Once they were out of the woods, the airbase was in plain view, the glare from the runway lights casting a bright halo into the sky. As they neared the perimeter and the cover grew more and more sparse, the fugitives dropped into a crawl, slithering through the dark bush like wraiths.

'Blast this belly-crawling lark,' Jones grumbled. 'I'll end up with housemaid's knee.'

'A few pints when we're back in London will soon put you right,' Vaculik shot back at him, reminding them of the reason they were there. All being well, from this very airport lay their route home. 'Now shut up and keep your eyes peeled.'

A dark, blocky mass reared up ahead of them. It had to mark some kind of perimeter fortification. As they paused to watch, a sentry appeared in silhouette, then slipped from view again, before reappearing a few moments later. There was one guard at least up ahead, treading a regular beat back and forth along the wire. With the wind blowing in the watchers' direction, not a sound had carried across to the sentry, and he seemed oblivious to their presence.

'I could just about do him,' growled Paddy Barker. 'What'll you bet me?'

'Save it for tomorrow,' Vaculik hissed. None of them were out to kill any Germans tonight.

Glancing left, another blocky shape was visible – a second sentry post, around 200 yards away. They figured they should aim for the midpoint, and see if they could cut a path through. Inching ahead, they reached the first coils of vicious barbed wire without any sign that their presence had been detected. One by one, they snipped the strands, each bite of the steel cutters making a sharp click as it sliced through.

Once the way was clear, the three wormed past, wriggling into a patch of long grass on the far side. Having taken stock, they decided to make for a nearby patch of trees. From there they should be able to get a proper look at the airstrip with little danger of being spotted. But when they reached the copse, they had the shock of their lives: the 'trees' were entirely fake. Utterly lifelike at anything other than close quarters, their trunks and limbs were artificial, and the foliage seemed to consist of chicken feathers spray-painted to imitate leaves – green for new growth and brown for those on the wane – mounted on what looked like chicken-wire frames.

'You've got to hand it to them,' whispered Jones, grudgingly, as he studied the ingenious *getarnte Bäume* – camouflaged trees. The fake woodland must have been placed there to obscure something from the air, and moments later one of the fugitives spotted it. 'Look! There's a plane!' hissed Jones.

Stealing through the ghostly terrain of this false forest, weapons very much at the ready, they crept towards the first massive airframe. Instantly recognisable, it was the distinctive form of a Junkers Ju 52 'Tante Ju', a tri-engine transport aircraft that was the workhorse of the Luftwaffe, the third engine forming the plane's stubby pug-like nose.

The three men eyed it hungrily. It was just too tempting. 'Mustn't forget to blow that tomorrow,' Vaculik whispered. He'd just given voice to what was on all of their minds.

'It's as good as done,' confirmed Paddy Barker.

'Mightn't be a bad idea to put a match to it right now,' added Jones. 'Give us something to see by.'

Beneath the bravado, it was fortune alone that had led them to the enemy warplane, which at anything other than close quarters would have been obscured by the fakery. Had they not headed for the 'woodland', they might never have found it. There were sure to be others, equally carefully concealed. But the three musketeers had to remind themselves of the purpose of tonight's mission: it was to recce the airbase, to see how they might best be pulled out of there. They weren't looking for targets. But still . . .

'I wonder if we've got enough plastic?' Vaculik mused. Plastic explosives. Surely they must have. Garstin was bound to have kept a little in reserve.

They darted across to an adjacent 'copse', just to test their theory. Sure enough, the fake trees concealed a bomb dump. What more could any of them have wished for? As long as they had some explosives remaining, they didn't doubt that Garstin would want to leave a little fiery carnage in their wake. He wasn't the kind who could ever say no, especially when such juicy targets were so close at hand. It was also a truism that a few good men on the ground could achieve so much more than a fleet of aircraft at altitude. After all, that was exactly why the SAS had been sent in: to find, fix and destroy.

Repeatedly in the run-up to D-Day, Étampes airfield had been targeted by the Allies, US bomber fleets leading the charge. In one such raid, on 14 June '44, sixty-nine B-17 Flying Fortress heavy bombers had rained down munitions, but they'd only succeeded in destroying one Ju 52 and damaging one other. It was little wonder that the Germans had gone to such lengths to camouflage their airframes, but what the Allied bomber fleets had failed to do the SAS might have a crack at, with what meagre supplies of explosives they still had to hand.

Either way, it was time to press on. They needed to check out the runway and any defences that might impede an incoming – mystery – aircraft. To do so involved breaking cover from the fake forest, and belly-crawling through a stretch of deep grass. Ten minutes of such work, and they had eyes on the runway itself. Before them lay a wide expanse of billiard-table-flat grass, a good 1,500 yards or more from end to end. Two separate flare paths were visible, delineating two distinct runways.

They'd seen enough. With the right kind of warplane, flown by an aircrew with balls of steel, the way was clear to nip in and out again, pausing briefly to pick up a dozen shadowy figures dashing out from the cover of the long grass. If the RAF were crazy enough to try it, the three musketeers figured they had no option but to give it a whirl. And if they could spread a little carnage in the process, so much the better.

Recce done, they retraced their steps. But as they stole back towards the perimeter, they feared that Murphy's Law might well have come into play: *if it can go wrong, it will.* Thick cloud scudded across the moon, making it all but impossible to find the spot where they had cut their way in. They could of course slice their way out again, but that doubled the chances of being caught. Finally hands groped their way to where the strands had been severed and as quickly as possible they slipped through. As the others stood watch, Jones twisted the strands back together again, so the fence would appear as if it was still intact.

It was 4 a.m. by now, and as they hurried away from the air-base the fatigue began to hit. The three fugitives longed for their sleeping bags 'like a tired horse longs for the stables'. Perhaps for that reason – they were stumbling along minds intent on sleep – the first Vaculik, Jones and Barker knew of being back at their camp was when those on sentry rammed the muzzles of their Sten guns into their ribs. There was a password of course, but a string of the most colourful curses from Jones served just as well. Few were those who could master the accent and the sheer bloody-minded ribaldry of the former miner from Wigan, and for sure no German ever could.

Moments after reporting to Garstin on all they had found, Vaculik, Jones and Barker crawled into their sleeping bags and were dead to the world. While the three musketeers did their sleeping beauty act, Howard Lutton went a-hunting. By the time Vaculik, Jones and Barker were awake, he'd managed to trap four fat rabbits.

'There's no one can snare like he can,' Lieutenant Wiehe told them, admiringly, of Lutton's work. 'He was a bit of a poacher before he joined the army, you know.'

At times there was a strange otherworldliness to the Mauritian, a quaint naivety that seemed so at odds with this most bloody and brutal of wars. In a sense, it made the camaraderie between Wiehe and Jones, the born fighter from Wigan, seem all the more bizarre. But as David Stirling had averred, the ranks across the SAS were all of 'one company' and any sense of class was 'alien and ludicrous'. In that spirit, Jones and Wiehe's was a friendship that would endure, come what may. Equally, Wiehe had proved his mettle when it mattered most – dispatching the sentries back on the rail tracks at Dourdan. Beneath his courteous, old-fashioned demeanour there lurked a core of inner steel. He would need it for what was coming.

It was around dusk that evening when the first of the sentries came dashing in to raise the alarm. 'Make yourselves scarce! There's a Jerry patrol coming!'

Within an instant, the figures in that clearing had melted into the trees, hearts pounding, Stens at the ready. The seconds ticked by, before the heavy tramp of boots came echoing through the trees. Garstin had set their camp a good distance off a winding path, which was fortunate, for that was the way the column of grey-uniformed infantry came. They appeared alert and focused, scanning the undergrowth to either side, but equally they weren't inclined to stray from the path. As they stomped past, it struck the watchers how easy it would be to wipe them out with a few well-aimed bursts. But they had neither the ammo to waste, nor the inclination, for that would only serve to draw the enemy's ire.

Not a minute after they had appeared, the column of German

troops was gone, swallowed into the trees, and all was silence once more. Garstin gathered his men. It was time to head for the airfield. Tonight, either they would pull off the mother of all extractions, or they'd be ensnared within the mother of all battles. He was clear about one thing: whichever way it might go, they would be sure to plant the few charges that remained on the juiciest of targets.

Whatever fate might hold in store, Garstin was determined that SABU-70 would go out with a bang.

Chapter 9

With unerring instinct, Jones had led the raiders right to the hole cut in the wire. It was a night like that which had gone before, with dark clouds blanketing a hidden moon – all the better for what Garstin and his men had in mind. There wasn't a breath of wind in the skies, which should prove perfect conditions for what one adventurous – some might argue crazy – RAF aircrew had planned for tonight. Once all had crawled through the gap, Jones pushed ahead like a bloodhound on the scent. Otherwise something of a grouchy, unruly rebel without a cause, there was no one better when on the trail of the enemy.

Moments later they were in amongst the fake trees. The stark, angular form of the Junkers Ju 52 loomed before them, the distinctive black cross superimposed upon a white background seeming like a target emblazoned on the fuselage. Gathering his men, Garstin eyed the aircraft, appraising where best to plant his charges. With a wingspan just short of 100 feet, and a length of over 60 feet from the stubby nose to the swastika adorning the sharp tail, the three-engine Junkers was only a little smaller than a Stirling. On one level, it was almost beyond belief that no sentries had been placed on such a target. It looked to be a case of the Dourdan ammo dumps all over again: the enemy still could not conceive of Allied troops operating so far behind the front lines.

'Give it a Lewes bomb with a four-hour fuse,' Garstin ordered, in hushed tones.

The Lewes bomb was one of the SAS's very own inventions, a work of genius in terms of its efficacy and simplicity. During the earliest days, when operating in North Africa, the SAS had realised it needed a new kind of sabotage weapon, one light enough for a man to carry several in his pack, but potent enough to destroy a swathe of enemy warplanes – then their chief targets. It was Lieutenant John 'Jock' Lewes, one of David Stirling's stalwarts, who'd found the answer, inventing a DIY blast-incendiary device, which combined plastic explosive, diesel fuel and thermite, a metal-based gunpowder.

The resulting 'Lewes Bomb', as it became known, proved highly effective. Encased in a small canvas bag, it could be secreted inside a cockpit or on the wing of an enemy warplane, in close proximity to the fuel tank, so that when it detonated the resulting fire spread with dramatic consequences. Made up by hand in the field, the Lewes bomb didn't look like much – a stodgy lump of plastic that resembled bread dough and was distinctly oily to the touch, stuck with a timer pencil. But when detonated in the vicinity of the fuel tank, it would render the aircraft into a seething fireball.

That was exactly what Garstin intended now, with the Ju 52. Or at least in four hours' time, as that was the length of fuse they would set – hopefully giving them plenty of time to be whisked away, prior to the real fireworks getting started. With the Ju 52 rigged to blow, Garstin asked Jones to lead them to the ammo dump, plus any other targets that might be close at hand, after which they'd crawl into the cover of the long grass to await whatever miracle might materialise out of the dark skies.

'Supposing our plane doesn't come?' Lieutenant Wiehe whispered, as the men set about lacing the ammo dump with charges.

It was a reasonable question. If the RAF failed to show, presumably the twelve fugitives would be triply hunted, once the Lewes bombs went off, and with almost nothing left – no bullets nor bombs – with which to fight.

'If it doesn't come, it doesn't,' replied Garstin, fatalistically. 'That's all. You can only die once.'

That last remark – *you can only die once* – epitomised the SAS captain's steely resolve. After the long years at war and his numerous brushes with death, the Grim Reaper had become something of a constant companion for Pat Garstin, as it had for many of the more experienced SAS commanders. Death lurked on your shoulder, scythe at the ready, especially when on operations deep behind the lines, and in particular when bearing in mind the intent, if not the fine detail, of Hitler's Commando Order.

It was twenty minutes to midnight by the time all their remaining charges had been set: time was running, and Garstin needed to get his men into position. As they crawled through the long grass, weapons at the ready and making for the runway, there was the distant grumble of what sounded like an aircraft high in the heavens.

'What's that?' Garstin hissed. 'Sounds like a plane.'

Sure enough, there was an aircraft up there somewhere. If it was their RAF pick-up, it was a good quarter of an hour early. Garstin urged his men onwards, worming their way towards the very fringes of the mown strip. But as they hurried ahead on knees and elbows, the air above Étampes airbase was filled with a deep, throbbing thunder. It wasn't just one aircraft that was inbound, that was for sure.

Left: 6 June 1944: as Allied troops stormed ashore to seize the D-Day beaches, the men of the Special Air Service were dropped far behind enemy lines, tasked with a crucial do-or-die mission.

Hitler had ordered his armoured legions – including the 9 SS Panzer Division Hohenstaufen, 10 SS Panzer Division Frundsberg, and 2 SS Panzer Division Das Reich – to the beachheads, to hurl the Allies back into the sea. The SAS were charged to stop the Nazi armour in its tracks.

Right: Legendary SAS commander Colonel Blair 'Paddy' Mayne, DSO, commanded 1 SAS, which spearheaded the D-Day operations. He urged his men: 'Before they surrender, the Germans must be subject to every known trick, stratagem and explosive which will kill, threaten, frighten or unsettle them: but they must know that they will be safe and unharmed if they surrender.'

Left: Major Ian Fenwick (centre, with binoculars) and Captain Cecil 'Jock' Riding (right of photo), prepare the men of D Squadron 1 SAS for Operation Gain, one of the most daring and audacious of the D-Day missions. Sadly, Fenwick would die when his jeep hit an enemy ambush, leaving Captain Riding to take overall command.

In Scotland, rigorous training got fresh SAS recruits into shape for the D-Day missions. Mayne had set his men the 'around Britain challenge' – to cross the nation begging, borrowing and stealing whatever they might need, for there was no better way to teach behind-the-lines survival techniques.

Below: Riding in Short Stirling warplanes, the men of D Squadron were parachuted to the south of Paris, in the depths of night, as the SAS prepared to cry havoc and let slip the dogs of war.

Above and below: Heavily-armed Jeeps were dropped to the Op Gain raiders, along with supplies of weaponry, explosives and ammunition. Moving by vehicle and on foot, and linking up with the French Resistances, the raiders began to blow up trains laden with armour, plus road convoys, just as Mayne had urged.

Right: Churchill had urged massive supply drops, to arm the French Resistance prior to D-Day. Once Mayne's raiders had parachuted in, they brought confidence, audacity, command and raw firepower, the combined SAS and Resistance teams proving 'extremely successful' on the ground.

Left: From their hideouts set in thick woodland to the south of Paris, the Op Gain raiders struck time and time again, causing 'considerable material damage' to 'rolling stock and railway lines.'

In areas hosting the SAS there was a 'carnival' atmosphere, as locals sensed their hour of liberation was close at hand. But with German military units harassed at every turn, they turned their ire on the villagers, wreaking savage vengeance.

Twelve men formed the sabotage team codenamed SABU-70, commanded by Captain Patrick 'Pat' Garstin MC (above). Garstin and his second in command, Lieutenant John 'Rex' Wiehe (right), had been ruled unfit for frontline duties, but had managed to hide their injuries and blag their way into the SAS.

Under cover of darkness, Captain Garstin, Lt. Wiehe and their raiders blew up a steam-train laden with war materiel bound for Normandy, plus scores of ammo dumps piled high with tank and artillery shells.

Pat Garstin and his men found themselves hounded by a vengeful enemy, hunting them cross-country in fast moving patrols. Cut off from the French Resistance, they faced all-but-certain capture, unless …

Left: In Britain, a pilot and his crew readied a C47 'Dakota' to execute one of the most daring and audacious rescue missions of the entire war.

Flying into Etampes airfield, a Luftwaffe airbase lying to the south of Paris, the aircrew landed under intense fire, plucking Captain Garstin and his raiders to safety. (Photos above and below show a second August '44 landing by C47 deep in enemy territory, to relieve a sister SAS patrol: a USAAF photographer just happened to be aboard and managed to snap these remarkable images).

S A S
Special Air Service

THE train was a long one. It carried men and ammunition to help Rommel hold the Allies near Caen.

Still nearly three hundred miles from the fighting, the troops on board smoked, played cards and ate their rations while they raced through the Forest of Orleans.

The engine hooted as it neared a clearing in the trees. Ahead the drivers could see the straight stretch where a road ran parallel with the line.

As the train entered the clearing, three jeeps appeared on the road and drove at breakneck speed alongside it.

Standing in the back of each jeep, khaki-clad figures spotted streams of incendiary bullets at the train from twin medium machine-guns.

Not until the train was on fire front and to and and had been derailed did the attack cease. Then the jeeps disappeared back into the forest as quickly as they had come.

Once more Rommel had lost valuable men and material to an impudent British unit that had been harrying his rear ever since he had battered his way down the road that led to Alexandria.

How Rommel Rattled

Rommel knew quite a lot about the Special Air Service. He may not have known that it was formed by a young Scots Guards Lieutenant, David Stirling, from Commando troops disbanded in the Middle East, nor that its first operation in November, 1941, was through bad luck a failure.

But Rommel did know that throughout 1942 little parties of British troops had appeared mysteriously hundreds of miles behind his lines in the African desert and attacked airfields, lines of communication, dumps, headquarters and any other promising target.

These early operations of the Special Air Service cost Rommel dear. When the RAF was too weak to hold his Luftwaffe in the air over Libya and Egypt, SAS parties had sneaked up to his airfields and destroyed between 400 and 500 planes on the ground.

They had smashed much valuable Wehrmacht material, sent back prisoners and information. They had created chaos on the Italians of his arrogant Afrika Korps; yet the carried of his super-trained troops on edge and caused panic in the ranks of his jittery elite.

One Man — 100 Planes

It was to do just this that in August 1941 Stirling was given authority to form I, Det, SAS, with 100 of all ranks. They were to strike deep behind the enemy's lines, by land, sea or air, and cause so much damage and confusion as possible.

The sort of men he picked for this job were men who had a strong sense of responsibility, initiative and individuality, coupled with strong discipline.

These men were in those days was the Luftwaffe, and in one of these 1942 raids alone, at Kabrit, north of Benghazi, they destroyed 100 German planes.

That particular raid brought into prominence an athletic young Lieutenant named Mayne. A giant, he personally destroyed 37 planes that night. Not satisfied at this, he reached for more than 100 aircraft himself, immobilising one by tearing out the control panel with his bare hands when he had run out of bombs.

Feats like these and the occasion when he paid a quiet, unhurried visit to a German officers mess and "liquidated" it before leaving brought him an almost legendary reputation in SAS. Today, as Lt. Col. R. B. Mayne, DSO and two bars, he commands the senior SAS regiment.

By the beginning of 1943, when its founder, now Lt. Col. Stirling, DSO, was captured near Mareth while attempting to reach the First Army from the Eighth, I, Det., SAS, had grown to be nearly 700 strong and had been formed into I SAS Regiment.

Shortly afterwards I SAS Regiment was split into a Special Raiding Squadron, commanded by Mayne, and a Special Boat Squadron, commanded by Major David Jellicoe, each of about 250 of all ranks. Men who had been raiding the French coast from Channel Islands went out to Africa from home and, with locally recruited personnel, were formed into 2 SAS Regt.

First into Sicily

Major Mayne's Special Raiding Squadron was the first force to touch shore in Sicily, near Syracuse.

They made an assault landing against coastal batteries, which they destroyed, taking 500 prisoners. From there they rushed up the coast to storm and hold Fort Augusta. They took it at the first attempt, and when they came to cross the causeway to the mainland they were engaged by a concentration of all kinds of weapons. For most of the night, until relieved by the main British force, they held the enemy — and in the morning it was discovered that they had been facing and containing half a division. Up in north-eastern Sicily small SAS parties were landed by sea on scouth-east Sicily.

In Italy 2 SAS Regt carried out a whole series of successful operations and in addition to their offensive function helped to get escaped prisoners of war back to the Allied forces, either by sea or through the enemy lines. The SAS, with a detachment of 2 SAS, also took part in the successful Termoli landing.

Typical of SAS work on the Italian front was operation "Tombola" carried out early this year in Northern Italy.

Dropped in the mountains in the Reggio Nell'Milia province, Major R. A. Farran, DSO, MC and two bars, formed an SAS battalion with 40 British parachutists, 100 Russians who had either deserted from the Wehrmacht or escaped from P.o.W. camps, and 100 Italian partisans. After training and equipping, their four major operation was to attack the German 11 Corps HQ at Bottego.

Piper Dropped Too

Helped by a thick mist, they filtered through German positions to the turning-up point and lay up for the day while Italian women conducted enemy dispositions.

The targets were a villa in which were the German Corps Commander, a visiting Divisional Commander, and 17 other Germans; and a second villa in which were the HQ registry and documents, operations rooms, map room and a Staff Colonel.

While the Russians formed a defensive ring outside, 110 SAS parachutists forced their way into each villa, followed by 20 Italians.

As soon as the first shot was fired, Piper D. Kirkpatrick, who had been dropped to Major Farran's force, began to play his pipes.

At the Corps Commander's billet the 10 British parachutists ran through machine-gun fire after the shots had been given, killed the four sentries and took the ground floor. The Germans resisted strongly from the upper floors and two attacks up the stairs were repulsed. So Germans who tried to force their way down the stairs were killed. SAS men tried to start a fire in the kitchen, then the lights were shot out and the attackers got away after 20 minutes, carrying their wounded.

At the other villa four sentries were killed and the door forced after it had been weakened by Bren fire. As in the generals' villa the ground floor was taken, but it was not possible to get up the stairs.

'That's not a plane,' a voice whispered. 'It's a whole ruddy squadron!'

In rapid order the lights of the airbase were doused, as the German defenders must have realised what was coming. Moments later, the air was rent by the sharp reports of gunfire, and explosions erupted high above Étampes airbase. The anti-aircraft batteries had kicked into action, the ferocious barrage creeping ever closer, as the gunners tracked the inbound fleet of warplanes.

The very heavens seemed to scream in agony now, as the first sticks of bombs plummeted down, blinding flashes pulsing across the airfield and throwing all into stark relief, the air ringing with powerful detonations and the ground beneath shaking with each blast. It looked as if the RAF had mounted some kind of diversionary raid, during the chaos and confusion of which Garstin and his men were supposed to get plucked to safety. Or at least, so the twelve fugitives had to presume.

Mayhem engulfed Étampes aerodrome, as the guns of the *Luftschutz-Rgt zur besonderen Verwendung* – the air defence units – blazed away and the air howled with bombs raining down, the twelve fugitives finding themselves caught right in the very heart of it all. As the staccato flashes seared across their place of hiding, Garstin kept checking the dial of his watch. With one hand he readied the flare gun with which he intended to call the RAF warplane in – a guardian angel descending from the war-torn skies.

As the second hand swept around to midnight, Garstin lifted the gun and fired. In rapid succession three green Very lights sailed into the sky, forming three distinct arcs like the fronds of a palm tree, the trunk of which was rooted in the SAS team's place of hiding. Nothing like advertising their presence to an enemy already on high alert. But this was it now: do or die.

Twelve figures waited with bated breath for something to happen, for some sign that their signal had been seen; that the pick-up was due, and that they hadn't by some bitter twist of fate been caught up in an Allied air raid simply by coincidence . . . and forgotten. All of a sudden, a 'great black mass appeared out of the darkness', executing a dramatic pass over the heads of Garstin and his men. To the watchers it had the unmistakable silhouette of a C-47 Dakota, although it had almost the exact same dimensions as a Junkers Ju 52, and they'd have to hope the troops manning the airbase might mistake it for one of their own.

A signal lamp blinked from the C-47's open side door: 'PEACH to ROMO 47, can we land? PEACH to ROMO 47, can we land?' 'Peach' was the aircraft's agreed call-sign, 'Romo 47' that of the waiting SAS party.

Wiehe lifted a powerful torch, flashing a reply skywards: 'ROMO 47 to PEACH, you can land. Wind nil.'

The dark form of the C-47 swept low across their position, before swinging around to line up with the runway. But as the shadowy warbird dropped towards the strip, the utterly unexpected happened: twin beams of light speared out from the Dakota, harshly illuminating the length of grass ahead of it. The pilot had switched on his landing lights, each set midway along the wings. It looked as if rather than trying to sneak in under the cover of the air raid, he'd decided to bluff his way down, as if he had every right to be there.

By the fierce glare, the watchers could see that the C-47's landing gear was already lowered. Moments later, the aircraft's wheels bumped once or twice on the grass strip, before it settled, the nose lifting as it slowed, and it came to a rest on the single tail wheel situated at the rear. Like that, the C-47 taxied across the grass, the pilot coming to a halt no more than a hundred yards from Garstin and his men, the open side door just aft of the wings offering a tantalising promise of safety.

Somehow, the RAF warplane was down and waiting, without a shot having been fired.

But as Garstin ordered his men to their feet, there was the grunt of heavy engines and the distinctive forms of several German Army trucks powered out of the darkness. Their head-lamps speared the gloom, nailing the C-47 in their glare, the telltale red, white and blue insignia of the RAF clear for all to see now. A machine gun opened fire, a blaze of bullets tearing up the airstrip in a cloud of blasted dirt and grass all around the warplane. The C-47 was a sitting duck, unless Garstin and his men could do something, and fast. The time for hiding – of remaining covert – was over.

'FIRE!' roared Garstin. 'Stop them destroying the plane! Whatever you do—'

His last words were lost in a deafening blast, as Jones levelled his trusty Bren and opened up, emptying an entire magazine into the lead vehicle. The truck's headlamps erupted in a shower of shattered glass, as bullets raked the chassis from end to end. Within a matter of seconds, Jones had unleashed all four of the remaining Bren mags, hosing down the enemy convoy with mur-derous fire. Presumably the soldiers riding in those vehicles had had no idea that a British patrol was positioned in the heart of their airbase, so getting hit by this mystery force must have added to all the chaos and confusion.

Seizing the advantage, Garstin ordered one man to make a

dash for the C-47's open doorway, to get the pilot to hold steady, as they dealt with the enemy. All they needed were a few precious seconds. It would be such a bitter disappointment, to be so close, 'and to be stopped by a handful of Germans!' As one of his men broke cover and dashed across the airstrip, Garstin ordered those remaining to redouble their attack on the trucks, although they were desperately short of ammo by now.

'Anyone got a grenade left?' he yelled.

By way of answer, his men lobbed the last of their pineapple-shaped projectiles, one falling directly onto the nearest lorry, where it detonated in a searing blast. The enemy truck 'burst into flames, casting a sinister, flickering light all around'. Other vehicles were raked by a storm of shrapnel as grenade blasts tore into them. Even as the last of the explosions died away, Garstin ordered his men to make a run for the waiting aircraft, at which all eleven broke cover and took to their heels.

Having dashed across the grass strip, one by one the fugitives vaulted inside, ducking low to make it through the oval-shaped doorway, and helped aboard by the welcoming arms of the RAF aircrew. More gunfire rang out across the airstrip, as a machine gun began to chew up the terrain all around the aircraft, the surviving enemy troops regrouping to attack. The C-47's dispatcher was just about to give the pilot the clearance to move, when Ginger Jones let out a wild cry.

'Paddy! Paddy! Where are you?'

There were eleven passengers in the hold of the C-47, where there should have been twelve. One, the unmistakable form of Paddy Barker, the giant, always cheerful Irishman, was missing. Even as enemy fire tore into the aircraft's exposed flanks, Jones dived out and was gone. As figures leaned out of the side door, searching for the missing men, the twin engines of the warplane began to rev and to roar, the pilot preparing to get underway. Moments later, Jones was back, half-carrying and half-dragging Barker with him, and the two men – one of whom, Barker, was injured – were hauled aboard.

The C-47 jerked into motion and began to gain speed. Even as it did, a vehicle – smaller, faster than the trucks; a *Kübelwagen*, perhaps – came tearing onto the dirt strip, in an effort to block the plane's path. The pilot just kept rolling, the speed increasing all the time as the twin Pratt and Whitney radial engines howled at maximum revs, the propellers clawing at the air. The progress still felt painfully slow to those riding in the hold, as bursts of fire hammered into the airframe. The reinforced military version of the DC-3 airliner, the C-47 had an ability to take battle damage and punishment that was legendary, but that was little consolation to those aboard right now.

Seeming to defy all logic – surely, it was about to be torn to pieces on the runway – the C-47 accelerated along the grass strip, lifted off just above the vehicle that was attempting to block her path and tore its way into the dark skies. The climb seemed to take forever, for the enemy were still spraying the warplane with fire, which 'splintered woodwork and ricocheted off metal'. But at last the impossible seemed to have transpired and the C-47 was over the perimeter of the airbase, at which point the pilot roared away at low level, hiding the warplane amongst the shadows and the trees.

Like that – 'hedge-hopping to avoid the ack-ack and the night fighters' – they turned for home. It took some time for those riding in the hold to get their pulses back to something like normal, and to grasp what had just happened. Twelve SAS – two of whom, Lieutenant Wiehe and Captain Garstin, had been ruled unfit for frontline duties – had just pulled off one of the most daring escapes of the war. Even Paddy Barker's injury turned out to be nothing more serious than a flesh wound. Not only that, they found themselves marvelling at the sheer neck and nerve of the RAF aircrew. Unarmed and defenceless, they had somehow pulled it off. Simply incredible.

Once they were well on their way, Garstin went forward to have words with the pilot, who by anyone's reckoning had to be one hell of a flier. 'Good work, old man,' he announced, his words laced with emotion. 'But what on earth did you switch the lights on for? I thought you were quite mad.'

'What a question,' the pilot retorted, his voice an exercise in phlegmatic cool and calm. 'It was because I couldn't see, of course.'

Of course. What a silly question to have posed.

Not only had the C-47's aircrew just pulled off an utterly audacious rescue mission, they had set the tone for more such operations to come. In early August '44, an SAS squadron engaged in Operation Bulbasket – another behind-the-lines mission in France – would be betrayed, ambushed and badly mauled by the enemy. The survivors would be pulled out by the RAF, being relieved in place by a fresh contingent of SAS troops. In preparation, a farmer's field would be recced as a DIY airstrip, one on which an RAF Lysander had landed previously, in 1943, carrying SOE agents. 'One excellent strip can be cleared, hedges trimmed to 2 metres and one tree felled,' the SAS had radioed back to base, regarding the proposed landing site.

In due course they carved out a 1,000-foot airstrip, codenamed Bon Bon – 'sweet' in French – which was to be tested first by a pair of twin-engine Lockheed Hudsons, an American-built light bomber, converted in this case to carry cargo or paratroopers. The Hudsons had flown in packed with arms for the French Resistance and with fresh SAS troopers, to prove that the strip was viable. That done, a C-47 Dakota flew in with heavy weaponry and more relief forces, pulling out those who remained.

There would be more such daring missions, dashing in and out of hostile terrain under the enemy's very noses. But for now, Garstin and his men rested their exhausted limbs, knowing they were the trailblazers, as the pilot set a course for home. Some two hours after their miraculous rescue, the C-47 touched down at Fairford, after a flight that had proven largely uneventful. Shortly after that, Garstin and his men could raise a celebratory glass of beer, knowing that not only had they made it out alive, but that soon their Lewes Bombs would be exploding amongst the Ju 52s and the ammo dump of Étampes airfield.

True to his promise, Garstin and his men had very much gone out with a bang.

Chapter 10

Having made it home against all odds, the SABU-70 raiders might have reckoned they deserved some down time. But there was to be little let-up. There was a war to be fought and already the actions of the SAS in France had proved a spectacular triumph. A report from the time – dated 19 June 1944 and stamped *top secret* – concluded that SAS operations in the field had 'succeeded in delaying the departure of 2 SS divisions for over a week,' including their heavy armour. Of course, those delays would prove absolutely critical.

The actions of Operation Gain/Cain were seen as being especially disruptive to the enemy, in terms of their efforts to repulse the Normandy landings. In particular, SAS raids had 'proved extremely successful' amidst terrain and in conditions 'which might have been expected to be very difficult'. Much of this was down to the 'daring, energy and initiative' with which the commanders and their men had operated in the field.

To the south of where SABU-70 had deployed, other Gain raiding parties had been at work. Under the command of Major Ian Fenwick, a well-known cartoonist prior to the war – a 'mad bugger' who could 'get anything done' – the main body of D Squadron had taken out a series of targets, including blowing up several trains and petrol tankers, cutting numerous railway lines, and at one point shooting up a convoy of German trucks in the marketplace of Dourdan town itself. They had also called in a number of RAF airstrikes, one of which had hit a million-gallon fuel dump in Orléans.

In the process they had taken a German dispatch-rider prisoner, who they had named 'Fritz' and proceeded to make the cook and general dogsbody at their deep forest camp. 'Fritz' seemed perfectly happy to be out of the war. Most regular German soldiers expressed a deep mistrust of Hitler, blaming the war on the 'Nazis, SS and propaganda'. In his downtime, Fenwick busied himself with sketching an entire new book of cartoons – his first, *Enter Trubshaw*, was just about to be published – and with introducing bow-and-arrow training to his Robin Hood warriors.

General Dwight D. Eisenhower, the senior American commander in Europe, would write to the SAS's senior command, lauding the unit's role in France. 'The ruthlessness with which the enemy have attacked Special Air Service troops has been an indication of the injury which you were able to cause to the German armed forces . . . Many Special Air Service troops are still behind enemy lines; others are being reformed for new tasks. To all of them I say, "Well done, and good luck."'

In wreaking such havoc, Fenwick had been ably assisted by his deputies, Captain Cecil 'Jock' Riding and Lieutenant James 'Jimmy' Watson, both of whom were former room-mates of Lieutenant Wiehe. But the Germans had begun to lose patience with being hit from all sides, unleashing a storm of savagery. According to a report by Watson, the French had given 'invaluable help' but had paid a heavy price. In just one incident, 'Six Parisien [sic] refugees were ordered to move on by the Germans, and on being ready were sub-machine gunned.' In another particularly brutal case, a store of fuel was discovered in a house owned by a member of the Resistance. German troops shot the man in the leg, after which they burned him alive. In numerous locations, French villages would pay a heavy price for helping the Resistance and SAS forces.

In many ways, Major Fenwick was ideally suited to guerrilla warfare, despite its harsh and bloody reality. A kindred spirit to Colonel Mayne, he'd been recruited from the Auxiliaries, a top-secret British resistance organisation founded at Churchill's urging under the SOE. The role of the Auxiliaries was to resist the anticipated invasion of Britain by Nazi Germany by all possible means. It was Brigadier Colin McVean Gubbins, chief of SOE, who Churchill had charged with founding a nationwide net-work of Auxiliary units. Under the motto *Valiant but Vigilant*, Gubbins had laid out their creed.

In his plan for a very British form of guerrilla warfare, Gubbins advised: 'Surprise first and foremost by finding out the enemy's plans and concealing your own . . . Break off the action when it becomes too risky to continue . . . Choose areas and localities for action where your mobility will be superior to that of the enemy, owing to better knowledge of the country . . . Confine all movements as much as possible to the hours of darkness . . . Avoid being pinned down in battle . . . Retain the initiative at all costs . . . When the time for action comes, act with the greatest boldness and audacity.'

Having been schooled in such warfare, the Auxiliary units had proven fertile hunting ground for the SAS when the invasion of Britain – *Unternehmen Seelöwe* (Operation Sealion) – failed to materialise. In early '44, Mayne had given a talk to 500 Auxiliaries in the Curzon Cinema, in London's Mayfair. Daunted by speaking in front of such a large crowd, Mayne had seemed somewhat quiet and withdrawn. He'd offered little but 'hard work and action' but his words must have impressed. Some 130 officers and men had volunteered, Major Fenwick included.

Now Lieutenant Colonel Mayne himself planned to parachute into France, to join Fenwick and the Op Gain party. Taking command, he would ensure that the energy and derring-do of these raiders would remain undimmed. For those like Garstin and his SABU-70 raiders, the knowledge that their commanding officer would be dropping into theatre was hugely heartening, especially as they were about to be redeployed themselves, heading back behind the lines.

The battle for France had reached an absolutely pivotal juncture, senior Allied commanders concluded. 'The Resistance situation . . . is now entering a very critical period. The Germans, after a certain amount of confusion following the initial landings, are now organising concentrated attacks.' Unless isolated Resistance bands could be 'supplied with considerable quantities of arms and ammunition, they are likely to be dispersed and suffer severe losses'. There was more – much more – to be done.

The men of SABU-70, battle-scarred and worn though they might be, were about to be re-formed for a new task. As they had prowled around Étampes airbase so comprehensively, who better to send back in, charged with putting out of action the fleets of warplanes based there. As a bonus, this time they would no longer need to drop blind. The local Resistance were apparently raring to go. In short, they would parachute back into the Étampes area armed to the teeth, on a month-long sabotage mission working closely with the locals. As they had gone out with a bang, so SABU-70 were to be sent back in again.

The twelve men – Garstin, Wiehe, Vaculik, Jones and Barker

amongst them – wandered off to their separate quarters, to digest the news: they were returning forthwith, and to assault the very same airbase that had so very nearly proved the death of them. Some, predictably, turned to the beer barrel, others to their sweethearts. They figured they'd earned a good few hours downtime, even if strictly speaking no one was allowed off the base.

Vaculik, very much the ladies' man, had recently wed the daughter of an English noblewoman, in secret and wholly against the family's wishes. In true SAS style, he stole away from the confines of the Cage for a few precious hours in 'Lady Nicky's' company. Lieutenant Wiehe, meanwhile, turned to the camaraderie of his mates in the mess, and late at night, once the carousing was done, he retired to his tent and his journal.

That book, page after page of which was covered in a neat flowing hand etched in fountain pen, had been with him since his departure from Mauritius. As he contemplated their death-defying Dourdan/Étampes experiences, Wiehe flicked through previous entries, searching for inspiration. He read over the day when he'd learned that Eda, his fiancée, had volunteered for the Mauritius Red Cross, readying parcels containing all 'the necessities of war' to be sent to Allied POWs. She'd done so in an effort to better empathise with his own journey into the dark heart of war.

He reread the notes he'd made of Churchill's warning issued to the British people, prior to D-Day. The public needed to avoid 'excessive optimism regarding the price of victory', and to be warned about 'the enormous losses that our Army is going to suffer in terms of human lives'. Churchill had averred that there would be a high cost to be paid for liberating Europe, and Wiehe didn't doubt it one bit, especially after their recent adventures and their seat-of-the-pants rescue.

He reread the diary entries about his evenings in the mess, prior to setting out on their first mission, when, at age twenty-seven, he'd been surrounded by men far, far younger, some looking entirely like 'adolescents'. They were all so young, and by comparison he had felt aged beyond his years. Reading the entry for 9 April 1944, he was reminded of how precious was family. Family was simply 'irreplaceable and one of the most beautiful things ever given to a man'.

Wiehe had lost his father in 1928, when he was just twelve years old. In time, he'd come to view it almost as a blessing, for it had brought him face to face with death, preparing him at an early age for war. 'Everything passes,' he had noted in his diary. 'We pass.' All was vanity in a world that would end. Those sentiments seemed to echo the words of Captain Garstin, as they had stolen onto Étampes airfield: *You can only die once.*

After his father's death, Wiehe had resolved to become a priest. His family were devout Catholics. But then had come the war and so had begun the relentless desire – the thirst – to do his duty. He had felt compelled to play a frontline role, come what may. Well, now he'd ventured behind the lines and as his pen hovered over his journal, Wiehe could only find trepidation in his heart and a darkness muddying his mind. Tonight, the words – any sense of clarity – just wouldn't come. He left the pages unwritten.

Wiehe left the previous jottings – the last words scribbled before deploying first time around, which had ended in the Stirling's crash-landing – as his final entry. 'Now I close this notebook probably for a long time,' Wiehe had noted, adding that he was awaiting 'departure for France, into occupied territory, far behind the enemy lines . . .' Then, as if in afterthought, he'd written: 'Or are these notes that I am writing now the last?'

Somehow those words seemed as fitting now as they had then. After all, what had changed? What else was there that needed saying?

For their next mission, Garstin and his men would be highly dependent upon their local reception party. A 'Progress Report SAS Operations' from 24 June stressed that wherever possible SAS patrols 'should be dropped to reception so that guides and information about enemy dispositions and targets can be supplied'. In theory, it was a win-win situation. The SAS would parachute in container-loads of arms for the Resistance, and could instruct them in their use. The locals would point out enemy targets and strengths, and could stiffen the SAS's ranks when undertaking missions.

It was crucial not to lose momentum, and to avoid the 'danger that, after the initial wave of enthusiasm raised by the Allied landings ... Resistance will tend to fall off considerably as a result of casualties'. The Resistance needed to be 'wholeheartedly supported with arms and equipment, and where possible by the presence of Allied troops'. Keeping up morale was essential, 'and its value cannot be sufficiently stressed'. In an effort to stiffen spirits, 'news of successes of Resistance elements in other areas' needed to be broadcast into France. Providing weapons and training was key, if Resistance bands were to stand firm when faced with German armoured units.

Captain Garstin and his men were slated to drop into a DZ adjacent to the tiny French village of La Ferté-Alais, an area with a long history of Resistance activities. It offered fine territory from which to wage guerrilla warfare, despite the fact that it was situated less than 40 miles from the centre of Paris. Sixteen miles to the east of Étampes airfield, the beauty of La Ferté-Alais as a base of operations was its position within the Forest of Fontainebleau – a 400,000-acre expanse of ancient woods, heath and wetlands. It should prove a perfect setting from which to strike at Étampes airbase, and to retreat to once the damage had been wrought.

Of all the Operation Gain parties, Garstin and his men were to be dropped closest to Paris, at the northernmost tip of the Gain area of operations. Their mission would acquire its own separate codename, 'Toby 3'. The details of this, and their wider objectives, were laid out in a report entitled 'SAS/SOE Plans', which called for 'sabotage, disruption of communications, individual guerrilla action, etc., all designed to harass the enemy and giving him no organised forces to take action against'.

Melting away into the Forest of Fontainebleau should achieve just those kind of results. The cover of that report was emblazoned with a veritable profusion of security stamps, including a massive red 'X' emblazoned across the entire front page. Added to that were 'BIGOT. Most secret. To be kept under lock and key,' plus the following caution: 'It is requested that special care may be taken to ensure the secrecy of this document.'

Oddly, at some stage the document's title, 'SAS/SOE Plans', had had the 'SOE' part scrubbed out, by what appears to be an official's angry pen. For some reason the SOE's role, working in partnership with the SAS in organising the Resistance, was seen as worthy of being expunged. But whatever the reason or the timing for the striking out of one partner from the record, it seemed ominous. And certainly, for Garstin and his men it would not augur well.

Dropping with containers stuffed full of weaponry, Garstin's force would be highly dependent on their SOE-organised reception party, for they were going in without the means to make radio contact with the UK. Deploying without a Jed set, they would rely on the Resistance radios for establishing contact with their Moor Park signals headquarters. In case of emergencies, one man – poacher Howard Lutton – would take carrier pigeons strapped to his chest, complete with sachets of bird food. It wasn't uncommon for SAS parties to take pigeons as a back-up means of sending messages home. As the Resistance were in regular contact with SOE by radio, Garstin and his men should have no reason to send any pigeon winging its way back to British shores.

Strictly speaking, the SOE was not a part of the British armed forces. Deliberately so. Churchill believed that the Second World War was a 'total war' that needed to be fought with no holds barred. The forces of Nazi Germany had already demonstrated as much, in their lightning seizure of nearly all of western Europe – an exercise in unprovoked aggression and bullying almost without compare. Churchill was convinced that Hitler – 'that guttersnipe', as he referred to the Führer – would only understand one thing: an opponent willing to fight fire with fire. Hence the need for SOE.

Formed under the Ministry for Economic Warfare, SOE would operate under a series of cover names – including the anodyne-sounding 'Inter-Services Research Bureau', and, more tellingly, 'the Baker Street Irregulars', 'the Firm' or 'the Racket'. Officially, the SOE did not exist, which made it perfectly placed for carrying out ultra-secret and deniable operations, such as assassinations, economic sabotage and the raising of guerrilla armies. It could break all the rules of war, and be denied by His Majesty's Government if and when all went awry.

Unlike the men of the SAS, SOE agents – both male and female – deployed into Nazi-occupied Europe dressed in civilian clothes. As they weren't in uniform, they could expect to receive none of the protections extended to bona fide prisoners of war. But even SOE agents – spies, by any other name – were entitled to a fair trial under international law. And despite their obvious differences, the SAS and SOE made for perfect bedfellows, especially when tasked with joining forces with the Resistance to help liberate France.

So why the striking out of the SOE's name from that summer 1944 report? Why the need to hide that singular partnership? Why the desire to deny it; to expunge it from the record?

Very possibly because something had gone terribly wrong at the heart of SOE's operations in France.

Chapter 11

SS *Sturmbannführer* (Major) Hans Josef Kieffer was preparing his report on the present *Funkspiel* operation, to file with his superior in Berlin. SS *Sturmbannführer Kriminaldirektor* (Major Chief Inspector) Horst Kopkow ran one arm of the RSHA (Reich Security Main Office), the Gestapo and SS security headquarters, in Berlin, which wasn't so far removed from the Führer himself, as Kieffer well appreciated. Horst Kopkow had first come to Hitler's notice in the aftermath of the assassination of SS *Obergruppenführer* (General) Reinhard Heydrich, a mission orchestrated by the British and their wily SOE.

As Hans Kieffer was fully aware, the SOE – his nemesis – was divided into individual country sections. So, for example, F Section, his direct adversaries, dealt with France. It was Kieffer's job, operating out of his Paris headquarters, to confound and defeat them. It was the Czech section of SOE that had trained the agents for Operation Anthropoid, the assassination of General Heydrich. On 27 May 1942 they'd struck, ambushing Heydrich's staff car on the streets of Prague, the Czech capital, and wounding the SS general. Heydrich was both a Hitler acolyte and one of the Führer's favourites, and it was Kopkow who was called in to investigate the audacious ambush.

Ironically, Operation Anthropoid would be the making of Kopkow, not to mention his direct subordinates. Flying into

Prague on the very afternoon of the attack, Kopkow quickly set about making his arrests, tracing the bomb fragments and the weapons used . . . to Britain. The SOE assassins, Czech citizens Jozef Gabčík and Jan Kubiš, were duly tracked, and would die in a last-stand shootout with German troops. On 4 June, SS General Heydrich – the de facto ruler of Nazi-controlled Czechoslovakia – died of his wounds. In the savage reprisals ordered by Hitler, thousands of innocent Czechs were murdered.

Two days after Heydrich's death, Kopkow's Berlin department was elevated to dizzying heights, being placed in charge of combatting all 'parachute agents, terrorists and saboteurs [whether] English, Soviet Russian or any other agency.' Across the length and breadth of Nazi-occupied territories, and within Germany itself, Kopkow was responsible for the fight against the SOE and their Russian counterparts, and any other Commando-type forces that might operate alongside them.

As more and more SOE agents were dropped into France – clearly where the Allies planned to launch their D-Day landings – Hitler had become obsessed with the French Resistance and their British associates. It was almost as if each mission, each act of defiance, was a personal insult against the Führer. Once captured, SOE agents were to be classed as *Nacht und Nebel* – 'night and fog' – prisoners, Hitler decreed. They were to be subjected to the very worst and made to disappear without trace. Neither their families, their loved ones nor their associates would ever learn of their fate.

Not only their lives but even their very identities would be forever snuffed out. But first, they would be made to suffer terribly. 'The agents should die, certainly, but not before torture, indignity and interrogation has drained from them the last shred of evidence that should lead us to the others,' SS *Reichsführer* Heinrich Himmler, the all-powerful chief of the SS, had declared. 'Then, and only then, should the blessed release of death be granted to them.'

The prescribed treatment for captured Allied parachutists and agents fell to the SS. Under Nazi dogma, all SS members had to be certified as 'pure Aryan', making the SS the elite of the elite, the cream of the *Übermenschen* – the so-called master race. By summer '44, the SS had grown to a million-strong force – a state within a state, boasting its own police service, the Gestapo, its own military, the 600,000-strong Waffen SS, and its own slave labour force some 700,000 strong, spread across hundreds of forced-labour *Konzentrationslager* (concentration camps). For the SS, subjecting a few captured Allied Commandos to the very worst was child's play.

But Hans Kieffer didn't necessarily agree that this was the right approach. Quietly, he believed there was another way – a less violent, more 'collaborative' means, one that he did his best to encourage at his Paris Gestapo headquarters. By apparently befriending SOE agents, and by convincing them that all was lost – that their agency had been penetrated to the very highest levels – he argued he could gain so much more. He didn't just seek usable intelligence. Kieffer was far smarter than that. He sought a *partnership*. He aimed to turn captured agents, so they could be used as a weapon against the very people who had sent them in the first place.

In this, he believed he had been uncommonly successful, as the present *Funkspiel* (radio game) operation should prove. As the man charged with hunting down all SOE agents throughout France – and, more recently, the SAS and Commandos working hand in glove with them – Kieffer was at the peak of his power.

Born in 1900, Kieffer, the humble son of a barrel-maker from Offenburg, had followed his brother into the German police force. He first came to his superiors' notice when he was found to possess an uncanny skill at getting information out of suspects, and was quickly moved into intelligence work.

At war's outbreak, Kieffer had been transferred to the Gestapo. Ironically, he'd won his plush Paris posting due to the fact that Offenburg lay on Germany's western border with France, and his superiors had presumed that Kieffer would be reasonably fluent in French. In truth, he spoke not a word. But he and his wife were long-standing Nazi party members, and all their children were enrolled in the *Deutsches Jungvolk*, a section of the Hitler Youth, so he believed himself deserving of the very best that Nazi Germany might have to offer.

With his family's impeccable pedigree, plus his charm and his fine physique – Kieffer, a talented sportsman, believed himself striking-looking, with a shock of wavy hair and deep-set, dark eyes – Kieffer was highly ambitious and driven, and he felt himself destined for great things. Now, as the chief of anti-sabotage and *Funkspiel* operations across the length and breadth of France, his was a pivotal role.

By the winter of 1943, some 500 clandestine radio sets had been detected transmitting out of France, which equated to a similar number of radio operators. Most, though not all, of those sets were sending messages to SOE in London. But rather than seeking to do the obvious – to smash the network – Kieffer had decided to try to co-opt it, and wherever possible to turn it against the enemy. The means to do so was the *Funkspiel* – the radio game – at which he and one of his deputies would prove past masters.

SS *Untersturmführer* (2nd Lieutenant) Dr Josef Goetz, a myopic, bespectacled former teacher, was that deputy. On 13 April 1943 Kieffer's men had arrested one of the SOE's most high-profile radio operators, Marcus Reginald Bloom, seizing his radio and associated ciphers. Upon learning the news, Kopkow, in Berlin, ordered Kieffer, in Paris, to attempt the first ever *Funkspiel* operation from French soil. Kopkow was a merciless taskmaster, and Kieffer was under huge pressure to get results. Ideally, Bloom would have to be made to talk, if the *Funkspiel* were to be successful.

Bloom, the son of British Jews living in London, had dropped into France in November 1942, and he had been transmitting ever since. He'd kept constantly on the move, to avoid the German detector vans, and it was a combination of loose talk and betrayal that had led to his capture. He was incarcerated in the dreadful confines of Fresnes prison, in Paris, and interrogated. When Bloom refused to cooperate, Kieffer was forced to abandon his softly-softly approach. Bloom was beaten remorselessly, but still he revealed nothing.

Kieffer delegated Goetz to carry out the *Funkspiel*, and both men felt under huge pressure. 'The greatest possible importance was attached to this scheme, both by Berlin and Paris.' Deprived of Bloom's help, Goetz went ahead anyway, powering up Bloom's radio set and sending a series of decoy transmissions to SOE headquarters in London. As far as possible, he attempted to mimic Bloom's 'fist' – the individual style of his Morse – encoding the messages via the ciphers that they had captured, along with Bloom's radio set.

The aim was to make it appear as if the Resistance network for which Bloom had been the radio operator was still operational, and as if Bloom remained at large. If the *Funkspiel* was successful, Kieffer's team could not only send London disinformation, but – crucially – they could also call for more supply drops and agents, to be parachuted directly into their hands. For four weeks Goetz persisted, but without Bloom's help the *Funkspiel* proved a failure. For whatever reason, London hadn't swallowed the bait.

Two months later, things were to prove very different. On 15 June, two French-speaking Canadians – both SOE agents – were captured by the Gestapo, along with their radio and codebooks. So would begin one of Kieffer's most successful *Funkspiel* operations, which would last twelve long months. The two agents had been charged with setting up a new SOE circuit to the east of Paris, codenamed 'Archdeacon'. Using the captured equipment, Goetz started transmitting as if all was well, and this time SOE's F Section was well and truly hoodwinked.

For months on end, agents and supplies were parachuted into France, supposedly for the Archdeacon network, but actually at the behest of the Gestapo and falling directly into their hands. Success breeds success. By that summer, Kieffer had two such *Funkspiel* circuits up and running. On occasion, Kieffer himself would attend the drop-zone entrapments, as men and war materiel appeared as if by magic from the night skies. Over the six months to December of that year, and urged on by Kopkow in Berlin, Kieffer ramped up such operations, capturing some forty SOE agents.

It wasn't just SOE that Kieffer was netting. He'd also ensnared agents of the Office of Strategic Services (OSS), the equivalent agency in the United States. The failure of SOE's French Section to realise they were being played for fools via the *Funkspiel* would have been laughable, if the consequences hadn't proved so dire for those on the sharp end. SOE's radio traffic was supposed to have failsafes built into it – so called 'bluff checks' and 'true checks'. These were specific snippets of information known only to the agent and his SOE handler, which were to be inserted into a radio message as proof that all was well.

But all too often, when an initial *Funkspiel* message was dispatched by Kieffer's men, F Section would reply: 'My dear fellow, you only left us a week ago. On your first message you go and forget your true check.' Or: 'You forgot your double security check – be more careful.' Again and again this would happen, SOE London offering 'a blundering reply that gave the game away'. The result was that captured agents faced ever more brutal questioning, to force them to reveal the failsafes with which subsequent *Funkspiel* transmissions could be made ever more convincing.

On occasions, Kieffer had even resorted to executing a 'soft sabotage mission' – blowing up a largely unimportant target in France, but one that he could trumpet to London via radio messages as a supposed triumph for one of his ghost circuits. It was well worth suffering a little damage in those mock sabotages, for the supposed authenticity they provided boosted the *Funkspiel* massively by convincing London that all was going well with a particular network.

So successful had the *Funkspiel* proven that Kieffer had to turn over an entire floor of his headquarters at 84 Avenue Foch, Paris, to sorting, cataloguing and distributing captured SOE equipment. It didn't just include weaponry, ammo, bullets and bombs; there were also huge amounts of cash being parachuted directly into the Gestapo's hands. One of his deputies, *Hauptscharführer* (sergeant major) Karl Haug, a First World War veteran and a master of reliability and order, had been placed in charge of the cache of captured SOE stores.

The *Funkspiel* operations were an intensely guarded secret known only to a top coterie of Nazi officials, and any unauthorised communications about them were a treasonable offence. Regular reports to the Führer were made regarding this 'partisan combat'. Captured agents were kept alive, simply so they could be forced to assist with further *Funkspiel* plays. So extensive was such trickery that by the summer of 1944, when the SAS started deploying into France, it was arguably safer for such parties to drop 'blind', rather than risk meeting a Gestapo reception party on the ground.

Kieffer knew that other national *Funkspiel* programmes were in operation, the one in Holland being said to rival his in France. In every sense, the race was on. And tonight, 4/5 July 1944, yet another SOE consignment was due to fall into his hands. Tonight's shipment was only supposed to consist of containers, or so the transmissions from SOE London had led him to believe, but still it would represent another feather in his cap. His greatest hope was that a SOE radio and codebooks might be included, offering scope to start yet another *Funkspiel* circuit.

The drop was due to take place a few dozen miles to the south of Paris, and Kieffer had given it the codename 'Marbois'. As only supplies were due – not any live agents – he had delegated the capture operation to his deputies. *Hauptscharführer* Haug, Kieffer's captured-kit quartermaster, plus several other Gestapo agents – Woerle, Teschner, Stork and Vogt amongst them – would oversee Operation Marbois, ensuring 'the reception lights and signals should be shown correctly'.

That afternoon Haug had set out, in the company of his

Gestapo cohorts, and with a strong escort of Waffen SS troops. While they weren't expecting too much trouble in the Forest of Fontainebleau, you never knew quite what to expect with a *Funkspiel* entrapment. Haug had the procedure down to a tee. He'd made sure to bring the guide lights for the RAF pilot, and was well practised at this: the men with lights would stand 'in a straight line in the direction of the wind, about 80–100 metres apart. A fourth man stood 10–20 metres to the side of the first man . . . and gave the necessary flash signal.'

Upon arrival at the Forest of Fontainebleau, Haug and his Gestapo colleagues proceeded to check out the terrain. The drop was scheduled for an isolated cornfield, surrounded on three sides by thick woodland, known locally as the Bois de Bouray. Under the Waffen SS commander's supervision, the entire 'place was encircled . . . [as] a security measure against a possible surprise attack by members of the Resistance'. With the cordon in position, Haug and his fellows settled down to await whatever tonight's drop might bring.

Earlier that day the BBC had twice broadcast a message into France, to warn the Fontainebleau Resistance that the Bois de Bouray drop was on. As dusk descended, a party of Frenchmen, all armed, crept towards the darkened DZ. But instead of finding it deserted, as they'd expected, a hidden party of gunmen opened fire on them. Two of their number were killed, and after a short but fierce firefight the Resistance party melted away, realising they were outgunned. One, a dogged and courageous individual, volunteered to remain, crawling deep into a thicket so as to wait and to watch.

With that, silence descended over the Bois de Bouray drop-zone.

*

Back in Britain, Captain Garstin and his men readied themselves for departure for tonight's mission – Operation Toby 3. All seemed well both at their Fairford base and on the ground at their DZ. 'The reception party was arranged by SF Baker Street, and mounted by a BBC message,' it was reported, 'SF Baker Street' being a code for SOE. As far as Garstin and his men could tell, fair stood the wind for France.

At the last minute, Ginger Jones realised that his military-issue watch was on the blink . . . again. Of course, a watch was a vital piece of kit on an operation wherein split-second timing might be everything. So Jones, the former miner from Wigan, confessed to Wiehe, the scion of a landed and wealthy colonial family, his dilemma. As Wiehe owned several timepieces, it wasn't a problem, the SAS lieutenant declared. He'd loan his friend one of his own.

For tonight's mission, Wiehe had decided to carry with him a tiny pocket-book, in which he planned to keep a diary of sorts. Deploying for a month, he felt compelled to keep some kind of a written record. He'd already made the first entry. Each page was printed with basic details. This one read: 'Tues 4 July. Sun Rises, 3.49; Sets 8.19 (GMT).' Below that Wiehe had noted: 'Left Fairford AFB [Air Force Base] with Pat. Garstin and ten men for France.'

Prior to departure there had been an eleventh-hour change of plan. SAS veteran Lance Corporal Billy Hull, from Belfast – another Royal Ulster Regiment stalwart – had been slated to deploy, alongside Garstin's men. But at the last minute, Mayne had had a change of heart. Hull was the SAS commander's driver, and Mayne had him earmarked for another role. He planned to parachute in to join the Op Gain party himself, and he wanted a trusted pair of hands at the wheel of any vehicle he might beg, borrow or steal on the ground, so he could visit his various patrols. Hull was that man.

Regardless of that last-minute change of personnel, Mayne was on hand to give Captain Garstin and his men a final update and a personal send-off. This patrol had already proven one of his most hard-hitting in the field, and once again the SAS leader had high hopes for Garstin and his men.

At 23.34 the twelve raiders mounted up their Stirling aircraft, for their third flight into France in as many weeks. Garstin's stick retained many of the old faces, plus a smattering of newbies. Wiehe, Vaculik, Ginger Jones, Paddy Barker and Howard Lutton were all present, plus there were also a Sergeant Varey, plus Troopers Walker, Young, Morrison, Norman and Castelow. The recognition signal to be flashed from the La Ferté-Alais drop-zone was 'B for Bertie', without which none of the men were likely to jump. As before, they might fly in only to have the mission aborted.

Of those on the patrol, two were from Ireland – in addition to Captain Garstin, Paddy Barker and Howard Lutton. Troopers William 'Billy' Young and Joseph 'Joe' Walker were both Royal Ulster Rifles, so they shared that regimental tradition with Captain Garstin and Lieutenant Colonel Mayne. For tonight's mission, Garstin had formed an 'Irish patrol'. Splitting his stick into two units of six, he'd kept all the Irishmen under his command, plus Vaculik, the lone Frenchman. Lieutenant Wiehe had got the remainder, including the redoubtable Ginger Jones.

In his Irish patrol, the SAS captain had a spirited bunch of fighters, Paddy Barker and Howard Lutton included. As with Garstin himself, Trooper Joe Walker had had a real battle on his hands to make it as a frontline soldier. A former farm labourer from County Down, Walker had spent considerable time in the brig, due to his restless soul. But once he'd volunteered for the SAS and been sent for airborne training, his 'cheery disposition' and hard-working nature won through. A year earlier, Walker had lost his older brother, Isaac, who'd been serving in Tunisia with the Irish Guards. Like Garstin, he had every reason to be hungry for action and driven to fight.

Trooper Billy Young, the eldest of five sons from County Antrim, was a dairyman by trade. He'd volunteered for 1 SAS on the same day as Walker, and they had passed through airborne training together and into Garstin's patrol. Young's father and four of his uncles had soldiered in the First World War, and he had a brother in the RAF, plus five cousins also serving. For all of Captain Garstin's Irish patrol, soldiering ran deep in the blood.

Sergeant Thomas Varey, from York, was Wiehe's second-in-command. As with Major Fenwick, Varey had served with the Auxiliaries, volunteering for the SAS when the threat of a German invasion had receded. With a younger brother in the RAF, Varey was the 'old man' of the patrol, being all of twenty-nine years of age. Also on Wiehe's stick was Trooper Herbert Castelow, a former brick-maker from Stockton-on-Tees and another of the 'old men', being just a year younger than Varey.

The final two on Wiehe's stick were Troopers Morrison and Norman, the latter being a 'taciturn' individual, according to Vaculik – a still-waters-run-deep type. As matters would transpire, Troopers Norman, Morrison and Castelow would prove themselves possessed of a rare tenacity and endurance in the face of extreme jeopardy, but all of that lay some time in the future.

For now, these twelve men were heading into France on a mission to spread carnage and mayhem across familiar ground to many – Étampes airbase.

A thirteenth man had joined them on the Stirling, but only for the flight in. An SAS original and renowned desert navigator, Captain Mike Sadler had taken up the bomb-aimer's seat in the aircraft, so he could better see Garstin and his men make their drop. Now serving as part of the SAS's intelligence set-up, Sadler aimed to fine-tune such drops, by observing them for real in the field. That way, the SAS could learn from any mistakes and seek to do better in the future. On tonight's mission there would be an awful lot to observe and to learn.

As the Stirling climbed to altitude, it proved cold on that warplane. The twelve raiders sat in silence, each wrapped in his own thoughts. As if sensing the danger they were heading into, Wiehe found himself playing with his rosary beads, and mouthing a silent prayer: 'Holy Mary, Mother of God, pray for us sinners now and at the hour of our death.' The rosary was very dear to him. It had come into his possession in the most special of ways. It had been a gift from a Father Arrowsmith-Larkin, an army chaplain, in March 1942, when Wiehe's then unit had been serving in the North African desert.

Father Arrowsmith-Larkin had told him that he'd placed the rosary on the Rock of Agony at Gethsemane, where Jesus was said to have prayed the night before his crucifixion. He'd given it to the young lieutenant at a time when he was at his lowest ebb. Wiehe had tried to volunteer for special duties the first time around by arguing that his bilingualism would be an asset to British forces behind the lines. But his kindly commanding officer had put the kybosh on it, arguing against him volunteering for a post wherein the 'risks would surely be greater', Wiehe had noted in his diary.

After such a let-down, the gift of that precious rosary had lifted the lieutenant's spirits mightily. Ever since then he had turned to it, whenever he was faced with his greatest challenges – as he did now, on a Stirling heading into the darkness and the unknown. *Holy Mary, Mother of God, pray for us sinners now and at the hour of our death . . .*

After running the gauntlet of the German ack-ack over the French coast, the Stirling droned onwards, mercifully unharmed. Shortly after 1.40 a.m., Garstin and his men felt the aircraft begin to lose altitude, which had to signify they were approaching the DZ. Momentarily, there was a distinct sense of the warplane hitting some turbulence, as it bumped and bucked its way across what appeared to be another aircraft's slipstream.

This near to the drop, it was ominous. What could another plane be doing right here, if not waiting to pounce? But despite the pilot's warning that there was 'another aircraft around', no cannon fire erupted from the dark night sky; no white-hot lead came tearing through the Stirling's flanks. Instead, the pilot brought his aircraft down to 800 feet, with all seeming well. Studying the configuration of lights below on the ground, and the recognition signal, all appeared perfectly correct. Whoever was down there, they sure knew their craft well.

Moments later the jump-light winked red, and Garstin and his fellows hurried to the trap. It switched to green, and one after the other twelve men plummeted into the aircraft's slipstream. The Stirling turned for a second pass over the DZ, a dozen containers stuffed full of weaponry, ammo, cash and other supplies being thrown into thin air, each falling beneath its own parachute.

But even as those containers were shoved into the night, Sadler caught sight of something far below – the blaze of a muzzle flash, amongst the darkened terrain. It was not unknown for high-spirited Resistance types to greet a drop with bursts of celebratory fire. Sadler had to hope this was that. If not, then Garstin and his men were in some kind of trouble.

Barely had Sadler had time to entertain such thoughts when the night-fighter was upon them, howling out of the darkness. The Messerschmitt Bf 110 *Zerstörer* (destroyer) came at the Stirling head on, its 20mm cannons and machine guns blazing. The combined velocity of the two warplanes meant that they blazed past each other at a speed in excess of 500 mph, meaning the exchange of fire was over in a flash. If it had come at them from behind, and given them a long burst, they might well have been done for.

Instead, the Stirling's pilot dived to gain speed in an effort to lose the hunter, but the Bf 110 was still on their tail. 'We dived down pretty rapidly into the clouds,' Sadler recalled. 'I thought the wings were going to come off.' As the Stirling raced for the coast, the night-fighter began hammering out bursts of fire. The pilot kept weaving dramatically, in an effort to shake off his tormentor. By the time they'd reached British shores and had succeeded in losing the enemy warplane, the Stirling had taken a serious pasting. Still, they managed to make their home base with no loss of life.

All hoped that Garstin and his men had fared better, as they had tumbled into the darkness.

Chapter 12

Conditions on the night of 5 July '44 would prove unkind to Captain Garstin and his men: the twelve figures drifted to earth amidst an eerily bright and moonlit scene. Garstin and his Irish patrol had jumped first. They'd been followed by Wiehe, Varey, Ginger Jones, Morrison, Norman and Castelow, who was jumper number twelve. The order of the drop would prove critical. The first seven, Wiehe included, would land in the open cornfield. The last five were swallowed by the Bois de Bouray, with Troopers Morrison, Norman and Castelow landing deep in the woodland.

At first, there appeared little that was wrong with the drop. As the lead figures touched down in the open and clipped out of their chutes, they could see the rest of the stick drifting towards them, and the Stirling making its second pass, disgorging the containers. All seemed peaceful and quiet. Garstin – typically, first down, expecting to be the rallying point for his men – spied a figure hurrying out of the woodlands. Instantly recognisable as a civilian, the man approached the SAS captain, crying out: 'Vive la France!'

This was not an unusual way for a Resistance man to issue a salutation, and as they were expecting a reception party Garstin reached out to shake the man's hand. But as soon as he was close enough the Frenchman hissed a desperate warning: 'Be careful: there are Boches all around!' No sooner had he said it than the stillness of the night was torn apart by a rattle of gun fire. Confused, but sensing trouble, Garstin allowed himself to be led by the Frenchman towards the cover of the dark fringe of trees.

For SS *Sturmbannführer* Hans Kieffer's men – Haug first and foremost – this was not what they had been expecting at the Bois de Bouray. Anticipating only a container drop, they'd been surprised – very – when twelve parachutists had descended from the moonlit skies, and they had been caught somewhat unprepared. 'At about the same time shooting broke out suddenly on all sides,' Haug observed.

Vaculik had dropped third in Garstin's stick, landing close on the SAS captain's heels. 'At once when I touched the ground I heard a burst of machine-guns [sic] coming in my direction,' he remarked, 'so I took my carbine ... and answered, in the direction of the firing ... They fired a few times like that and I answered. I wanted to get out of that field.' All seven of those who'd been dropped in the open were desperate to get out of the line of fire, whoever it might be that was doing the shooting.

Falling to his hands and knees, Vaculik crawled towards his leg-bag, rummaging inside for what had to be the most vital bits of kit right now – spare magazines and grenades. All the time, sporadic bursts of fire cut the night air. As he rifled through his equipment, he was trying to figure out just where the fire was coming from and who on earth was shooting at whom. The bursts intensified, tracers lacing the night sky above him, and Vaculik was hit by a blinding realisation: 'Suddenly, it occurred to me that we had dropped into an ambush. The Germans were expecting us.'

Like Captain Garstin just a minute before him, Vaculik decided to make for the cover of the trees – 'the only chance of safety'.

Abandoning the rest of his kit amidst the corn, he started the crawl of his life. He'd made around a hundred yards when a savage burst of fire tore out of the shadows. Ominously, it had come from the very patch of woodland for which he was making. Keeping low, he traded shots with an unseen enemy, moving after each burst so as to avoid making himself an easy target.

Shooting at night at hidden adversaries was no easy matter, as Vaculik well knew. He crept closer and lobbed two grenades into the dark wall of trees. The explosions ripped through the woodland, blasting off branches and leaves. Moments later Vaculik could hear panicked cries in German, plus the sound of boots crashing through the undergrowth, as if the enemy were retreating. On his feet now, he pushed forward, firing probing bursts into the treeline. Finally, he made the cover of the first of the trees, creeping ahead, 'my ears cocked for the slightest noise'.

But what he had hoped to be a sizeable woodland – enough, perhaps, to lose himself in – proved to be nothing more than a small copse. On the far fringes he detected hostile voices – there was no escape that way. He did a mental count of his remaining weaponry: six mags for the carbine, six grenades, plus his Colt with five clips of ammo. Enough to go down fighting. 'What could I do alone?' Vaculik wondered. Where were the others? If only he could link up with the rest, at least they could fight it out together.

He turned back, heading into the open once more. Towards the south of the DZ he'd spied another patch of woodland. Maybe that offered the chance of linking up with his fellows, or of escape. As he crept ahead through the dark trees, a voice cried out in German: 'Hands up! Drop the gun!' Vaculik's only response was to take to his heels, as a burst of fire slashed into the foliage behind him. Diving into the corn he crawled onwards, frantic to escape. In his mind a voice was screaming: 'I don't want to be taken prisoner. Not that, whatever happens.'

After he'd made a good few yards, Vaculik risked breaking cover, zigzagging through the field in an effort to avoid being hit. But suddenly his foot caught on something half-hidden in the corn, and he went sprawling. Reaching back, he tried to discover what had wrongfooted him. His hand touched ... something soft. He withdrew it in shock. A body was lying face down. Horrified, Vaculik manhandled it around, until he found himself gazing into the features of Howard Lutton – soldier by trade, poacher by nature.

Lutton had been hit by a burst of fire, and the blood from his wounds was still congealing on his uniform. 'His eyes were wide open and they looked astonished, as though he could not understand what was happening,' Vaculik recalled. By the scale of Lutton's injuries, Vaculik figured he wasn't long for the world, if he wasn't dead already. Reaching out, he closed those staring eyes. Lutton had jumped with four carrier pigeons strapped around his neck, held in special tubes designed for the purpose. They were lying close by.

Vaculik reached for the first, determined at the very least to send headquarters a warning message. They had dropped into a trap. Either they had been betrayed, or something else had gone wrong with the arrangements for the reception. For all Vaculik knew, he was the last of his stick left alive. Either way, SAS headquarters had to be alerted, or other parties might be delivered into the hands of the enemy.

Whatever dark skulduggery had transpired tonight, of one thing Captain Pat Garstin was certain: treachery was afoot in the Bois de Bouray. The first Frenchman to meet him on the DZ had been joined by a second, and together they had led the SAS captain towards what had seemed to be the safety of the woods. In truth, they'd delivered him into the hands of the enemy. Without warning, grey-uniformed figures had pounced out of the shadows, seizing Garstin and twisting his arms behind his back.

'Bring your men over here!' Garstin was ordered, at gunpoint.

The enemy were trying to get Garstin to call to his fellows, to lure them further into the trap. Unsurprisingly, he refused. One of his captors proceeded to rip Garstin's decorations and his rank slides from his uniform, declaring that the SAS captain was not a proper soldier, but a 'terrorist'. If he refused to help, he was a dead man. Bristling with defiance, Garstin made it clear he would offer the enemy not the slightest hint of any assistance.

'Right, we will shoot this officer anyway,' his captors declared, amongst themselves.

Realising that he had nothing left to lose, Garstin seized the moment and wrestled himself free, yelling for any of his men within earshot to make a break for it. As he tried to dash away, the German soldiers turned their MP40 'Schmeisser' sub-machine guns on him, and Garstin was riddled with fire. Two bullets struck him in the neck, two more in the arm, and a fifth tore into his shoulder, the burst of 9mm rounds throwing him to the ground. Grievously wounded, he was unable to get up again.

If anything, Garstin's second-in-command, Lieutenant Wiehe, had suffered even greater ill fortune: the trajectory of his drop had deposited him on the very fringes of the cornfield, right beside the enemy's guns. Once Wiehe had cut himself free from his chute, he'd noticed Paddy Barker just nearby. Together, the two men had crept towards the cover of the fringe of trees, but indistinct figures – 'vague shapes' – were moving in the shadows. They'd prowled closer, weapons at the ready, trying to make out if it was their people, or hostile forces.

The answer came when a volley of fire blasted out of the trees. Both men were hit, Wiehe falling in agony, and instantly 'losing the power of his legs'. Even as he'd gone down, he'd seen Paddy Barker – the always cheerful giant of an Irishman – likewise take a burst and get knocked to the ground. The rest of Wiehe's stick had been dropped further into the woods and they were as yet undetected, but upon hearing the bursts of fire, they tried to rush to their commander's aid.

Sensing their approach, Wiehe cried out a challenge: 'Who's there?'

On hearing the names of his men, he yelled at them to stay in the woods. He'd 'caught a packet', and was unable even to crawl. Wiehe's men insisted they venture out to fetch him, but he was adamant. If they broke cover, they would be easy targets, for the 'moonlight helped the enemy with his aim'. Instead, the SAS lieutenant gave orders that were as selfless as they were imbued with courage: his men were to head deeper into the woods to try to escape and evade, making for the Normandy beachheads if at all possible.

Troopers Norman and Morrison – jumpers ten and eleven – did as they'd been ordered, pushing deeper into the trees. At one stage, a burst of fire chased after them, but it went high, and by dropping to all fours they managed to slip away. Heading north, they emerged from the trees near the tiny hamlet of La Ferté-Alais, where they detected enemy troops moving on the road. Lying low until 'all was quiet again', they pressed on. Once they'd skirted around a few isolated houses, they figured they were through the enemy cordon. Maybe, just maybe, they had managed to slip the trap.

As for Trooper Castelow, number twelve in the stick, he had been deposited in the depths of the Bois de Bouray, where no enemy was ever likely to find him. Realising at once how badly things had gone, and sensing that none of his fellows were anywhere nearby, he decided to hunker down right where he was. 'I cut off my parachute and hid as quickly as possible,' Castelow noted. He would wait for the hue and the cry to die down, and then see what the first light of day might bring.

By now, sunrise was not so very far away. By the faint glow in the sky, Wiehe tried to inspect his injuries. Unable to stand, he felt himself all over. When he sensed hot liquid seeping through his hands, and saw that it was his own blood, he realised how bad things had to be. The blood didn't frighten him as much as the feeling of paralysis; of being trapped in a body that he could no longer control. As far as he could tell, he'd been shot three times – once in the shoulder, once in the thigh, and the very worst of all, in the base of his back, the source of a searing pain.

'My God, I am hurt!' he told himself. But at least he was alive. And where there was life, there was hope.

In the centre of the cornfield, Vaculik had finished scrawling his note to SAS headquarters. It read: 'Hard luck. Germans were waiting for us. God help us. Dupontel.'

Dupontel – it was Vaculik's French Canadian cover name: a name he'd been given in case of capture, in case of a moment like the one that had transpired, for he could see no easy way out of the trap that had been laid for them, with dawn fast approaching. He set the pigeons free, the messages fastened to their legs, wishing them Godspeed for England as they fluttered into the air.

That done, he crawled onwards through the corn, trying to find some avenue of escape. Now and again bursts of fire tore through the air, and not all of it seemed to be the enemy's. Vaculik just had to hope that some of his fellow raiders had survived and were putting up resistance. Of all the men in their number, he didn't doubt that Ginger Jones would fight to the last grenade and the very last round.

As the sky lightened, he detected the distinctive growl of a heavy engine. The Germans were bringing up some kind of mechanised weaponry. Soon he could hear a tracked vehicle quartering back and forth through the cornfield. It sounded like a machine-gun carrier – possibly a Vickers-Armstrong Bren carrier. Scores had been seized by the Germans during the Battle for France in 1940, and brought into the Wehrmacht via the *Beutepanzer* – their captured tank service.

Vaculik wondered how many other 'poor wretches' like himself were being hunted through the corn. Either way, he was finished if he remained in the open. Resolving to make the cover of the woods come what may, he took the last of his grenades, and one after the other he hurled them into the line of trees. As the explosions died away, he was on his feet dashing the 30 yards to the nearest cover. He made it, diving behind the gnarled trunk of an ancient-looking oak, even as the first of the enemy fire slammed into the far side.

In the silence that followed, Vaculik was surprised to hear a voice ring out in French: 'There he is. Behind the cover of that big oak, sir!'

It was Vaculik's first ever collaborator. He felt his blood start to boil. So this was the 'swine' who had betrayed them. Stealing a glance around the tree, he spied two figures lying prone in the undergrowth: the French traitor and the German soldier he had addressed as 'sir'. Acting on instinct Vaculik lifted his weapon and fired, seeing the bullets strike home, as each figure twitched with the impact and cried out in agony. Yet in a sense his action had been rash, for he'd well and truly given away his position now.

Rounds tore into the vegetation all around Vaculik, as he spied German soldiers in their distinctive *Stahlhelme* – coal-scuttle-shaped steel helmets – darting from cover to cover, closing resolutely for the kill. Firing burst after burst, he tried to fend them off, but eventually – inevitably – he heard a 'dry little click'. He was all out of ammunition. As he went to draw his Colt, figures seemed to rush in from all sides. Vaculik fired blindly with his pistol, but it was too late – a flurry of rifle butts pounded down onto him, there was a 'great spurt of fire' before his eyes, and all went dark.

Some time later, Vaculik came back to consciousness. He felt groggy and confused and his head was pounding. Even so, it didn't take him long to appreciate the full extent of his predicament. Altogether, it seemed seven of the SABU-70 raiders had been taken captive: Wiehe, Paddy Barker and Sergeant Varey, all of whom were injured, plus himself, and Troopers Young and Walker, who were more or less okay. And then there was Howard Lutton, who was absolutely at death's door.

The captives had been corralled together, hands bound tight with parachute cord, with a truck drawn up into which the injured had been loaded. From its open rear Vaculik could hear an agonised groaning. Glancing over, he spied Lieutenant Wiehe, his legs drawn up before him and his faced racked with pain.

'Got it badly?' he whispered.

'I've just about had it,' Wiehe replied. 'Just as I was landing, took a burst in the back. I'd give anything for a shot of morphine.'

Vaculik turned to the nearest German soldier, and asked if the wounded might be given something for the pain. He was told they'd have to wait until they got to hospital, whenever that might be. At that moment, more figures emerged from the trees. Most were German troops, but with them were a handful of figures dressed in dark civilian overcoats, with trilby-style hats. Those men in black carried lugers, and they propelled before them an unmistakable figure – Ginger Jones. His hands were tied behind his back, but 'his great shoulders were squared', Vaculik noted, his features set in resolute defiance. No surprises that Jones had fought it out to the last.

Those who could were ordered to stand, their faces to the truck, their backs to their captors. There was a series of ominous clicks, as weapons were made ready. 'This is it,' Vaculik told himself grimly. 'They're going to shoot us out of hand.' The seconds ticked by in silence, as all braced themselves for what they felt certain was coming. But their civilian captors – Gestapo, surely – began a systematic search, removing from the captives their maps, codebooks, compasses and money, which was quickly tucked away.

'How many of you were there in all?' one of the Gestapo men demanded. The question was barked at Vaculik, as he'd made it clear that he spoke French.

'Just a hundred,' he replied, straight-faced and serious.

'You're making fun of me,' the Gestapo man snapped, raising a fist as if to strike.

'Not at all,' Vaculik protested. 'There were several planes.'

'I see,' the Gestapo man replied. He seemed more interested now.

'Don't talk, Dupontel,' a voice pleaded from the truck. It was Wiehe, clearly worried that Vaculik was *cooperating*.

'Don't worry, old man,' Vaculik shot back, in English. 'Talk's a weapon, as well as silence. I want to see if I can get you a shot. How are you feeling now?'

'Pretty lousy. I think a bullet would be the best thing for me.'

Vaculik spun his lies with the Gestapo, inflating the drop into something far more extensive and thrilling than it had been. He could see the man's eyes glittering as he contemplated how quickly one of his captives seemed willing to talk. Finally, as a gesture of thanks, he untied Vaculik's hands and allowed him to fetch the first aid kit from the heap of captured equipment. With that, Vaculik, who'd had some basic medical training, was able to give Wiehe a shot of morphine, to take away the worst of the pain.

He'd just finished doing so when another group of soldiers emerged from the trees. They were dragging something – some individual – with them. It took a good few moments for anyone to realise who it was. Captain Garstin's uniform was soaked in blood, and he seemed barely conscious. For a moment his men tried to dash forward to help him, but they were dragged back violently by their guards.

Sensing where they were taking Garstin, Vaculik grabbed some of the sleeping bags from their pile of kit and threw them into the rear of the truck, laying them down. That way, at least when his captors lifted the SAS captain up and threw him aboard there would be something to cushion his landing. The sudden, jarring impact seemed to bring Garstin to his senses, and he began to beg for water. There was none, but Vaculik had some whisky in a flask, and he managed to get a little through Garstin's cracked lips.

He followed that with a shot of morphine, after which the wounded SAS captain began to talk, his words coming in short, breathless gasps. Having given a brief account of how he had been captured, he encouraged those of his men who were still conscious not to lose heart: 'Do your best to let London know what's happened,' he urged. And tell—' But his last words trailed away to nothing as he drifted back into oblivion ... leaving his men wondering just what they were supposed to let London know.

To one side of the truck a group of the German soldiers began to dig a pit. Bodies were dragged out of the woods and flung into it unceremoniously. These were none of the SAS party, which begged the question, exactly who were the dead? Had the Resistance provided some form of reception party after all, only to meet with a bloody end when the German troops had attacked? It was impossible to tell. All they did know was that the truck loaded with the nine of them was about to get underway.

Vaculik heard orders issued with 'Paris' in the sentence, before two of the Gestapo men clambered onto the rear of the vehicle. There, with their weapons at the ready, they remained, as the engine coughed into life and the lorry ground its way along a rutted track, crawling out of the woodland, a vehicle-load of German troops bringing up the rear.

Wiehe lay in the truck, each jolt causing a bolt of agony to shoot through him, in spite of the morphine. He glanced to left and right, where the other injured lay, one man – Garstin – 'stained with blood', the other, Lutton, 'already unconscious, maybe dead', plus Paddy Barker bleeding profusely from a thigh wound. A part of Wiehe realised then how close so many of them had come to death that morning, in the Bois de Bouray.

As the truck turned north on that 5 July morning, pulling onto the tarmac for the short drive to Paris, *Hauptscharführer* Haug reflected upon what had transpired over the past few hours. He had fought in the First World War, been taken captive and held by the British for eighteen months as a POW. Now, utterly unexpectedly, he had nine British prisoners in the rear of his truck. How the wheel of fortune turned.

The vehicle had closed sides, but an open rear. From that, Vaculik – who knew Paris well – was able to keep track of their progress. On the outskirts of the city the convoy came to a halt at a modern-looking military barracks, the Paris HQ of the Waffen SS – the 'Armed SS', the military wing of the SS and Nazi Party. This had to be the unit that had set the ambush at the Bois de Bouray.

A German officer wearing the Waffen SS's distinctive death's head and runes proceeded to inspect the captives, or at least those who were able to stand. He seemed apoplectic at their treatment, and demanded of the Gestapo that the prisoners' hands be untied. As that was being done, Vaculik managed to raise the issue of their wounded, who were in need of urgent medical attention if they were to stand any chance of survival.

By way of response, the Waffen SS officer clambered into the rear of the truck to see for himself. He emerged with his face set in stone, ordering his men to offload their equipment as fast as possible and to unload their weapons. Just as soon as that was done, the convoy was sent on its way again, heading due north towards the heart of the city and presumably hastened on its way to a hospital.

A short drive took them to the 13th arrondissement, to the southeast of central Paris. Sure enough, the second stop for the convoy turned out to be the vast edifice of the Hôpital La Pitié-Salpêtrière. Originally a gunpower factory– saltpetre being a constituent of explosives – it had, ironically, been transformed into a hospital in 1789, becoming the largest in all of France. The convoy ground to a halt at its ancient portals, where four men – Captain Garstin, Lieutenant Wiehe, Lance Corporal Lutton and Trooper Paddy Barker – were offloaded.

Sadly, Lutton was pronounced dead upon arrival, and the other three were in little better shape. Few expected Garstin or Wiehe to make it, especially with what they would face now. Although the French nurses tried to demonstrate a little 'cautious' sympathy for the wounded men, none of those left aboard the truck felt any great hopes.

'We said good-bye sadly to our wounded comrades,' Vaculik noted, and as the truck got underway again, 'no one said a word'.

Chapter 13

The convoy turned west, following the course of the Seine, the main artery of Paris. It rumbled across one of the main bridges spanning the river, before pulling onto the grand expanse of the Avenue Foch, the widest in all Paris, running from the famous Arc de Triomphe to the Porte Dauphine metro station. Prior to the war, the Avenue Foch had hosted some of the grandest residences in France, boasting palaces and mansions owned by some of the world's foremost dynasties. But much had been taken over by the machinery of the Nazi state, and since January 1943 number 84 Avenue Foch had served as headquarters of the Paris Gestapo.

Indeed, numbers 82–86 had been taken over by the organs of the Nazi security apparatus, with other buildings housing the *Sicherheitsdienst* (SD), the Nazi Party and SS's bespoke intelligence service. It was at number 84 that the trucks ground to a final halt. In the shadow of the chestnut trees that lined the grand boulevard, the five remaining captives – Vaculik, Jones, Walker, Varey and Young – were made to dismount. Before them towered a grand stone edifice several stories high, each floor boasting fancy balconies with ornate wrought-iron railings, set before floor-to-ceiling windows.

There was little to mark the building out as the sinister abode that it had become, but as their Gestapo captors actually announced to the SAS captives where they had arrived, all knew the grim reality. They had been brought to Gestapo central, and few doubted what would follow, just as soon as they stepped inside. The Gestapo had methods to make practically any man – or woman – talk. Indeed, no one was expected to hold out forever. As with the SOE, SAS captives were asked to remain schtum for a minimum of forty-eight hours, to give their comrades time to cover their tracks. As the five captives stepped through those grim portals, they just had to hope they could hold out . . .

Naturally, *Sturmbannführer* Hans Kieffer – the son of the barrel-maker from Offenburg – greeted the news of that morning's captures with undisguised glee. Today's *Funkspiel* – Operation Marbois – had well and truly come up trumps. Never had he seized such a large group of British captives in one fell swoop. This was unprecedented: a quite extraordinary outcome. With the prisoners safely in custody at Avenue Foch, Kieffer sent an exultant message up the chain of command to Horst Kopkow in Berlin.

The reply came back more or less immediately: they were to await 'further decisions and orders on this matter. On the express orders of Berlin, Paris could not give any instructions concerning the Commando [sic] men. They were in fact in the power of RSHA.' Berlin – Kopkow – had seized control of the SAS captives, and nothing could happen without his say-so.

Each floor of 84 Avenue Foch performed a distinct function. The basement was *Hauptscharführer* Haug's domain, and right now he had a new batch of captured SOE equipment to process into stores. The top – fifth – floor housed the guard-room and the all-important cells, in which those being interrogated were held. The fourth floor housed the quarters of *Sturmbannführer*

Kieffer, the master and commander of much that went on in that building.

Below that, on the third floor, an equally powerful individual, SS *Standartenführer* (Colonel) Helmut Knochen had his offices, from where he oversaw security matters across a swathe of western Europe, stretching from France to Belgium. Nominally, Knochen was of a senior rank to Kieffer, but with the latter's thrusting ambition and his ruthlessness, he was seen by many as the man in charge. Much of Knochen's duties involved the rounding up and deportation of Jews to the concentration camps, but he also had the blood of hundreds of French patriots on his hands, those in the Resistance who had stood firm against the Nazi occupation and paid the ultimate price.

Below Knochen, the entire second floor was dedicated to *Funkspiel* operations, making it Goetz's domain. This morning it was abuzz with excitement. Out of the blue, today's *Funskpiel* had netted nine British agents, or rather parachutists dressed in military uniform. Berlin had been informed. Already, there was talk of the Waffen SS commander of the operation, *Obersturmführer* Schubert, receiving a decoration, the *Kriegsverdienstkreuz II. Klasse* – the War Merit Cross, 2nd Class – for his brave actions. Now to begin the questioning, from which who knew what might follow.

On the fifth floor the five SAS captives awaited the inevitable, with a heavy sense of dread. Exhausted, hungry, battle-worn and demoralised, they were locked together in one cell, Vaculik begging the others 'not to betray the fact that I was French'. It wasn't long before they were marched out again, and taken below, to Kieffer's domain. There, they were led before the SS *Sturmbannführer* himself, who had with him SS *Untersturmführer*

(Lieutenant) Alfred von Kapri, a former languages student who spoke faultless English, as well as being a die-hard Nazi.

Kieffer's key focus today was 'to determine whether a radio-deception plan was possible' as a result of the captures. Having checked through the captives' personal effects, he'd already deduced that both officers on the patrol – Captain Garstin and Lieutenant Wiehe – had been hospitalised. From studying the captured radio cipher pads, he knew that the man he would need to turn, if a *Funkspiel* were to be possible, was Lieutenant Wiehe.

The softly-softly Gestapo man was wont to offer his English captives tea and biscuits, to better reel them in. But in terms of a *Funkspiel*, the five men ranged before him now could offer little, he suspected. His questioning soon confirmed his suspicions. Due to their rank, none of the five 'were able to give the necessary details for carrying out a radio deception'. Still, having had men of the SAS fall into his hands was a first, and Kieffer had high expectations of their subsequent interrogations.

As one of the captives was already under suspicion of being a Frenchman – a treasonous swine, playing at being a bona fide member of the British armed forces – they would concentrate on breaking him first. Kieffer detailed one of his toughest and best, SS *Hauptsturmführer* (Captain) Richard Schnur, assisted by the very capable von Kapri, 'to proceed with a detailed interrogation . . . and to submit a comprehensive report'.

At the same time Kieffer dispatched two of his men to the Hôpital La Pitié-Salpêtrière, to check if either of the SAS officers was fit enough to face questions. Their news was dispiriting. Unfortunately, 'there was little hope of keeping the men, and particularly the officer [Captain Garstin] alive'. For Garstin and Wiehe, those conclusions wouldn't have come as any great surprise. But in his wisdom, Kieffer begged to differ: Kopkow had demanded daily reports on the case, and at the very least Wiehe, the radio man, *must* be made to talk.

From the moment of their entry into the hospital, Garstin, Wiehe and Paddy Barker had faced a nightmarish scenario. Stripped of everything, they were taken to a 'special room reserved for wounded terrorists and partisans'. It resembled little more than a prison cell. While Garstin was barely conscious, Wiehe remained surprisingly alert and lucid, considering the severity of his injuries. In his fluent French he was able to ask why they had been segregated from the other Allied soldiers held at the hospital. The answer was chilling: the SAS men were regarded as 'spies', in spite of their 'wearing British uniform'.

Worse was to follow. While their injuries were roughly bandaged, it was made clear that that was going to be the sum total of their treatment. It looked as if their wounds would be left to fester and rot, in which case it would take a miracle to save them. For Wiehe, the questioning began almost immediately. Despite his parlous state, he faced a grilling by a visiting Gestapo officer, the thrust of whose interest was all too clear: he was seeking to learn all he could about their means of communicating with headquarters.

Despite hours of such questioning, Wiehe refused to talk, even when his interrogator resorted to hitting the badly wounded man around the face. Finally he was wheeled into the corridor. There the Gestapo man made a new and chilling threat. Of the three bullets, one was lodged in Wiehe's femur, another at the base of his spine. If he refused to talk, the Gestapo man would order the medical staff to remove the bullets without any anaesthetic. Such treatment, Wiehe knew, might kill him. But he was at death's door anyway, and no matter what, he was determined not to break.

For hours the interrogation continued. When his inquisitor finally tired, Wiehe was wheeled into a new room. There were several beds inside, and none of them held any of his SAS comrades. Indeed, he would never get to see either Paddy Barker or Captain Garstin again. Instead he was to be incarcerated with members of the French Resistance. One, he learned, was called Georges Leroux. Fifty-two and grey-haired, Leroux hailed from the village of Breuilly, south of Paris, and he was a blacksmith by trade.

As with Vaculik, it seemed that the Gestapo were convinced that Wiehe was French – another 'traitor' masquerading as a British soldier. And as he quickly learned, the French 'patients' were in line for particularly brutal treatment. An *Unteroffizier* (sergeant) of the Wehrmacht was in charge of security on the new ward – a bald-headed, bull-necked individual, who wore his Iron Cross on a ribbon around his neck and his Eastern Front medals with equal dash. At any time that *Unteroffizier* was wont to reign down flurries of kicks and blows upon his 'patients'. Wiehe's only defence was the truth – to argue, doggedly, that he was a British soldier and should not be there at all.

The one possession the SAS lieutenant had managed to keep hold of was his tiny notebook. Despite his terrible injuries, he somehow managed to enter a first few words in spidery-looking, almost illegible pencil. On the page headed 'Wed 5 July. Sun Rises, 3.50; Sets, 8.18 (GMT)' he had managed to scribble: 'Parachuted 2 a.m. near Étampes. Whole party with exception of 3 of my section POW. 4 wounded included Garstin and self.'

Lieutenant Wiehe had last visited Paris when he was aged just six, on one of his few overseas trips before the war. He had never imagined returning here, like this. But equally, he had wrestled with the meaning of death early in life, when he had lost his father. Since then, he'd seen any number of his friends die on the field of battle. He'd weathered exploding mines, bullets and bombs, not to mention his own injuries from parachuting. He was prepared for his death, but strangely, he felt that now was not to be his time.

Late on the day of their capture, the first of the five men held at 84 Avenue Foch was called for individual questioning – 'Jean Dupontel' was ordered to step from the cell. The guard marched Vaculik down a flight of stairs, to Kieffer's floor, where he was led into a large, sunlit room that opened onto the Avenue Foch. By the window stood a youngish-looking man, in an immaculate SS uniform – von Kapri. Before Vaculik was seated an older figure, in a dark civilian suit, with 'hard, clear-cut features and a rather aquiline nose' – Kieffer's chosen inquisitor, *Hauptsturmführer* Schnur.

From the very outset, it was clear that the Gestapo man knew Vaculik was French. 'You say that your name is Jean Dupontel and that you were born in Quebec,' Schnur began, removing an envelope from his desk that contained Vaculik's few documents. 'If so, why do you have such a strong accent?'

'That's because I'm French-Canadian,' Vaculik replied, running through his cover story in his head.

'You are quite sure you are French-Canadian?' Schnur queried.

'Of course. I was born at number 33, the High Street, Montreal, where my father was a lawyer.'

'I don't believe you,' Schnur countered. 'You're lying. Name me three hotels near the main station in Montreal.'

By way of answer, Vaculik asked for a piece of paper and pencil. With that he drew a sketch of downtown Montreal, pointing out the Tremaine, the Royal and the St George. Vaculik hoped he'd remembered the hotel names correctly from when he'd been briefed on his cover story, especially as Schnur pocketed the sketch, promising: 'I am going to double check all this.' Then he seemed to change tack completely. 'How long have you been in the army and what is your rank?'

'Two years, and I'm a corporal.'

'Then why is your paybook so new?' Schnur queried, indicating the (false) document lying on his desk.

'I lost the other one, that's all.'

Schnur smiled, patronisingly. 'You may as well admit that you're French. It will go better for you.' His tone had softened, sounding almost friendly, as if he was giving a piece of kindly advice. 'We don't treat the French so badly. We're not at war with them. Now come on, be sensible. Admit it.'

'I'm not,' Vaculik replied, sticking doggedly to his story. 'I'm a British subject, although of course my ancestors were French.'

As Vaculik wouldn't talk, things were about to get nasty. While Kieffer claimed not to sanction violence, in truth he oversaw a 'don't ask, don't tell' policy at 84 Avenue Foch. He expected his interrogators to get results. What means they employed to secure them were their own affair, and Avenue Foch boasted all the accoutrements of the dark art of torture. 'I was beaten up and slapped during my interrogation,' Vaculik would later report. But first would come the mind-games.

Without warning Schnur sprang to his feet and slammed his fist onto the desk. 'That's enough!' he yelled. 'You're a dirty Frenchman, making common cause with the English.' He knew very well the captives were SAS, Schnur warned, especially as he had 'other SAS prisoners' in his custody already. Vaculik didn't doubt that the Gestapo knew what unit they were from, but having other SAS prisoners – surely he had to be bluffing.

Schnur reached for a Luger he had lain in a desk drawer. 'Now, you will tell me exactly what you came here to do, or I'll shoot you out of hand.'

Staring down the barrel of the 9mm pistol, Vaculik felt his innards turn to ice. He just had to hope the Gestapo man was acting out a part, although it didn't exactly look that way. There was spittle at the corners of his mouth, like a rabid dog. Schnur thrust the Luger forward until it was pressed into Vaculik's ribs. Still Vaculik refused to admit anything, and moments later the interrogator's whole demeanour changed again.

Reaching into his pocket, he pulled out a packet of Gauloises. He offered one to Vaculik. Accepting a cigarette wouldn't hurt and at least it might help settle his jangling nerves. But taking it proved nigh-on impossible, for Vaculik had been handcuffed along with the others, just as soon as they were inside the building. As Schnur offered Vaculik a light, the Frenchman asked if his cuffs might be removed. To his surprise, his interrogator agreed.

For a few seconds the two men – inquisitor and captive – puffed away in silence. Schnur exhaled a long cloud of smoke at the ceiling. His expression had apparently softened. 'I don't like being unpleasant towards you,' he began again. 'You're being silly. Pig-headed. All you have to do is tell me why you were sent and the code you use to keep in touch with London . . . and you'll be treated decently.' He eyed Vaculik for a long moment. 'Otherwise . . . you'll be treated as a terrorist. And I dare say you can guess we've a short way with terrorists.'

Vaculik gestured at how he was dressed. 'I am a soldier in uniform, and I ought to be treated as a prisoner of war.' As he'd been briefed in England, this was one of his only defences, if captured.

'We don't regard parachutists as soldiers, and we don't treat them as ordinary prisoners of war,' Schnur countered. 'For us they are bandits who creep up from behind and slit our throats.'

'I am a soldier in uniform,' Vaculik repeated, showing Schnur his red beret and cap badge, as proof. 'And I demand to be treated as—'

'Swine!' Schnur suddenly exploded, a fist full of heavy rings smashing into Vaculik's face. Schnur hit him three times in quick succession, knocking the half-smoked cigarette from Vaculik's mouth. He let the blows unseat him, as if he'd been knocked to the floor. By the time he clambered to his feet again, he'd managed to grab the remains of the Gauloises and palm it, hoping he could keep it hidden for later.

Von Kapri stepped across the room and clouted Vaculik for good measure, before forcing him roughly back into the chair. Schnur brought his face very close to Vaculik's, his voice dropping to a whisper. 'You are one of those dirty terrorists, saboteurs and murderers who spring on our men from behind . . . You'd better make up your mind to talk, or it will go very hard for you.'

'I can't say any more than I've already said,' Vaculik countered.

Schnur turned to von Kapri. 'Take him away.'

The younger man reached forward and dragged Vaculik out of the room, propelling him back to the cell, whereupon he was handcuffed once more and thrown inside.

'Walker!' von Kapri cried. 'You're next!'

With that, Trooper Walker, the former farm labourer from County Down, was led away. Ever since joining the British Army, the high-spirited twenty-one-year-old had spent considerable time in various military prisons, due to his unruliness and high spirits. No one doubted that Walker would give a very good account of himself, and Schnur was unlikely to get anything out of the tough Irishman.

With Walker gone, Jones eyed Vaculik's swollen face. 'They're a nice bunch, I must say.'

'Never mind about that, look what I've got,' Vaculik announced, revealing the crumpled remains of the Gauloises.

Jones practically broke into a jig at the sight of it. Having straightened it out as best he could, he grabbed a match from his pocket, lit up and drew in a huge lungful of smoke, holding it in as long as he could, before letting out a regretful gasp. Just then, their guard slid an eye up to the peephole in the door. There was a flurry of bolts being flung back, before he stamped in furiously.

'My god! Who's smoking?' he exclaimed. 'It is forbidden! You'll be punished! Who's smoking?'

'No one's smoking,' Jones replied, all innocence. He'd palmed the cigarette butt, just as soon as he'd heard the key in the door.

'Maybe it's smoke from the chimney,' Vaculik added, facetiously.

The guard swore. He knew when he was being made fun of. He slammed the door, making sure to lock it firmly behind him.

Beneath the bravado, Vaculik ached from head to toe. Over the past twenty-four hours he'd been shot at, clubbed with rifle butts and beaten up, but the very worst was seeing men he respected and revered being gunned down. With neither Captain Garstin nor Lieutenant Wiehe on hand, both the patrol's officers were gone. And while the SAS stressed the importance of self-reliance and inner strength amongst its men, regardless of rank, it would have been an enormous relief to have had at least one of the officers still in their company.

Jones helped Vaculik onto one of the thin beds. His body trembled and he felt as if he were falling ill. They'd had precious little food or water since taking off from England, and in truth Vaculik was both physically and emotionally shattered. Jones urged his friend to try to get some rest, but as he laid down sleep just wouldn't come. Instead, he was back in that cornfield, with bullets and grenades bursting all around, and everywhere the death rattle of machine guns.

Soon it was Jones's turn in the interrogation room. If anything, the ornate, seemingly civilised surroundings of 84 Avenue Foch lent the questioning and the associated violence an even more twisted and sinister feel. It was almost as if this kind of treatment could not be happening in this kind of setting. Of course, Jones – the SAS original, former miner and trained boxer – carried his attitude on his sleeve. This was a man who was very much bloodied but unbowed.

From the very moment they'd been thrown into the cell, Jones had taken to berating their guards in his thick Wigan accent, employing the most colourful curses imaginable. As the jailers couldn't understand, there was little they could do about it. But when he was taken down for questioning, his inquisitors took the extra precaution of tying him to the chair, in spite of his handcuffs. That done, von Kapri – tall, clean-shaven and well built – took up a position hovering on Jones's shoulder.

It was done with maximum intimidation in mind. 'If I failed to answer, [he] would walk round and hit me in the face with the back of his hand,' Jones recalled, of von Kapri's behaviour. Every time he refused to cooperate – which Jones did in his own, inimitable style – the SS *Untersturmführer* would punch him. For a man like Jones – a trained boxer – it must have been utterly infuriating to have to sit there and take it.

Jones was faced with 'all kinds of threats', in an effort to extract the information Schnur sought. He was asked about the nature and objectives of their mission. He was asked about the 'doodlebugs,' the V1 flying bombs that had been raining down upon London and other British cities, as Hitler's riposte to the Allied landings. Nazi propaganda was trumpeting the V1, the first of the so-called *Vergeltungswaffen* (vengeance weapons), and further such ground-breaking weaponry – chiefly the V2 – as the means to reverse the tides of the war.

Finally, the SS *Hauptsturmführer* seemed to grow as angry and frustrated with Jones as he had been with Vaculik. The SAS corporal was dismissed, with dark threats ringing in his ears: 'We cannot waste any more time on you.' But instead of being returned to the cell, Jones was led directly to Hans Kieffer's office, whereupon the contrast with Schnur's approach couldn't have been starker.

Kieffer had with him his secretary, Käthe Goldmann, with whom he was reputed to be close. He had a wife and four children back in the German city of Karlsruhe, where he had first forged his career in the Gestapo. But he'd argued that they should remain there, rather than accompanying him to Paris, for the children were in good schools. With Kieffer's pretty young secretary on hand, the atmosphere of Jones's second questioning was almost 'homely'. Of course, Kieffer had spoken to the captives already, as a group. But this one-on-one chat was his speciality – the supposedly pally approach.

Kieffer regaled Jones – the keen sportsman – with stories about how he had once played rugby in England. Whether there was any truth to it, who could say. His questions, slipped in almost as asides, were all about SABU-70's officers, Garstin and Wiehe. Kieffer seemed to want to know every minor detail, no matter how seemingly insignificant. Of course, this was all for a purpose. Apparently trivial personal details – parents' occupation, schooling, favourite sports, type of car one drove – were invaluable in building up a sense of a radio operator's persona. That was crucial for a successful *Funkspiel*, for those were just the kind of details SOE London might inquire about, to verify a person's identity.

Securing such minutiae could also be used against the individual in question, during interrogations. Small personal details, slipped into the flow of questioning, could prove hugely unnerving, leaving the captive wrong-footed and wondering how on earth his inquisitor might know *that*. By apparently befriending his captives – finding aspects of common ground, like sport, with Jones – Kieffer sought to inveigle and beguile. But in truth, any who fell for Kieffer's charms were only 'befriended' for as long as they served his ends: the *Funkspiel*'s ends. Once any usefulness had been exhausted, the captive was shipped off to Germany, to be sucked into the *Nacht und Nebel* – the night and the fog.

Supposedly befriending such captives when they were at their lowest ebb, feeling terribly fearful and vulnerable, was of course the cruellest cut of all. Those 'befriended' were to be disposed of – without mercy; without trial; without trace even – once they'd served Kieffer's ends. By comparison, those German agents captured on British soil – and there were many – were given a stark, but fair choice. Swap sides and work for the Allies, or face trial before a properly constituted court as a spy, for which the sentence was death. If they chose the former option, their lives would be spared and at war's end they would be repatriated to Germany as 'undesirable aliens'.

Incredibly, there was one SOE agent – codename 'Emile' – who had been acting as Kieffer's 'friend' for many months now. He had even been granted the dubious honour of being allowed to reside at 84 Avenue Foch full-time. A graphic designer by trade, on occasion he was allowed to dine with his Gestapo pals at fine Paris restaurants. But most often, he could be spied at 'his' desk in the 84 Avenue Foch guard-room, working on detailed sketches of the Gestapo's operations, delineating both their *Funkspiel*-controlled 'ghost circuits' and those still genuinely in SOE hands. That shadowy figure was present at 84 Avenue Foch, even as Vaculik, Jones, Walker, Young and Varey faced their interrogations.

And he would go on to play the most extraordinary role in the SAS captives' fortunes.

Chapter 14

Even as the Avenue Foch captives were facing their first, brutal inquisitions, the three of the SABU-70 raiders still at large were intent on executing their getaway. Having skirted around the hamlet of La Ferté-Alais, Troopers Morrison and Norman – numbers ten and eleven on the drop – discovered that a second, more daunting obstacle lay in their path, the wide sweep of the main Orléans to Paris railway. Oddly, only two of the six sets of tracks seemed to be polished with use. The rest looked unused.

In truth, due to sabotage operations by Major Fenwick's raiders – located to the south of SABU-70's DZ – 'considerable material damage was done to rolling stock and railway lines'. Indeed, SAS reports would conclude of Operation Gain that 'the German Army . . . was not safe from attack in the middle of villages from Dourdan to Orléans', a stretch of terrain some 50 miles across.

Even more surprisingly to Morrison and Norman, no guards seemed to have been set, and the railway looked deserted. Seizing their chance, the two fugitives crept across, on the far side finding themselves on the outskirts of Bouray-sur-Juine, some 3 miles to the northwest of their DZ. They had two options: turn back, or brazen it out and push through the darkened streets. As north towards the Normandy beaches lay their only hope, they turned in that direction, heading deeper into the sleeping town.

At first Morrison and Norman tried to make their way from garden to garden, vaulting railings and gateways. But the cacophony of dogs barking and the inevitable curses from those rudely awakened soon dissuaded them from that course of action. Neither man understood the slightest French, but they clearly were not making the townsfolk of Bouray-sur-Juine particularly happy. So they took to the open road and dashed north at speed, making for the comparative safety of the fields on the far side of town.

Shortly a new obstacle blocked their way – the River Juine. Morrison waded in to see if it could be forded, but within the first few steps he was waist deep, the riverbed proving soft and treacherous underfoot. By now it was getting light and the two fugitives urgently needed to find a crossing point and somewhere to lay up in hiding. They spied a mill that forded the river, but shadowy figures could be seen moving about in the half-light. Nearer at hand lay a rowing boat, fastened by a sturdy padlock. For a few moments they considered trying to cut the chain using their 'issue escape file' – part of their escape kit – but the time it would take and the noise it would make dissuaded them.

As luck would have it, a small track lay a little further ahead, which crossed the river via a narrow bridge. It seemed deserted. The two men flitted across, skirted around a house lying at the bridge's far end, dashed across the main road beyond and made for the forest on the other side. The terrain rose steeply, and having climbed to a vantage point Morrison and Norman decided 'to make this their lying-up point'. They searched around and found an ancient-looking cave that seemed ideal for their purposes.

Having crawled inside, the two men – famished and

exhausted – tried to take stock. Given the small amount of food they had on their person, they discussed cutting their daily rations to the bare minimum, 'one tin of milk and bar of chocolate each' per day. But with 150 miles lying between where they were now and the Normandy beaches, as the crow flies, that clearly wasn't going to be enough to keep them going. Desperate times called for desperate measures. Norman volunteered to head off in search of some extra provisions, while Morrison stood guard at the cave.

Norman disappeared deeper into the woods. A mile from the cave he came across a house, and as he watched from the trees a woman came out to feed her chickens. Seeing no other option, he beckoned her over. Via sign language and gestures, Norman managed to make her understand that he and another British parachutist were hiding in the woods. Having checked that they were unobserved, the woman led Norman into her house, where she proceeded to press upon him some 'bread, milk and some very fat bacon'.

Hardly daring to believe his good fortune, Norman returned to the cave, where he and Morrison soon had 'the old Tommy cooker going hard at it' – their portable stove. Knowing that the enemy was bound to have patrols out in force searching for any escapees, they decided to lie up all that day plus the following night, 6 July, and to see what the fates might bring thereafter. And so, having feasted courtesy of the farmer's generosity, they settled down to an exhausted sleep.

Meanwhile Trooper Castelow – number twelve on the jump – was busy executing a lone escape and evasion that would prove even more of a daredevil enterprise. As soon as the hue and cry had died down, the sound of enemy vehicles fading into silence,

Castelow had got moving. Pushing north – the only sensible direction to take – he'd crept along the marshy, thickly vegetated banks of the Essonne, a tributary of the Seine. After covering a good 10 miles, he'd reached the small village of Vert-le-Petit, where he was duly introduced to the head of the local Resistance, who 'gave me civilian clothes and a French pass'.

With the massive urban expanse of Paris lying directly to his north, there was little point going any further that way. Instead, Castelow – who would go on to be awarded the Military Medal – was about to join the locals in their battle to expel the Nazi occupiers. 'I remained . . . and worked with the Resistance,' Castelow would report, of his time with the partisans of Vert-le-Petit. He would put his SAS training to very good use now: 'We were mainly engaged with ambushing transport on the roads.'

Eventually, the Gestapo would learn of Castelow's existence and role, and he would be forced to move on. But for now, he was relatively safe and engaged in the kind of activities that would wreak suitable vengeance for what had transpired at their DZ. For all Castelow knew, he was the only one of Garstin's stick to have made it out of the ambush alive.

After several visits to the Hôpital La Pitié-Salpêtrière, *Untersturmführer* von Kapri appeared convinced that none of the wounded men was likely to pull through. Despite receiving 'the best treatment and care', they were barely fit for any further questioning, he reported to his boss, Kieffer. *The best treatment and care* – Captain Garstin, Paddy Barker and Lieutenant Wiehe would beg to disagree. Denied any official recognition as POWs, they had been informed they were 'terrorists' in the eyes of their captors, and were to be treated as such.

Lieutenant Wiehe – the suspected Frenchman – was subjected to the very worst. His treatment was torture, pure and simple. The Gestapo plagued his bedside like devils, seeming 'determined to make him speak by all means, but the worst torture he had to endure was the lack of medical care'. Still fully conscious, he knew that the wound at the base of his spine was 'serious and getting infected', and he cried and winced in pain. But all care was reserved for the German patients, who filled up the vast majority of the hospital.

There was one notable exception to this, as surprising as it proved uplifting. *Unteroffizier* (Corporal) George Richard was a German orderly serving on Wiehe's ward. In the deepest of ironies, Richard – 6 feet tall, bespectacled, and a student in Munich before being conscripted into the Wehrmacht – was a fervent anti-Nazi. 'He did everything he possibly could to help me and to make life easier,' Wiehe reported. But his greatest single gesture of kindness was to return to the grievously injured man his rosary. That simple act reminded the SAS lieutenant that while he had lost everything – his dear friends and comrades, his freedom, his very mobility – 'his heart was still beating', and 'life-blood pumped through his weakened body'.

The return of the rosary gave Wiehe 'tremendous courage' to endure. Whenever he found himself drifting into a 'state of semi-coma', or twisting in agony and trying 'desperately to find a more comfortable position to relieve his torment', his hand would reach involuntarily for that precious string of beads. He thought then of his fellow captives: where were they now? What were they enduring? He imagined them being spirited away to Germany, to face unimaginable horrors. And he thought of those back at SAS HQ, 'wondering how they were reacting to news of their capture'.

In truth, no one at SAS headquarters was any the wiser as to what might have happened to Captain Garstin and his men. The sole means of their discovering the grim truth – those pigeons set free by Vaculik – had never reached Britain. Instead, before they were able to properly take flight, the messenger-birds had been scooped up by the Gestapo . . . and unfortunately their fate would propel Vaculik deeper into the darkness.

'You had carrier pigeons,' *Hauptsturmführer* Schnur announced, his voice smug and self-satisfied. 'We've got four of them. I suppose you don't know anything about them either?'

It was the afternoon of his second day in captivity, and Vaculik was back before his chief inquisitor. At midday, they'd been given some coffee, 'a black and bitter brew', plus soup and coarse bread. It wasn't much, and the five captives had wolfed it down. The questioning had begun shortly thereafter, and mostly Schnur had been asking about their signals. From somewhere, he'd produced a Jed set, and he kept demanding to be shown how it worked. Vaculik played dumb, arguing that he was nothing more than a 'pot and bottle washer'. But now had come the issue of the birds. Somehow he felt utterly cheated that even those pigeons had failed to make a bid for freedom and for home.

'We brought them with us to supplement our rations,' Vaculik retorted. 'To eat.' It was a piece of barefaced insolence, and he knew it, but he hadn't felt able to resist.

His reward was a blow around the face from Schnur, which was delivered with all the force that he could muster. 'Perhaps that will teach you to behave yourself,' he snarled, his face puce with anger. Then he turned to his SS assistants. There were two now. 'Take him away, and brighten up his ideas a little, will you.'

Vaculik was propelled into a neighbouring room, where

there were two baths filled with water. One was steaming hot, the other ice cold. Schnur, who had followed him in, ordered Vaculik to strip. He refused, so Schnur's lackeys beat him until he had no choice but to obey. Naked, Vaculik stood before them, his mind clouded with fear. The two flunkies grabbed him and dumped him in the scalding water, forcing his head under, until he felt as if he were going to drown. When he was on the verge of blacking out they dragged him out, and shoved him into the ice-cold bath.

The freezing water after the boiling was sheer torture, and all the while Schnur was yelling at him to talk. The process continued until Vaculik lost consciousness. It wasn't until the following morning that he properly came to. He was back in his cell. There was vomit on the bed and his head was ringing horribly. By now, all five of the SAS captives were in 'bad shape, depressed and full of aches and pains'. For hours they sat in silence, no one finding the energy or spirit to talk much.

Vaculik drifted off again. Sometime later he was woken by the guard. Midnight. Interrogation time. The questioning went on for hour after hour, until Vaculik lost all sense of night and day. The torture became more inventive, more sinister and agonising. Cigarettes were stubbed out on Vaculik's flesh. Other means were used to cause unspeakable pain. All the while Schnur kept warning Vaculik to talk, or he was very likely going to breathe his last. Finally, Vaculik realised he would have to say something – to invent some credible story – or they would finish him.

He signalled that he was ready to speak. 'Our mission was to prepare the way for an airborne division,' he whispered, exhaustedly. 'It was to be dropped shortly, near Paris, to take the German troops in Normandy in the rear.' It was complete rubbish of course, but he just had to hope and pray that Schnur would find it convincing.

A smile flitted across the Gestapo man's features. 'That's better. Now, what about the radio codes?'

Vaculik shook his head. 'I've already told you. I wasn't anything to do with communications.' Vaculik had repeatedly argued that radio procedures were well above his pay grade. 'I didn't know the codes.'

Schnur studied Vaculik for a long moment, sizing up what to do next. Then he turned to the guards. 'Put the handcuffs on him and let him go to the devil.' With that, Vaculik was dragged from the room 'with trembling legs' and propelled back to the cell.

Schnur had been personally trained by Horst Kopkow, the Berlin maestro, in 'radio counter-espionage' (*Funkspiel*). As he was finished with the five SAS captives, he issued a detailed report, based in part on the questioning, but more on a close study of the captured maps, kit and the 'one-time pad codes', the means by which SABU-70's radio messages would have been encoded. From that he had deduced several things. The SAS unit was a sabotage squad: that was clear from the amount of captured explosives. The lack of a Jed set and the SAS's intentions to link up with the Resistance reflected their plans to rely on local French forces for communications back to England.

'The squad had no wireless connection to their own to headquarters,' Schnur concluded. 'The transmission set of the Resistance group ... was to be used.' The plan at 84 Avenue Foch was to continue with the Op Marbois 'decoy transmission, which had been sent out many times by the Commander of Paris [Kieffer]'. If possible, the *Funkspiel* that had led to Captain Garstin and his men's capture was to be amplified, but the key to that lay with the wounded Lieutenant Wiehe, and there was little help he could provide right now. As for the rest of the captives, it was for Berlin to decide their fate.

The immediate priority was to get them out of 84 Avenue Foch. They would be sent to a nearby Gestapo detention centre, just a few minutes' drive away. Kieffer was adamant that if prisoners whose assistance might be required for a *Funkspiel* were kept together, it was 'at the cost of prejudicing the security of individual radio deception projects'. Accordingly, each of the SAS captives was to be placed in 'solitary confinement', if room could be found, for 'all the cells were occupied by prisoners'.

There were three main Paris holding centres for captured SOE agents, Resistance members and, more recently, Allied special forces. One was Fresnes, where SOE radio operator Marcus Reginald Bloom, source of Kieffer's first ever *Funkspiel* attempt, had been held – the largest and longest-established such facility, on the southern fringes of the city. Then there was Cherche-Midi, a former French military prison, but that was used mostly by the Wehrmacht; and then there was 3 Place des États Unis, where the SAS captives were destined to go.

In the greatest of ironies, 3 Place des États Unis was the former residence of the American ambassador to France. The historic square of the same name housed numerous memorials to Franco-US relations, including a bronze model of the Statue of Liberty, a statue of George Washington and, most recently, the Memorial to the American Volunteers (dedicated in 1923), those US citizens who had stepped forward to fight on behalf of France in the First World War.

Since the seizure of 3 Place des États Unis, its large airy rooms had been converted into bricked-up holding cells. But with space there limited, Kieffer had wanted to send the SAS captives to the much larger Fresnes, where conditions were notoriously – *suitably* – harsh. Berlin had intervened. A teleprint – a typed message, sent via the telephone network – had arrived from Kopkow, ordering Kieffer to place the prisoners in individual cells at the nearest detention facility: Place des États Unis. Berlin was taking a very active interest, and clearly wanted them kept close at hand.

On the morning of their fourth day in captivity, one by one the five captives were taken from their cell, bundled into a waiting car and driven off at speed. It was barely a five-minute ride to Place des États Unis, but still it provided time for Vaculik to glance around 'at all the people . . . going about their business in freedom while I was a prisoner held by armed men who would not hesitate to shoot if I attempted to escape'. Upon arrival, each of the captives was frogmarched through the wrought-iron gates, and propelled to the top floor, where five cells had been readied for them.

The rooms were sparse: one wooden bed, a mattress and a bucket beside it. Each had iron bars set across the windows. They looked out over the unmistakable form of the Eiffel Tower in the distance, while nearer at hand young girls played in the court-yard of a convent, situated on the Rue de Lübeck. A spyhole had been fitted into each of the doors, and every fifteen minutes or so 'an eye became visible as the SS gaoler looked in to see whether everything was in order'.

In fact, here at their new prison the guards would turn out to be somewhat less hardline than those at Avenue Foch. Mostly they were former Russian POWs, who'd been presented with a harsh choice by their captors: either join the cause of Nazi

Germany, or be worked to death in the concentration camps. They were known as 'Hiwis' – an abbreviation of the German word *Hilfswilliger*, meaning 'those willing to help'.

'They were prisoners of war . . . captured somewhere on the Eastern Front,' Ernst Vocht, another of the Avenue Foch interrogators, remarked of the Hiwi guards. Vocht, who walked with a pronounced limp, had taken six bullets in a shootout with an English SOE agent, yet still he remained a tireless Gestapo agent. 'They never learned German properly . . . I know Kieffer regarded them as a liability, not from the point of loyalty but that an accident might occur because they had not been able to understand their orders. They knew the difference between us and our English and French prisoners, that they must not let the prisoners go.'

Vaculik could speak a smattering of Russian, and he worked at building bridges with the Hiwi guards, many of whom had realised by now which way the fortunes of the war might be blowing. This was something that Vaculik and Jones would take advantage of, to execute their first daring attempt at escape. But before any such thing could happen, the fickle hand of fate was to twice intervene in the fortunes of the SAS captives. Both would be as the result of attempted assassinations – the first of Field Marshal Erwin Rommel, the second on Adolf Hitler himself. In each, British special operators were seen as having their hand at the very throat of the German high command, and the SAS captives would reap the whirlwind.

The highly respected Field Marshal Johannes Erwin Rommel – known as *der Wüstenfuchs*, the Desert Fox – had forged a formidable reputation in the battle for North Africa, and more recently commanding German forces opposing the Normandy landings. A long-time antagonist of Allied high command, it was as the result of a recent SAS operation that Rommel was seen as being unusually vulnerable. To the southeast of the Op Gain area, A Squadron 1 SAS had been executing a contemporaneous mission, codenamed Operation Houndsworth, with similar objectives – to block German armour and reinforcements from reaching the Normandy beachheads.

In the process, Major Bill Fraser, Houndsworth's commander, had learned that Rommel himself had his headquarters at the Château de la Roche-Guyon. Fraser had a personal reason to want to 'get Rommel'. Two and a half years earlier, in Operation Flipper, a group of Commandos had landed by submarine in North Africa to attack Rommel's then HQ. All but two of the raiders were killed or captured, and they'd failed to kill Rommel, who was absent at the time. Fraser's commanding officer, Lieutenant Colonel Geoffrey Keyes, had died during the raid, earning a posthumous VC.

Though Rommel's French château lay some 250 miles away, Fraser radioed headquarters, asking to have a crack at the German commander. Instead, SAS command stood up its own mission, which was given the fitting codename of Operation Gaff, a gaff being a large barbed hook used to land captured fish. Op Gaff would be commanded by a twenty-four-year-old Franco-American, 'Jack William Raymond Lee', whose real name was Raymond Courand. Courand – variously a French Foreign Legionnaire, a decorated war hero, a sometime gangster, and a veteran of the SOE and the Commandos – had been shot in both legs during Operation Chariot, the 1942 raid on St Nazaire, but had survived.

In the spring of 1943 Courand had been recruited into 2 SAS.

A year later, Brigadier McLeod – the hunting, polo-playing, pig-sticking SAS commander – figured that Courand was the man to lead Operation Gaff. Courand's hand-picked assassination squad consisted of four fellow ex-legionnaires, including a German sergeant named Marx (or 'Mark' in some reports) and a Russian named Fedossof, with the sixth man being an English lance corporal called Moore.

In his orders for Op Gaff, McLeod charged Courand and co.: 'To kill, or kidnap and return to England, Field Marshal Rommel . . . If it should prove possible to kidnap Rommel, and bring him to this country the propaganda value would be immense . . . To kill Rommel would obviously be easier than to kidnap him, and it is preferable to ensure the former than to attempt and fail in the latter.' Any successful assassination was to be 'reported by pigeon'.

Courand and his team duly parachuted into France at St-Rémy-lès-Chevreuse, some 50 miles from their target, carrying sniper rifles, the intended means of assassination. But in a belt-and-braces approach, the RAF's 193 Squadron flying Hawker Typhoons attacked Rommel's HQ, overturning his staff car and seriously injuring the German field marshal. It was only when Courand first reported into SAS headquarters by radio that he learned that the RAF had beaten him to it and that 'Rommel had been got'.

With their target hospitalised and out of reach, Courand and his team – undeterred – turned their attentions to freelance raiding instead, hitting several trains, and even tracking a senior enemy commander to his headquarters before attacking it, while Marx yelled out orders in German to confuse the defenders. Finally, with their ammo and explosives exhausted, Courand and his men had escaped to Allied lines.

As fate would have it, the injured Field Marshal Rommel

had been brought to the Hôpital La Pitié-Salpêtrière. There Lieutenant Wiehe, still stubbornly hanging onto life, learned of Rommel's admittance from Corporal Richard, the anti-Nazi orderly. Richard spoke no English and only broken French – but it was enough for the two men to make each other understood. As all knew, Rommel was a high-profile German commander and a hero of the nation. With the Allies targeting such senior figures, it didn't bode well for those who had fallen into the enemy's clutches. But worse was coming.

Three days after Rommel's injury and hospitalisation, the attempt on Hitler's life was made. On 20 July a bomb concealed in a briefcase was detonated at the *Wolfsschanze* ('Wolf's Lair'), one of Hitler's top-secret headquarters, situated near Rastenburg in what was then East Prussia (present-day Poland). Four senior Nazi figures were killed, but Hitler suffered only minor injuries.

As the attack was classed as sabotage, it fell to SS *Sturmbannführer Kriminalrat* Horst Kopkow to investigate, just as he had done with the attempt to assassinate General Reinhard Heydrich, two years earlier. Kopkow rapidly established that the bomb had 'English chemical-mechanical timer' components, plus firing pins and detonators. The hand of Britain's covert agencies – of her sabotage and assassination specialists – was seen as being at work.

Over time, the 20 July plotters – senior military figures who had planned and executed what would become known as Operation Valkyrie – were rounded up and some 200 would be executed. At the same time Hitler and his coterie of Nazi loyalists took an even firmer grip on power. The Führer himself declared: 'Having escaped death in so extraordinary a way, I am now more than ever convinced that the great cause I serve will survive its present perils and that everything can be brought to a good end.'

At 84 Avenue Foch, the fallout from Operation Valkyrie would be felt most personally. SS *Standartenführer* Helmut Knochen, who ran operations on the third floor, quickly fell under Berlin's suspicions. Suspected of being an accomplice of the Valkyrie plotters, Knochen was arrested and accused of 'behaving in an unsoldierly, not to say cowardly manner'. Shortly, he would find himself demoted to the SS equivalent rank of a private and sent to the front line, to fight.

In the meantime, all staff at 84 Avenue Foch were ordered to wear their SS uniforms, as opposed to their much-preferred civilian clothing. 'I felt I was putting on fancy dress,' remarked one. 'Then Kieffer had us all photographed, told us we were to assemble below. It was the whole staff of 82–84 Avenue Foch, Gestapo and *Sicherheitsdienst* together . . . Just before the shutter clicked, the colleague standing beside me whispered: "Is this to make sure the British will know us, to hang us?"' The Gestapo and SD men knew what they were guilty of. They feared a reckoning was coming.

The cumulative effect of such repeated assassination attempts – Heydrich, Rommel, Hitler – was a thirst for revenge at the very highest echelons of the Nazi regime. While Kopkow was caught up in the exhaustive and swingeing investigations into Op Valkyrie, the SAS captives in Paris had gained a little breathing space. For now. But when the focus returned, it would do so with a vengeance.

It would be from Hitler himself that their fate would be decided.

Chapter 15

It was when poking around at the bars to his window that Vaculik first sensed the possibility of escape. Of course, solitary confinement is designed to do what it says on the tin – to deprive an individual of all other human contact. In the SAS captives' case, they were supposed not even to know the fate of their fellow prisoners. But Vaculik had managed to befriend Vassiliev, a Russian guard who had been captured two years earlier, during the Battle for Moscow, opting to join the German military rather than be shot, and Vassiliev was proving helpful.

From Vassiliev, Vaculik had managed to scrounge the odd cigarette. More importantly, he'd learned that Ginger Jones was being held on the same floor, as were Walker, Young and Varey. The five were together, but apart. He was determined to get a message to his friends, to stiffen their spirits. Via Vassiliev's good offices, Vaculik managed to broker a trip to the lavatory with a brief stopover at the door to Jones's cell. After checking the coast was clear, the Russian flipped aside the peephole and beckoned Vaculik over.

'Ginger!' Vaculik hissed, as he forced a partly smoked cigarette through the narrow aperture. 'Here's a dog-end for you.'

'Good lord!' Jones cried. 'How goes it? I thought you were dead.'

'Not quite, but they fixed me up alright.'

'We'll make 'em pay for it later,' Jones growled.

The guard hurried Vaculik away, but on hearing those few words of defiance he had felt his spirits soar. Later, in the privacy of his cell, he took a careful look at his watch, which by chance his captors had failed to confiscate. With infinite care, he managed to dismantle it, removing the mainspring, the coil of toughened steel that, when wound, provides power to the timepiece's mechanics. With the spring straightened, Vaculik broke it into two pieces – the kind of lengths that might serve as a makeshift file – and hid the remains of the watch deep in his mattress.

That done, he crept to the window and began to work on the bars. Luckily he could hear the guard's approach, whenever he came to check via the peephole, and could break off from his sawing in good time. After two hours' work, and with fingers rubbed bloody and raw, he'd managed to sever the first bar. The cut from the narrow 'blade' was all but invisible. He figured there was little chance it – and subsequent cuts – would be discovered.

The following day he managed to slip a length of the spring through Jones's peephole, under the cover of grabbing a few quick words. He felt sure his friend would know what to do with it. While the food at 3 Place des États Unis consisted of little more than a hunk of coarse black bread, a bowl of thin soup and a mug of bitter coffee, if they could only keep their strength up escape was possible: Vaculik felt sure of it. With time, he and Jones could saw through the bars, 'and escape one night into the convent garden' that lay below.

Vaculik felt compelled to make the attempt, no matter how slim were their chances: 'Life was sweet and I wanted to live.' That desire was driven by the conviction that sooner or later, he would be 'taken out . . . and shot without a soul knowing what had happened'. He felt sure the other captives would be feeling and acting likewise.

With twelve of the bars cut, and 'day five' of his solitary confinement scored on one wall of his cell, Vaculik was feeling guardedly optimistic, but all his hopes were about to be dashed. A hatchet-faced SS sergeant arrived at his door, making a routine inspection. Vaculik had rubbed in some chewed-up black bread to hide the cuts to the bars, but one shake by the SS man was enough to reveal his handiwork.

Furious, the man span around and thumped Vaculik in the face, delivering a blow that almost made him swallow the length of steel spring he'd secreted between his top lip and gum.

'*Donnerwetter*! That's you, I suppose.'

'Me? I don't know anything about it. Someone else must have done it. What do I have to cut it with?'

The sergeant scowled. 'I don't know, but for sure we'll find out.'

Vaculik's room was turned upside down and he was thoroughly searched. Fortunately neither the dismantled watch nor the hidden spring was found. That night Vaculik lay on his thin mattress feeling frustrated and disheartened. There would be no more sawing through the bars. Then another idea struck him. There was a cupboard in his room. It was locked, but he could use the spring to pick the lock. Once inside, he could try to tunnel through the wall. He'd need some kind of digging tool, but surely he could find one.

The following morning he searched his cell from end to end. There was nothing remotely capable of chiselling through masonry. Downhearted, Vaculik glanced out of the window. His eye was drawn to a girl who had appeared on one of the convent balconies. She looked about seventeen or eighteen years old. With her chestnut-brown hair and sparkling eyes, she was arresting, and she had a wonderful air of freedom and defiance about her.

As Vaculik watched, she held up a blackboard on which she had written: 'My heart is with you. Have courage. Henrietta.'

Vaculik felt his spirits soar. 'I no longer felt so utterly alone,' he remarked of the moment. There were others in Paris who knew what was going on at 3 Place des États Unis. At the same time he was painfully aware of how dishevelled and dirty he must look. Repeatedly he'd been tortured and beaten, and he'd not washed or shaved for days. Even so, Henrietta's brave gesture – her spirit of resistance – spurred him on. He must escape. He must.

Later, he got a visit to the bathroom. It wasn't Vassiliev on duty, and the guard forced him to use the lavatory with the door wide open, so as to prevent him from trying to escape. Even so, Vaculik's eyes were drawn to a thick iron nail driven into the bathroom wall. It looked perfect for his plan to tunnel his way out. On the way back to his room, Vaculik risked a momentary peep into another of the cells. For his pains, he was shoved violently by the guard and assailed with a string of curses.

But it had been worth it. Vaculik felt shocked at what he'd just seen. Momentarily, like some scene from a horror movie, he'd caught a glimpse of a young woman sitting on her bed in that bare cell, reading. When Vassiliev came on duty later, Vaculik redoubled his charm offensive.

'Dobrý večer, tovarich,' – good evening, comrade. Vassiliev returned the greeting. 'Tell me,' Vaculik continued, 'what's that young woman doing locked in the cell along there?'

'She's a spy. She's waiting to be shot. The Germans don't wear kid gloves, even with women.'

Vaculik asked if he might speak with her. Vassiliev stressed that it was strictly forbidden, but when he next took Vaculik to the lavatory he promised they might give it a try. A while later they made the short journey. Once in the bathroom, and with the door firmly closed, Vaculik wrestled the thick nail free from the wall and slipped it into his pocket. On the way back, the Russian paused at the door to the woman's cell, before reaching out, unbolting it and swinging it open.

Vaculik knew he only had a few precious seconds. 'My name is Jean Dupontel,' he announced, hurriedly. 'I'm being held prisoner here with a number of English comrades.'

'I'm Charlotte L.,' the woman replied, 'an agent of Free France. I was captured a month ago and I am to be shot soon.' She spoke the words calmly, the ghost of a smile playing across her lips.

'You are very brave, mademoiselle.' Vaculik reached out to her. 'I am proud to shake your hand.'

They shook hands briefly, before Vassiliev hustled Vaculik away. That night the Gestapo came for the condemned prisoner. Vaculik heard her cell door being opened and the sound of Charlotte being marched away, defiant to the last. Instinctively, he sank to his knees. There were no words for such inhumanity.

The following morning, he etched another grim score in the wall of his cell – eight days at 3 Place des États Unis. While Charlotte L.'s horrible fate proved hugely dispiriting, it was also a spur to his anger and his courage. He inspected the cupboard, and within thirty minutes had the lock open. He swung wide the door, and was delighted to discover it was more than deep enough to work inside. He vowed to start his excavations that very night.

Each evening the guard would order him to strip, taking

away his British uniform as a disincentive to escape. No bother: he would work in his underclothes through the night hours. He'd place the bolster and the bucket tucked under the blanket, to mimic a person asleep in the bed, while he beavered away in secret. That first night Vaculik slaved away, feverishly attacking first the plaster, and then the brickwork, catching all the debris and lowering it to the floor. As the hours passed, he saw the light of the guard periodically glint through the peephole, but each time the bucket-and-bolster deception seemed to pass muster. At one stage he heard a lump of masonry tumble away from the far side, and land on a neighbouring roof with a tremendous clatter.

Vaculik froze. Surely the guards must have heard. He swept up the plaster and debris and shunted it to one corner of the cupboard, before closing it with fevered hands and diving back into bed. For long minutes he waited, fearing discovery. But no one came. No one seemed to have noticed. Even so, Vaculik felt too shaken to continue. He tried to get some rest, but sleep wouldn't come.

Dawn found him back at work on the wall. By the time the guard arrived with his uniform and his morning mug of coffee, Vaculik was kneeling by his bed, hands clasped together. The guard seemed amused at Vaculik's devoutness. In truth he was praying for God to give him the strength to make the escape attempt.

Later that morning Vaculik received a huge boost, which could not have come at a better time. All of a sudden, an unmistakable voice rang out through the corridor. It was Paddy Barker, the irrepressibly good-humoured giant of an Irishman. He was yelling out news to the others, despite the guards doing all they could to silence him. From Barker, Vaculik learned that 'Lieutenant Rex' – Wiehe – was going to have some kind of operation for his injuries, and that Captain Garstin was on the mend, and was very likely going to join them.

Vaculik felt his spirits soar. It seemed like impossibly good news right then. A while later, when Vassiliev came on duty, he learned that the SAS captain had indeed been moved into one of the nearby cells. It happened to be the room that Charlotte L. had been taken from, for her execution. On the way to the lavatory, Vaculik was allowed a few hurried words with the newly arrived prisoner. As the door swung open and Captain Garstin spied Vaculik, his face lit up in a brave smile. For each, it was as if the other had come back from the dead.

'Hello, old boy,' Garstin began, with an air of forced jollity. It was so good to see him again, but Vaculik could tell how weak and sickly he was. The SAS captain was hardly able to stand and his breath came in short, painful gasps. 'The swine didn't attend to me in hospital,' he remarked, by way of explanation. 'Just questioned me and questioned me, twisting my arms. My wounds open and festering. Treated me as if I were a spy. Cut off my ribbons and shoulder pips.'

Vaculik clenched his fists in helpless rage at seeing his commander like this. Vassiliev was standing watch at the end of the corridor and it was obvious they didn't have long.

'If I don't get away and you should happen to, let my wife know, will you,' Garstin added. 'You know the address.'

'Of course I will, ' Vaculik assured him. He felt so frustrated. There was nothing he could do to help a man he revered and counted as a dear friend. 'The dirty louts will pay for this later,' was the best he could manage.

Garstin gave a smile of recognition for the other man's fighting spirit. Several times the SAS captain had pointed out to their captors that he and his men were bona fide soldiers, he explained. It hadn't seemed to do much good. 'If you end up in a prisoner-of-war camp, let the English commander know. He'll get a message through to London.'

'I will,' Vaculik promised. 'You can rely on me for that.'

Vassiliev signalled they had to go. The SS sergeant was making his rounds, and moving in their direction.

Later, spurred on by everything that had happened, Vaculik went to work on his excavations with a vengeance, timing his digging to the sentry's rounds. But somehow he must have made more noise than he'd imagined, for all of a sudden the door to his cell was flung open and four SS men rushed inside. In a flash, Vaculik was seized and bludgeoned over the head with a cosh, collapsing unconscious in the heap of telltale debris lying at the bottom of the cupboard.

Some time later he came to. He seemed mired in a thick and suffocating blackness. He barely knew if he was dead or alive, and then an unmistakable voice cut through the shadows.

'What have you been up to? To have the honour of being dumped in the cellars?'

It was Ginger Jones, and Vaculik felt his heart skip with joy. 'I tried to escape,' he replied, as he felt his head tenderly, where the cosh had struck. If Jones was also locked here in the dark, he too must have 'incurred the Germans' displeasure for some reason', Vaculik supposed.

Jones laughed. 'I was halfway up the chimney when they dragged me down. The swine didn't even give me a chance to clean the soot off.' Jones had been trying to climb onto the roof, to make a break for it, just as Vaculik was attempting to tunnel through the wall. 'Got a dog-end by any chance?' Jones added, hopefully.

Vaculik scrabbled around in his pockets and managed to retrieve a few strands of tobacco. He presented it to his friend. 'But I haven't got any cigarette papers, Ginger.'

'All right, we'll ask for some.' They were locked in the cellar of 3 Place des États Unis, and Jones made his way to the low door, rapping on it noisily. A light flickered on, and a voice yelled out: 'What is it?'

'Paper, Russky! Paper for cigarettes!' Jones yelled.

'No, no!' the guard shot back. 'No paper!'

The light was extinguished, as Jones heaped every insult imaginable on the head of the guard.

'Is it day or night?' Vaculik asked, once the rumpus had died down.

'Night. Must be about two or three in the morning.'

From that Vaculik determined that he'd been unconscious for most of the day. Jones was still inclined to berate the Russian guard, and every now and then he fired a string of invective in his direction. 'And to think that up to now I've always thrown my dog-ends away,' he lamented. 'I swear I'll never do so again. They're too precious.'

'Just like the time you swore you'd give up beer,' Vaculik needled him.

Despite their predicament – the cellar looked utterly escape-proof – it was great to be back in the company of his old friend. Still, after his beating with the cosh, Vaculik felt shattered. He told Jones he was going to try to get some rest, wishing his friend sweet dreams.

'I can only dream with a pint of beer in front of me,' Jones objected, 'and plenty more where that came from.'

In due course Jones was able to acquaint Vaculik with some more news. He'd got to speak with Paddy Barker direct. Barker seemed to be making a half-decent recovery, despite the lack of any medical treatment. Jones had also managed a few snatched words with Garstin. The SAS captain had heard that one of their number had died at the hospital. If it wasn't Howard Lutton, who'd been judged dead-upon-arrival, it could only be Lieutenant Wiehe. Jones was particularly saddened that such a gentleman and a gentle soul – his good friend – might have succumbed to his injuries.

Jones needn't have worried. Despite his parlous state, Captain Garstin was taken away for three days' interrogation at Avenue Foch, and when finally he returned his spirits seemed to have brightened. He brought good news. Lieutenant Wiehe appeared to be through the worst. It was Howard Lutton who had died at the hospital. Otherwise, all eight of the captives seemed to have survived their various ordeals.

Not only that, but Captain Garstin had argued most forcibly that far from being 'terrorists', he and his men were soldiers serving in uniform, and were entitled to all the protections due prisoners of war. He was convinced that their captors at 84 Avenue Foch had finally decided to listen. By way of response, they had promised to organise a prisoner exchange, whereby the SAS would be swapped for some German agents held by the British. All they were waiting for was Lieutenant Wiehe to get better, whereupon 'the whole party would be moved to England'.

On one point at least the Gestapo – Kieffer – had been truthful. Wiehe seemed to be through the worst. In a poignant diary entry, under the page headed 'Tues. 25 July, St James. Sun Rises, 4.12; Sets, 7.59 (GMT)', he'd written: 'Operated on by German surgeon who removed two 9mm bullets.' They had let twenty days pass before attending to Wiehe's injuries, but at least finally they had done so. Indeed, the German surgeon had performed a laminectomy, opening up his spinal cord to relieve pressure on his damaged nerves, removing two bullets from his open wounds.

'Garstin was convinced that everything would be alright, it was only a matter of time,' Jones noted. While some were visibly lifted by the news of Wiehe's miraculous recovery, plus that of the promised prisoner exchange, Vaculik and Jones remained sceptical. Rather than any prisoner swap, they feared they were still for the hatchet.

Locked in the hot, airless cells of 3 Place des États Unis, the days seemed to merge into one. In such conditions, Garstin's injuries were hardly about to improve. Apart from the difficulty he had walking, one arm was hanging limp and 'almost useless', Jones observed. Via a mixture of pleading and browbeating the guards, he secured permission to help Garstin 'dress and undress, morning and night'. The SAS captain's injuries were proving too debilitating to manage on his own.

By now it was the dying days of July '44. Though none of the Paris captives could know it, Trooper Castelow – parachutist number twelve – was still at large, wreaking havoc with the Resistance band at Vert-le-Petit. And to the north of there, Troopers Norman and Morrison – numbers ten and eleven – were still at liberty. For several nights they'd pushed north through forest and village, dodging enemy patrols. At one stage they'd bedded down in a wood, only to have an entire German infantry column camp up in the very same location. They'd spent the night with scores of enemy troops barely a dozen yards away.

On another occasion they'd gone to cross a major road, only to dash out into the path of a German sentry. By sheer luck he happened to be looking in the opposite direction and they'd made it into some cover without being seen. Surviving mostly on gifts of bread, milk and eggs from friendly farmers, plus the chocolate from their rations, they'd discarded all but the bare necessities, to lighten their loads. Like that they'd pressed on following a compass bearing, carrying only their haversacks and their sleeping bags.

On the night of 13 July they'd reached a patch of woodland west of the town of Saint Chéron, to the southwest of Paris, where they threw themselves down to rest. Parched, they searched for water, but could find none. The following morning they approached a nearby farm, where the occupants proved hugely helpful. Having pressed ample food and drink upon the two SAS men, the farmer did his utmost to persuade them to stay. Allied forces could not be so very far away, and all the two would achieve if they headed onwards was to risk getting caught by the enemy.

They could camp in the woodland in comparative safety, and he would see to it that they were fed and protected. Norman and Morrison agreed to stay as 'guests' of the French farmer, but there would be several near misses in the days that followed. On one occasion, they were invited to lunch with the farmer, and were just leaving his house as a German officer strode up the garden path. Fortunately, both SAS men had discarded their uniforms by now, and were dressed in clothes provided by the locals.

Spying the enemy officer – who had come to buy eggs – Trooper Morrison calmly walked past and slipped out the garden gate, while Trooper Norman shooed some ducks out of the way of the jackbooted visitor, before disappearing around a corner of the farmhouse. Both got away with it. A little later, a local school-teacher, who had become their main source of intelligence and morale, was caught by the Gestapo. In an act of selfless bravery he gave neither of the SAS fugitives away, but was shot for his courageous refusal to talk.

Trooper Castelow, meanwhile, had fallen under the Gestapo's spotlight. They had got wise to his presence amongst the Vert-le-Petit Resistance, whereupon 'it became too dangerous to remain'. Castelow's only option was to try to make Allied lines. Dressed in a gendarme's uniform – that of the French police force – the lone fugitive set off, bicycling towards Normandy, around 150 miles away. He made fair progress, until he was caught up in a massive German military convoy.

To make matters worse, his bicycle was stolen, and 'unfortunately, upon discovering this, I swore in English', Castelow would report. He was overheard by some German troops, who pounced upon Castelow, threatening him with immediate execution as a spy. But a senior German officer intervened, deciding to send Castelow under escort further into German-occupied territory, 200 miles east to Verdun. There Castelow was imprisoned, interrogated and tortured, but he declined to talk.

'I refused . . . to tell them what I had been doing or that I was a paratrooper.' From there, Castelow was loaded aboard a truck, to be dispatched to Germany. If he was spirited into the Fatherland itself, the lone fugitive feared that he was done for. He would need to make a break for it, and quickly, for the German border was less than 100 miles away.

At 84 Avenue Foch meanwhile, Hans Kieffer was getting more

than a little anxious and frustrated. Twice he had sent messages to Berlin, asking for guidance on the fate of the SAS captives. Twice Kopkow, still dealing with the fallout of Operation Valkyrie, had failed to respond. Berlin's decision 'was overdue for a long time', Kieffer noted, which riled him considerably. The Gestapo's Paris jails were full to overflowing as it was, and he needed rid of the SAS men, who had become something of an encumbrance.

Finally, Kopkow sent a response by teleprint. Kieffer gathered with *Standartenführer* Knochen, plus several others of the Avenue Foch higher echelons, as they read the missive from Berlin: 'The Führer and Supreme Commander of the Wehrmacht has ordered that the men of the enemy Commando, which collaborated with the French Resistance movement, are to be shot. The sentence has to be previously made known to them. They are to be shot in civilian clothes.'

'Report of completion is to be made within twenty-four hours,' the order continued, 'so that higher headquarters may be informed.' For the avoidance of doubt, the order was to be carried out in the 'strictest secrecy'. After weeks of silence, Hitler himself had intervened, as all in that room understood perfectly now. Of course, they were well aware that none of the SAS captives had faced any kind of trial or due legal process. No charges had been prepared, no prosecution appointed, no defence lawyers hired, nor any hearing held before any kind of judges, military or civilian.

But at the same time they knew that in the case of Allied troops caught behind the lines, supposedly Hitler's word *was* the law. All had been acquainted with *das Kommandobefehl* – the Commando Order – issued on 18 October 1942 from the Führer's headquarters. 'Henceforth, all enemy troops encountered by

German troops during so-called Commando operations ... though they appear to be soldiers in uniform or demolition groups, armed or unarmed, are to be exterminated to the last man ... If such men appear to be about to surrender, no quarter should be given to them.'

German officers were charged to 'Report daily the number of saboteurs thus liquidated ... The number of executions must appear in the daily communications of the Wehrmacht to serve as a warning to potential terrorists.' Any such troops were to be held captive only for as long as the Gestapo or SD needed, in order to interrogate them. The Führer's order ended with a telling threat: 'I will summon before the tribunal of war all leaders and officers who fail to carry out these instructions – either by failure to inform their men or by their disobedience of this order in action.'

Since the *Kommandobefehl's* issuance, certain developments had forced the Nazi hierarchy to consider holding show trials for those facing execution. In December 1943, the first German war crimes suspects had stood trial – not in the west, but in the city of Kharkov, in the Soviet Union. Three German officers, including an SS lieutenant, were tried for mass murders committed in the city, along with one Russian collaborator. After the city of Kharkov's seizure, the *Einsatzgruppen* – Hitler's mobile death squads – had killed tens of thousands of Jews, communists and Soviet POWs, as well as other Nazi 'undesirables'. Shootings, hangings and mobile gas vans were the means of liquidation, and the victims were thrown into mass graves.

The conviction of the four accused and their subsequent public hanging had made headline news around the world, including in Germany. Hitler and his propaganda minister, Joseph Goebbels, had mooted a riposte. They'd proposed holding show trials for captured Allied agents, who would be tried for acts of sabotage and the targeting of German soldiers – including senior commanders – behind the lines. But it seemed that cooler heads had prevailed. In term of propaganda, this risked backfiring most spectacularly. Such actions, when weighed against the mass murders of thousands on the Eastern Front by Hitler's *Einsatzgruppen*, paled into insignificance.

Then, in the run-up to the D-Day landings, a group of senior German commanders – Colonel Knochen included – had sought to challenge the legality of the *Kommandobefehl* itself. Surely, they argued, the order had to be rescinded. 'The military operations caused by the invasion [the D-Day landings] would bring about fluid fronts,' they pointed out, whereupon the implementation of the Commando Order would prove impossible. Such a fast-moving situation would leave individual commanders 'uncertain as to how they should deal with the order in individual cases'.

But Hitler was unmoved. Indeed, the Führer went one step further. His office issued a supplementary order, which read: 'In spite of the Anglo-American landings in France, the Führer's order of 18 October 1942, regarding the destruction of saboteurs and terrorists, remains fully valid . . . all parachutists encountered outside the immediate combat zone are to be executed.'

In an attempt to reconcile the new order with the realities of the Allied landings, 'a line was determined a certain number of kilometres away from the front', Knochen noted. 'What came down behind that line was to be treated according to the Commando Order. The group that parachuted near Paris had, at that time, jumped far behind that line.' In other words, as far as the Paris

Gestapo were concerned the case was clear cut: the SAS captives would face death, due to the simple fact of where they had landed in France.

As the teleprint from Berlin had called for the 'strictest secrecy', they would need to restrict knowledge of the coming executions to the smallest possible circle. Knochen – no virulent Nazi, certainly; a man accused of being a part of the Operation Valkyrie conspiracy to assassinate Hitler – let Kieffer take full charge. For secrecy's sake, Kieffer set about ensuring that 'the preparations, particularly the change into civilian clothes, should be carried out by men of my section who were already acquainted with the case'.

The execution party would consist of several of his stalwarts. In command, Kieffer placed his acolyte, *Hauptsturmführer* Schnur, the man who had done such a thorough job of interrogating the SAS captives. Schnur was 'instructed to make out a verdict, to be communicated to the members of the SAS, that based upon the fact of their having parachuted in connection with a group of the Resistance Movement . . . they were to be shot . . . on order of the Führer and Supreme Commander of the Wehrmacht'.

Under Schnur, Kieffer selected von Kapri to translate the death sentence into English, for the order from Hitler had specified that 'the sentence has to be . . . made known to' those condemned to die. As for Haug, the Avenue Foch quartermaster, he would furnish the captives with their civilian clothes, chosen from amongst the captured SOE stores. Kieffer appointed SS *Hauptsturmführer* Julius Schmidt as the chief executioner. As well as being Gestapo, Schmidt was a Waffen SS officer, so had widespread military experience and should be quite capable of leading the shootings.

Schnur was left to select others for the firing squad as he saw fit, but keeping it all as far as possible to those already in the know. They would need transport. Drivers. They would need an execution spot. Somewhere private, isolated, unseen. But all of that could be arranged.

And then, the fate of the surviving SAS captives would be sealed.

Chapter 16

SAS Captain Garstin was a thoroughly decent and upstanding individual, who believed there could still be honour in war. To him it was inconceivable that the story SS *Sturmbannführer* Kieffer had told him of the prisoner exchange could be anything other than genuine. To have concocted such a tale out of thin air in an effort to mollify his captives and to render them more pliant and willing to cooperate was anathema. Kieffer was a major, Garstin a captain, and both served in the forces of foremost martial nations. In the SAS captain's view, such deliberate subterfuge was simply unthinkable.

Back at their home in Canterbury, Pat Garstin's wife, Susan, was just about to celebrate their son, Patrick Beresford Sean Garstin's, first birthday. But for Captain Garstin, without anything particular to distinguish one from another, all the days seemed to merge into one. Time seemed to crawl in the dark and claustrophobic cells at Place des États Unis. The muggy days of Paris in summer meant that often the captives felt they could hardly breathe.

Over time, Jones and Vaculik settled into something of a routine. The narrow windows to their cell were kept permanently shuttered, but in one they had discovered a small hole. It was large enough to get an eye to, and taking turns they would gaze out onto an unsuspecting world. Nearby there was a bench, set in the shade of some trees. As regular as clockwork an elderly gentleman would arrive, open his newspaper to peruse it, then after a while check his watch and hurry away. Each evening at six o'clock a pair of lovers would take the seat. The young man was always dressed in the same dull brown suit, but the woman seemed to have an expansive wardrobe, and Jones and Vaculik would 'make bets as to what colour dress . . . she would be wearing'.

At one stage, Allied warplanes wheeled overhead, hitting targets somewhere in the city. It prompted Vaculik to ask Jones what he would do if a squadron of American tanks thundered into the square. A part of Jones resented the 'Yanks', for with their dollars they tended to 'drink all the whisky and there's not much left for us'. But upon reflection, he figured if American troops did roll into Place des États Unis, at the very least he would 'offer 'em one of my dog-ends'. That was saying something, for right then a cigarette butt was about Jones's most precious possession.

The SS sergeant who oversaw security at Place des États Unis still appeared convinced of the omnipotence of Hitler's Reich. He checked on Vaculik and Jones obsessively, just to ensure they weren't somehow trying to tunnel their way out. He'd taken to berating them, throwing the words 'terrorists', '*kaputt*' – finished – and a derogatory term for Jew in their faces. In the same breath, he'd trumpet the supposed wonders of the Nazi Reich and the invincibility of the Teutonic warrior. He claimed that the Wehrmacht had launched glorious counter-offensives both against Russia in the east, and to repel the Normandy landings, which would finish the Allies once and for all.

'We shall win this war in the end,' he crowed. 'And do you know why? Because we are braver and more disciplined.'

In truth, the SAS captives found it hard to argue. For weeks on end they'd heard little of the Allies' fortunes. For all they knew, the D-Day landings might well have been flung back into the sea. In spite of the promised prisoner exchange, their morale was at an all-time low, which was why Jones's discovery with the broken watch-spring was so special and so timely. Since their escape attempts, Jones and Vaculik had had their handcuffs fastened especially tight. But one morning, Jones discovered that he was able to pick the locks. All he had to do was force the narrow thread of steel between the teeth and the cog that wound them tight, and he could work the mechanism free.

For now, it meant they could loosen their hands at night, making it far easier to sleep. There was one small broken-backed bed in their cell, which they were forced to share. If they kept their newfound freedom secret, it had to boost their chances of making a getaway. Having made the discovery about their cuffs, Jones and Vaculik hatched a scheme of sorts. One night they would call the guard, feigning sickness. They'd overpower and kill him, take his weapon and release their fellow captives, whereupon they'd resort to barefaced bluff: they'd walk out of the prison 'wearing German uniforms'.

The captives were able to speak to each other a little more freely, especially when 'the good Vassiliev' was on duty, and the word on everyone's lips was escape. But when they discussed their plans to break out, the problems appeared insurmountable. The chief issue was Captain Garstin. It was clear that he couldn't manage 'a hundred yards without dropping', and even then far too slowly to make a getaway. All seven of the captives were adamant: if one was to go, all were to go. They would break out as one band of brothers, united, or not at all. In any case, the signs were that the prisoner exchange was happening, or so their guards kept saying.

On the afternoon of 8 August – five weeks after they had set out for France aboard the Stirling – the blustering SS sergeant paid a visit to Vaculik and Jones's cell, with some associates in tow. They carried with them soap, towels and razors, plus bundles of what looked like civilian clothes. The prisoner exchange had got the green light, the SS man explained, and it would be taking place in neutral Switzerland. They were to be swapped 'for nine German agents held in London'. Vaculik and Jones would need to wash and shave for the journey, plus he had need of their uniforms, so they could be cleaned – hence the civilian clothes. To underscore his intent, he put his hand to his nose, to indicate how they and their uniforms reeked.

As the SS man had been speaking to Vaculik in French, Jones hadn't understood much, but he was instinctively suspicious. As for Vaculik, he didn't believe a word. He asked when they might be starting their journey to Switzerland. The answer: they would depart at 1 a.m.. That cemented his fears, for it left nowhere near enough time to launder and dry their uniforms. Sensing what dark motives had to lie behind all this, both men refused to change their dress. By way of response, the SS men forcibly stripped the two captives at gunpoint.

In short order, Jones and Vaculik were deprived of their British Army battle dress, complete with the 1 SAS Regiment shoulder flashes, shirt and tie, plus boots and gaiters, and the thin veneer of protection it had all provided. They were stripped of every last vestige of their military identity: even their army-issue underwear and socks were taken. In their place, they were left a pair of dark, moth-eared suits, a shirt each, and great clodhoppers for shoes. Though fearful of what was coming, the two men set to with the hot water and shaving kit – for this was their first chance at any kind of a freshen-up since the day of their capture.

'I enjoyed that wash,' Jones remarked, simply.

Oddly, when Vassiliev came to take their clothes later that evening – as he always did, to dissuade any escape attempt – he left their cell door slightly ajar. Vaculik took the opportunity to nip out, on the Russian's heels. Did Vassiliev mind if he had a quick word with Captain Garstin, Vaculik asked, especially as this was their last night in the jail. As long as he was quick, the Russian guard cautioned.

Vaculik dashed along to the SAS captain's cell. In hushed tones he outlined the worst of his fears: there was no time to launder their uniforms, and he didn't believe the prisoner exchange was for real. Forcing them to dress in civilian clothes was all part of a trap. Garstin looked feverish, and it seemed as if his condition was rapidly deteriorating. His teeth were chattering, as some kind of infection took hold. It was hardly surprising, considering the extent of his untreated injuries, and where he was being held.

The SAS captain made a visible effort to gather his wits. Taking a grip on himself, he explained how he'd been given solemn assurances that the prisoner exchange was genuine. 'Make a dash for it if you like,' he added, trying to force a smile, 'but I'd far rather you stayed and took your chance with us.'

Vaculik recognised these were the words of 'an honest and upright man . . . a chivalrous soldier', one who 'just couldn't imagine that anyone could be so vile. He didn't know much about . . . the SS and the Gestapo.' But upon reflection, maybe the SAS captain was right, he reasoned. Maybe they should stay together. Maybe it was all or nothing.

Once back in his cell, he explained everything to Jones. 'But perhaps he's right in a way,' Jones reasoned, of Garstin's all-or-none stand. There was little chance of making a break for it in the few remaining hours, especially as the place was crawling with SS, making ready for their early-morning departure.

'Let's see if we can get some sleep,' Vaculik suggested. 'Sleep brings counsel, they say.'

Jones snorted. 'We've been sleeping in this ruddy place for weeks now, and it hasn't done much good.'

A few hours later an engine coughed into life. A mile across the sleeping city, SS *Obersturmführer* Otto Ilgenfritz pulled onto the midnight streets of the blacked-out city. Even the sleek Opel staff-car's headlamps were hooded, so as to shield it from any marauding Allied warplanes. It was a short drive to number 22 Avenue Foch, where the Gestapo and Waffen SS officer he was scheduled to collect had his luxurious apartment. Upon arrival, *Hauptsturmführer* Julius Schmidt slid quietly into the passenger seat, before instructing Ilgenfritz to drive to the nearby Place des États Unis.

Ilgenfritz's orders for today had come from out of the blue: a phone call from Schmidt, late the previous afternoon, instructing him to prepare a car plus a convoy of trucks for 'an action against terrorists', the details of which were most secret. From June 1941 Ilgenfritz had served as the chief of motor transport for the Avenue Foch Gestapo and SD, with several hundred vehicles in his charge. It was a rare occasion when he got to leave his Paris depot to undertake any kind of mission, and he presumed that the present undertaking had to be against the French Resistance.

Unbeknown to Ilgenfritz, it was Kieffer himself who'd suggested him as the driver for the death squad, for a man of his rank and stature should appreciate and respect the need for secrecy. On reaching 3 Place des États Unis, in the sweep of his muted headlamps Ilgenfritz could see that the truck he'd ordered was ready and waiting. Most of the vehicles required for today's mission would be packed full of troops, but one had been reserved for a party to be collected here.

Ilgenfritz had allotted SS *Oberscharführer* Fritz Hildemann as the driver of that truck, a good, solid, reliable individual. When Hildemann had asked him about the nature of the mission, Ilgenfritz had promised 'it would be interesting', while repeating the warning that it was top secret and not be discussed. It was Ilgenfritz's first visit to the Place des États Unis. Schmidt led him inside, and on the ground floor introduced him to *Hauptsturmführer* Schnur – the Avenue Foch interrogator – plus a figure who was busy making up parcels of sandwiches, presumably for the coming journey.

Ilgenfritz noticed a group of men dressed in a motley collection of civilian clothes being led to the waiting truck. It confirmed what he'd suspected: they were bringing some French prisoners with them, which was not so unusual. Doubtless they were collaborators of one sort or another, and would be used as translators and to flush out the Resistance. Seeing parcels of sandwiches loaded aboard the truck, it reinforced in Ilgenfritz's mind just who the passengers were.

The car and truck formed up in a small convoy and headed through the deserted streets to Avenue Foch. En route, Ilgenfritz asked Schmidt what exactly the nature of today's mission was. Seven 'captured terrorists' were to be shot, Schmidt explained, and both he and Ilgenfritz were to be part of the firing squad. Somewhat taken aback, Ilgenfritz asked for fuller details, but was warned that the undertaking was *geheime Reichssache* – top-se-cret Reich business – and that he wasn't permitted to know more. A two-to-three-hour journey lay ahead of them, Schmidt added, and urging Ilgenfritz to stick close behind the truck in front, he lapsed into silence.

Forming the guard on the rear of the prisoner truck were von Kapri and *Hauptscharführer* Haug, the Avenue Foch quarter-master. Of all those tasked with today's mission, Haug was the only one who had been present from the very beginning – when the 5 July *Funkspiel* had brought down twelve human parcels to the Bois de Bouray drop-zone, and not just containers as they'd expected.

Haug, a First World War veteran who'd been held as a prisoner of the British, didn't feel entirely comfortable right now. He'd been ordered by Kieffer to deploy on an anti-Resistance oper-ation, so why were these British prisoners there, and why were they dressed as civilians? He'd recognised them immediately, having spoken to some of them directly after their capture. Back then, they'd all been dressed in distinctive 'English khaki uni-form'. So why the transformation? He resolved to ask von Kapri, for the more senior SS and Gestapo man was sure to know.

As the vehicles rolled east through the sleeping city, Haug broached the subject. What were the SAS prisoners doing there? Von Kapri seemed almost surprised at the question. They 'were being taken away to be shot', he explained. Still, the penny had yet to drop with Haug. He presumed they were transporting the captives to 'some camp or prison' to face 'a firing squad especially chosen for the purpose'. As far as he knew, such executions were always held in 'the yard of a fortress or a prison'.

An hour or so earlier, the seven SAS captives had been woken and ordered to dress. There was no sign of their uniforms, but equally it was clear that 'resistance would have been useless', surrounded as they were by heavily armed SS. As they pulled on the worn civilian clothing, Vaculik and Jones made sure to keep their lengths of steel spring hidden. At the last moment one of their captors spied another prize – Jones's watch, the one that he'd been loaned by Lieutenant Wiehe – and forced the prisoner to hand it over. Jones absolutely hated losing it, for it wasn't even his to give away.

Once the precious watch had been confiscated, the seven prisoners were hustled into a room in the cellar – the first time all had been together since their capture. Despite their wash and shave, in their shabby clothes they made a sorry sight, especially after spending so many weeks as guests of the Gestapo. Even so, Paddy Barker, Walker and Young – the Irishmen – tried to crack the odd joke, in an effort to lift spirits.

Garstin was silent, his state of physical decline clear for all to see, as Jones helped him dress, pulling on the blue tweed jacket with which he had been issued. After suffering multiple injuries, and given the lack of medical treatment, it was a miracle that the SAS captain was still alive. The last thing the former miner from Wigan did was lace up Garstin's footwear. Somehow he'd managed to retain his rubber-soled Commando boots. Maybe the Gestapo had run out of civilian shoes.

With Garstin dressed, the seven captives were marched up stairwells and along corridors lined by SS men, weapons in hand. On the first floor Schnur – the interrogator and torturer-in-chief – was waiting. Brusquely he read out the captives' names, ticking off each in turn, before their handcuffs were checked and they were taken outside. Everywhere grey-uniformed figures rushed to and fro. Just as soon as Jones spied the number of guards assigned to their party, he 'knew what was in store'. As for Vaculik, he felt like they were 'cattle being . . . moved into the slaughter-house'.

The prisoners were chivvied into the waiting truck, whereupon two figures, weapons across their knees, climbed into the rear: one, Haug, was not a bad man when all was said and done; the other, von Kapri, was a nasty piece of work and a die-hard Nazi. Bundles of sandwiches were thrust in the captives' direction. What was this – a last supper? It certainly felt that way.

'But none of us was interested in eating,' Vaculik remarked. 'The lorry started up and the sound of its engine was very loud in the silent night.'

They pulled up at Avenue Foch, where several cans of petrol were loaded aboard. The captives felt their hearts skip a beat. Surely that was a positive sign? Surely it had to signal a long journey lay ahead of them? Maybe Captain Garstin was right. Maybe they were bound for Switzerland after all. Maybe, just maybe, freedom – sweet freedom – beckoned. Hope flares eternal in the living man's heart.

The truck got underway again. Via the open rear the captives saw it join a larger convoy – perhaps a score of military vehicles. What did that mean? Did it take this many troops to escort one truckload of captives to Switzerland for a prisoner exchange? At first the column thundered through the ghostly streets, moving in entirely the right direction – south and east, towards Switzerland, some 300 miles away. But after a twenty-minute drive they pulled up at a familiar stop – the Hôpital La Pitié-Salpêtrière.

They could only be there for one reason – to collect Lieutenant Wiehe. Surely the prisoner exchange was looking more likely than ever, if all were being collected, even the worst of the wounded? For ten minutes all stood idle, waiting, and then there was a slamming of doors from the truck cab, a muffled order was given and the vehicle got underway again. Jones had been convinced his good friend was about to join them, but not any more, for there was no sign of the SAS lieutenant at all. 'Why the stop at the hospital I never found out,' he noted, sadly.

In the Hôpital La Pitié-Salpêtrière Wiehe was recovering from the laminectomy – his spinal surgery. In fact, for days now he'd been hovering between life and death. And amongst the French medical staff were secret members of the Resistance. They understood exactly where the Gestapo would be taking the British captives, and they had conspired to ensure that when the lorry came to collect him, SAS Lieutenant John H. Wiehe was nowhere to be found.

It was around 3.30 a.m. as the convoy set off once more. The moon was high and bright, casting an eerie light over the city. Of all the captives, Paddy Barker seemed to have landed the most outlandish dress. Maybe it was all the Gestapo had been able to find, to fit his big, rangy frame. Irrepressibly cheerful, despite the wound that he was carrying, Barker began making fun of his look – he was dressed in plus-fours, short socks and brown shoes, showing off a good length of hairy ankle. As for the others, Walker had holes in his strange, low-cut shoes, Varey was dressed in plus-fours above heavy boots, and Young had been issued with a white cyclist's jacket that was far too small for him.

Despite the forced humour of the captives chaffing each other, Vaculik felt increasingly troubled. Instead of pushing further south and east, the convoy had reversed course. One by one the vehicles passed through the Arc de Triomphe and rumbled onwards through the city, until they reached the suburb of St Denis, some 6 miles to the north of central Paris. As Vaculik well knew, this was completely the wrong direction of travel for Switzerland.

He asked the guards where they were heading. He would learn soon enough, was the curt answer. What was he supposed to tell the others, Vaculik wondered. The convoy pressed on, passing through Sarcelles, Montsoult and Chambly – moving northwards all the while. They were fifty-odd miles out of their way by now, and Vaculik figured it was time to warn his comrades. There was no way they were making for Switzerland, he told them. No one made any particular comment. 'Heads lowered, we were jolted along, each occupied with his own thoughts,' remarked Vaculik. 'They were not particularly pleasant ones.'

But they were still alive, and while there was life there was still hope.

Chapter 17

Turning away from the guards, Vaculik pretended to blow his nose, while carefully slipping the length of watch-spring from its hiding place in his mouth and forcing it into the mechanism of his handcuffs. It made every sense to be ready. He managed to signal for Jones to do likewise – loosening their cuffs to the degree that they could still keep them on, but slip out of them in a flash. Surreptitiously, the lengths of steel spring were passed from man to man, as Jones tried to show each what to do.

Vaculik meanwhile did his best to distract von Kapri, the young SS man who had done such a fine job of assisting *Hauptsturmführer* Schnur in the Avenue Foch interrogations and torture. Feigning amity, he asked whether the SS man had ever been to London, to learn such fine English.

'No,' von Kapri told him. 'I learned English as a student in Munich.' He spoke it as fluently as he did French, he added.

'You look young to be in the military,' Vaculik observed.

He was in his twenties, which was young to be an officer in the SS, von Kapri explained, proudly.

'Seen any fighting?' Vaculik asked.

'I was on the Russian front,' von Kapri replied haughtily.

The SS man paused to light a cigarette, and as the smoke drifted through the vehicle, Jones made a comment about what he wouldn't give for a puff or two. Von Kapri ignored it, but not so his companion, Haug. Vaculik overheard a quick exchange between the two men, the subject of which was obviously whether to offer the prisoners a cigarette or not. Von Kapri clearly wasn't persuaded, but Haug quietly removed a packet from his pocket and handed them around.

As Vaculik sucked in a greedy lungful of smoke, his mind was a whirl of thoughts. They'd been on the road for a good ninety minutes by now, and nothing seemed to make any sense. If they were going to be executed, why the interminable journey? Why not shoot them in the cellars of the Place des États Unis, or at one of the many other places of execution the Gestapo boasted – a Paris barracks block, prison or rifle range? Vaculik had noticed that both Schnur and Schmidt formed part of their escort – the former riding in the truck cab, the latter in the Opel car that was sticking close on their tail. Why were two SS captains required, if not for a prisoner exchange?

With the first blush of dawn already lightening the sky, Haug and von Kapri lowered the canvas rear of the truck. The roads were smaller and more rural now, and it was getting noticeably dusty. The vehicle rumbled over badly made surfaces, each jolt throwing the captives about, as the cuffs made it almost impossible to hold on. Through a rip in the canvas enough light filtered in to illuminate the pale and drawn faces of the seven men.

At one stage Vaculik caught sight of a road sign through the torn canvas: 'Noailles' – a town lying some 50 miles to the north of Paris, amidst lush forest and farmland. Why on earth had they been brought here?

Up front in the truck cab, Schnur had dozed through most of the journey, relying on the driver, Hildemann, to dumbly follow the line of vehicles in front. Finally, seemingly in the middle of nowhere, the column ground to a halt. Ilgenfritz, Hildemann's boss, came over to the truck, ordering him to let the Opel take the lead now. Ilgenfritz made it clear he had no idea where they were heading – they were just to follow orders.

'The car . . . drove off along a different road,' Hildemann noted. 'I followed with the truck . . . After about ten minutes the car halted . . . near a projecting piece of woodland. I had then to drive the truck along a field track.' After bumping over rough ground, Hildemann pulled over where indicated, several dozen yards from the road.

Without a word of explanation, Schmidt and Schnur – the two SS captains – set off on foot for the nearby woods. A few minutes later they were back. 'Get out,' they ordered Hildemann. They indicated that he should unfasten the rear of the truck, for the prisoners were to be unloaded here. Hildemann did as ordered, whereupon Haug and von Kapri vaulted down, and voices began calling for the prisoners to get down.

'Schnell! Schnell! Schnell!' Suddenly everyone was in a massive hurry, it seemed.

It was light now, the sky above the truck a clear, duck-egg blue. Armed figures surged around the captives, some – oddly – carrying Allied weaponry, mostly Stens and US carbines. There was a momentary pause, as Jones tried to help Captain Garstin down from the truck, and in that instant Vaculik seized his chance.

He turned to von Kapri. '*Somme-nous sur le point d'être abbatus?*' – are we about to be shot?

Von Kapri sniggered. '*Bien sûr, vous allez être abbatus*' – of course you're going to be shot.

Vaculik had entertained few doubts. In his heart he'd known the dark truth. But still, to hear it on the lips of one of their would-be executioners – 'the brutal words added to my horror'. Before he could react, Schnur gave the order: 'Right turn, march at ease!'

With that each of the prisoners was hustled into motion by the butts of their captors' weapons and the line of figures began to trudge across the field. As Haug joined up, forming one of the escorts, it suddenly occurred to him that *this* was where the British soldiers were going to be shot, and that he was going to be a party to their execution.

Schnur led the way, the gold braid of his epaulettes glinting in the early-morning light, his neatly pressed grey tunic over a gleaming white collar and tie, below which his breeches bagged out above high leather boots. His large peaked cap, of matching grey and complete with a *Totenkopf* (death's head) symbol, topped off the SS full regalia. It made it all the more incongruous that the SS man was carrying a British Sten gun in his arms.

For a moment Schnur signalled a halt in the open, not far from the truck. The seven captives were lined up, but as the SS captain studied the scene he clearly didn't find it to his liking. It was too near the road. Too visible. He ordered them onwards into the trees. As if in afterthought, Schnur turned and yelled for the truck driver, Hildemann, to join them. He should bring up the rear, where Jones was desperately trying to help Captain Garstin to stay on his feet and to keep going.

As the SS commander yelled for all to keep up, Haug hung back with Jones and Garstin, which made them the last of the group to enter the shadows of the woodland. The ground rose before them in a shallow incline. It slowed Garstin's progress still further. Up ahead, sunlight filtered into a clearing, and the first of the captives – Young, Walker, Barker and Varey – could be seen forming up in line, facing their armed guards who were ranged in a half-circle, weapons at the ready.

There was no mistaking any more what was about to happen. For a moment Garstin paused and stared, aghast. 'My God, they're going to shoot us,' he exclaimed in horror.

Prods and yells from Hildemann got him moving again, as the last men in line were propelled into the clearing. A beautiful dawn chorus of birdsong filled the air. So this was 'Switzerland', Vaculik told himself, grimly. They joined the line – first Vaculik, then Captain Garstin and finally Jones.

In the distance, a church clock chimed five times. It was time. The would-be executioners readied their weapons, as Schnur produced a piece of paper from his pocket. Oddly, several of the gunmen had pulled on white gloves. The captives turned to each other to exchange a final look – they all knew what was coming.

'So you were right after all,' Garstin remarked, quietly, to Vaculik. Then, under his breath, to all: 'I'll distract them . . . On my signal, be ready to make a run for it.'

Everyone knew what the desperately sick SAS captain intended. He would stand firm in line and take the fire, so the others might make a break for it. Schnur cleared his throat. He began to read from the paper in German, as von Kapri, standing by his shoulder, translated.

'On the orders of the Führer, having been tried and found guilty of collaborating with French terrorists and endangering the security of the German Army, you have been sentenced to death by shooting.'

Both Ilgenfritz and Hildemann – the drivers – felt a jolt of shock upon hearing von Kapri start to translate. Until now they'd had no idea that any of the captives were British. They'd learned enough English in school to realise what language the death sentence was being translated into. But there was no time to process any of that, for hardly had von Kapri finished the first line of his translation than all hell let loose.

Even as von Kapri pronounced the word 'shooting', Garstin signalled – *NOW*.

To his right, Vaculik leapt like a coiled spring, emitting a deep animal yell, one filled with rage and a burning hatred, Jones doing the same to Garstin's left. Throwing off his handcuffs as he charged, Vaculik launched himself at the nearest figure, von Kapri, as hard as he could. Bursting through the cordon, he made a few more yards before his foot caught in a tree root and he went sprawling. Moments later he heard gunshots, bullets hammering past above his head.

On the words 'death by shooting', Jones had likewise broken away. 'I found myself running and stumbling, shots and screams ringing out,' he recalled. But as he'd not yet managed to fully free his handcuffs, he lost his balance and fell, having made only a few dozen yards. Most likely, that is what saved him, for a burst of fire went tearing across his fallen form, rounds chewing into the trees just beyond. There Jones lay, playing dead and praying for the best.

For all his glittering SS insignia, Schnur hadn't made a particularly good executioner. As the first of the prisoners had broken free he'd fumbled to get the paper from which he'd been reading the death sentence back into his pocket. That in turn had prevented him from opening fire. By the time he'd readied his weapon, several of the captives had taken to their heels. Panicking, Schnur yelled at his men to give chase. If any got away, he dreaded to think what might happen, once Berlin was informed.

Leaping to his feet, Vaculik blundered onwards, tearing through brambles and with branches whipping at his face. 'Behind me I heard a heavy volley and I knew what that meant: they had executed my comrades.' He was driven on by a blind fury now and gripped by the desire to survive, so that he could 'bring back the story, and see the murder of my comrades avenged'. As he raced deeper into the woods, zigzagging to avoid being hit, he 'heard bullets pass . . . and whistle through the trees'. The knowledge of just who was chasing him and why seemed to lend him wings.

Jones, meanwhile, lay where he'd fallen, 'not daring to move . . . Would I feel anything when they walked up to shoot me? It was useless trying to get up . . . if I'd tried I would have been riddled.' There was the pounding of heavy feet, as his would-be executioners gave chase. Expecting at any moment to take a burst in the back, Jones held his breath in fear. Moments later the boots had thundered over and past him, angry curses ringing through the trees.

It took nerves of steel, but still Jones forced himself *not* to move. To play dead. 'I lay on, the shots . . . ringing out. Still a lot of shouting and running. After a while . . . I raised my head from the ground. I could see a matter of fifty yards from me two of the Jerries – they seemed to be searching. I couldn't hear any movement near me, so I got up slowly and moved towards a tree . . . I made it without being seen and got behind it for some cover.' There Jones slipped out of his handcuffs.

He glanced around, trying to work out where best to run. In the process, he caught sight of several bloodied bodies lying in the clearing. At the very least the killers had got five of his comrades: Varey, Walker, Young, Barker and Garstin, by the looks of things. From the position of the bodies, it was clear that some had tried to make a run for it. With the injury he'd been carrying, Paddy Barker would have stood little chance. As for Captain Garstin, weakened by his injuries, he had stood firm to draw the enemy's fire.

The sight of his comrades gunned down in cold blood made Jones's blood boil, spurring him into action. He made a bolt for it, his heart 'thumping fit to burst', dashing through the woodland until he all but 'passed out on the ground. The few weeks in prison hadn't done me any good.' There he remained, lying low in a thicket and hoping he'd made it clean away.

A little distance away, Vaculik was still being hunted through the trees. From behind he could hear curses, boots crashing through undergrowth and the dull thud of 'bullets hitting tree trunks . . . They were coming to kill me . . . If only they didn't get me with a bullet I'd stand a chance.' Despite the weeks of torture, the starvation diet and the lack of exercise, 'I never ran so fast in my life and the fear of death urged me on.'

Finally he burst out of the woods into open farmland. But it was now that a seemingly insurmountable barrier barred his path. Before him lay a tall, thick hedge, as high as any man. It stretched to left and right without a break, and 'the Germans were almost on my heels'. Vaculik – 'caught like a poor beast in a trap' – did the only thing he could think of. In their Battle Course training in Scotland, they'd learned to surmount similarly daunting obstacles. With a superhuman effort, he launched himself at the high green barrier, wormed his way onto the top of it and vaulted down the far side.

A horse, startled by his sudden appearance, galloped off, whinnying wildly. That was sure to alert the enemy. Vaculik took to his heels, as bullets zipped and snarled through the hedge. His pursuers had to be firing blindly now, which surely gave him the edge. He raced at full tilt across the open field, a ragged fringe of woodland drawing him onwards. It was maybe 500 yards away, but if he could just make it without being caught, he should be well out of range of the killers' weapons.

He reached the line of trees, pausing for an instant to catch his breath. Glancing back, he saw that one of his pursuers had found a way through the hedge. He was kneeling, taking aim. Vaculik dived for cover, though from all his experience he knew the gunman had almost no chance of hitting him at this kind of range. The SS man unleashed a long burst, but the bullets whistled past high, tearing into the uppermost branches of the trees. Moments later Vaculik dashed into the cover of the woods, finding what seemed to be a well-worn bridlepath that snaked ahead into the shadows.

It was around 5.30 a.m. by the time those pursuing Vaculik finally gave up the chase . . . for now. Back at the botched execution site there was much angry cursing, especially as one of the five captives who had seemingly been shot had miraculously disappeared. 'There were now only four corpses,' the SS men observed, with mounting alarm. Then, someone spotted 'a track, made by crawling or dragging along, leading up into the woods'. It looked as if one of the captives, though injured, had managed to stagger away from the kill-zone.

Haug had found it impossible to gun down prisoners with whom he'd formed a soldierly bond of sorts. He'd unslung his weapon and opened fire, but he'd deliberately aimed high. Ilgenfritz, by contrast, seemed to indulge no such qualms. The SS men spread out in line abreast and began to comb the undergrowth through which the injured captive had fled. After covering around 500 yards Ilgenfritz, together with his driver, Hildemann, spotted a figure hiding behind a pile of wood.

'He must have been wounded and dragged himself there,' remarked Hildemann. As Ilgenfritz raised his weapon, the man broke cover and began to run. Ilgenfritz yelled out an order for him to stop. 'Halt! Stand still! Halt! Stand still!' As the fleeing man 'did not comply with my call, I made use of my weapon', Ilgenfritz would report. Taking aim at 'the prisoner running', Ilgenfritz proceeded to 'shoot him down'.

The dead man was carried back to the clearing. Now there were five corpses, where by rights there should have been seven. Beside himself with dread, Schnur began to argue that 'one of the bodies had been carried away by . . . members of a Resistance or sabotage group', which left only one escapee. Seeing the drift of Schnur's argument, Schmidt and Ilgenfritz backed him up. For sure, only one man could have got away. Haug thought this was utter rubbish, but he wasn't about to argue. Schnur had already begun to blame him for supposedly allowing the one captive to flee.

Hildemann was dispatched to guard the vehicles, in case the escapee tried to steal one and make good his getaway. Shortly, Ilgenfritz joined him. Schnur had ordered them to drive to the local Luftwaffe base, to seek reinforcements. They set off in the Opel, heading for a nearby château where the Luftwaffe had their headquarters. They returned, a short while later, with a truck full of airmen in tow, who proceeded to load the five corpses onto their vehicle. The Luftwaffe men had been told that some 'saboteurs' had been surprised and killed in a gun battle in the woods. One had escaped and the surroundings needed to be searched most thoroughly. And so the circle of deceit and lies was closed.

Or at least, it should have been. Against all odds, two men had got away. One, Jones, was lying low in the depths of the woods and would not break cover until nightfall. The other, Vaculik, was even now stumbling exhaustedly into a French village, desperately seeking anyone who might hide and succour him. Both men had every intention of seeing the murder of their brothers in arms avenged, if only they could evade the enemy and somehow make it back to Allied lines.

It was far from being a happy drive back to Paris, late that afternoon, as Schnur and the other SS killers contemplated the wrath of Berlin. By orders of the Führer, all the SAS captives had been condemned to be shot, in a top-secret operation. Despite that, they had allowed one at least to get away. There was bound to be an investigation and surely heads would roll.

But by chance, fortune was to come to the execution party's rescue. As luck would have it, news of the botched executions was about to be buried by the coming cataclysm. Just ten days after the Noailles Wood shootings the battle for Paris would begin. The city was liberated by the Allies in short order.

Soon Kieffer, Schnur, von Kapri, Ilgenfritz and their ilk would be burning their files and fleeing towards Germany, seeking safety.

Chapter 18

As Vaculik bicycled his way towards the house of Fernard Bourgoin, a local woodsman, he still harboured serious doubts. Across France, the *gardes de forêt* – the French foresters – were known to form the backbone of the local Resistance, but there was always the exception that proved the rule. All it would take was for this man's incredible story to be a concoction of lies, cooked up on behalf of the Gestapo, and Vaculik might be about to fall back into the hands of those from whom he'd only recently fled. The thought didn't fill him with any great sense of happiness or ease.

Bourgoin claimed to be sheltering an English soldier who had escaped from an enemy firing squad. The description the forester had given – of a redheaded individual who spoke not a word of French, but who had by gestures indicated he'd fled from a German death squad – could only be Ginger Jones. But that was impossible, as far as Vaculik was concerned, for he was convinced that he alone had made it out of the Noailles Wood alive.

Indeed, over the past few days his dreams had been plagued by bloody images of his six fellows being gunned down. 'I could imagine their bodies sprawled in line under the trees in that clearing and tears came to my eyes,' Vaculik remarked, of the visions that haunted his night hours.

It was a week after his miraculous escape, and in the interim Vaculik had endured a series of heart-stopping adventures, during which he'd realised that his 'nerve seemed to have gone'. Upon shaking off his SS executioners, he'd made his way into the nearest village and headed for the church. In their briefings the SAS men had been told that if in desperate straits, they should seek out the local priest. As with the *gardes de forêt,* the *curés* – the Roman Catholic priests – tended to be staunchly anti-Nazi. But not this one: Vaculik was summarily turned away, for there were German troops nearby.

With his handcuffs still stubbornly affixed to one wrist – he couldn't seem to free one of the clasps – Vaculik wrapped a scarf around the contraption, in an effort to hide it, before hurrying onwards. He realised what a state he must look. His trousers were torn and had bullet holes in them, and blood was running down one leg from where a round had nicked him. One ankle was swollen and turning blue, and he figured he must have twisted it when leaping over the hedge. Fear must have blanked his mind to the pain.

Tearing down a branch to form a makeshift crutch, like a wounded and hunted animal he'd stumbled on across open country. As German Army trucks rumbled by, he hoped and prayed that he hadn't been spotted, for there was no way that he could outrun any pursuers now. Finally he'd come across an isolated farmstead. In desperation he'd approached it and told the farmer and his wife his story. They in turn had fetched the local butcher, whose 'plump red face' and 'jovial' air Vaculik had instinctively warmed to.

Vaculik had begged the man to help link him up with the local Resistance. It turned out that the butcher and his cousin were diehard anti-Nazis, and with their assistance Vaculik was spirited by horse and cart to the nearby town of Bresles. There, to his shock, he was brought before the local gendarme – resplendent in his French police uniform – together with his young assistant. They had various official-looking papers spread out on a desk before them. Fearing a trap, Vaculik learned to his relief that the gendarme – known to all simply as 'Rouillard' – doubled as the local Resistance chief.

Even so, Rouillard had proceeded to subject Vaculik to a robust interrogation, in order to establish his bona fides, during which he was asked to write down the answers to a list of detailed questions. They were taken off to be checked with 'friends'. It turned out that a downed British airman was being sheltered by the Bresles Resistance. He had scrutinised Vaculik's scribblings, declaring that the escapee had passed with flying colours. That being the case, Rouillard was keen to discuss with Vaculik 'the military situation' and the 'best ways and means of carrying out sabotage'.

Vaculik appreciated how badly Rouillard and his Resistance fighters needed help, but first he felt compelled to confess how seriously he 'had the wind up', and how his nights were plagued by the 'sweat of fear'. Rouillard told him that was only natural, with all he had been subjected to. After a little rest and recuperation with the good people of Bresles, he should be fine.

'Don't worry too much,' the Resistance chief had reassured him. 'You'll be alright.'

Not a day or two later had come the shock news of the seemingly miraculous coming-back-to-life of Ginger Jones. Early one morning Rouillard had burst into the house where Vaculik was billeted. 'Quick! Get up and get dressed. Something extraordinary has just happened. Can you ride a bike?' And so they had set off pedalling furiously the 3 miles or so to 'Old Bourgoin' the forester's home.

En route, Rouillard had outlined his plan to confound any possible Gestapo subterfuge. They'd bring the mystery man into Bourgoin's kitchen, while Vaculik would remain in the next room, where he could overhear things. They'd need to present the man of mystery with a series of questions that only he could answer.

'What are the best things to ask?' Rouillard queried.

'Ask him his name, his number, unit, rank, the name of his CO, where he was born and the name of the Frenchman who was in his group,' Vaculik told him, 'and, above all – above all, mark you – the name of his favourite local.'

By the time they'd reached the forester's cottage, the target of all their interest and suspicion was already in the kitchen. Vaculik was made to stand in the corridor, with the door a little ajar. But at the very first answer to the very first question Vaculik didn't need to hear any more. There was no mistaking Ginger Jones's thick Wigan tones – no Gestapo agent, however talented, could mimic those.

Without waiting for an invitation, Vaculik burst through the door. Once inside, he just stood there, staring, as though he'd seen a ghost; a man who 'really had come back from the dead'. As for Jones, he seemed even more dumbfounded. His eyes were like saucers and his mouth hung open in slack-jawed astonishment. Vaculik could see how Jones's ordeal had affected him – his 'untidy ginger hair seemed to have lost its vitality and for the first time I noticed streaks of grey in it. He seemed to have aged twenty years.'

'Is it really you, old man?' Jones murmured, his eyes filling with tears. 'It can't be. I was sure you were dead.'

Vaculik reassured Jones that he was no apparition, at which the two men stumbled forward to embrace.

Finally, Jones eased the two of them apart, until he had Vaculik held at arm's length. 'I can't understand it,' he murmured. 'I saw you go down when they fired into your back.'

'I did go down,' Vaculik confirmed, 'but I tripped over a root. I was up again in an instant.'

For a while the two men talked over each other, as they tried to make absolutely certain that neither of them was dreaming. Bourgoin, meanwhile – a tough, upstanding-looking figure, in his smart forester's uniform – broke out a bottle of rum. Together, they drank to a miraculous reunion, as each man regaled the other with the story of his escape.

Jones's flight through the woodland had taken him to a small road. In a field on the far side he'd spied two farm workers. Managing to attract their attention, he'd explained as best he could who he was and that he needed to make contact with the local Resistance. Jones was told to stay where he was, lying low in the forest. Someone would come to fetch him.

He'd remained there until eight o'clock that night, his stomach a knot of fear, until 'three fellows came along to take me to the house of the forester'. He'd spent the next week camped out in the woods, with Bourgoin bringing him food and drink whenever possible. And now, unbelievably, he'd been reunited with his 'dead' friend. 'I thought I was seeing a ghost,' Jones concluded simply, of Vaculik's miraculous reappearance.

When Jones was done telling his story, Vaculik translated the gist of it for Rouillard, who'd been standing by looking as astonished as anyone. It was decided that Jones should return with them to Bresles. He would be billeted in a house near where

Vaculik was staying, with another family who were likewise friends of Rouillard's. No one doubted that soon they would be getting busy, for together, SAS escapees and Bresles Resistance, there was much work to be done.

The 24 June 'Progress Report SAS Operations' – marked *BIGOT Top Secret* – had called for 'Bren Guns (ratio one per ten men) and rifles, with an assortment of PIATs and BAZOOKAs in addition to Stens', to be dropped to Resistance parties. The PIAT – Projector, Infantry, Anti-Tank – was a British-made shoulder-launched anti-armour weapon, with a range of just over 100 yards; the Bazooka was an American portable anti-armour rocket-launcher, with a range a little over that of the PIAT.

In the month of May, 1,006 Sten guns, 1,877 incendiary bombs (for sabotage) and 4,489 grenades had been parachuted into the French Resistance forces, plus scores of the heavier weapons called for. Over July and August, such armaments drops would continue. But getting hold of weaponry was of little use if there was no proper training, without which it could prove more of a curse than a blessing. Luckily, the Bresles Resistance had just had two of the best possible weapons instructors fall into their hands.

Within days of their miraculous reunion, Jones and Vaculik – with Rouillard's help – had got an air-drop of weaponry delivered to the Bresles Resistance. The two escapees proceeded to teach '120 men how to use Bren guns, bazookas, grenades and other arms'. The Bazookas in particular needed careful handling, for they 'could be dangerous in ignorant hands', the SAS men warned. In addition to weapons instruction, Vaculik and Jones proceeded to deliver a crash course in 'elementary battle tactics': how to advance and withdraw over differing terrain, how to mount an ambush, how to take cover, how to scale obstacles and how to master the all-important craft of sabotage. Jones – a natural with any weapon – became the de facto armourer. 'His big hands were gentle and almost caressing when he was handling our Colts and Sten guns,' Vaculik observed.

But it was all very well sneaking out at night to cut telephone wires and to bring down telegraph poles – the kind of sabotage work Rouillard and his men were accustomed to. They needed to move onto bigger and better things. It was via repetitive, dogged reconnaissance work that the first opportunity was identified: a German staff car was spotted, passing daily on the road to Clermont, a town lying to the east of Bresles, in the late afternoon. It ran like clockwork and never seemed to have an escort, which made it a perfect opportunity to cut the head of the Nazi snake.

A ten-man ambush force was selected. Vaculik and Jones would go, of course, the latter with a battered old hat pulled low over his shock of red hair. Rouillard would be there, as well as de Rouck, a former soldier in the French Army who had fought against the invasion in May 1940, and who had proven himself an excellent weapons instructor. A position just outside Bresles was selected for the ambush, where thick forest lined the road, providing ample cover to melt into once the job was done.

One man was concealed in the fringes of the woods, with a Bren to provide cover. The others took up hidden positions along the road. Rouillard was at the forefront, resplendent in his best gendarme's uniform. At 4.15 p.m. on the dot the big black staff car became visible in the distance. Rouillard strode into the road, waving a gendarme's flag to signal the approaching vehicle to stop. In theory, the gendarmes were still the French nation's police force – especially in more rural areas, such as this – and the staff car, though packed with German officers, dutifully ground to a halt.

The driver's window wound down. 'What is it?' demanded the young-looking SS officer in the front passenger seat, impatiently.

'You're prisoners,' Rouillard declared by way of response, drawing his Colt and levelling it at the driver.

As if by magic, the rest of the gunmen swarmed onto the road, weapons at the ready. Seeing they were surrounded, the car's occupants decided discretion was the better part of valour. They got out of the vehicle, hands in the air. There were five in all, one – the most senior in rank – wearing the gleaming uniform of an SS colonel.

'You'll be shot for this!' he threatened.

Jones, who was the nearest, didn't know exactly what the SS colonel said, but the tone was clear enough. He booted the man hard in the backside. 'Pipe down, laddie,' he growled. 'If we want you to talk, we'll ask you to.'

If the captives hadn't realised there were Englishmen amongst their captors, they were sure to know now. As the five prisoners were frog marched into the woods, one of the Resistance men slid behind the staff car's wheel, ready to drive it off to a pre-arranged hiding place – a remote barn, where it could be covered with bales of straw. Before that, the car was searched. There was a leather briefcase lying on the rear seat: it was found to contain various official-looking documents, plus a selection of photos.

From those, it was clear that the captives weren't just SS. They were also Gestapo. Upon learning of this, something inside Jones just seemed to crack. The big, solidly built redhead launched himself at the immaculately dressed SS colonel. It took several men to drag him off, for he'd clearly intended to strangle the man on the spot.

Cursing furiously, Jones demanded he get his shot at revenge. 'What's the matter with a bit of our own back?'

For now, Rouillard, Vaculik and all needed the captives alive and well enough to face questioning. Vaculik explained as much to Jones, although of course he appreciated exactly how his friend was feeling.

Later in the war, as a column of SAS jeeps pushed into the heart of Nazi Germany, Jones would get his 'payback' for real. Colonel Mayne was in command of the patrol, and an SS officer, arrogant and unrepentant in his pristine uniform, was captured. While Mayne had long known that 'the days of noblesse oblige and the Knights of King Arthur stuff had . . . drawn to a close', he had always striven to respect the niceties of war. But by then – April 1945 – he'd learned of the extent of the atrocities perpetrated by the enemy. He handed the SS officer over to Jones, who exacted his own form of vengeance.

But right now in the woods outside Bresles, it was vital to get as much intelligence out of the captives as possible. Rouillard began a thorough search, turning out their pockets and winkling out their secret hiding places. Amongst the most interesting finds was a photo marked 'Minsk, 3.11.42'. It showed a number of figures who'd been hung from trees, and posing beside them, smiling proudly, was the SS captain on whose person the photo had been found. Clearly he carried it as some kind of macabre trophy.

The fate of the city of Minsk had become notorious. On 22 June 1941, Nazi Germany had invaded the Soviet Union, opening a second front in the war. Minsk was one of the first cities to fall, with victorious German forces marching into its streets, whereupon a reign of terror had descended over the city. Minsk was designated the administrative centre of *Reichskommissariat Ostland* – an area covering mostly the Baltic States – which had been designated as *Lebensraum* (living space) for German nationals. Amongst other policies, the entire Jewish population was to be annihilated, and any remaining locals were to be forced to leave, or face forced Germanisation.

With thousands left to starve and with their homes requisitioned by the invaders, the largest Nazi-run ghetto of the war was established in Minsk, enclosing some 80,000 Jews within its limits. They were used as slave labour in German-run factories and on construction projects, but increasingly efforts to work the Minsk Jews to extinction gave way to the professional killers. Via the efforts of the *Einsatzgruppen* – the Nazi death squads – over a millions Jews would be exterminated across *Reichskommissariat Ostland*, and the entire Minsk ghetto would be wiped off the face of the earth. In one horrifying episode, the ghetto's orphanage was emptied and the children buried alive in a pit of sand.

But Minsk had also became famous for its spirit of resistance: some 10,000 of the city's inhabitants had managed to escape to the surrounding forests, from where they waged a highly effective guerrilla war, with support from the Soviet equivalent of the SOE. By the time the Soviet Red Army and the Resistance forces retook Minsk, in early July 1944, of the city's original 300,000 inhabitants, fewer than 50,000 – one-sixth – remained.

Clearly, some amongst those captured at Bresles had practised their dark arts at Minsk, targeting the city's *Untermenschen*, those the Nazis classed as 'sub-humans' – Jews, communists, homosexuals, Resistance fighters and anyone else who had stood against the Nazi machine. Worse still, 'they were proud of their murderous work', Vaculik noted. At the sight of the Minsk hangings photo, he felt swept up in a fierce rage. His mind flipped back to the interrogations and torture at the Avenue Foch, and what had followed thereafter: 'I saw again my dead comrades sprawled in the woods.'

Vaculik turned on the SS colonel, his eyes blazing. 'Where were you going?'

At first the man refused to speak. 'A German officer does not answer the questions of a terrorist.'

'I am a British parachutist,' Vaculik shot back at him, teeth gritted murderously. 'I have been tortured by your people and I escaped from one of your execution squads, along with my companion here, Corporal Jones . . . We came to France in our red berets. You took away our uniforms in order to shoot us and pretend that we were really terrorists.'

'I didn't,' the SS colonel stammered, his face a deathly pale now.

'No, you didn't. But you've done the same to plenty of others. And what about him?' Vaculik nodded towards the SS captain. 'He's the fellow on the pretty Minsk photo, isn't he? In any case, you'll do perfectly well.'

Turning to Rouilland and the others, Vaculik asked them to bring picks and shovels – enough for each of the captives. They were to be made to excavate their own graves.

'You'll each dig a deep hole,' Vaculik ordered the SS colonel.

'We'll do nothing of the sort,' he stammered.

'Then you'll be shot.'

'But that's against the laws of war.'

'You're a fine one to talk of the laws of war,' Vaculik retorted, disgustedly. 'You'll do as you're told or else.'

'Let me have a crack at 'em,' Jones pleaded, his hand gripping his weapon.

'No. Let them dig their own graves.'

As the captives set to work, Vaculik, Jones, Rouillard and de Rouck discussed what exactly they should do with the prisoners. Jones had made his views abundantly clear. Vaculik was all for roping them to the nearby trees, once the digging was done, so they could stare into what they believed were to be their own graves for a good few hours. After that, they should be locked up under guard, to face justice once the day of liberation was at hand, which couldn't be long now, from all the reports they were hearing.

But Rouillard objected. 'Too dangerous. Bump them off straight away and they can't talk.'

Eventually it was decided to leave the captives roped to the trees, but with armed guards to watch over them. It was dark by now, and all were in need of sleep. They'd decide the captives' fate come morning, when they should be in a far better frame of mind to talk, having spent a night staring into their own graves.

Back in Bresles, Vaculik, Jones and Rouillard were woken in the small hours. There had been a shock development at the woods. Together they hurried through the darkened terrain, the moon hidden behind thick cloud. They reached the site of the ambush, only to find the guard bound and gagged. He'd been rushed by unknown assailants, he explained. For a moment, all feared that the captives had escaped, but Jones discovered otherwise.

'We're too late,' he announced, having been to check. 'They're all ruddy well dead. The lot of 'em. Come and see.'

The three men headed for where they'd left the prisoners. A grim sight met their eyes. Each figure was slumped forward, his head hanging down on his chest. Each had been ungagged before having a bayonet thrust into his chest. With no other option, Vaculik, Jones and Rouillard untied the corpses and rolled them into the graves that they had dug earlier, throwing in the soil to cover them.

'Have you any idea who could have done it?' Vaculik asked Rouillard. In spite of everything, he felt deeply unsettled by what had transpired.

Rouillard shrugged. 'Some of our own people, I should think.'

As no one else had any suggestions all fell silent, and they finished the grisly task of the burials. The Germans were in the habit of visiting savage reprisals on civilian populations, whenever sabotage work or related activities came to their attention. The French Resistance tended to act in kind. Few doubted that it was some amongst the Bresles partisans who were responsible for tonight's dark acts of murder. But there was a war to be won, and as all concluded, 'dead men tell no tales'.

With the BBC radio reporting the liberation of Paris, the arrival of Allied troops could only be a matter of days away now. In the interim, Vaculik and Jones had to prepare their band of fighters for what they knew was coming. Increasingly, columns of retreating German troops were crawling through the town, moving mostly at night in an effort to avoid Allied warplanes. But a squadron of heavy Tiger tanks had taken up defensive positions in Bresles, positioning themselves as close as possible to civilian homes, and with German troops billeted all across the town.

At one stage, Vaculik was woken early in the morning by the woman in whose house Jones was staying. German soldiers were in her kitchen demanding a bed, she blurted out in terror, and 'the Englishman' was still asleep upstairs. What was she to do? There was a back entrance to the house, with a hole in the garden wall that Jones should be able to squeeze through, Vaculik explained. If she could get him out unseen, Vaculik would be waiting. The woman went off trembling, but minutes later the plan had been executed to perfection, and a semi-dressed Jones was whisked out of harm's way.

'If this goes on I'm going to have all my hair shaved off,' Jones swore. 'I'll just go nuts otherwise.' Being a redhead did tend to make him stand out.

When flights of Hurricanes and Typhoons roared over the town, the pilots realised they couldn't attack the German armour, for fear of killing the townsfolk. By hiding amongst the civilian population the enemy troops and their tanks were escaping unscathed. A means would need to be found to unseat them, Vaculik and Jones reasoned. They set a plan of battle: even as Allied forces advanced on Bresles, so the Resistance would rise up in the enemy's rear. All were ordered to 'hold themselves in readiness for immediate action'.

It couldn't be long now, and Vaculik, Jones and Rouillard looked forward to their day of vengeance.

Chapter 19

On 31 August 1944, American troops advanced towards Bresles. In one day of fierce fighting, the town's main church would get pounded by artillery barrages, as the opposing forces fought for every inch of territory. American soldiers, Resistance fighters and the townsfolk of Bresles would lose their lives, as would German troops, but by the end of that day the battle-scarred French town would lie in Allied hands. One small band of men-at-arms, striking in the enemy's rear, would play their part in enabling the Allied breakthrough, and at their vanguard would be the rump of the SABU-70 raiders.

But before that could happen, news of SABU-70's dark fortunes would finally filter through to all at SAS headquarters, including to the man who had sent them off on their ill-fated mission, Lieutenant Colonel Mayne. In the interim, the SAS commander had himself parachuted into France, to take the helm of Operation Gain, for the mission's overall leader, Major Ian Fenwick, had been killed in fierce action against the enemy.

On 7 August some 600 German troops had surrounded Major Fenwick's forest base, but in a textbook example of guerrilla operations his men had managed to slip the enemy's noose. Fenwick was absent on a jeep-based mission at the time, and the following morning he was misinformed that dozens of his men had been killed, including his very capable second-in-command,

Captain Cecil 'Jock' Riding. Enraged at the news, Fenwick had set off without delay to investigate, little realising that the progress of his lone jeep was being shadowed by a German military Fieseler Fi 156 Storch spotter plane.

On the approach to the village of Chambon, an elderly woman had waved Fenwick to a stop. The SS were in the village and they had been forewarned of Fenwick's approach. They were preparing to ambush his speeding vehicle. Not only that, but they had rounded up all the men and boys of Chambon, who had been herded into the church, with threats that unless information was handed over about the saboteurs, all were going to be shot. Fenwick remained utterly undeterred, declaring to the elderly Frenchwoman: 'Madame, I intend to attack them.'

No doubt his subsequent actions were driven by the rage that he felt at the supposed loss of so many of his men, but they were very likely also inspired by the knowledge of what horrors the inhabitants of a small French village were facing. Regardless, with himself at the wheel, and SAS Corporals William Duffy and Frank Dunkley manning the guns, Fenwick steered the lone jeep towards Chambon at top speed.

They hit the initial ambush doing 60 mph, according to Corporal Duffy, 'all guns blazing'. The SS, in well-prepared positions, met fire with fire. Fenwick was almost past the first of the enemy's guns when a 20mm cannon round struck him square in the forehead, killing him instantly. 'Major Fenwick fell across the wheel,' Corporal Duffy reported. 'I felt the blood, which I found later was his ... just like water sprinkling on my face, and he flopped at the same moment ... from then on I lost consciousness, I was hit.'

Driverless, the jeep careered onwards, coming to a final rest in a nearby patch of woodland. In the process two Resistance figures riding in the vehicle were killed, and Corporals Duffy and Dunkley were injured and taken captive. Dunkley would be executed by the SS, along with two other Op Gain captives, Troopers Leslie Packman and John Ion. As for Duffy, with the aid of brave French medical staff working at the hospital where he was sent to be treated, he would execute one of the most audacious escapes of the war.

With Fenwick dead, leadership of the surviving Operation Gain raiders had fallen to twenty-eight-year-old Captain Jock Riding, who would go on to win a Military Cross for taking command of the mission under such difficult circumstances. On 10 August, Mayne himself would parachute into France, carrying with him a wind-up gramophone, plus some records by the Irish singer-songwriter Percy French, including 'The Garden Where the Praties Grow' ('pratie' is Irish slang for a potato), and 'Come Back, Paddy Riley', plus his all-time favourite, 'Mush! Mush Mush! Tural-i-addy', a fine Irish song about drinking and fighting.

After so long spent behind the lines, and having lost a commander of Fenwick's stature, 'the morale of certain of the men cracked a trifle', Captain Riding would report. Mayne recognised that the fighting spirit of his men would need stiffening, and he was there both to raise morale and to steady the ship. At their new forest base he played the homely Irish ballads on his gramophone and sent out reconnaissance patrols, seeking targets, calling in RAF airstrikes to hit the most vital ones. Not long after he deployed, their area of operations was liberated by advancing US forces, many of whom could not countenance that British 'jeeping' parties had been operating for so long so far behind enemy lines.

On 28 August, Captain Riding and Sergeant Almonds were 'captured' by US forces, who simply refused to believe they were who they claimed to be. Riding and Almonds explained that the jeeps had been parachuted behind the lines, and that this was actually the first time they had ever been stopped, when buzzing around the French roads at night in their heavily armed vehicles. The American commanding officer scrutinised the pair with obvious disbelief, promising they'd be taken before General George S. Patton the next day, to explain themselves.

Sure enough, the following morning they were driven to the nearby US Army HQ, to face 'Old Blood and Guts' Patton himself. A statement was read out to the American general, outlining just who Riding and Almonds claimed to be. At the end of it the American general eyed the two men. 'If you're Brits, you'll be okay,' he growled. 'If not, you'll be shot – even if I have to shoot you myself.' They were promptly handed over to Patton's British liaison officer, who was eventually persuaded of the veracity of their story.

Mayne himself would go on to have his own altercation with the famously hard-charging US general. In France, the SAS commander had felt hunted, having to keep constantly on the move. He'd admitted that at times he was scared. But Mayne never became paralysed with terror: he always kept a grip on it, mastering his fear and using it to fuel his fighting spirit. Upon the liberation of the city of Le Mans, Mayne, together with Mike Sadler, drove through the streets firing off their guns in a wild celebration. For their pains, they were arrested and taken before General Patton. Mayne mastered the situation in an instant, asking of the US commander: 'I hope we didn't frighten your men?' Making it quite clear that of course his men hadn't been scared, General Patton let the two SAS officers go with a suitable warning ringing in their ears.

Days later, Mayne was flown back to Britain, knowing fully well what a heavy price the enemy had paid at the hands of his raiders. SAS operations in France that summer had caused havoc and carnage across a wide swathe of territory, especially when working in partnership with the Resistance. Reports estimated that some 3,500–4,000 enemy troops had been killed; 15–20,000 enemy had surrendered, as a result of such actions; 750–1,000 vehicles were damaged or destroyed; fully 25 trains were blown up; and it proved impossible to enumerate all the railway lines put out of action.

In addition, the morale boost to the Resistance, and the corresponding adverse impact on the morale of the enemy, spoke volumes. In fact, 'the greatest single value of SAS activities' was seen as being the morale effect, plus the gathering of crucial intelligence. But a heavy price had been paid by those killed in action, and – as was increasingly becoming clear – in the dark fates of those men taken captive. In late August '44, Mayne would receive the first, definitive proof of the fate of one of his captured patrols – news that would shape the fortunes of the SAS in the months and years to come.

On 15 August, SAS Troopers Norman and Morrison – jumpers ten and eleven in the SABU-70 stick – learned that US troops had arrived in their vicinity. They'd been hiding out in the woods around the town of Saint Chéron for fully thirty days. On hearing the news, the two men 'dug up their uniforms, had them dried at the farm . . . and set off in search of the Americans'. After a brief interrogation at the US Army headquarters, they were dispatched to the coast riding in a captured enemy truck, and then placed aboard 'a homeward-bound ship'.

At 'approximately 2230 hours on Monday 19 August', Norman reached Fairford camp, the base from which he had set out, having spent forty-three days behind enemy lines. After a brief stopover in London, Morrison would join him. Theirs would be one of the longest escape and evasions in SAS history. Of course, one of the first things that Trooper Norman was able to do was to alert all at Fairford to the fate of their wider patrol. In a report entitled 'Operational State of SAS Troops 22 Aug. 1944', the first intimation of the ill fortune that had befallen Captain Garstin and his men was noted: '2 offrs 10 ORs in NORTH GAIN area are possibly missing'.

Of course, even with Norman and Morrison's eyewitness testimony, the remainder of Garstin's stick could only be listed as 'possibly missing'. Their true fate remained unknown. But even that was progress of sorts. Prior to Norman and Morrison's miraculous return, Garstin and his men had simply disappeared into the void, as far as all at SAS headquarters had been concerned. 'After they jumped that was the last we saw or heard of them,' reported Captain Sadler, who'd seen the SABU-70 raiders off from the Stirling that had dropped them.

When not parachuting into France, Colonel Mayne had become something of a welfare officer for 1 SAS, writing a seemingly endless stream of letters to the parents, wives and other close family of those he had dispatched into harm's way. He did so with a simple elegance of phrase and a heartfelt empathy – especially with those killed or missing in action – that might seem surprising for a man with such a fearsome reputation. But all he did during his time in the SAS was out of a deep compassion for his fellow warriors: to stand tall in their view, to stand firm at their side, and in an effort to bring them home.

Colonel Mayne felt each failure – each loss – very personally. When he learned of Captain Garstin and his stick's fate, he vowed that something had to be done. These were men that he had in many cases recruited personally, and had twice – some might argue three times – dispatched behind enemy lines, on some of the most challenging missions. Their loss did not sit lightly on his shoulders.

Shortly after Norman and Morrison's return, Colonel Mayne charged Mike Sadler, together with Major Harry Wall Poat, another of the SAS originals and Mayne's second-in-command, to investigate the fate of Garstin's patrol. They were to leave for France post-haste, to visit the areas where the SAS personnel had 'disappeared', in an effort to investigate what exactly had happened. Even now, a year before the end of the war, Mayne and his fellow SAS commanders had an eye to a full and proper reckoning.

Meanwhile, in France, two of the objects of that investigation were even now embroiled in the fight of their lives. On paper, the original battle plan for the Bresles Resistance had been a sound one: they had built a fortress-headquarters of giant haybales, each weighing about 220 pounds, to the rear of the German positions. To any casual observer, they'd appeared to be just another group of farm labourers laying in a store of hay for the winter. But inside the haystack, they'd built up their armoury and prepared to wage war.

The haybale fortress was to form a fire platform, from which they would strike at the enemy from behind. Initially, it performed just as intended. As the American forces assaulted Bresles from the north, the Bresles Resistance – plus the SAS men embedded in their number – opened fire from their haystack fortress. The

German troops eventually cottoned on, at which stage they launched a ground assault. But with its thick walls the haystack soaked up bullets, leaving those perched atop it a fine vantage point from where to rain down fire upon the approaching enemy.

The haystack defenders held firm 'for three hours against a party of 40 German paratroopers', Vaculik noted. All seemed well until the enemy troops sited a machine gun in a nearby tree, with the elevation to rain down fire. With the defenders taking casualties, something had to be done. After several near misses, the haystack warriors managed to slot a Bazooka round directly into the branches of that tree. 'There was a violent explosion . . . [and] at least one body [was] flung into the air,' reported the SAS men. 'The machine gun nest had been rubbed out.' But more trouble was coming.

A German mortar team began to lob in rounds. Soon they had the haystack's range. A direct hit set the bales alight. Fighting for their very lives now, the haystack warriors faced either being burned alive if they stayed where they were, or exposing themselves to the enemy guns if they broke cover. It was clear that the German troops hadn't exactly appreciated being hit by surprise from the rear, and it was now that the fearsome form of a Tiger tank rumbled onto the scene.

'It rolled towards us with its long sinister muzzle pointed in our direction,' Vaculik observed. The very sight spread panic amongst the Resistance fighters, who began to drop their weapons as if ready to flee.

'The very first man to run I'll shoot,' de Rouck, the former French soldier, roared, his gun levelled.

The effect was salutary, especially since the figureheads of the Bresles Resistance – SAS brethren included – were determined to stand and fight. As thick smoke billowed up from the burning hay, it spread a smog across the battle scene. All of a sudden, the haystack defenders realised it could serve to hide their escape. Using it as a makeshift smokescreen, the entire force dashed to a nearby cluster of farm buildings, making the cover of the farmhouse to find it deserted. For now at least they should be out of the Tiger's line of fire.

The enemy kept slamming the haystack fortress with fire, unaware that their prey had moved. But it was now that the dynamics of the battle began to shift markedly. A second tank rolled onto the scene. This was an American Sherman, and just as soon as the haystack warriors spotted it, so too did the crew of the Tiger. They watched, aghast, as the Tiger swung its 88mm gun around and fired. The Sherman had been taken by surprise, and it was hit fair and square, a jagged hole appearing in its side. Moments later it erupted into a blaze of smoke and flame.

Enraged, four of the haystack warriors decided the Tiger had to die. Vaculik led the charge, as they scuttled from patch of cover to cover, weaving in and out of the shifting miasma of smoke, creeping closer all the time. But by the time they were within range and had readied the Bazooka, the Tiger was on the move. Its exhausts belched smoke, as it swung around and began to thunder southwards, away from Bresles. The town was being abandoned to the Allies. Vaculik fired a round, but it 'whistled through the air and exploded harmlessly in a clump of trees'. Already, the Tiger was out of range.

Not long thereafter church bells began to peal out from Bresles, ringing in the changes, and the men of the Resistance made their way into the centre of the town. By three o'clock the first American troops rolled onto the scene, and the roads were clogged with US military convoys – Sherman tanks, armoured carriers, truckloads of infantry and vehicles piled high with all types of war materiel. Cigarettes, chocolate and gum were handed out by the American soldiers, as people shook hands and marvelled that the hour of liberation had finally come, after four dark years.

In the town square Vaculik came across a bizarre-seeming confrontation. Ginger Jones had accosted a US infantry sergeant. There was tension in the air, and Jones kept repeatedly trying to thrust something into the American soldier's hands.

'You smoke it, you bloody Yank!' Jones declared, threateningly. 'I saved it up for you.'

The American soldier seemed completely at a loss. 'But what do I want to smoke that dirty little stub for?' he asked. 'I've got plenty of cigarettes of my own.'

Vaculik stepped in now, explaining to the US infantryman the promise that Jones had made all those weeks back, in the cellar of the Place des États Unis prison – that at the very least he would offer the American liberators one of his precious dog-ends. He was simply trying to make good on that oath now.

'In that case, here goes!' declared the sergeant. He grabbed Jones's dog-end, sparked up and with 'terrible grimaces' smoked it to the very end, with Jones slapping him on the back delightedly all the while.

Here and there groups of German troops stood around, hands clasped to their heads. The American commander approached the Resistance leaders. He needed to speak to the town mayor, he announced. His forces must roll on real quick, and he would have to hand over security and administration to the local authorities. Vaculik explained that the town's mayor had been deported by the enemy, so there wasn't one right now. The US commander wanted to know who Vaculik was, a guy dressed like a French Resistance fighter but who spoke such good English. Vaculik explained.

'If you're a parachutist, how come you're not in uniform?' the commander demanded.

'We were taken prisoner by the Germans and escaped,' Vaculik said, gesturing at Jones. 'This is Corporal Jones, of the same unit.'

The US commander declared that Vaculik would make the perfect stand-in mayor, while Jones and the Bresles Resistance leaders should organise a security force for the town. And that was exactly what happened. Over the next few days Vaculik heard a flood of denunciations against supposed collaborators, as figures presenting themselves as stalwarts of the Resistance kept coming forward. Meanwhile, the real Bresles Resistance – a redheaded fighter foremost amongst them – patrolled the streets, and sent parties to comb the surrounding forests, from where groups of German captives were brought in.

But for Jones and Vaculik, something else was preying on their consciences. As the tide of war turned, in the back of both men's minds there was the hunger for a reckoning; for justice. Though they had no idea exactly how it might be achieved, somehow justice ought to be done for Captain Garstin, Paddy Barker, Varey, Young and Walker – men in the prime of their lives, gunned down in cold blood – and very likely for Lieutenant Wiehe too, a man left to die in a Paris hospital.

A week after the liberation of Bresles, Jones and Vaculik took action. Having bid farewell to their friends, on 6 September, in a car driven by the local garage owner, they set off for the site of their would-be executions, which lay some 15 miles south of town. They headed first for Noailles itself, where they made contact with the local Resistance leader, who rejoiced in the magnificent name of Louis Gaston Emile Liger de Chauvigny.

De Chauvigny was a forty-six-year-old former French military officer, and he'd heard rumours about the mystery executions of 9 August at the time. They'd taken place in an area of woodland known as the Bois de Mouchy, around a mile outside Noailles town. Apparently, the bodies had been buried in the grounds of the nearby Château de Parisis-Fontaine, which had served as the headquarters of a local Luftwaffe unit. De Chauvigny offered to take Jones and Vaculik to both locations.

After a short drive, they pulled over in the same place where the Gestapo's Opel staff car had halted, almost a month earlier. From there, the small party retraced the steps of the death march. Struck dumb with emotion, Jones and Vaculik stepped into the woodland, seeking the very spot where five of their number had met such a brutal end. Finally, they arrived. 'On the trees there were some fine marks of the bullets,' de Chauvigny noted, and as they searched amongst the fallen leaves Vaculik and Jones retrieved spent casings.

This was the place alright. From there, the two SAS men traced the route along which they had fled. Jones showed Vaculik the tree behind which he had taken cover, after playing dead. Vaculik showed Jones the tall hedge, marvelling at how the devil he had 'managed to get over such a formidable obstacle'. With a handful of 'empty cartridge cases' – those unleashed by the killers – stuffed deep in their pockets, Vaculik and Jones turned away from the grim scene. There was an even darker task ahead of them, but it had to be done.

Back in the car, they drove the few miles towards the Château de Parisis-Fontaine, situated on the outskirts of the village of

Berthecourt. En route, they were joined by a Monsieur André Lemain, the director of the local gasworks, and a mover and shaker in the Berthecourt Resistance. The thirteenth-century chateau lay within a grand sweep of deciduous woodland, the ornate stone entranceway rising before them, wrought-iron gates barring their path. No one was present, save the caretaker and his wife, and de Chauvigny signalled the car to a halt at their cottage.

An aged figure, weighed down by the war and his advanced years, Monsieur Paul Clément received the unexpected visitors graciously. After being told why they had come, Madame Berthe Clément, the caretaker's wife, proved particularly forthcoming. She'd been at the chateau when the truckload of bodies had arrived, she explained, and she knew of the burial site. Even then, there had been dark rumours that the dead were British parachutists. In a mark of respect, she'd started taking flowers to the grave, which was set a way into the woodland.

Madame Clément led the small party along the route that she had grown accustomed to using. It looped around the chateau, past a clutch of farm buildings and some 400 yards into the woods. Lying to the right of the track, about 20 yards away, was the gravesite. She indicated the patch of bare earth that showed where the men had been buried.

Jones and Vaculik – plus de Chauvigny and Lemain – came rigidly to attention as they stood there, silent, choked up, contemplating all that had led up to the moment when the bodies of five brave SAS soldiers had been dumped here in an unmarked grave. 'Garstin, Paddy Barker, Varey, Walker and Young,' Jones enunciated, his voice choked with emotion, listing the names of their dead comrades. Tears that they could no longer hold back rolled down the cheeks of both men.

Left: Expecting to link up with the Resistance, Captain Garstin and his men dropped directly into enemy hands. During the fierce firefight that followed, Garstin and Lieutenant Wiehe suffered terrible injuries, while Free French SAS man Serge Vaculik (left), plus SAS original Thomas 'Ginger' Jones (front of photo, with Garstin, below) fought to the last grenade and the last round.

Above: The SAS patrol's capture had been masterminded from the Gestapo's Paris headquarters (pictured). SS Sturmbannfuhrer Hans Kieffer (fifth from left, front row) was the grandmaster of the Funkspiel – the 'radio games' – using captured radio sets and codebooks to lure in Allied airdrops, while his boss, SS Standartenfuhrer Helmut Knochen (left) rounded-up thousands of Resistance members, Jews and other 'undesirables', to be sent to the death camps.

Above: Assassination attempts by British-trained special agents – including Operation Anthropoid, in which high-ranking SS commander Reinhard Heydrich's staff car was blown up (pictured) – had enraged Hitler. The Furhrer issued orders that Captain Garstin and the other SAS captives were to be dressed as civilians and executed …

Facing a firing squad in a patch of dark woodland, Garstin – pictured with wife Susan and with their infant son – was too weakened by his injuries to break away. Instead, he ordered his men to flee, as he stood firm to take the fire. Only two men, Vaculik and Jones – pictured right, in the civilian clothes the Gestapo had forced them to dress in – managed to make a daring getaway.

Having escaped death, Vaculik and Jones linked up with the local Resistance, training and arming them and ambushing a German staff car. But the thing they hungered for most was justice for their murdered SAS comrades. The trouble was, there were no leads to go on: the Gestapo had managed to hide their identities.

SOE agent Captain John Starr provided the breakthrough. Captured and held at the Gestapo's Avenue Foch headquarters, Starr was fully aware of who was responsible for the SAS murders. At war's end he made it back to Britain alive, and gave chapter and verse on the Gestapo killers.

WANTED reports were issued, but in the chaos of post-war Germany the suspects had to be found. Enter Major Eric 'Bill' Barkworth (above left), seasoned SAS man and fluent German speaker. Together with his trusty deputy, Sergeant Fred 'Dusty' Rhodes (above right), they set out for Germany in May 1945 driving a battered SAS jeep and truck, to become some of the most successful Nazi-hunters ever.

From a commandeered villa in the German city of Gaggenau, Barkworth's Nazi-hunters got to work. Very quickly they realised that hundreds of captured SAS, SOE and downed Allied aircrew had been murdered under Hitler's 'Commando Order', which decreed that all such captives were to be 'exterminated to the last man'. Thirsting for justice, Barkworth, Rhodes (third from left, below) and team would break all the rules to track down the killers.

Even as they rounded up the suspects, the SAS itself was disbanded in October 1945. Colonel Mayne (second from right), and Colonel Brian Franks (fourth from right) – 2 SAS's commander – remained determined to track down those who had murdered their men. With Churchill's backing, Barkworth and his team went covert, becoming 'The Secret Hunters'. Quietly recruiting more men – like Sgt Peter Drakes (driver of the jeep, below) – they combed Europe, from Italy in the south to Norway in the north, and as far east as the Russian Zone of occupation.

By spring, 1947, the Secret Hunters had captured all of the Gestapo/SS who had murdered Captain Garstin and his men, including *Hauptscharfuhrer* Karl Haug (here in his arrest photo), plus Gestapo commanders Hans Kieffer and Helmut Knochen. On April 22, 1947, all were sentenced to hanging or given long custodial sentences.

The top-secret operations of Barkworth (above, sketched in pastel, by an unknown artist during his Secret Hunters days), Rhodes (above right, in suitably irreverent pose) and team lasted through to summer 1948, during which time they tracked down and brought to trial over one hundred Nazi war criminals.

In hunting down the Nazi war criminals, the SAS reclaimed the Swastika – originally an ancient symbol from the East, denoting spirituality and peace – in freedom's cause.

Today, there are regular reunions to commemorate Operation Gain, including one in 2015, when British and French parachutists dropped into one of the original WW2 landing zones, including James Irivine (centre photo, beige beret), grandson of Trooper Leslie Packman who was murdered on Op Gain.

Of course, there was still just a chance that this was not the final resting place of the SABU-70 murder victims – just a chance. Vaculik and Jones needed to be certain. They asked the caretaker to show them around the chateau. It was locked and shuttered, but even so they managed to pry their way into the ground floor. Yet it was in the hallowed grounds of the chapel, which was attached to the chateau, that they made the crucial discovery.

Jones was searching one corner of the building when he called out to Vaculik: 'Hey, this looks like the boots he was wearing.'

Before him sat a pair of footwear. It was instantly recognisable to Jones, being the pair of rubber-soled Commando boots that he had spent so many mornings lacing up, when helping the wounded Captain Garstin to dress at the Place des États Unis dungeon. Jones would know them anywhere. Outside, in the chapel grounds, they found the shoes that the Gestapo had issued to Trooper Walker – the ones with the odd low-cut profile, and which had holes in them.

There was little doubt any more. The bodies of their comrades had been brought here, where some at least had been stripped of their footwear, before being buried in the chateau's grounds. Jones and Vaculik had the answers they had come for. But were they any closer to a reckoning, to securing justice for their fallen comrades, which was what they hungered for with a vengeance? Very possibly not.

As they took the road north towards the beaches at Arromanches, they ruminated on all that they knew, and just what they didn't know. They knew the identity of those murdered and their final place of resting. Of course, of Lieutenant Wiehe's fate they were none the wiser, and likewise of the whereabouts of those who'd escaped capture at the DZ. But most frustratingly of all, they had little idea of the identities of the Gestapo killers.

At all stages – capture, incarceration, questioning, torture and during the final death drive – their captors had been careful not to use their names in front of the captives. Rack their brains as they might, neither man could remember any of the identities of the Avenue Foch killers. They could remember their hideous faces – how could they forget? – but what was a face without a name to put to it? How was a hunt to be launched, how were suspects to be sought, without even one name to go on? How was anyone to be brought to justice without a name for a wanted poster or an arrest warrant? Whichever way they looked at it, there were no obvious leads. They seemed to have reached a dead end.

Even so, upon arriving at the Normandy coast, they managed to get the first formal report of their discoveries telegraphed to SAS headquarters, ahead of their own arrival. Dated 7 September 1944, it read: 'SECRET ... two from 1 SAS Cpl JONES and NU PONTES reported ... to 60 Transit Camp ... they state SEVEN captured and put before firing squad near NOAILLES' ('Nu Pontes' should of course have read Dupontel, Vaculik's Canadian cover name). The first official record of the Noailles atrocity had been filed. But to what end?

The Avenue Foch killers seemed to have slipped away into the shadows, like ghosts.

Chapter 20

Barely two months after their return to Britain, Vaculik and Jones found themselves in a London courtroom. For Jones, who was not unaccustomed to having the odd brush with the law, it made a refreshing change to find himself in the witness box, giving evidence in such a high-profile case and amidst such rarefied surroundings. Once they had made it back from France to SAS headquarters and been debriefed in detail, the wheels had spun into motion remarkably quickly.

On 7 November 1944, Major Thomas Langton, MC, a longtime stalwart of the SAS, had written to the Under-Secretary of State at the War Office concerning 'the deaths of the 1st SAS party under Capt. Garstin'. His letter included detailed statements from Vaculik and Jones on the Noailles Wood killings, plus one from Captain Mike Sadler, who, along with Major Poat, had completed his own investigation on the ground in France.

Sadler and Poat had reached the area on 20 September, barely two weeks after Vaculik and Jones. For both men this had been an intensely personal quest, for Captain Garstin had been a close friend. That had proven particularly useful when they had come to open the grave at Château de Parisis-Fontaine, in order to identify the bodies. De Chauvigny, the Resistance leader, had acted as their guide, and there had been fresh flowers on the graveside when they had reached it, courtesy of the caretaker's wife.

Fittingly, De Chauvigny had fetched some German prisoners to do the spade-work. Even though the POWs were made to do the lion's share of the exhumations, 'digging up Pat Garstin and his men wasn't particularly pleasant,' Sadler remarked, with typical understatement. In truth, it proved a harrowing experience, especially as the suffering endured by the SAS captives was plain to see. Sadler observed that 'the men's wrists had been close together at the time of their death and have stiffened in that position', showing how they had been handcuffed when they were gunned down.

The bodies having been in the ground for seven weeks, 'the stink was enough to knock you over,' noted Major Poat. Captain Garstin's corpse was 'readily identifiable' owing to his distinctive head of thick, curly dark hair, but the other four were not. Though the bodies were badly decomposed, Sadler could tell that Garstin's 'right arm was quite broken . . . almost detached. I think his leg was broken as well. They were in a hell of a mess.' Garstin's suffering, during those weeks spent incarcerated in the Paris hospital and the Gestapo dungeons, did not bear thinking about.

Other grim discoveries were made in that woodland in September '44. 'While Capt. Garstin's grave was being opened, we found two other diggings of the same size in the wood,' Sadler noted. 'They were older, but were almost certainly graves, probably of the FFI.' The French Forces of the Interior – FFI – was the formal name given to the Resistance during the latter stages of the war. It seemed as if Captain Garstin and party were not the only victims to have been buried in the chateau's grounds.

The bodies of the five SAS men were taken from the chateau to the nearby town of Beauvais, and buried in the Cemetery Marianne, in graves numbers 325–9. But even then, Sadler and Poat's investigations were far from done. They were particularly keen to learn how the SABU-70 party had dropped right into the hands of the enemy. 'It was the first flop we had had,' remarked Poat, 'and the thing that interested us was how the Germans had got there and what happened when our men landed.' If they could work out how it had all gone wrong, they could try to prevent any more such disasters, for many long and punishing months of operations lay ahead.

In the La Ferté-Alais area they made contact with Jean Bourget, the local Resistance leader. Bourget had received several arms drops organised by SOE, with whom he had been in regular – if not always reliable – wireless contact. He confirmed that a BBC message had alerted them to the 5 July drop, but that the DZ had been staked out by the enemy long before they had reached it. The Gestapo and Waffen SS cordon thrown around the area had been impenetrable, the trap being well baited and set.

'The Gestapo had been at great pains to cover their tracks, and it was only possible to discover a little about the Germans who occupied the chateau and who buried the bodies,' Sadler and Poat concluded. They'd uncovered three names – 'Captain Hans Carling, Sous-Officier Hans Zool, Oberfeldwebel Gall' – all of whom served with the Luftwaffe signals squadron. But the very most any of them could be charged with was being an accessory to the crime of murder, and they could very reasonably argue that they'd believed the dead men they had buried were French saboteurs.

Still there were clamours at the highest level for justice to be done. The Under-Secretary of State for War was one Henry Page Croft – Baron Croft – a decorated veteran of the First World War who had been appointed to his present post directly by Churchill. A respected politician from the inter-war years and an unofficial leader of the House of Commons, Croft had been a die-hard proponent of resisting Nazi Germany's ascendancy under Hitler. Commenting on the Blitz, he'd observed: 'Every class of Londoner responded defiantly to the long, long period of attack and from the Royal Family to the . . . dustman all vied in showing contempt of danger . . . London is a grand city with a big heart.'

Like Churchill, a long-standing critic of German rearmament prior to the war and of Britain's comparative military weakness, Croft was a champion of the rank and file. In his view, Nazi war crimes were an abomination, especially when perpetrated against soldiers serving in uniform. The Noailles Wood case was exceptional in that two witnesses had survived to tell their tale. Two of those whom Hitler had ordered to be gunned down and sucked into the *Nacht und Nebel* – the night and fog – had got away from their executioners. That made the case unique.

The full title of the hearing in London that November was something of a mouthful: 'Supreme Headquarters Allied Expeditionary Force Court of Inquiry re Shooting of Allied Prisoners of War by the Germans near Noailles, Oise, France, on 9th August, 1944'. However, it lacked for nothing in terms of scope, power and reach. The court's mandate had come from the very top: it was convened 'by Command of General Eisenhower' himself – General Dwight D. Eisenhower was then serving as the Supreme Commander of Allied forces in Europe.

Both Captain Sadler and Major Poat appeared in person at the court, to give evidence. Describing the murder scene, Poat related how 'Captain Garstin said: "Make a break." He could hardly stand up at all . . . He was far too ill to move . . . The Germans began to spray the men with bullets.' Major Poat then pointed to Vaculik and Jones, the star witnesses in the courtroom: 'These two corporals had a most amazing escape, in spite of their handcuffs, they managed to get away.'

The execution spot had been carefully chosen, Poat explained: 'the wooded ground went right up . . . almost like a wall, so that if you stood men halfway up the bullets, if missing them or whizzing past . . . would go into the ground behind.' Glancing around the courtroom, he added: 'I should say the clearing was the size of this floor. It was just comfortable enough to line up seven men with a good space between so that there would be no chance of them sort of making a leap behind the nearest tree.'

On the orders of the court, a military pathologist, Lieutenant Colonel Robert MacKeen, of the Canadian Armed Forces First Canadian Base Laboratory, had carried out post-mortems on the Noailles Wood massacre victims. MacKeen, a pathologist of twenty years' standing, had carried out sixty post-mortems on behalf of the Canadian Army, so was well versed in such work. His testimony before the court proved utterly sobering.

On examining Captain Garstin's clothing, he'd found seven bullet holes in the SAS commander's jacket. Garstin had taken a veritable fusillade of fire, suffering wounds to his stomach, back and limbs. The one consoling factor was that death would have been 'almost instantaneous', MacKeen concluded. But at some stage Garstin's right jaw had suffered a powerful blow from 'a blunt instrument', and was found to be missing all of its teeth. It looked as if efforts had been made by the Gestapo killers to smash in their victims' features, to further hide any evidence of their crimes.

There were no signs that any of Garstin's original injuries suffered at the La Ferté-Alais DZ had been treated. Indeed, a 9mm round was still lodged in his arm, where it had fractured his humerus, the long bone in the upper arm, during the ambush on 5 July. When asked about the appearance of that bullet, MacKeen described how it was 'almost untouched. I have it here.' He proceeded to show to the court the 9mm round. 'Bullet produced by witness is marked Exhibit "A,"' the court recorder noted.

MacKeen was unable to identify the next four bodies, but with each he described the means of death, distinguishing them by their grave numbers. Body 326 had been killed by a single shot to the neck, causing 'fracture of mandible and vertebrae'. Body 327 had also been killed by a shot to the neck, after which 'the missile track continued upwards, penetrating the palatal bone' – the top of the mouth. Body 328 had suffered two bullet wounds to the side of the head, causing 'massive fracture and fragmentation'. Body 329 had been killed by 'a bullet wound of the skull and brain from below'. All the men had been buried fully dressed, but minus their footwear.

After MacKeen, two French witnesses were called, a Madame Simone Vignes, who had worked as a cook for the Luftwaffe squadron stationed at the Château de Parisis-Fontaine, and a Monsieur Félix Duband, the mayor of Noailles. They were able to give a little more information about the Luftwaffe unit, but that was all. The chateau's caretaker and his wife, the Cléments, also gave evidence. 'My wife and I discovered the little hillock,' Monsieur Clément related, 'and rumours had been going on that soldiers had been buried there.' But they had little more of any substance to add.

The final witness was Commander de Chauvigny, the Resistance leader who had shown Vaculik and Jones, and then Sadler and Poat, around the sites of the killings. He was crystal clear about how Garstin and his men had been captured: 'The Germans had been warned of the expedition (indiscretion from London) and were waiting for the parachutists, upon whom they opened fire.' He also gave evidence that four of the dead men had had their faces 'crushed, so as to render them unidentifiable'.

'I put his body in the coffin,' de Chauvigny told the court, of Captain Garstin's reburial. 'He had a Military Cross and his name was in the coffin . . . I took the body in the lorry and the lorry followed my car which arrived at the cemetery. There was an attachment of American and British soldiers and French FFI and an American chaplain . . . Military honours were rendered and a religious ceremony was performed.'

With that, the witness evidence was complete. The court's findings were unequivocal. Issued on 19 April 1945 – the delay had been caused by the court visiting the site of the crimes – they listed the five dead men as follows:

P. B. Garstin, MC Captain 95531 SAS Regiment

T. Varey Sergeant 811752 1 SAS Regiment

T. Barker Trooper 6986237 1 SAS Regiment

J. Walker Trooper 7019954 1 SAS Regiment

W Young Trooper 7018947 1 SAS Regiment

The court concluded that 'the killing of the . . . five British soldiers . . . was in violation of the well-recognised laws and usages of war and the terms of the Geneva Convention . . . and was murder.' The court refused to accept 'the reading of the so-called sentence as authorising a shooting, which was in fact murder. All five victims were British subjects wearing British uniforms at the time of their capture and were engaged upon a legitimate military action. They had been brought before no court and given no trial.'

Vaculik and Jones had been able to provide detailed physical descriptions of the killers: 'smaller than I am . . . round face with a childish look, about twenty, and . . . spoke affectedly. Perfect English' – their description of von Kapri. 'Silver braid with silver button on shoulder, smart grey uniform, tie and white collar, big light grey cap, breeches with line down side, high boots' – their description of Schnur. Vaculik vowed of his tormenters and killers: 'If I saw them, I could recognise them. My description will not be very good, but I could recognise them.'

No one doubted that he could. But while the court was certain that those 'who ordered and are responsible for the said murders were members of the German Gestapo at Paris', they were equally clear that 'the identities of the individuals who ordered and/or carried out the said murders are not known'. With no names and no identities, the court had next to nothing to go on. It was pretty much back to square one.

The court's recommendations were that the three known members of the Luftwaffe signals squadron should be sought, in the hope that might lead in turn to the Gestapo killers. At the same time the French authorities should be approached, to check any records of the Gestapo who had served in Paris, to see if they answered the descriptions given to the court. The final recommendation was that if any 'members of the German Gestapo are identified and come into Allied hands, and are shown to be implicated in the killings, they be brought to trial . . . on charges of murder'.

By the autumn of 1944, a tsunami of German prisoners had fallen into Allied hands. A report in August 1944 described just one of the POW cages springing up across liberated France: 'The sight that greeted us will never be forgotten . . . Acres and acres of the Chosen Race were parked behind barbed wire. Their one desire in life at that time was a drink of water.' On 9 August alone some 351 German officers and 18,109 men had been captured, during fighting around the Falaise Pocket; by November of that year, some 750,000 POWs were in Allied hands.

Searching for the three named Luftwaffe suspects was going to prove something of a needle-in-a-haystack exercise, to put it mildly – if they had even been taken captive. In the interim, there was a war to be fought and won, during which the SAS would have a seminal role to play. Of the SABU-70 survivors, some would be returning to the fight. And one, miraculously, would be returning to Britain, as if from the very grave.

After a little r&r, Jones and Vaculik would turn to offensive operations, volunteering first to drop into Arnhem, in September 1944, in an effort to help relieve those airborne troops cut off and besieged by enemy forces. Allied commanders had miscalculated, believing the fight had gone out of the Germans. Operation Market Garden, and the loss of so many courageous parachutists and glider-borne troops, would prove otherwise. Indeed, every inch of occupied Europe would have to be fought for tooth and nail, and even more so when Allied troops punched into Nazi Germany itself.

In due course Jones and Vaculik would deploy into Belgium, close to the German border, dropping into thick winter snows. Forming part of a jeep-bound force, they skirmished far behind the lines, shooting up columns of retreating enemy troops. 'The

Germans fought with courage and despair, as we ambushed their convoys along tree-lined avenues and at cross-roads,' Vaculik reported. He would end up being wounded by a German sniper near Bremen, and he spent VE Day in hospital. As for Ginger Jones, he would fight through to the absolute bitter end.

Castelow, meanwhile – jumper number twelve of the SABU-70 stick – had endured a remarkable series of adventures to get back to Allied lines. Having fought with the Vert-le-Petit Resistance and having attempted to escape dressed as a French gendarme, Castelow had been captured and dispatched by truck towards Germany. On 9 September '44 the lorry crossed the Moselle River, the largest tributary of the Rhine, just a few dozen miles short of the border. That night, Castelow had been locked in a room with one SS guard for company.

Realising that it was now or never – the following day they would enter Germany – at one minute to midnight Castelow 'killed the guard and took his rifle'. Having got out of the building where he was being held, he scaled the outer wall and made his way through darkened streets towards the river, which at that point was several hundred feet across. 'I swam the Moselle,' Castelow recounted, in his escape report to MI9 – the British military intelligence's so-called 'escape factory' – 'and started walking back towards the Americans. I met their forward units around 1900 hrs on 10 Sept.'

Castelow's had been a truly remarkable escape, one told with studied understatement and humility. For the SAS in the Second World War, this is just what they did. But if anything, Lieutenant Wiehe's tale of survival – coming back from the very brink – was perhaps the most astonishing of all. The last hint any of Captain Garstin and his party had had of the SAS lieutenant was the short stopover during their journey of death, on 8 August '44, at the Hôpital La Pitié-Salpêtrière.

The next official record of the desperately sick SAS man was a hand-scribbled note: 'Lt Jean Hyacinthe Wiehe . . . Missing, known to be wounded, believed POW. Now located at 217 Gen Hosp HQ Sqdn Base Section USA. Shell fractures, wounds multiple . . . with spinal injuries.' That note must have been written after the Allies liberated Paris, and once US forces had been able to establish a field hospital at La Pitié-Salpêtrière to care for their wounded – so towards the end of August, at the earliest. But what had happened between that date, and when the Gestapo murder squad had failed to collect Lieutenant Wiehe so he could join the Noailles Wood line-up, some three weeks earlier?

On 16 August, just as the forces of Nazi Germany were evacuating Paris, the enemy had come for SAS Lieutenant Wiehe. 'Gestapo agents came to the hospital, threw me some clothes . . . and took me away,' Wiehe would report. 'I could not of course dress myself as I was permanently lying on my back. They took me in a Gestapo car, accompanied by an officer in uniform and a civilian who covered me with an automatic, to the Jewish hospital . . . A French doctor on the staff told me that I was to be taken away by the Gestapo shortly . . . The Gestapo never came back for me.'

That move courtesy of the Gestapo had taken Wiehe from the left bank of the Seine, across the Pont de Bercy to the Hôpital de Rothschild – 'the Jewish Hospital' – on the right bank. Though it was no more than a fifteen-minute drive, to transport a man in Wiehe's delicate condition had been a high risk indeed. It remained a total mystery as to why the Gestapo had orchestrated such a move, after which they seemingly abandoned the SAS lieutenant to his fate.

Either way, once Paris was liberated, Wiehe was shifted back to the Hôpital La Pitié-Salpêtrière. His own entries in his pocket notebook – the same as had survived all the calamities so far – provide a record of sorts. On 16 August he noted: 'Transit from German hospital to Rothschild French Hospital.' And then, on 9 September: 'Transferred to 217 American General Hospital La Pitié.' Six days later, another entry simply noted: 'Flew over from Le Bourget. Admitted Wroughton RAF Hospital.' Paris Le Bourget is an airport just to the north of the city centre, while RAF Hospital Wroughton was a thousand-bed facility set up on the Wiltshire airbase of that name in 1941.

On 15 September 1944 Lieutenant Wiehe finally made it back to Britain. On 22 October he was able to send a short telegram to Mauritius, giving his family the news: 'My dearest mum, I write to send you my most affectionate best wishes. I'm getting better. I'll try to write more soon. I kiss you all very affectionately.' The Wiehe family had their proof of life. Their son/brother/uncle/fiancé was alive. As he lay in his hospital bed in Britain, the SAS lieutenant marvelled at how he had survived the initial ambush and the terrible treatment in the Paris hospital, and then evaded two Gestapo round-ups. Truly, his life had been blessed.

Against all odds, Lieutenant Wiehe had cheated death many times over. Discounting those five men buried at the Château de Parisis-Fontaine, and Corporal Howard Lutton, who had been pronounced dead upon arrival at the Paris hospital, the last of the SABU-70 raiders had been brought home. Six out of twelve had survived a cunning *Funkspiel* entrapment, a carefully set ambush, deliberate neglect in hospital, interrogations and torture, and a murder sentence delivered on behalf of the Führer.

Now all that remained was to find and nail the culprits: Kopkow, the dark lord ruling out of Berlin; Kieffer, the cunning Paris ring-master; Dr Goetz, the myopic *Funkspiel* virtuoso; Schnur, the cold-hearted Avenue Foch interrogator; von Kapri, his die-hard Nazi sidekick; plus Schmidt, Haug, Ilgenfritz and Hildemann – those who had done the Noailles Wood killings. Right then, none of their identities was known to the Allies, but by an incredible stroke of good fortune all of that was about to change.

Against all odds, in January 1945 a man would step out of the shadows with one of the most controversial and divisive records of the war. After his capture, SOE agent Captain John Ashford Renshaw Starr had spent eleven months living at 84 Avenue Foch, and was either an outstanding SOE double agent or a stand-out traitor, depending on who one tended to listen to. Either way, Starr knew the Gestapo's Paris operations inside out and back to front by the time he was dispatched to Mauthausen concentra-tion camp, for 'final disposal'. As he had many times before, Starr miraculously survived.

And in his interrogations back in Britain, Starr would deliver chapter and verse on the Noailles Wood killers.

Chapter 21

A graphic artist before the war, Captain John Starr – aliases Emile, Bob and Bobby, amongst other cover names – had deployed twice for the SOE, and being a clandestine operative in France had become something of a Starr family pastime. His older brother, George – codename Hilaire – ran one of the most successful ever French circuits, with twenty SOE agents under his command. But three months into his second mission, John Starr was arrested by the SS in Dijon, in July 1943, being shot in the thigh while trying to escape.

Following standard practice, Starr was dispatched to 84 Avenue Foch as a guest of Kieffer and his cronies. But before that, his Dijon captors subjected the wounded SOE agent to a horrific beating and interrogation – 'the full treatment'. Once he arrived in Paris, Starr reached some kind of an accommodation with Kieffer, which had enabled him to take up residence at the Avenue Foch, where he became the subject of one of the Paris Gestapo's greatest ever *Funkspiel*. In short, for months on end no one in London would have the slightest idea that their star agent had been captured.

As a demonstration of how utterly SOE had been hoodwinked, on 17 April 1944 Starr's promotion to major, for 'important operational work in the field', was signed off by the head of SOE's F Section, Colonel Maurice Buckmaster, plus SOE's director himself, the long-experienced Brigadier McVean Gubbins. In truth, of course, Starr had been in Gestapo captivity for fully *nine months* by then. How was this even possible? And how was Starr's double life finally rumbled?

On 27 September 1944 a letter arrived at SOE's Baker Street headquarters on 'Box No. 500' letterhead. The euphemistic title was how MI5, Britain's domestic intelligence service, was known, due to its wartime London address – PO Box 500. Allegations had surfaced about Starr, and they were of sufficient weight to warrant MI5 asking SOE for 'full particulars' of their agent. By the spring of that year, SOE had got wise to Starr's capture, and that his circuit – codenamed Acrobat – had been penetrated, which made it all the more concerning that for months on end they had continued to dispatch sensitive messages, supplies and even agents to what they had believed was their man in the field.

By November 1944 the depths of the allegations against Starr were becoming increasingly clear. In a report dated 13 November, based upon the interrogation of a French prisoner – a suspected Avenue Foch collaborator – Starr was said to have cut a deal. 'Kieffer proposed to him that if he played with the Germans, he would be completely free on condition that he continued his W/T communications with the UK and helped with the arrest of parachute agents and the collection of parachuted arms and ammunition.' (W/T stood for wireless telegraphy – Morse Code sent by radio means). Starr had 'betrayed all the W/T agents of whom he had knowledge', the report continued, 'made accurate drawings of all British . . . officers of which he had knowledge . . . and of all landing grounds in England and France that he knew.'

If true, this was devastating. But there was more: 'The last people who were arrested thanks to him were twelve to fifteen soldiers who landed with a number of pigeons.' Could Starr's betrayal – if it was betrayal – have extended even to the capture of Captain Garstin and his men? Certainly there was no other parachute patrol of anything like that number that had dropped directly into the Gestapo's hands, in the summer of '44 in France. It seemed inconceivable that this could have been anything other than the SABU-70 raiders.

On 15 November 1944, SOE wrote to MI5 that 'Bob Starr has quite obviously been proved to have been working for the Germans.' A day later, Starr was being referred to as 'the notorious Bob Starr'. By the twenty-seventh of that month, a Major John Delaforce, who ran the Paris based SPU-24 – one of SOE's field security units – reported how the Avenue Foch Gestapo had maintained 'approximately fifteen false WT traffics with the home station' – in other words, *Funkspiel* – although he was unsure if 'they were all the result of traffic maintained through' agent Starr.

By early January 1945 MI5 was actively seeking to get their hands on Starr, though no one had the slightest idea where he might be or even if he was still alive. He was by then officially listed as 'a British renegade' by Supreme Headquarters Allied Expeditionary Force (SHAEF), whose role it was to track down 'British traitors and suspect traitors' across Europe. The hunt was very much on.

For months the trail went cold. Then, on 7 May 1945, Captain John Ashford Renshaw Starr appeared from out of the blue in Bern, Switzerland, as one of a shipment of 'French' prisoners who had been spirited out of Mauthausen by the Red Cross. His very survival was close to miraculous. No one would ever know how many perished at Mauthausen, a Nazi concentration camp in the hills above the Austrian market town of the same name. Estimates are between 120,000 and 320,000, most of whom were worked to their deaths in a network of subterranean weapons factories, mines and aircraft plants.

Yet somehow Starr – as an SOE agent, one who would have been earmarked for the very worst; for *Nacht und Nebel* treatment – had emerged from Mauthausen very much alive. Instructions were telegraphed to Bern: 'RETURN HIM UK IMMEDIATELY . . . ADVISING US ETA AND PLACE OF ARRIVAL.'

By 9 May John Starr was back in Britain and facing his first interrogation at the hands of his employers. But from the very start, Starr presented a markedly different figure from what his accusers might have been expecting. As far as he was concerned, he had done nothing wrong. Quite the contrary: the long months he had spent at the Avenue Foch were all to one purpose – to gather intelligence on the depths of the Gestapo's penetration of the SOE, and to escape and bring that to London.

While Starr accepted that he needed to provide a full account of himself, and was 'only too willing to write it', he resented his chilly reception by SOE. 'I do feel that above all, I would like to see my family if only for a few hours,' he objected. Starr was married with one daughter.

In due course he would present a case for his own actions that would prove very hard to disentangle and disavow. Yes, he had lived at 84 Avenue Foch for eleven months. Yes, at times he had dined with his Gestapo captors at fine Paris restaurants. Yes, he had used his skills as a graphic artist to draw maps of the various SOE circuits. But all of this was done with one purpose in mind – to gauge the depths of the Gestapo's duping of SOE, learning all of their secrets so he might spirit them away to Britain.

Starr's in-depth interrogation took place between 28 and 30 May 1945. In it he described the two key reasons why he had started drawing the SOE circuits for Kieffer. Firstly, he hoped 'to glean a lot of information that would be extremely valuable' if it could be got back to London. The second reason, he openly admitted, was for his own personal gain: conditions at Avenue Foch were infinitely more comfortable when compared to the Gestapo's alternative places of incarceration.

During his eleven months as a guest at Avenue Foch, Starr argued he 'never saw an Englishman ill-treated there'. On the *Funkspiel* side, he claimed that he 'never did any coding or decoding'. Sometimes the Gestapo brought him a *Funkspiel* text, 'perhaps to ask him how to spell a word, or occasionally to discuss a message'. As to the coded BBC signals the Gestapo intercepted, while he 'used to take these to Kieffer', he claimed he never aided the Gestapo in their interpretation. 'I might have made a slip once or twice,' he conceded, 'but I tried not to.'

Starr was quite open about how cosy were his relations with his Avenue Foch captors. On his birthday, 6 August, he 'was given presents by the Germans and flowers were placed in his room'. That evening they threw a party, and 'the Commandant [Kieffer] came up to the cell and brought a bottle of champagne and a bottle of cognac'. In Starr's view, 'Kieffer was very decent and usually brought round, personally, chocolate and cigarettes for the prisoners.' On a few occasions he and Kieffer had had a swim together at 84 Avenue Foch, 'in a static water tank which had been built in the grounds'.

Starr's interrogation report read like a bizarre cross between a confession and a case for the defence. The aces up his sleeve, Starr argued, were his two escape attempts, which were unarguably courageous and spirited. The first, just hours after his capture, had ended in his being gunned down on the streets. The second was even more demonstrative of his supposed good intentions and unimpeachable motives. In December 1943 he'd made contact with a female agent codenamed Madeleine – real name, Noor Inayat Khan – a British SOE agent and unarguably one of the bravest ever to have served. Together with another Avenue Foch captive, they would undertake a daring escape attempt.

To that end, Starr offered to repair the Avenue Foch's vacuum cleaner. To do so he'd needed tools. He'd managed to spirit those into his cell, and to that of his fellow captives on the building's fifth floor. With those they had loosened the bars to their windows and in the dead of night the three escapees had crawled onto the roof. But by ill fortune, an Allied bomber squadron had chosen that night to launch a raid over Paris. The city's searchlights blazed into life, catching the three fugitives as they crawled to safety. In short order they were dragged down, at which stage 'Kieffer was furious and said they were going to be shot'.

Noor Inayat Khan and the other escapee were dispatched to Germany, Inayat Khan to Dachau concentration camp, where she would face an unspeakable death, having never once cracked or breathed a word of any use to her captors. The first female radio operator ever sent to France, she would be posthumously awarded the George Cross, Britain's highest civilian decoration for valour. Starr, meanwhile, had been presented with an ultimatum by Kieffer. He could choose either to be shipped to Germany or to remain at Avenue Foch, but for the latter would need to 'give his word of honour never again to attempt to escape . . . while in France'.

Faced with such a stark choice – Germany almost certainly

spelled torture and death – Starr gave his word. In his SOE interrogation report, he stressed that when trying to escape he'd taken with him 'a number of documents containing much valuable information, which he hoped to get over to England'. That, he maintained, was his foremost reason for doing as he had done at Avenue Foch.

In August 1944 Starr had been informed of his imminent dispatch to Germany, 'in view of the approach of the American forces'. Starr seemed convinced that Kieffer had 'taken a good liking to him and that was the main reason for his good fortune ... three times already Berlin had demanded that he ... should be shot, but the Commandant had managed to put it off'. Starr was duly sent to Mauthausen, and in due course had somehow managed to convince the camp authorities that he was French, and to wangle a place on the Red Cross prisoner convoy to Bern, from where he had been returned to Britain.

At the end of Starr's interrogation, SOE and MI5 compared notes. To prosecute or not to prosecute, that was the question. On balance, the two agencies had to weigh up 'whether such traitors can be prosecuted without doing more harm than good'. While Starr had definitely worked with the enemy, SOE's Major Delaforce concluded, he had also made those two escape attempts. If the second had succeeded and he'd made it back to Britain, Starr would doubtless have been hailed as the hero of the hour. Delaforce suspected that prosecuting Starr 'would not be worthwhile from an SOE point of view, as it would result in a certain amount of mud being raked up'. That 'mud' chiefly concerned the extent to which SOE had been duped by the Avenue Foch's *Funskpiel* operations.

In weighing up whether to send Starr for trial, charges were considered of 'materially aiding the enemy', which carried the death penalty. But establishing Starr's culpability in the *Funkspiel* operations would be key, and how could that ever be proven? Certainly, his status almost as a 'member of staff' at Avenue Foch was unconscionable, SOE argued, especially when other captured agents became aware of it, as invariably they did. It had proved devastating to their morale, and on that basis alone Starr 'acted very wrongly'.

He was a 'conceited type and considers he was extremely clever in making the Germans take such a fancy to him', his SOE interrogators concluded. 'Clever as Starr thinks his behaviour was, I am sure that the Germans at Avenue Foch were far cleverer . . . and he was undoubtedly useful to them in many ways.' In the final analysis, the decision was taken not to prosecute. SOE had far too many skeletons in the closet to risk the blaze of attendant publicity. As for MI5, an elegant argument was found to justify taking no action: it would be bad for recruitment and the retention of agents.

'It would be said . . . that a trained agent ought to be able to deceive the enemy . . . in order to save his own life,' MI5 argued, in a July 1945 letter on the Starr case. 'It might be a very bad thing if it were to be thought amongst prospective agents that any effort to double-cross the enemy . . . were tolerably likely to result in a trial by Court Martial on their return.' In short, no prosecution was to be brought against Starr. It was case closed.

For the ghosts of the SABU-70 raiders, it didn't much matter either way. What was crucial to them was what John Starr knew and could tell. And on that front, his insider information would prove revelatory. Starr had been present at Avenue Foch at the same time as Captain Garstin and his men, and what he didn't know about the circumstances of their capture, and the identities of their captors/killers, wasn't worth knowing.

On 8 October 1945 Starr gave a detailed statement: 'In the matter of the shooting of British prisoners of war near Noailles, France, 9 August 1944'. In it, he confirmed that he'd been told of the 5 July '44 *Funkspiel* operation, and of the subsequent – surprise – capture of the SAS men. He'd seen the captives brought to Avenue Foch, including the SAS captain 'who wore a decoration'. Starr even claimed he'd 'been able to give these prisoners some cigarettes', but that he was forbidden from talking with them, although there is no record of anything like that happening in any of the SAS captive's own accounts.

More importantly, Starr was able to furnish chapter and verse on the identity of their captors. On SS *Sturmbannführer* Hans Josef Kieffer: 'The chief of the Gestapo ... was an SS man and had been one of the earliest NS [Nazi] recruits. He is reputed to have been an athlete, aged about 40, height about 5 ft 7 in, hair dark, turning to black, plentiful and inclined to be wavy. His eyes were light blue and deep set; complexion fresh; prominent forehead, small nose, square type of face, smallish chin. He wore glasses for reading and was close shaven. He had broad shoulders, thick chest, stocky build. He could not speak English.'

On SS *Untersturmführer* Alfred von Kapri: 'about 25; height 5 ft 6 ins; hair dark; complexion pale; oval type of face; clean shaven ... He spoke Romanian, German, Russian, Italian, French and English fluently ... He was at Avenue Foch for the whole of the period I was there, and I last saw him in August, 1944.' On *Hauptscharführer* Karl Haug: 'aged about 40–45; height 5 ft 8 ins; thick dark wavy hair; dark eyes; thick eyebrows; thick lips; complexion sallow; square face; very thick set in build. He had been a prisoner of the British in the last war. He was married with four children.'

And so on and so forth.

By an absolute freak of fate, a suspected British traitor, or a courageous double agent – depending on how you tended to look at things – had managed to escape almost certain death at Mauthausen, and to return to Britain with the intelligence that the ghosts of the SABU-70 raiders had so needed, not to mention the patrol's survivors. Vaculik and Jones had begun to fear that their quest for justice had hit the buffers. In truth, the next stage of that long and tortuous journey was only just beginning.

The day after Starr's bombshell testimony, ten 'Wanted Reports' were issued in London. They were for Kieffer, Goetz, von Kapri and Haug, plus six others whose role in the Noailles Wood massacre was not significant, although no one knew that yet. The descriptions given in those wanted reports were basically carbon copies of what Starr had provided in his statement. Somewhere across post-war Europe, some of the wanted surely had to be in custody, or at least they should be.

Allied policy was for all former SS to be arrested, no matter what their rank or role. Post-war prosecutors charged the SS with being 'the very essence of Nazism. For the SS was the elite group of the Party, composed of the most thorough-going adherents of the Nazi cause, pledged to blind devotion to Nazi principles, and prepared to carry them out without question and at any cost.' The SS was deemed a criminal organisation, the very membership of which was enough to make one an automatic target for pursuit, capture and interrogation.

Interestingly, a 'Wanted Report' was also issued for George Richard, the German soldier who had done so much to help

Lieutenant Wiehe in hospital. 'The wanted person is described as about 6 ft tall . . . close-shaven, wore glasses . . . Spoke broken French but no English. In Aug 1944 he was employed as an orderly at La Pitié Hospital, Paris. He is wanted for interrogation only as he may be able and willing to describe Gestapo personnel who are wanted in connection with the murder of five British POWs.'

On 13 March 1945 Lieutenant Wiehe had been 'pronounced permanently unfit for any form of military service'. A month later the War Office had written, thanking him for 'the services which you have rendered . . . during a period of grave national emergency . . . the Army council fully appreciate the patriotism which led you to give your services in this way'. Sadly, Lieutenant Wiehe would never fully recover from his injuries and would be wheelchair-bound for life. Even so, shortly after being ruled unfit for duty, Wiehe felt well enough to give his own statement in support of the Noailles Wood case.

'I am now a patient in the Emergency Hospital, Leatherhead', he began. 'In the early morning of 5 July 1944 I was dropped by parachute behind the German lines . . . northeast of Étampes, together with Captain Garstin and other SAS personnel. We were ambushed by the Gestapo and I myself was seriously wounded.' And so it continued, chronicling all that had followed. Wiehe's statement provided yet more ammunition for those seeking the Noailles Wood killers. Now it only required a team with the tenacity and dedication to hunt down the suspects.

It was time for the SAS to prove how they would look after – and avenge – their own.

Chapter 22

In August and September 1944, an eighty-strong SAS team had parachuted into the Vosges Mountains, on France's border with Germany, on a mission codenamed Operation Loyton. The heavily fortified western wall of the Vosges was to be the Wehrmacht's last bulwark against Allied forces, for beyond that lay the Fatherland. Hitler had urged his forces to mount a last-ditch stand in the Vosges, to prevent the Allies from punching through. Fittingly, the objective of Op Loyton was to spread havoc and chaos in the enemy's rear, with the aim of convincing the German rank and file that Allied forces had broken their lines.

During operations in Nazi-occupied Europe, the SAS had developed a new technique for waging the kind of warfare at which they excelled. It was encapsulated in the phrase 'cutting the head off the Nazi snake'. By targeting senior enemy officers deep behind the lines, it served to strike terror into the ranks, for not even those at the top of the chain of command were safe, no matter where they might be. On Operation Loyton, the SAS would excel at just such a strategy.

From their base at Les Bois Sauvages (the Wild Woods), deep in the densely forested Vosges Mountains, they struck time and time again, in fast, jeep-mounted operations. On 8 October 1944 – eight weeks into the mission – they ambushed their final German staff car, making eleven in total that had been blasted to pieces. In short, no enemy officer had been able to travel the precipitous, winding roads of the Vosges in safety, or devoid of fear. Amongst many of Loyton's daring exploits, SAS man of steel Lieutenant Ralph 'Karl' Marx and his small team would cross the border to blow up a train, in what was the first mission of its kind to strike on German soil.

The reaction of the enemy was extreme. The very presence of the winged-dagger raiders was enough to send the German high command apoplectic. Their response was to launch Operation *Waldfest* – 'party in the forest' – in which two complete German divisions were sent to hunt down eighty British paratroopers. As Colonel Mayne had done on Op Gain, the commander of 2 SAS, Lieutenant Colonel Brian Morton Forster Franks, had parachuted in, to lead Op Loyton on the ground. But on 9 October '44, with little ammo, explosives, food or cold weather gear remaining, he had bowed to the inevitable.

'I decided to end the operation,' Franks recorded in the Op Loyton war diary, 'and instructed parties to make their way to American lines as best they could.'

Weeks later, back in Britain, Colonel Franks was counting the cost of the mission. The French populace had paid a terrible price for hiding, and supporting, the SAS raiders operating in their midst. Thousands of villagers had been rounded up and carted off to the nearby concentration camp, Natzweiler-Struthof, which sat high in the hills just to the French side of the border, as German commanders sought to 'exterminate this alarming terrorist band'. So few would return at war's end that the area would become known as the 'Valley of Widows' and the 'Vale of Tears'.

There were also thirty-one SAS listed as missing in action – more than a third of the Op Loyton force. Colonel Franks was determined to find out their fates and if possible to bring them home. He assembled a team to investigate, and if necessary hunt down the guilty parties, if indeed the missing SAS men had met with a dark and bloody end. There was only one possible candidate to lead such an effort, as far as Franks was concerned – Major Eric 'Bill' Barkworth, the unflappable SAS intelligence supremo, who had been fond of marching up and down on his Cairo hospital bed to matron's great annoyance.

Barkworth had forged a reputation as being brilliant, tireless, eccentric and scrupulously fair, but with a streak of the ruthless to boot. He'd also demonstrated a healthy lack of respect for unnecessary rules, hierarchies and bureaucracies, which were just the kind of qualities that Franks felt he needed in the man to head up his grandly titled 'SAS War Crimes Investigation Team' (WCIT). In truth it consisted of Barkworth, plus the SAS major's trusty cohort, Sergeant Fred 'Dusty' Rhodes, together with half a dozen other long-standing SAS veterans – truth-seekers on a mission.

Rhodes had left school at age fourteen with no qualifications, to start work with his father as a gardener in Locke Park, a 47-acre green space in Barnsley. He was just twenty years old when he signed up in February 1940. Slim, wiry, sandy-haired and blue-eyed, Rhodes spoke with a strong Yorkshire accent in tones that were surprisingly firm and commanding, considering his youth. In 1942 he'd volunteered for 'special duties', discovering in the SAS 'a marvellous organisation . . . the work and ideas and the creative ideas . . . were tremendous'. It was a unit of 'loners [who] didn't believe in relying on other people. They relied on their own men.' It suited the tough, phlegmatic Yorkshireman absolutely, and 'promotion in the ranks came quickly'.

The contrast with Barkworth's upbringing could hardly have been more complete. The SAS major hailed from an independently wealthy family – his father, who'd been a student of law, had listed his profession simply as 'Gentleman'. Having studied at Oxford and then Freiburg University in Germany, Barkworth was fluent in seven languages. He'd spent much of the pre-war years travelling Europe, at one time meeting Hermann Goering, the future *Reichsmarschall* – the most senior ranking member of Germany's armed forces and Hitler's chosen successor. Goering had inquired of Barkworth what the English thought of him.

In a rare act of diplomacy, Barkworth had decided not to tell Goering the unvarnished truth. 'They say you are a very good pilot,' he'd demurred. Goering's response was to slap his own thigh, uproariously.

Barkworth didn't just aim to learn a language: he immersed himself in it. He used to maintain that the best way to imbibe a new tongue was to go to the marketplace in the morning, in order to listen to bartering and everyday conversations, then to the law courts in the afternoon, to hear the formal, well-spoken form, and then to the nightclubs in the evening, to learn the latest in-vogue expressions – in the process imbibing the national culture too. He'd done all of that and more in Germany, where he liked to challenge himself by conversing with someone in a language other than English – French, say – while listening in on a neighbouring table where they were speaking German.

Upon volunteering for special duties, Barkworth had been asked to phone a certain number, and when the caller answered, to speak only in German. This he had proceeded to do. On the other end of the line was a German-speaking Swiss woman who worked for the British. She reported back to Barkworth's recruiters that she 'was sure he must be German, his language skills were so convincing'. He combined all of that with an unconventional and ingenious mindset, which meant that nothing was out of bounds. That combination – in-depth language skills and cultural familiarity, plus the ability to think outside the box – would make Barkworth a Nazi-hunter almost without compare.

During the war Barkworth and Rhodes – these two men from such very different backgrounds – had grown inseparable. The Barkworth clan's roots lay in Yorkshire, so perhaps that was what drew them together. The family home had been in Tranby, Yorkshire, and the last Barkworth to live there had been Uncle Algernon, who typified the family's do-or-die spirit. A first-class passenger on the *Titanic*, he'd proceeded to jump overboard wearing a thick fur coat over his lifejacket, even as the ship went down. He'd found an overturned lifeboat, clambered aboard and stood on the keel all through the night, until he was rescued by the RMS *Carpathia* come daybreak.

Or perhaps Barkworth and Rhodes had bonded most over taking the surrender of seventy SS officers, using nothing more than a good dose of bluff and chutzpah, plus a little long-lived regimental tradition. In May 1945, the SAS intelligence teams had 'moved to Germany, to have one grand slam at the Nazis', Rhodes recorded, in his handwritten notes of the war years. In the process, they'd stumbled across a squadron of SS holed up in an ancient castle. In his fluent German, Barkworth had talked his way inside, seeking the garrison's capitulation. The commanding officer had retorted that Barkworth was now *his* prisoner, and that he would surrender to nobody but a member of the 'Brigadier Guards,' a colloquial term for the Brigade of

Guards, the parent unit of a dozen Guards battalions, generally held in high esteem by the German armed forces.

'That's alright,' Barkworth had responded, 'I've got one right here for you.' He'd promptly thrust forward Rhodes, for by luck the Yorkshireman's parent unit was the Coldstream Guards.

'Right, then, Dusty, come on, here goes,' Barkworth had enthused, 'show them what the Brigadier Guards can do!'

The 'whole bloody lot surrendered', Rhodes recalled, in astonishment. 'This officer surrendered, and he surrendered the whole garrison to one former member of the Brigadier Guards.'

Barkworth would be awarded an MBE for this action, the citation for which read: 'On 1 May 1945, Major Barkworth . . . was ordered to interrogate an SS officer . . . Major Barkworth went . . . with the German officer to the SS HQ in an attempt to negotiate a surrender. Final negotiations broke down and Major Barkworth found himself disarmed and a prisoner. Nevertheless, he escaped and returned to our own lines, bringing with him 70 SS troops whom he had persuaded to surrender.' By the time the MBE was awarded in early 1946, Barkworth and his team would be deep inside post-war Germany, hunting war criminals.

In May 1945 Sergeant Rhodes had found himself at home, enjoying some rare leave – 'a pint or two' – as the war in Europe was over. But not for long. 'Major Barkworth was ordered to see Colonel Franks, who then ordered him to reform his team and return to France and Germany and not to return until the 31 missing SAS men had been found, plus the people who had in any way been responsible for the deaths and disappearances.' A copy of Hitler's Commando Order now lay in Allied hands, and all feared the worst, 'knowing the instructions from the top people in the German Army and Adolph Hitler, [to] the Gestapo – that SAS were to be murdered, were to be shot.'

Franks had every reason to spur Barkworth and his team on. A mass grave had just been discovered in the Erlich Forest, in Gaggenau, southwest Germany, and it was thought to hold the bodies of some of the Op Loyton missing. With Germany split into British, American, French and Russian zones of occupation, Gaggenau lay under the French purview, and British troops were not often to be found there. It would take all of Barkworth's and Rhodes's particular skills to negotiate – or force – a passage through. There was no time to delay: no one knew what state the bodies were in, for the purpose of making identifications.

On 16 May the small team set out, driving one war-worn jeep and one battered British Army truck. There were strict regulations about travelling through post-war Europe. 'Authority to move . . . had to be approved by the military,' Rhodes noted. 'Six men, one officer, and one sergeant made light of the journey.' As would become their trademark, the SAS WCIT circumvented the regulations wherever possible. From the start, Barkworth appreciated that if you were hunting Nazi war criminals, it was best not to forewarn them of your intentions. 'Extreme care should be taken to ensure that no news that the SAS are searching for [X suspect] should reach the wanted man's ears,' Barkworth cautioned. Far better to pitch up out of the blue, having flitted through the backroads and avoided any checkpoints, to take him by surprise.

On reaching Gaggenau, Barkworth and his team made themselves known to the town's authorities. Of their arrival Rhodes noted: 'Gaggenau Rathaus [town hall]. Bürgermeister [mayor] good chap. Row between Captain B. and jumped-up French Lt.'

As all who knew him appreciated, Barkworth tended not to suffer fools. 'No digs for the night. Told the men . . . to find their own and if any man returned 0700 hrs without a smile on his face, some 252s would fly about.' A '252' was slang for an army charge sheet, otherwise known as being put 'on jankers'.

Expecting the men to beg, borrow or steal their lodgings was fine for the first night, but clearly something more permanent needed to be found. The answer lay in the town's Villa Degler, the expropriation of which had about it a delicious irony. The imposing house was home to the Degler family, who owned the local brewery. A prominent Nazi, Herr Degler had been arrested by the French. In a neat role reversal, Barkworth took the villa over, co-opting Herr Degler's wife and daughters as his and his team's domestic staff. As a bonus, the Villa Degler possessed a deep and roomy cellar, which was perfect for what Barkworth intended – to fill it with prisoners.

The next entry in Rhodes's notes reads: 'The bodies cemetery Gaggenau.' During the war, the main employer in Gaggenau had been the Daimler-Benz factory, which produced trucks for the Wehrmacht. In the Bad Rotenfels district of Gaggenau, a camp had been built to house 1,500 prisoners – slave labour for the Daimler-Benz vehicle plant. The Rotenfels labour camp was actually a satellite of Natzweiler, a concentration camp some 80 miles to the west, in the Vosges Mountains. Prisoners were shipped east to Bad Rotenfels to work, then back to Natzweiler when they were too exhausted and sick to be of any use, for 'final disposal'.

Germany in early June 1945 was a land of utter chaos and misery. The nation's cities had been pounded into rubble. Across the British zone alone there were eighty concentration camps, work camps and sub-camps. At the Bergen-Belsen concentration camp some 15,000 inmates had died following liberation, from starvation and typhoid. An entire population was on the move, as families returned to ruined cities and towns, carrying what few possessions they could cram onto rickety carts. Everywhere famished civilians queued for what little food the Allied powers were able to muster, as mass starvation threatened. In the fields, hundreds of thousands of German POWs laboured under the watchful eyes of guards, working to bring in the harvest.

As Gaggenau's Daimler-Benz factory had proved a magnet for Allied air raids, some 70 per cent of the town had been flattened. Amongst this morass of human suffering, Barkworth had somehow to start the hunt. Fortunately, it was a very concrete lead that had drawn him to Gaggenau. Adjacent to the vehicle factory lay the Erlich Forest – the site of the recently discovered mass grave. On 25 November 1944 the commandant of the Rotenfels camp had received an order to liquidate all Allied prisoners held there. Ten British and American POWs, plus seventeen French citizens – three of whom were priests and one of whom was a woman – were taken to the Erlich Forest and shot, their bodies tumbling into a bomb crater and being heaped over with earth.

Upon taking control of Gaggenau, the French authorities had excavated the grave, leading to the first reports reaching Lieutenant Colonel Franks that there might be SAS men amongst the dead. But the evidence had been fragmentary. Shortly after their arrival in Gaggenau, Barkworth, Rhodes and his team began the horrendous task of unearthing the mass grave for a second time, to carry out rigorous, forensic identifications that would stand up in a court of law. Fortunately they had on hand a team of American military pathologists, photographers and legal experts, commanded by Colonel David Chavez Jr. As Gaggenau lay just a few miles west of the border with the American zone of occupation, it was easy enough for Chavez and his team to get there.

Fittingly, the former managers of the Daimler-Benz factory were made to dig up the bodies, as the steely figure of Rhodes stood over them. 'We felt that they had been responsible for the people being shot and killed,' Rhodes remarked. 'So many of them said that they didn't know anything about it. Well, I don't believe that.' In the nearby *Waldfriedhof* – a cemetery located in the Erlich Forest – the chief US pathologist, Lieutenant Colonel Edwards, set up a temporary morgue in the Chapel of Rest, which in normal times was where families would come to view the body of the deceased, before burial.

Rhodes asked the helpful and friendly Gaggenau *Bürgermeister* to 'produce some men to . . . carry the bodies to the morgue, where Lieutenant Colonel Edwards was doing the autopsies – a man smoking a meerschaum [clay] pipe and wearing a rubber apron. Men's skulls were being sawn in half, searching for the cause of death (a bullet). Identification by teeth, broken bones . . . This was a task that was beyond what had been expected but must be done. Several bottles of Schnapps were consumed each day, all put down to the *Bürgermeister's* expenses.'

It was grim work. 'The bodies were three-quarters decomposed,' Rhodes noted. 'What a terrible sight and smell. The Germans knew we were after them. We had word through the system that they were spreading out. They knew that stones would be turned to find them. The Major was now planning ahead – looking for clues and information.' The wanted men were busy changing names, procuring fake identity cards – the black market for false ID documents was booming – and altering their appearances, in an effort to avoid getting caught. But as the twenty-seven dead were exhumed and painstakingly identified, the hunt proper was about to begin.

First of the SAS to be named was twenty-year-old SAS Lieutenant David Dill, a man who'd parachuted into the Vosges on the night of 13 August 1944, on the initial Operation Loyton drop. The hugely capable and keen-spirited Lieutenant Dill had been tasked to command the rear party, as the main body of raiders had split into smaller groups, to slip back to Allied lines. Dill's mission had been to link up with some of the missing – Op Loyton's second-in-command, Major Dennis 'Denny' Reynolds, first and foremost – and to 'kill a German before he left', to make it appear as if the SAS were still operating in the area.

Instead, Lieutenant Dill, together with his six men and one young Resistance fighter, had been captured when the Germans had surrounded their base. After a prolonged firefight, the Waffen SS officer who took Dill captive shook his hand, and declared: 'You are my prisoner. You are a soldier and so am I.' But the initial, supposedly gallant and honourable treatment had somehow ended with the SAS lieutenant being dumped in the Gaggenau mass grave. It didn't exactly bode well for the rest of Dill's men, who were also numbered amongst the Op Loyton missing.

Lieutenant Dill had been identified by his military-issue wristwatch, which had a unique serial number. That on Dill's timepiece matched his records. Alongside Dill were buried several US airmen, including Curtis E. Hodges and Michael Pipcock, plus the very man that the SAS lieutenant had been ordered to wait behind for, Major Dennis Reynolds. Reynolds had been injured in a firefight with the enemy, and forced to take refuge in a cave in the Vosges, in the company of Captain Andrew Whately-Smith.

The latter's corpse was also present in the Gaggenau grave. Both men were easy to identify, as they still had their military-issue dog tags.

From his dental records, Captain Victor Gough was also identified. Gough had served with the Jedburghs, a unit set up to liaise with the French Resistance and most often consisting of three-man teams, including a Frenchman, an American and a Brit. The specific mission of 'the Jeds' had been to act as what would now be termed 'military advisers', calling in supplies of weaponry and advising on targets and tactics. As such, Captain Gough had been only loosely tied in with Op Loyton.

Two other SAS men – Troopers Maurice Griffin and Christopher Ashe – were also identified by their dental records. For Barkworth and his team, the gruesome work proved intensely emotional. In many instances, they had known personally the murdered men and counted them as friends. In Barkworth's case, he had personally seen Whately-Smith off from Fairford, when the SAS captain had boarded his aircraft to deploy into the Vosges.

Though neither Barkworth nor Rhodes had deployed on Op Loyton, Rhodes had ridden on a number of the resupply flights, dropping in desperately needed food and arms to the men on the ground. 'Sometimes, there was just the faintest resemblance,' Rhodes remarked of those they had exhumed. 'You could pick out the features of certain people you knew so well. You could say: "Yes, this is Captain so-and-so." But you couldn't always do that.'

In November 1944 Colonel Franks had received a letter from the Red Cross, listing Major Reynolds, Captain Whately-Smith, Captain Gough, Lieutenant Dill and the US airman, Pipcock, as being present at the Schirmeck *Sicherungslager* (security camp) – a satellite facility to the Naztweiler concentration camp in the Vosges. They had certainly been alive then. Now, some seven months later, they had been positively identified in this Gaggenau mass grave. Barkworth and his team's role was to trace what had happened in the interim, and to track down those responsible.

It was 20 June 1945 by the time the exhumations were complete. There were many who would argue that Barkworth's was a true mission impossible. But in the Gaggenau case, he and his team were blessed with having former camp inmates, and in many cases former camp guards, step forwards to give evidence. Barkworth's star witness was Abbé Alphonse Hett, a young Catholic clergyman who'd been held at Rotenfels as a suspect member of the Resistance. He was an eyewitness to the forming up of the execution party. He'd seen the ten prisoners dressed in British and American uniforms loaded aboard a closed truck, little doubting what lay in store for them.

A French POW, Albert Arnold, had been forced to drive that truck. He provided eyewitness testimony to the shootings. The prisoners were marched into the Erlich Forest in threes, by German soldiers Ostertag, Ullrich, Zimmermann and Neuschwanger, where they were shot dead. A group of Russian POWs were made to bury the bodies. One had removed a photograph from one of the corpses. That had also made its way into Barkworth's hands, and it showed the loved ones of the murdered SAS Trooper Maurice Griffin.

Within days of the exhumations, Barkworth had secured detailed eyewitness accounts of the crime, and the names of his first suspects: Ostertag, Ullrich, Zimmermann and Neuschwanger. According to the French priest, Abbé Hett, that last man was a notorious torturer and sadist. SS *Oberwachmeister* (Lieutenant) Heinrich Neuschwanger had excelled in unleashing savagery on Allied prisoners. Strung up by their hands, they were beaten until the bones showed through their skin. Neuschwanger extracted great amusement from doing so. He had been nicknamed 'Stuka', after the distinctive German dive-bomber, due to his predilection for stomping on prisoners.

At Rotenfels, Major Denny Reynolds had confided in Abbé Hett about his own beatings, remarking how 'he would not have thought it possible for the body to withstand such pain without death occurring'. Somehow Reynolds *had* survived the beatings, but not his Erlich Forest executioners, as Barkworth would discover. His 15 July report on the killings stressed 'the urgency of bringing the German criminals to justice'. Barkworth had realised that he had stumbled across 'the full machinery for the elimination and destruction of prisoners', just as Hitler's Commando Order had called for.

First blood fell to Barkworth and team, and quickly. 'Weber. First arrest,' Rhodes scribbled, his notes reading like those of a Scotland Yard detective, though he had no formal training, of course. 'In between identification and official burials, the local businessmen were now to be involved to track down SS.' The arrest in July '45 of Sigmund Weber – a man whom Barkworth and Rhodes described as the 'Rotenfels camp Quartermaster', and a 'beater' of SAS captives – was the first real milestone. Weber was dragged into the Villa Degler basement, the first of many such prisoners to partake of its hospitality.

There, he faced Barkworth. Unfailingly polite and eschewing violence, somehow Barkworth would prove himself an inquisitor without compare. 'Few Germans interrogated by him ... even the most hardened of Gestapo men have failed to comment on his courtesy and consideration,' remarked one of Barkworth's colleagues. 'Some have even mistaken him for the ex-Gestapo chief of the area, whose physical likeness and even the German accent is so like Bill that it startles the prisoners.' Shortly after interrogation, Weber would attempt suicide – testimony to the psychological rigour with which Barkworth broke his captives.

Weber would go on to serve seven years' hard labour for his crimes. But shockingly, he had been 'traced by Major Barkworth . . . living in comfort with a pass signed by a junior French officer stating that he, Weber, was a "harmless German"'. This would prove typical. Even at this early stage of proceedings, there seemed little appetite for apprehending Nazi war criminals, and what systems did exist were a complete shambles. Such issues weren't restricted to the French zone. If anything, the problems Barkworth would experience at the hands of the British occupation authorities were even worse.

In early August, a team of 'official' war crimes investigators was sent south from the British zone to 'assist' with Barkworth's efforts. Fresh from investigating the horrors of Belsen, the team didn't stay long. Their commander, Lieutenant Colonel Leo Genn, confided to Barkworth: 'The difficulties of organisation are so great that I am only marking time.' The SAS major – driven, resolute and deeply personally motivated – had no time for such an attitude.

After Barkworth had sent Lieutenant Colonel Genn and his team packing, Genn would pen a report concluding that Barkworth's efforts 'have now reached a dead end . . . missing members of 2 SAS still remain untraced and . . . no avenue remains which can be usefully followed up'. Barkworth countered

Genn's criticism with the perfect putdown: 'It is not agreed that no avenue remains; it is however agreed that [Genn's team] is perhaps most usefully employed elsewhere.'

Barkworth's detractors upped their criticism, declaring that 'only a miracle' would lead to the missing SAS being traced. Hearing of this, Franks felt deeply frustrated: 'I very much doubt whether even a small percentage of the perpetrators of these crimes will be brought to justice. I feel personally responsible, not only to the families of these officers and men but also to the men themselves. There are no lengths to which I would not go to ensure that action is taken.' At Gaggenau, Barkworth shared Franks' steely conviction. There were no lengths to which he wouldn't go, either.

Having got Weber, at the top of Barkworth's wanted list sat *Oberwachmeister* Heinrich 'Stuka' Neuschwanger. But Barkworth was soon to add another suspect, this being a senior member of the *Geheime Staatspolizei*. On the liberation of Paris in August '44, the Avenue Foch Gestapo had retreated east, re-establishing itself in and around the Vosges. The Gestapo unit that had fallen under Barkworth's spotlight was named *Gruppe Kieffer*, after the man who commanded it – SS *Sturmbannführer* Hans Josef Kieffer. As Barkworth discovered, it was Kieffer who had dispatched Major Denny Reynolds and Captain Whately-Smith to their torture and death, and he had done so in the most devious of ways.

One morning in mid-September 1944, Captain Whately-Smith and Major Reynolds had been sent to reconnoitre a new base of operations in the Vosges. In the process of doing so they were ambushed, and Reynolds was shot and wounded. While hiding in a cave and being helped by French villagers, Captain

Whately-Smith had scorned all opportunities to escape, as to do so would have left his wounded brother officer in dire straits. Having lost contact with the main Op Loyton force, the two men had carried out a little freelance raiding, before setting out on 30 October to try to make it back to Allied lines. In the process, they had been captured by a unit of regular German troops.

The two SAS officers were initially treated with all proper consideration due to Allied prisoners of war. But after forty-eight hours Kieffer had appeared on the scene. Upon arrival he had promised that the SAS men would be treated as bona-fide POWs, and not executed under Hitler's Commando Order, as their captors feared would be the case. Indeed, the Wehrmacht officers were 'convinced that we had by our opposition saved the two officers from being shot as spies ... both British officers were very pleased with the treatment accorded to them ... and both hoped to see us after the war. What became of them after they were taken by Kieffer in his car I have no idea.'

Kieffer had pledged to take 'personal charge' of Whately-Smith and Reynolds. His idea of doing so involved driving the two SAS officers direct to Schirmeck, after which their hellish treatment and murder had followed. In short, an attempt to extend to two SAS officers operating in uniform the rights and protections they were due had been scuppered, at SS *Sturmbannführer* Kieffer's hands. Of course, Whately-Smith and Reynolds were just two such victims consigned to the *Nacht und Nebel* by Kieffer – but it was their case that had brought him under Barkworth's unyielding glare.

Barkworth felt under particular pressure to solve Major Reynolds's case, for the SAS major was both a close personal friend of Lieutenant Colonel Franks and a well-known and colourful character within SAS circles. Born to Irish parents, Reynolds had owned and bred racehorses before the war, riding many winners himself. Of his Sandhurst officer training, it was recorded: 'Has any amount of character and grit, is cheery with it all and will make an excellent officer. Grade A.'

After Sandhurst Reynolds had joined the King's Royal Rifle Corps, along with Major Ian Fenwick, the SAS commander who would be killed on Operation Gain. Fenwick had made Reynolds the subject of many of his cartoons, captioning one, in which Reynolds is about to execute a parachute jump: 'Had been a pre-war amateur steeplechaser, and hence was unfit through multiple injuries. Later he was passed fit, learnt to parachute and joined he SAS . . . was a charming shooting companion at Strensall (snipe and partridge) and a perfect team worker.'

Franks felt Reynolds's loss most personally, writing of the thirty-five-year-old major's death: 'Everyone in the SAS Regiment who knew Denny had a sense of personal loss. He was the best second-in-command anyone could wish for and he was a great friend and it is difficult to say how much I miss him.'

Barkworth and Reynolds had also shared a particular bond. One of Reynolds's most infamous exploits had been to try to drop into the Vosges with his dog, Tinker, whom he had taught to parachute. He was only stopped when Franks radioed: 'We don't want a bloody dog here.' Reynolds went everywhere with Tinker, which was something that Barkworth could relate to, for he had picked up strays all through the war years. In Italy he'd found a beautiful – abandoned – Apulian sheepdog, and had had it flown back to the family home in Britain, so he could adopt it at war's end.

Both Barkworth and Reynolds had never been without a dog

if they could help it. Now Barkworth had had to exhume the semi-decayed corpse of his murdered SAS comrade. Halfway through the grim work, Colonel Franks had radioed, asking: 'Have you any more clues Denny etc.?' Barkworth had replied: 'Bodies of Denny and Andy [Whately-Smith] identified.' It was Rhodes himself who'd got down into the grave, to remove the SAS officers' identity tags. They had also retrieved 'a shoulder strap bearing the insignia of a crown, as worn by a major in the British Army, also a black button bearing the insignia of the King's Royal Rifle Corps, which was major Reynolds's parent unit'.

By the autumn of 1945 SS *Sturmbannführer* and Gestapo man Hans Josef Kieffer was firmly on Barkworth's radar, particularly since *Gruppe Kieffer* was found to have orchestrated other murders in the Vosges in which the SAS victims had been forced to change into civilian clothing, just as had Captain Garstin and his men. A modus operandi was emerging here of how Kieffer and his Gestapo henchmen endeavoured to bury forever – *Nacht und Nebel* style – their heinous crimes.

For Barkworth and his team there was much to be done, and as they repeatedly proved their mettle, the scope of their work kept expanding. Tracing the Op Loyton missing was the trigger that had led to the SAS war crimes team being dispatched. But as Rhodes noted, it was also the catalyst to 'three years spent by SAS War Crimes in tracing' those wider Nazi suspects 'who had committed the terrible acts'.

With both the Gaggenau mass grave and the Noailles Wood murders, Kieffer and his Gestapo team were the common thread: Barkworth had double the reason to want to nail them. But there was a problem, as unexpected as it was to prove potentially disastrous. In September 1945 the decision was made that the SAS was to be disbanded. In wartime, the unit had served a vital purpose. In a time of peace, there was no role for the winged-dagger raiders, or so the military and political hierarchy argued.

And that meant that the SAS War Crimes Investigation Team was slated to die with it.

Chapter 23

At the end of September 1945 there was a surprise visitor at the Villa Degler. Captain Yuri 'Yurka' Galitzine was an Anglo-Russian nobleman in his early twenties who'd served with the SOE during the war. In autumn '44 Galitzine had commanded the search team that had discovered Natzweiler – the first Nazi concentration camp to be found by the Allies. Shocked, sickened and enraged at what he had found – the first thing that had struck him was the sickly sweet smell of burned human flesh hanging heavy in the air – Galitzine had been an overnight convert to the pressing need to hunt down the Nazi war criminals.

Now he was here at Villa Degler, at Lieutenant Colonel Franks' urging, bringing both good and bad news. The bad news was the coming disbandment of the SAS, which by then was very much official, and had an air of absolute, nail-in-the-coffin finality about it. An 'Urgent Memorandum' had been issued by the War Office, which read: 'It has been decided to disband the Special Air Services Regiment . . . Disbandment will commence on 5 Oct. 45 and will be completed by 16 Nov. 45 . . . Complete disbandment will be reported to the War Office.'

Free-wheeling, free-spirited and unorthodox, the SAS had rarely proved popular with those in high places, and for the very reasons that had made it such a spectacular success waging war behind enemy lines. Indeed, Winston Churchill was one of its few dedicated and unrelenting backers. But in that July's general election Churchill had been voted out of power, and so the SAS's greatest benefactor was no longer in an unassailable position to safeguard the unit's future. In short order, the naysayers had got their way and the axe had come down. Of course, disbandment was made all the easier in that the SAS had been so secret. There had been precious little news reporting of their daring operations and few people had even heard of the unit, so who was there to object to their passing? There was hardly likely to be a public outcry.

While work had already started on destroying the SAS's most sensitive files, questions had been raised about a certain bespoke unit working overseas. 'Will you please say in the case of Major Barkworth and his team what was the originating authority for dispatch and to what headquarters or unit are they accredited,' wrote the War Office, in a letter dated 29 September. Franks had little intention of answering, or at least not in any direct fashion. Instead, with Galitzine's help, he intended that the entire Villa Degler team would go dark – becoming a secret, deniable and covert unit, one that officially did not exist.

In the Villa Degler's plush drawing room, and with a bottle of spirits set on the polished wooden table between them, Barkworth and Galitzine plotted. Around the room sat Rhodes and others, one man using his Commando knife to slice off hunks of bread, as the candlelight flickered around the walls and a smog of cigarette smoke hung thick in the air, conspiratorially. Galitzine explained that Franks had paid him a visit, in light of the coming disbandment of the SAS. 'I'm going to ask you a very big favour,' Franks had told Galitzine. 'Is there any means by which you can keep this team going?' By 'this team' he meant the Villa Degler outfit, and Franks – who was 'extremely well connected' – had made it clear he had backing from the very top.

Churchill was a keen proponent of seeking retribution amongst the guilty across Europe. He was a die-hard backer of the SAS's Nazi-hunting team, and, with the assistance of his son, Randolph, he was determined to ensure that their operations continued unhindered. In short, it was inconceivable that they should let the SAS war crimes hunters die. Galitzine proposed that Barkworth and his men would drop from the record, ceasing to exist. He intended to 'hide' them amidst the post-war chaos and confusion. Galitzine was well placed to do so. Under public pressure following the horrors of the liberation of Belsen, the War Office had belatedly founded its own war crimes investigations team. It operated out of 20 Eaton Square, a grand Georgian building just a stone's throw from Buckingham Palace, under the cumbersome title of 'Adjutant-General's Branch 3 – Violation of the Laws and Usages of War' – or AG3-VW for short.

Captain Galitzine was a key figure at AG3-VW, and Barkworth and his team would henceforth be – secretly and covertly – controlled from there. Galitzine would massage budgets, equipment, transport and even personnel out of an unsuspecting War Office, which was still very much in post-war turmoil. Even as the SAS was disbanded and seemingly consigned to the dustbin of history, in Germany Barkworth and his team would continue to operate as if they had every right to be there, wearing full SAS regalia, while a radio operator working from the roof of Eaton Square would be the link to their secret headquarters.

Galitzine held Barkworth in the highest esteem, recognising him to be 'a man of enterprise and resource, who knew Germany well, talked the language like a native and was endowed with a complete disregard for higher authority. He started with the scantiest of evidence, persisted when others would have given up, and finally succeeded in such an uncanny way that British, French and Americans alike christened him "the Lawrence of Occupied Germany."' Come what may, it was imperative that his mission should continue.

There was one other key aspect to the plan. Quietly, the fight-back against the scrapping of the SAS had already begun. A Regimental Association had been formed, with Churchill as its patron, David Stirling as its president, Franks as its chairman, and Paddy Mayne as vice president, amongst others. Prime amongst its objectives was this: 'To provide a means by which the Regiment can keep in touch with one another and maintain *esprit de corps*.' Prior to the war, Colonel Franks had served as the manager of the Hyde Park Hotel (today's Mandarin Oriental), in Knightsbridge, London. He was returning as the managing director, now that the SAS was 'no more'. From there he planned to run a shadow SAS headquarters, 'requisitioning' a couple of rooms from which to do so.

Churchill, Stirling, Franks and others were determined that come what may, the SAS would rise again, phoenix-like, from the ashes. Barkworth's team was a key element of their survival plan, and they should expect to get the odd message on Hyde Park Hotel notepaper, from Franks. Wearing the distinctive SAS beret and cap badge, Barkworth's team would operate in the shadows until the time was right for the regiment to be re-formed, thus keeping its memory and spirit very much alive.

'They weren't mercenaries,' Galitzine would remark. 'They were being paid by the War Office; we were paying them alright.' But by October 1945 only a handful of those in the know were even aware of the existence of this unit, which would become known as 'the Secret Hunters'.

On 21 September 1945 the Belgian Independent Parachute Company (5 SAS) – which consisted mostly of Belgian volunteers – was subsumed into that nation's armed forces; days later the French SAS regiments also left the SAS family; and on 6 October, 1 and 2 SAS paraded before their commanding officer for what they believed would be the last time. No one knew why special forces were being got rid of, and so decisively and so quickly. It was simply a case of *thank you very much, you're on your way.* Men who had fought together and bled together for years swapped addresses, exchanged signature books and bade their farewells.

George 'Bebe' Daniels – one of the SAS's original training instructors, a tough, no-nonsense individual – handed his notebook to a distinctive, redheaded individual: Ginger Jones. In it Jones scribbled: 'Let's hurry up and get outta here, because I'm going to blow the bloody lot, Cheerio, Bebe, and all the best.' It typified the overarching, uncomprehending sense of loss felt by all. *Is this what it all came down to? Is this what it had all been for?* Fortunately, perhaps, Serge Vaculik missed the collapse of the SAS; this falling apart. He was in France, hobbling on his wounded leg with the aid of a stick and recuperating at his family's Brittany home. Little did they know it yet, but for each of these two men who burned for a reckoning, justice was coming.

Regardless of the snuffing out of the SAS, the Secret Hunters continued their work. If anything, they relished their newfound 'black' role. Now they could truly spread their wings, released as they were from all official constraints. Shortly the hunt would reach as far south as Italy, where SAS Captain Henry Parker would track the killers of several men, who had been captured on a sabotage mission behind the lines. Parker would demonstrate that old habits die hard. 'It is now two in the morning and I've been working the last two days on the Barkworth system . . . a mixture of whisky, Benzedrine and no sleep,' he would report to Franks, at his Hyde Park headquarters.

Even as Galitzine's Eaton Square office issued a missive, claiming that 'Major Barkworth will be winding up the investigation during December,' and 'Confirmed we agree disbandment of Major Barkworth's team,' the Secret Hunters were actually recruiting. By the turn of the year, Barkworth would have a team of twenty-four working under him, and a second house was commandeered in Gaggenau to furnish extra accommodation. In the coming weeks they would trawl POW camps across Austria, Czechoslovakia and France, and into the Russian zone of occupation, in search of the war criminals. Mostly, they would seek little official permission, blagging their way in their war-weary jeeps, which were averaging some 200 miles per day.

Fresh recruit Sergeant Peter Gervase Drakes – a veteran both of SAS Operation Keystone in the Netherlands and of the liberation of Belsen – was set to work scouring the length and breadth of northern Germany. Drakes had only just turned twenty-two when he joined the Secret Hunters, having falsified his age when signing up to the army: he'd been just short of his fifteenth birthday, but had claimed to be several years older. Further north still, Barkworth had men in Norway, seeking some of the key players in atrocities in the Vosges, who were posing as the crew of a surrendered U-boat. Day by day the cellars of the Villa Degler were filling up.

One of the star captives was *Hauptscharführer* Peter Straub, the Natzweiler camp executioner. Straub had, by his own admission, 'put four million people up the chimney', at Auschwitz and then Natzweiler. At the latter camp his victims had included four female SOE agents, Andrée Borrel, Vera Leigh, Sonia Olschanezky and Diana Rowden – the first such to be executed by the Nazis. After being given a supposedly lethal injection, one of the four had been placed in the camp crematorium while still alive. She'd reached up and raked her nails across Straub's face, in a desperate last act of resistance. It was that which would lead Dusty Rhodes to Straub.

Barkworth had been given an address in Mannheim. The city lay some 60 miles north of Gaggenau, inside the American zone. Knowing all systems were leaky, Rhodes took to his ageing jeep in the dead of night, flitting through darkened back streets and circumventing all checkpoints, dodging heaps of rubble and bomb craters. Upon his arrival at 1 a.m., the heavily armed SAS sergeant climbed the steps at the address, rapping on the door of the apartment. A woman answered, clearly surprised and shocked to find a British soldier calling at this hour. Behind her Rhodes spied a figure that just *had* to be Straub. Much as the man might wave fake papers under Rhodes's nose, the SAS sergeant was not to be denied. Straub 'still had the marks of that woman's fingernails' on his face. Still protesting his innocence, he was bundled aboard the jeep at gunpoint and whisked away to the Villa Degler's cells.

Rhodes was quite ready to fight fire with fire, at one point noting: 'Running and screaming by party who turned traitor on Sgt Neville's party – a few rounds from T SMG soon brought them to their senses.' 'T SMG' stood for the Thompson submachine gun – the 'Tommy gun' so popular with SOE agents,

Commandos and SAS alike. Sergeant Neville was one of the eight SAS who'd been in Lieutenant David Dill's party, the rear guard taken captive in the Vosges. Dill, an officer, had been separated from his men, and had ended up being shot at Gaggenau. Sergeant Neville and his fellow captives had been driven into a patch of remote woodland in the Vosges, and executed. The last to die had turned to his captors and told them simply: 'We were good men.'

Following the arrest of Straub, Rhodes's next note read: 'Dr Rhode Natzweiler.' Werner Rhode, the concentration camp doctor who had administered the supposedly lethal injections, had been tracked to the US zone of occupation. Working to a relentless and frenetic schedule, Rhodes and his team hunted down *Oberscharführer* (SS Company Leader) Max Kessler, who was wanted for the shooting and alleged burning alive of three SAS men in the Vosges. He was discovered hiding in a laundry basket in the cellar of a relative's home.

As the weeks flew by, Dusty Rhodes realised how many 'war crimes . . . were committed not only to SAS, but to Americans, Australians, New Zealanders – the reports on war crimes and the people who had suffered leads the SAS team into some bizarre places, also [to] some strange people'. No place proved stranger or more macabre than Strasbourg's main prison, where Rhodes was forced to inspect hundreds of body parts 'all preserved in formalin, in tanks', to ensure they weren't from any of their missing men. The bodies had been taken from Natzweiler and preserved by the Nazis in Strasbourg, as some kind of twisted 'medical' experiment.

But perhaps no undertaking was more bizarre than the snatch mission that Rhodes executed in the American zone, which would lead to Rhodes himself going into hiding. 'Fight in street,' Rhodes noted. 'This man . . . altered his rank and name and started work for the American legal department. Arrested when walking home. Dusty Rhodes put him on wanted list.' Again Rhodes had staked out the suspect's address covertly, arresting the wanted man as he walked home from the office. But as the captive had been working for the US authorities as a lawyer, and as the snatch mission had been executed with no clearance, Rhodes himself was forced to go into hiding, as the American sought to arraign him.

As for 'Stuka' Neuschwanger, the sadistic Nazi torturer and killer, Barkworth and Rhodes not only tracked him down, but they also took him back to the scene of his crimes – the Erlich Forest killings. There Barkworth forced him to look into the crater into which the bodies had tumbled – Major Reynolds, Captain Whately-Smith, Lieutenant Dill, Captain Gough and Troopers Griffin and Ashe, amongst twenty-two others. 'So, what do you feel now about the murders that took place here?' Barkworth demanded. When Neuschwanger refused to show the slightest hint of any remorse or regret, Rhodes cracked, unleashing a punch that knocked the SS lieutenant into the bottom of the crater. 'He was fortunate, because he was coming out again,' remarked Rhodes.

By the first months of 1946, dozens of the chief suspects of the Vosges killings had been dragged into the Villa Degler cells. By then Barkworth was tracking the killers of US airmen, French Resistance fighters, Commandos and Jedburgh team members, as well as the SAS – more than a hundred war crimes suspects in all. The more he studied the growing stacks of files, the more he realised there was one factor that bound them all together – the *Kommandobefehl*, Hitler's Commando Order.

'All the cases of War Crimes ... investigated by this team, have in one way or another derived from the Commando Order signed by Hitler on 18 Oct. 1942,' Barkworth noted.

How, he wondered, had such a thing come to pass, which was so obviously illegal, in a country that was otherwise so regimented? Many were the suspects who would use the Commando Order as the key plank of their defence: *they were only following orders from the Führer.* But 'only the slow-witted, the indifferent or the hidebound allowed reports of the capture of Commando men to be forwarded to Higher HQs,' reported Barkworth, knowing what would follow. Once such reports had been sent, 'the inexorable cogs of the German military machine, oiled with the emulsion of subservience and severe discipline, were set in motion by the touch of a button from above, and there was nothing to stop them.' Once a report was filed up the chain of command, the captives were basically dead men.

Barkworth calculated that a staggering number of men and women had fallen victim to the *Kommandobefehl.* 'In all, the death[s] of at least 160 British parachutists and Commando men ... have been a direct result of the Commando Order. Were the total of cases concerning Allied troops and the cloak and dagger British "Special Forces" to be added, the total would be over 250.' The ultimate responsibility lay at one individual's door. 'Perhaps the person most profoundly affected by Commando assaults was the Führer, who appeared to take them as a personal attack unworthily directed against himself. The war was his war, victory to be his victory, gained in the teeth of his generals and in spite of his people, who he was even then beginning to despise.'

The SAS major was also aware of the depths of subterfuge layered around the Commando Order, which suggested that its authors knew of its blatant illegality. In May 1943 the British government had protested to the German authorities about the killing of fourteen captured Commandos at Egersund, in Norway. They had been taken prisoner in November 1942, when their glider had crash-landed during Operation Freshman, an attempt to sabotage a vital part of Nazi Germany's nuclear programme. The protest resulted in an 'unseemly scramble' to formulate a suitable response, one to which 'Hitler gave directions for the main points' to be raised.

The Freshman raiders were British troops serving in full uniform and engaged in a military operation, but under the Commando Order they had been shot out of hand. The response from Nazi Germany involved creating a tissue of obfuscation and lies. 'The whole atmosphere that surrounded the production of this German answer was apprehensive, secretive and mendacious,' Barkworth noted. The *Kommandobefehl*'s authors spoke of how things 'could become very uncomfortable,' should the truth about the Commando Order get out.

Worse still, Barkworth himself had fallen victim to the falsehoods fabricated on high concerning the *Kommandobefehl*. When SAS Lieutenant James Quentin Hughes had escaped from captivity in Italy in May 1944, Barkworth had rightly treated his reports of being threatened under a 'Commando Order' with all due seriousness. He'd taken his concerns to London, but owing to the earlier Nazi lies and subterfuge over the Op Freshman victims, 'the sand lay thick in Whitehall's eyes'. The Nazi hierarchy had successfully duped London into believing that no such murderous *Kommandobefehl* might exist, and so Hughes's report was summarily dismissed.

Under the *Kommandobefehl*, prisoners – some of whom had

been wounded during the process of their capture – were to be done away with 'in circumstances which were as disgusting as they are obscure', Barkworth noted. Sadly, the issue of the Commando Order had begun to be taken seriously only 'when dead bodies of murdered prisoners had been found in France', as Allied troops had liberated that country. Rarely was that more the case than in the Noailles Wood killings, one of the files that sat most heavily on Barkworth's conscience, in his 'unsolved' ledger.

In the febrile atmosphere of the Villa Degler, anything was possible as far as Barkworth was concerned, especially when all leads had come to naught. Not only would no stone be left unturned, as Rhodes had promised, but no means was beyond bounds to hunt down the killers. At times when all seemed hopeless – and there had been many such times – Barkworth was happy to consult the spirits of the dead, to see if they might lend a hand. Galitzine had been caught up in one of Barkworth's Ouija board sessions, at first prudishly objecting to such a recourse, even in extremis.

'You can't mean you did this! I mean it's ridiculous,' Galitzine had objected.

'Well, why not?' Barkworth countered. 'If people were killed, I mean presumably they want to tell us what happened to them.'

Galitzine couldn't argue with the logic of that. That evening they set out the tools of the Ouija trade – numbered playing cards, the letters of the alphabet, plus the words 'yes' and 'no'. What the board told them that night would lead the Secret Hunters to more unmarked graves in the Vosges, and to another German posing as an innocent being unmasked by Barkworth and dragged into custody. Back in his Eaton Square offices, Galitzine would be upbraided most royally when the use of the Ouija board came to light. He was called before three senior War Office figures, some of the few who were 'in the know' about the Secret Hunters.

'How dare you do anything like this!' they remonstrated.

Galitzine held his ground. 'But sir, we've got two bodies and a prisoner.'

'Well, if you hadn't got two bodies and a prisoner you'd be court martialled,' they concluded, threateningly.

'He had a very open and enquiring mind,' Amy Crossland, Barkworth's daughter, would remark of her father, 'a willingness to examine all possibilities . . . including that of life after death . . . When I was a teenager I remember asking him about seances, and he said it was not an advisable thing to do as you never knew who you might get!' There spoke the voice of experience.

Fortunately, perhaps, Barkworth would need no help from beyond the grave to get his first break on the Noailles Wood case. While Kieffer – the mastermind of the Noailles Wood massacre, plus the murders of Captain Whately-Smith and Major Reynolds – had seemingly disappeared without trace, one of Kieffer's acolytes would fall into Barkworth's grasp, and all because he made the schoolboy error of returning to visit his wife and children. As Barkworth noted: 'The easiest Germans to find were those who stayed at home.'

For days on end and often wearing cunning disguises, Barkworth would have his men stake out the known addresses of his most wanted, in order to 'arrest him *bei Nacht und Nebel*' – by total surprise. That was how they got 'Stuka' Neuschwanger. Having heard that he'd been seen in Göppingen, a town in southern Germany, Barkworth and his team had removed their

SAS berets and regimental flashes, and dressed as locals. 'I wish you could have seen me,' Barkworth wrote to Galitzine, 'wandering around Göppingen in civilian clothes, with a pair of trousers belonging to the local chief of police, and which were big enough to hold me twice over.'

So it was that one of Kieffer's deputies blundered into Barkworth's clutches. 'Karl Haug of *Gruppe Kieffer* in 4 Civil Internee Camp Recklinghausen,' Barkworth reported via radio to the Secret Hunters' Eaton Square headquarters, having arrested the Gestapo man at the family home. 'Has given statement on shooting SAS Noailles in which he took part . . . Haug knowledgeable and willing witness.'

Haug, the former POW of the British from the First World War, was once again in British custody. Not only was he cooperating, but he was to prove the route via which to get to Kieffer. After their stint at Avenue Foch and then in the Vosges, SS *Sturmbannführer* Hans Josef Kieffer and *Hauptscharführer* Karl Haug had gone into hiding as the Third Reich had collapsed into fire and ruin. The two men had been childhood friends from when they'd been members of the same gymnastics club, and Haug was the godfather to one of Kieffer's children. After the war they had made some kind of unholy pact to help shield each other from the Allies. Thankfully, on Haug's side it proved far from unbreakable.

Under Barkworth's unflinching interrogation the full story began to emerge. After evacuating Paris – and having sent all of their prisoners, SOE agent Captain John Starr included, to all but certain death in the concentration camps – Kieffer had relocated his team to Strasbourg, just a few dozen miles east of the Vosges. From there, *Gruppe Kieffer* had done its bit on

Operation *Waldfest*, before retreating further into Germany itself. In Rosenfeld, a town in southern Germany, Kieffer was reunited with his wife and four children, who had been bombed out of their Karlsruhe home.

But with the collapse of the Reich, Kieffer had confronted his family one morning, telling them that this was goodbye. He'd left no clue as to where he was going, but was obviously running from the Allies and from justice. Together with Haug he'd headed for Garmisch-Partenkirchen, a quaint-looking ski town in southern Bavaria, right on the border with Austria. There they'd endeavoured to lie low, taking casual work as cleaners in hotels and the like. But eventually Haug, who had six children, felt compelled to return to his family, even though Kieffer warned him of the risk of being caught and forced to talk.

Sure enough, Haug was arrested at his home address, Horneburgerstrasse 110, in the town of Oer-Erkenschwick in northwest Germany, in the British zone of occupation. Haug's capture electrified London, or at least those charged by General Eisenhower and the Under-Secretary of State for War, Baron Croft, with bringing the Noailles Wood killers to justice.

'It is not unlikely that Haug will be able to give full details about the Gestapo,' declared a letter from the Judge Advocate General's office (JAG), the British military's dedicated legal service in London, 'and that his careful interrogation may throw some light on the murder at Noailles . . . These murders were particularly brutal and cold-blooded and so far all inquiries have produced a blank result, and much is hoped of the interrogation of Haug.'

In the spring of 1946 Haug underwent several interrogations, the results of which did not disappoint. He'd been a reluctant member of the Noailles Wood execution squad, and his words read more like a series of confessions, or a serial unburdening of his guilt. They would disclose 'fully the circumstances of the murders at Noailles, his own participation therein, and the names of other Germans who were implicated'.

Haug's testimony was the proverbial smoking gun.

Chapter 24

Haug began by explaining how he had ended up in the Gestapo, having been retired from the German armed forces in 1942, when he reached the 'age limit' for such service (forty-seven). A man of Haug's experience wouldn't be allowed to rest. He was soon called for a medical examination and 'was entered as "fit" for service with the police troops'. Haug was then given a choice of being posted either to a Gestapo team serving on the Eastern Front, or to the Paris unit run by his childhood friend, Kieffer. Unsurprisingly he chose the latter, taking up his post there on 28 July 1942.

Having detailed his route into the Gestapo, Haug described his role at Avenue Foch with disarming honesty as being a jack of all trades, 'but I greatly preferred it to lying in the muck somewhere on the Eastern Front'. He then proceeded to give the lowdown on the key players, including 'SS *Standartenführer* Dr Knochen ... SS *Hauptsturmführer* Dr Schmidt ... SS *Hauptsturmführer* Schnur ... SS *Untersturmführer* Dr Goetz ... SS *Unterscharführer* von Kapri ... SS *Obersturmführer* Ilgenfritz and SS *Sturmbannführer* Kieffer ... to whom I was directly subordinate'.

'During 1943 the Resistance movement in France grew stronger and stronger,' Haug recounted, which had led to more work for the Avenue Foch Gestapo. The *Funkspiel* teams 'listened daily to the wireless reports in French, and when there was an announcement that weapons were to be dropped at some place indicated, a number of men was immediately sent . . . I myself was very often detailed to do this.' As the amount of captured SOE equipment kept growing, 'the administration of the store of weapons, sabotage materials, radios, clothes . . . etc. which had been brought in, was entrusted to me by SS *Sturmbannführer* Kieffer'.

Turning to the capture of SAS Captain Garstin and his men on 5 July '44, Haug explained how 'we showed our lights repeatedly . . . the guide lights for the pilot, to let him know at which point he was to drop the drums. For this purpose three men each had a white or a red lamp (pocket lamp or torch).' Of course, it wasn't just supplies that would plummet out of the heavens from the belly of the Stirling. 'Late in the night a plane came and circled around the lights and then dropped something. We saw at once that there were not only drums hanging from the parachutes, but also men.'

Following the SAS patrol's capture, Haug's next contact with the prisoners wasn't until 8 August, when he was ordered to ride on the truck as one of their escorts. And it wasn't until marching the prisoners towards their place of execution that Haug had realised he was there to kill them. As Jones and Vaculik had broken away, 'everyone began to shoot; we each had a sub-machine-gun', Haug recounted. 'I found it impossible to shoot at these men with whom I had formerly been on such friendly terms. Three of the prisoners fell where they stood. The next two ran about 30 metres into the wood and they too crumpled up. Searching and swearing now began on a grand scale.'

Haug listed all those who had been involved in the killings and their roles, describing how Schnur, the commander of the murder squad, had had a 'hysterical crying fit from sheer anger', fearing the coming wrath from Berlin for the botched executions. But of course, the retreat from Paris had rapidly taken precedence, rendering Schnur's fears immaterial. On 7 March 1946 Haug scribbled his signature beneath the final, telling phrase: 'I have made the above statement voluntarily and without compulsion.'

Things began to move very quickly, now that the guilty parties had been exposed. Ilgenfritz was found to be in Allied custody. As a former member of the SS, he'd been arrested on 10 November 1945, at his home in Glashütte, a town in eastern Germany. In his initial interrogation report, Ilgenfritz had revealed nothing about his role in the Noailles Wood killings, stating only that he was 'in Paris and in charge of all SD and Gestapo transport'. But following Haug's bombshell statement, Ilgenfritz's file was marked in red 'For Special Interrogation', and orders were issued for his 'immediate removal to London District Cage'.

The London Cage was a top-secret detention centre run by MI9, housed in numbers 6–8 Kensington Palace Gardens. By March 1946 Haug was already there, and that opened up a whole world of possibilities. That month, Serge Vaculik received a letter from the JAG's office, inviting him to London. It came as a bolt from the blue, especially since Vaculik had spent the last several months recovering from his wartime injuries, and rebutting an unfortunate attempt by the French authorities to charge him with fighting on the side of the enemy.

When Vaculik had escaped from German captivity, following his capture at Dunkirk, he'd spent various periods in (Vichy) French, Spanish, Portuguese and British custody, as he endeavoured to get to somewhere where he could continue the good fight. Those stretches of imprisonment had come back to bite him. Called before a French court martial and accused of serving in a *Waffengattung* – a German military unit – Vaculik had to produce his British service records, and a note on his 'subsequent services in the Resistance', to prove how things had been very much the opposite. It was all explained away as being a case of mistaken identity.

When the JAG's bulky envelope had popped into his letterbox, it had come as a wholly unexpected – but very welcome – surprise. The letter explained how 'diligently pursued' had been the 'murder of Captain Garstin and 4 other members of 1 SAS', and suggested that 'the circumstances of the brutal murder of your 5 comrades will still be fresh in your mind'. It went on to explain that Haug had been arrested. A copy of his statement was enclosed. There were also photos of Kieffer and Schnur, together with this note: 'Do you recognise either of the men depicted in these photographs?'

The letter stressed how important it was for the suspects to be positively identified, and how Vaculik and Jones, as the sole survivors of the massacre, were the only ones who might do so. 'I sincerely hope that you will be willing to assist in bringing those responsible for the murder or your comrades to justice,' wrote the JAG, inviting Vaculik to London with that in mind. 'I may say I have had some difficulty in tracing you and I trust you will receive this letter. I should be grateful for an early reply.'

Vaculik's response reflected the relief and elation he felt at learning that somehow, life had been breathed back into the Noailles Wood case. 'I will never forget those frightful days, and I am at your obligation because I want [to ensure] that justice is done against those criminals.' He pointed out how 'Captain Garstin was my friend and I liked the other boys, and sometimes

336

when I am thinking about it I shiver and must say that I am lucky and grateful to be alive.' Vaculik confirmed that he recognised Kieffer and Schnur from the photos, adding: 'I still have the handcuffs. Must I bring them too?'

A similar JAG letter had also been sent to Ginger Jones, at his address at 3 Pagefield Street, Wigan. It stressed that with Vaculik in France, it was urgent that the former SAS man should go to London to identify Haug, so 'that justice may be done in this cold-blooded case of murder'. Jones replied that he was more than willing to do as asked, and he was duly issued with a slip of paper, giving him access to the London Cage: 'The bearer of this letter is Mr T Jones who I think will be in a position to identify Haug. Would you kindly allow Mr. Jones to see Haug for this purpose.'

Issued with a rail pass, Jones travelled to London to be the first of the Noailles Wood survivors to come face to face with his would-be executioner. A month later, Vaculik also made it to the London Cage, by which time Ilgenfritz was incarcerated there, alongside Haug. Vaculik recognised Haug instantly as the man who had given them cigarettes during the ride to their place of execution. As for Ilgenfritz, while he had conveniently 'grown a heavy beard and moustache', he had already confessed to his role in the shooting, his defence being that he'd only been obeying orders. Ilgenfritz also revealed the name of the death truck's driver, SS *Oberscharführer* Fritz Hildemann – meaning that the last of the execution squad had finally been identified.

Of course, the one other surviving eyewitness to Operation Marbois – Kieffer's codename for the 5 July capture and all that had followed – was Lieutenant Wiehe, but he was no longer on hand to help. In September 1945 the War Office had cleared the final hurdle to his return to Mauritius. A British nurse, sister Kathleen Ruscoe, who had lost all her family during the Blitz, was given permission to accompany Wiehe on the long sea journey, to provide medical care.

In December '45, she and Wiehe had sailed for Mauritius via South Africa. The *Johannesburg Star* newspaper reported: 'Parachutist's Return. Lieut. Hyacinthe Wiehe . . . was dropped into Paris the day the Allies landed in France and was completely paralysed when he received a burst of machine-gun fire in the back . . . Lieut. Wiehe, who is 29 years of age . . . was serving with the First Special Air Service when he was dropped into France. Although he had received grave injuries . . . he was questioned by the Gestapo and badly handled by them.'

Not long after Wiehe's return to Mauritius, the SAS Association published its second ever newsletter, on the front page of which was a report about the Secret Hunters, under the heading 'War Crimes Trial'. 'It had been hoped that Major Barkworth would have been able to write a short summary,' but 'a trial is proceeding at present and Major Barkworth has not had time'. Barkworth was indeed extremely busy. With the SAS having been disbanded for months now, the newsletter also detailed the fortunes of many members, including this: 'Lieut. Wiehe should now be safely installed at his home address which is Floreal, Mauritius, and would be glad to hear from old friends.'

Amongst the first to write would be Ginger Jones. His letter of 25 August 1946 began: 'I read in the News Letter of how you wished to hear from old friends – I do hope I'm included as one of those.' After providing a little personal news, Jones continued: 'Remember the watch you lent me for our operation – I tried to tell you when I came to hospital (at Leatherhead) to see you . . .

I kept that watch hidden until the very last day of our imprisonment, then when changing from uniform into civvies one of the guards saw it and took it away from me, that was the one thing I hated to lose and believe me I'm ever so sorry. I tried my best to keep it out of sight.'

Having apologised for the loss of that precious watch, Jones ended the letter with this: 'I'm expecting to go over to Germany on the trials, to give evidence.'

It was a poignant last line. It wasn't just a wristwatch that Kieffer's Gestapo had taken: it was Lieutenant Wiehe's youth and his physical abilities. Wheelchair-bound for life, he would die prematurely from the effects of his injuries. The Gestapo had also ended the lives of Captain Patrick Garstin, MC, Sergeant Varey and Troopers Paddy Barker, Young and Walker, and the many other victims that Kieffer and his team had dispatched into the *Nacht und Nebel*, SAS Major Reynolds and Captain Whately-Smith amongst them. For all, the time for a reckoning was long overdue. And while Lieutenant Wiehe would be absent from the trial, the very fact of his survival would prove key to its findings.

By now, the summer of 1946, Barkworth and his team were closing in on the last suspects. In July, they'd got one of their most-wanted – Schnur, the Avenue Foch interrogator-in-chief and the commander of the Noailles Wood execution party. In contrast to Haug, he seemed to show not a shred of guilt or remorse upon his capture. For Schnur, it had all been about following orders. Under interrogation by Barkworth, he complained that even as he'd read out the death sentence 'from the Führer and Commander-in-Chief', Garstin and his men 'undertook, in my opinion, a previously agreed upon attempt to escape'. Schnur had 'sent off a blaze of fire after the escaping [men]'.

With Haug, Ilgenfritz and Schnur in the bag, Barkworth turned to tracking the last of the SS men. Unfortunately, Alfred von Kapri would never stand trial. Though Barkworth had been sent an arrest report for a twenty-five-year-old SS *Rottenführer* Kapri, working as a 'kitchen helper' in the German town of Würzburg, that man had since disappeared. Instead, Barkworth discovered that von Kapri was believed 'to have been murdered and thrown into the Tegernsee', a lake in Bavaria, not so far from Garmisch-Partenkirchen where Kieffer and Haug had gone to ground. It was unclear exactly who had murdered von Kapri, or seen fit to dump his corpse in the depths of the lake. *Hauptsturmführer* Schmidt, the chief executioner at the Noailles Wood, was also believed to be dead, killed on the Eastern Front in the final months of the war.

With Kieffer, the number one most wanted, the Secret Hunters had precious few leads to go on. One of the reasons Kieffer had proved so hard to track down was that none of his subordinates appeared willing to help. Kieffer seemed to inspire such intense loyalty that even when facing a Barkworth interrogation, no one would shop him or even incriminate him. Yes, they argued, Kieffer had sent dozens to the concentration camps, but he never imagined they would face terrible torture and death there. It was Haug who finally let slip the vital clue: as he had gone to ground in Garmisch-Partenkirchen, possibly Kieffer might also be found there, he suggested.

In October 1946 the Secret Hunters fired up their ageing jeeps and set off on the drive south to the Bavarian ski resort. It was a long shot, but it was the only lead they had. Through snow-capped craggy mountains and dense pine forests they headed, until they reached the town itself, where they found chocolate-box streets dusted with snow. With his good friend Haug long departed, Kieffer had felt certain that sooner or later, the Allies would catch up with him. Maybe a part of him had wanted to get caught. Either way, he'd made little real effort to hide. He'd even registered with the town hall under his real name, except that he'd removed one 'f', so as 'Hans Kiefer'. The Secret Hunters could barely believe it: the former Gestapo chief might as well have walked around the streets with a huge pair of 'SS' runes pinned to his back.

From the town hall they traced 'Kiefer' to one of Garmisch-Partenkirchen's many hotels, where he was working as a caretaker. Upon his capture and unmasking, Kieffer seemed quite sanguine about it all: relaxed, almost. There was not much about him to suggest a man who was a fugitive from justice. The reason for this soon became clear: Kieffer did not believe himself guilty of any crimes. After all, he was only following orders from Berlin. With the dozens of SOE agents that he had dispatched to the concentration camps, how was he to know what dark fate they would face? He had sent no one directly to their deaths. No one had died at Kieffer's own hand.

But of course there was the one, glaring exception: the murder of SAS Captain Garstin and his men. It said much that it was Barkworth and his team – an SAS war crimes unit – that had resolutely kept on his trail and cornered him. As Kieffer knew well, there was a living witness to those botched executions – the SAS man who had broken free. (Kieffer believed that only one man had escaped, as that was what Schnur had told him.) If Kieffer had to face *him* in the witness box, what chance did he – and his Gestapo brethren – stand? For those murders in the Noailles Wood on 9 August 1944, a part of Kieffer feared very much that he would hang.

On 29 November 1946 Kieffer sat facing Barkworth for his full interrogation. The SAS major had left the man to 'stew' for several weeks in the Villa Degler basement, to help convince him to talk. In his statement, Kieffer would certify that 'I have put down the events in the "Marbois" case as they have come back to my memory after several weeks of reflection.' As he did with all his captives, Barkworth began by warning the former Gestapo chief that he was 'not compelled' to talk 'and that any statement he might wish to make would be taken down in writing and might be used in evidence'.

Whatever qualms Kieffer may have had about speaking, he would learn that in Barkworth he had truly met his match. He could be 'quite fearsome – verbally – when in full flight,' Amy Crossland would remark of her father. 'His skill in German language was a huge factor in obtaining information/securing confessions – not only his fluency . . . but also because he could sound like a German, and I think those he interrogated may well have found this very unsettling and unnerving. And because Pa didn't need to use an interpreter, this would have made his questioning much more effective and direct and relentless . . . the person being questioned hadn't got extra time . . . to think and plan his answers.'

In many ways, Barkworth used the same tricks of the trade as Kieffer had employed at 84 Avenue Foch, though there were no threats of beatings, semi-drownings or worse at the Villa Degler. Barkworth utterly eschewed all such violence, and in any case found it unnecessary to secure results. At one stage he'd been after a certain piece of information, which no one would divulge. He gathered a few of his captives and shared with them some oranges, which then were in precious short supply, of course. As they chatted away over the rare feast, Barkworth artfully steered the conversation to where he needed it to be, and one of them unwittingly let slip the information he sought.

In many ways, Kieffer's statement to Barkworth would simply confirm what those before him had already divulged, but while much had been hinted and guessed at previously, now it had the absolute ring of authority. Kieffer confirmed that his key role at Avenue Foch had been 'the execution of radio deception plans with fake messages' and that Operation Marbois, the capture of Captain Garstin and his stick, had come about 'during the course of a radio deception plan' – a *Funkspiel*.

When Garstin and his men were brought into Avenue Foch, Kieffer's prime interest had been to assess if a new *Funkspiel* might be possible, as a result of their capture. But with Lieutenant Wiehe, the team's radio operator, so grievously injured, nothing was doing, at least in the short term. Even so, careful study of the captured maps and communications kit 'provided a certain amount of information concerning those SAS groups that had already made an appearance', and Kieffer ordered a 'detailed interrogation'. By unleashing Schnur and von Kapri on the SAS captives, Kieffer had hoped to glean clues to lead him to other SAS teams already operating in France.

The final report on the captives' interrogations was dispatched to RSHA Berlin for *Sturmbannführer Kriminaldirektor* (Major Chief Inspector) Horst Kopkow's attention, amongst others. Kieffer's report revealed the SAS's teams targets: 'demolitions of railway tracks, road engineering and river regulation works . . . in the area south of Paris'. No one, it seemed, had breathed a word about SABU-70's real objective, to sabotage Étampes airbase. By way of response, Kopkow ordered 'that the SAS men should be segregated while in custody', and that all decisions regarding their fate would rest exclusively with Berlin.

With Allied forces advancing on Paris, Kieffer had pressed Kopkow repeatedly for a decision as to what was to be done with the men in his custody. The response, when finally it came, was that they were to be put to death on authority of the Führer, and that prior to 'execution, they were to be dressed in civilian clothes'. As the matter was absolutely top secret, Kieffer had had no option but to use his own men to carry out the shootings. 'The escape of one of the prisoners was truthfully mentioned,' Kieffer told Barkworth, and was reported up the chain of command to Berlin.

Kieffer rounded off his statement by emphasising that no one had been happy about what had transpired. 'Even on the days following the execution, I only mentioned very little concerning details to the men of my section who had taken part. Obviously, it was disagreeable to any one of them to have to speak about it.' Soon, though, Kieffer and his men were going to have to talk about it in very great detail, standing trial as suspected war criminals.

Barkworth combined characteristics that might at first appear contradictory: he was a ruthless and eccentric rule-breaker, whose tenacity on the hunt was legendary, yet at the same time he was a deeply humane individual, determined to see fair and proper justice being done. That Christmas, with the trial for the Noailles Wood killings fast approaching, he allowed his prime suspect a family visit. Hans Kieffer's wife, Margarete, had died of stomach cancer while her husband had been in hiding, so it was his youngest daughter, Hildegard, then aged nineteen, who travelled to see him. Upon arrival, Hildegard found her father's 'host', Barkworth, 'kind and reassuring'.

In many ways the Kieffer family had been close. During a visit home from Paris in 1943, he'd given his son, also named Hans, a gift – a trophy of his work. It was a hunting knife with the initials 'PC' engraved upon the hilt. It had belonged to SOE agent Peter Churchill, who'd been captured in France in April 1943, becoming one of Kieffer's captives. Peter Churchill had claimed to be related to Winston Churchill, and his captors had largely believed him – hence the trophy that Kieffer had delivered to his son. That simple ploy – achieved by a coincidental shared surname – would help Peter Churchill survive the war.

Since his capture, Kieffer had written often to his daughter Hildegard, addressing her as 'Meine liebe Moggele' – my dear squirrel – and he had a photo of her pinned to the wall of his cell. During her visit, Hildegard found her father quietly confident, especially as he didn't think that he had done anything wrong. His main concern seemed to be whether he would have his best suit ready in time for the hearing. Just prior to departure for his trial, Kieffer would remove the photo of Hildegard from the wall of his cell and ask for it to be mailed to his daughter, together with a note. It read, somewhat presciently, 'Moggele, I bless you in my last hour. Your father.'

Repeatedly, Barkworth had asked for the Noailles Wood case to be postponed. He'd done so to buy time in which to hunt down the full cast of suspects. He did so again now, at the cusp of the year. In Britain, the winter of 1946–7 would prove the harshest of the twentieth century: it was so cold and snowbound that families went to bed without food and suffering endless power cuts. In Germany, coal mines stopped working, factories closed, homes remained unheated and families were unfed, as transport across the nation ground to a halt.

But the Secret Hunters remained stubbornly active, as Barkworth sought one last suspect to stand trial for the 'deplorable incident' – the Noailles Wood killings – without whom he feared the entire case might collapse: SS *Standartenführer* Dr Helmut Knochen, who had been Kieffer's immediate superior at Avenue Foch, at least until he'd been accused of being part of the Operation Valkyrie conspiracy, the attempted assassination of Hitler in July '44. If Knochen failed to take the stand, it could 'cause extreme difficulties for the Noailles trial', Barkworth warned. The other accused would be able to claim it was all Knochen's fault, so why wasn't he on trial, especially as he was known to be in Allied custody?

For some time now Knochen had been held in France, where he was slated to stand trial for the deportation of thousands of Jews and French Resistance figures to their deaths in the concentration camps. As Barkworth was the first to admit, 'the French have an indisputable right to arraign Dr Knochen', but he remained a crucial figure for the Noailles trial. Barkworth proposed a solution: a trade. In British custody were Goetz – the Avenue Foch *Funkspiel* whizz – plus two other Gestapo men wanted by the French. Barkworth suggested that if they were handed over to the French, 'I take it ... our Allies would be willing to lend us Dr Knochen for short duration'.

In making that proposal, Barkworth also made it clear he hoped 'to be able to give some return for the help which my regiment received while it was operating in France'. The appeal worked. On 21 February 1947 Barkworth sat down to interrogate Helmut Herbert Christian Heinrich Knochen, who had been handed over from French custody. Amongst other things, Knochen was able to confirm how he'd been punished as a result of the Valkyrie accusations: 'I was dismissed from the position of Commander on 25 August on Himmler's orders'. Stripped of his rank, he was 'called up to the Waffen SS as an SS Grenadier (= private soldier)'.

Knochen's role in Operation Marbois – the SABU-70 stick's entrapment – had been marginal: at most he'd been a conduit between Kopkow in Berlin and Kieffer at Avenue Foch. But still his statement fleshed out some key details. He stated that he'd played an active role in challenging the *Kommandobefehl* after D-Day, arguing that a fast-moving front line made it impossible to implement the order on the ground. Hitler had responded by decreeing an arbitrary line, beyond which all captured parachutists were to be executed. As a result, Knochen argued, 'an immediate execution ought to have taken place' of the SABU-70 captives. 'I did not give such orders.'

By failing to do so, Knochen maintained that he had tried to buy the captives time. Once Kopkow and the RSHA took over, that had 'tied my hands'. As Garstin and his men had been seized as part of a *Funkspiel* operation, that made them automatically Berlin's concern – 'everything in this sphere had to be reported to Berlin at once'. And if Knochen had tried to resist the execution order, the consequences would have been dire: 'No one would have been able to have suppressed such a direct order of the Supreme Commander, or could have dared not to have such orders carried out.'

In case Barkworth had missed what would be the key thrust of Knochen's – indeed all of the accused's – defence, he rounded off his statement thus: 'Neither I, nor one of my subordinates, could have acted otherwise, without being condemned to death immediately.' Thanks to Knochen, it was crystal clear what all were going to argue at trial.

On pain of death, they had simply been carrying out orders from the highest authority in the land.

Chapter 25

The trial of the accused would take place from 7 to 14 March 1947, in the banqueting hall of the Zoological Gardens in the city of Wuppertal, in west-central Germany, within the British zone of occupation. It was presided over by six military judges. Barkworth, Rhodes and team would be billeted in an admin block adjacent to the courtroom, with the accused held in the local jail. Barkworth made it clear that he wanted the prisoners watched closely, especially when being transported to and from the court. 'Do not wish to have to look for them again,' he remarked, pointedly.

It was approaching two years since the work of the Secret Hunters had begun, and the coming trial would prove extraordinary on many levels – not least of which was that a foremost SS and Gestapo war crimes suspect would appear for the prosecution, giving evidence against his former comrades, and a high-profile SOE renegade, or war hero (depending on your view of things), would appear for the defence, giving evidence in support of his former captors.

A week before the case opened the star witnesses arrived in Wuppertal, in preparation for seeing those who had 'tortured us and murdered our comrades' stand trial. It was the first time that Serge Vaculik and Ginger Jones had seen each other since the end of the war. Jones had flown in from England, and his plane had almost crash-landed on the frozen runway. Even so, the reunion after so many months was a joyful one.

'Ginger!' Vaculik cried, giving the former SAS trooper a hug. 'Dear old pal, it's good to see you again.' Jones had been busted back to the rank of private – 'trooper' in SAS parlance of the time – for some misdemeanour, just prior to the disbandment of the SAS.

'Good old Frenchy!' Jones enthused. 'Damn glad to see you again too.'

But as they began to contemplate exactly why they had returned to Germany, their spirits waned. 'We were no longer . . . two light-hearted parachutists,' Vaculik remarked. 'We were sombre and silent.' Worse still, 'Ginger no longer swore whenever he opened his mouth, and that was a bad sign. His red hair seemed washed out and his once gleaming eyes had lost their sparkle . . . The war had turned him into an old man.'

The trial opened at 10.30 a.m. on 7 March, with the six accused – Knochen, Kieffer, Schnur, Ilgenfritz, Haug and Hildemann – being led in, and taken to a bench opposite the dock. The presiding judge was Lieutenant Colonel H. Bentley, OBE, a man who had previous form. In October 1946 he'd headed up a war crimes trial in which eight Germans were accused of ill-treating British prisoners at Stalag XI-B Fallingbostel, a POW camp in northwest Germany. Under Bentley sat four other British military judges and one French. Together with the six accused – all dressed in civilian clothes – sat their six German defence lawyers. There were also legal clerks, interpreters and at least eight armed guards.

Jones and Vaculik were seated in the witness gallery, just 'a few feet away from men who had murdered our comrades and so nearly murdered us'. It had taken two and a half years and a string of near-miracles to get to this point, where they could look the killers in the eye, knowing or at least hoping that justice was about to be done. But from the appearance of the defendants – Schnur in particular – convictions looked unlikely. As they chatted and joked with their lawyers that first morning, there was a high-spirited arrogance about the former SS men that was galling.

The six accused were facing charges of murder, and all were pleading not guilty. After the prosecution's opening address Vaculik was the first to be called to the stand. Under questioning, he described SABU-70's mission and their departure from Britain in 'full battle dress, a steel helmet and a beret. The objective was in the neighbourhood of Paris.' Point one had been well made: they had deployed in full uniform on a bona fide military operation. He went on to describe the ambush at the DZ: 'Some shots came from a wood. I lay down and took a rifle and a grenade from my pack.'

Vaculik spoke about the firefight, his capture, the wounded men being brought in, the incarceration at Avenue Foch, the interrogations and the fact that they were kept 'handcuffed all the time'. He explained how they'd been forced to change into civilian clothes, and the lies about the prisoner exchange. Then he recounted the moment of their departure to the Noailles Wood, and how he 'saw the accused, Schnur, by the truck. We were given sandwiches and told we were going on a long journey.' He told about the drive to the woodland, and being formed up for execution: 'The order of the line was Jones, Captain Garstin, myself, Varey, Barker, Walker and Young.'

'The Germans took up a line six paces away,' Vaculik continued.

'Opposite Jones was von Kapri. Opposite Captain Garstin was the accused Haug, whom I identify. Opposite me was accused Schnur, whom I identify. Next to Schnur was a German whom I think was Ilgenfritz, but I am not quite sure. Accused Schnur read from a piece of paper. Von Kapri translated it into English.' Vaculik went on to recount the shooting, and his escape, in as firm and commanding tones as he had started. By the time he was finished, the six accused didn't seem quite as haughty or self-assured any more.

The second witness was called – 'Mr Thomas Jones'. As Jones began speaking, he told a similar tale to Vaculik, but if anything his testimony proved even more powerful. He remembered particularly the ride in the death truck: 'Accused Schnur, whom I identify, was by the truck. Accused Haug, whom I identify, was in the truck. Accused Hildemann, whom I identify, got out of the truck when we reached the field . . . I helped Captain Garstin out of the truck, as he was sick. Accused Hildemann said, "Schnell! Schnell!" Captain Garstin was very weak and ill. No consideration was shown to him.'

'Accused Hildemann accompanied Captain Garstin and me up to the firing point,' Jones continued. 'He was armed. I do not know if he was in the line of Germans firing at us.' Jones then told of his desperate escape under fire, his fleeing through the woodland and taking sanctuary with the help of locals in a nearby French village. His words, simply and plainly told as any soldier would, proved electrifying.

On behalf of Schnur, defence lawyer von Bruch posed a question about how the SAS men had been supposed to make contact with Britain. 'The only means we had of communicating with England upon landing was by pigeon,' Jones answered. 'Our job was to do what we had to do and get out. We were not told in England that we might not be treated as prisoners of war,' he added, pointedly.

Apart from that one paltry line of questioning, there was no further cross-examination. It was almost as if the German defence team had decided to try to get Vaculik and Jones off the witness stand as quickly as possible. In a sense it was hardly surprising. Their eyewitness accounts had proved absolutely devastating. Rarely if ever had those facing a top-secret SS and Gestapo execution squad survived to tell the tale, and then to face their would-be killers in a court of law.

The third witness on that first day was something of a surprise – Fräulein Käthe Goldmann, one of Gestapo chief Kieffer's former secretaries at the Avenue Foch. The main value of her testimony was that she was witness to several reminders sent from Paris to Berlin, before the response finally came that 'the prisoners had to be shot within twenty-four hours and in civilian clothing'. In other words, if Berlin hadn't been chased, the captives might well have been overlooked, and could have been syphoned off to a POW camp, where all might have survived the war. And with that, at 6 p.m. on 7 March the court adjourned, pending more evidence to be heard the following morning.

At 9.30 a.m. on 8 March counsel von Bruch took to the floor, outlining the defence for the three most senior men – Knochen, Kieffer and Schnur. They accepted that the *Kommandobefehl* was 'contrary to international law' as ruled during the Nuremberg trials – a series of hearings from November '45 to October '46 for senior Nazi war criminals. But this case was different, von Bruch argued. The SAS men had been executed 'on a special order from Berlin aimed at this particular Commando [sic] . . .

the accused were unable to resist this order, because they would be shot if they did . . . The accused acted under duress and not of their own free will.'

This was clearly a well-thought-out and ingenious argument. Knochen was first to take the stand. He began by recounting how he had wanted to become a teacher after finishing university studies, but 'I had to become a member of the SS'. No reason was given as to why he'd been obliged to join. After that, his evidence pretty much echoed the statement he'd given Barkworth. There was one notable exception. Knochen tried to justify why Captain Garstin and his men had been forced to change into civilian clothes, before being killed. 'If the men had been shot in uniform, enemy intelligence might have reported the fact that the Germans had captured them.'

The cross-examination of Knochen pulled no punches, as the first of the accused was assailed by a volley of questions, and a copy of the *Kommandobefehl* was handed in to the court as evidence. Why were the men shot in hiding, in the depths of a woodland? Why were no efforts made to delay the order, with Paris facing evacuation? How was the wounded man, Lieutenant Wiehe, spared death, yet none of the Gestapo team punished or shot?

'I do not know why the men were taken away from a main road and shot where they could not be seen,' Knochen conceded. 'At a conference we decided not to execute the wounded men. We disobeyed the order, when we refused to shoot the wounded.'

Those two points landed hard. The SAS captives had been killed out of sight and in secret, and no explanation could be furnished as to why. The Avenue Foch Gestapo had got away without executing the wounded, so arguably the same mercy

354

could have been extended to the other captives, not that Captain Garstin wasn't grievously wounded in any case. Under cross-examination, Knochen had at first faltered and then tied himself in knots. If anything, Kieffer's performance was to prove even less edifying.

Kieffer took to the stand and began: 'The statement I made to Major Barkworth is correct.' He didn't intend to add a great deal more. The one point he did want to address was the change out of uniform for those facing execution. 'The civilian clothes were ordered, to ensure the strictest secrecy.' Kieffer added a last few lines, in which he clearly sought to appeal to the court's sympathy. 'I have three children. My son is a prisoner of war in France. I lost my wife during the war.' And with that, his evidence was pretty much done.

Facing cross-examination, Kieffer seemed to weaken and wither. Asked about the other parachutists that he had ensnared via *Funkspiel* operations and their fates, he mentioned some thirty agents who were 'wireless men and English officers in civilian clothes . . . I do not know what happened to them. This was the first time men in uniform were captured. I do not know why such men should be treated worse than men captured in civil clothes. As a human being, I have to say it was shameful to shoot the men without trial.' Needless to say, that last line was a telling – potentially catastrophic – admission.

Schnur – the unrepentant Nazi – was up next. Like Kieffer, he sought to rely on his statement to Barkworth, claiming to have little further to add. But under cross-examination Schnur began to writhe and thrash about, as he tried to argue that he could not possibly have killed any of the captives himself. 'I looked upon the prisoners with great respect, as they had undertaken such dangerous duties . . . It was impossible for me to have fired a burst . . . I brought my Sten gun to the firing position and intended to shoot. I did not have my magazine on and I could not fire. I must have lost it.'

As the questions came thick and fast, Schnur seemed torn between his stubborn belief that the killings were justified, and his desire to win acquittal by claiming that he'd never fired a shot. It was an unreconcilable tension. 'I knew it was forbidden for soldiers to operate with terrorists. The prisoners had been in cooperation with French terrorists . . . I pitied the fate of the courageous men, but I thought the sentence was a correct one . . . I chased two prisoners without any magazine in my Sten gun.'

With that – Schnur speared on the horns of a dilemma – day two of the trial was done. The court wouldn't reconvene until 10 March, for the ninth was a Sunday – meaning that the accused would have a day locked in their Wuppertal cells in which to contemplate their performances so far. Those can't have been the most relaxed and restful twenty-four hours. At 9.30 a.m. on the tenth the trial began again, with Ilgenfritz up next.

Instead of the SS *Obersturmführer* addressing the court, the statement that he had given to Barkworth was read out in both English and German. After that, Ilgenfritz added a few brief words. 'I am a motor mechanic by trade. The statements I have made are correct. I have nothing to add to them . . . I had no suspicions, before the sentence was read out, that I was concerned with Englishmen. I had no idea, before the shooting, that they were prisoners of war. I had no reason to believe that the sentence was illegal.' And with that he was pretty much done.

Under cross-examination, the prosecutor sought to pick apart Ilgenfritz's argument that he had no idea of the true identity of the captives. Finally the SS *Obersturmführer* admitted: 'From the moment I heard the translation in English, I knew the prisoners were English and not French. It was several minutes later that I shot the escaping prisoner. I shouted to him to stop. I thought it was my duty as a soldier to prevent the escape of dangerous prisoners, who had been sentenced to death by the proper sentence of a court.' Though somewhat contradictory and inconsistent, Ilgenfritz had if anything given a better account of himself than the three senior SS officers who had gone before.

Haug was up next, the man whose very capture had led to the rest of the accused being hunted down and arraigned. In contrast to those who had gone before, Haug chose to speak at length in a heartfelt plea. 'I am fifty-two years old and I have six children aged between eight and seventeen,' he began. 'During the 1914–18 war I was a prisoner of the English for thirty-seven months . . . I was conscripted into the SD in Paris. I was not a member of the SS.' As Haug was at pains to point out, he was the only non-SS man standing trial.

He spoke next of the capture of the SAS patrol on 5 July '44, being assigned as an escort on the truck that drove them to the Noailles Wood and how he 'gave them cigarettes at the place of execution . . . When Vaculik and Jones ran away, I did nothing at first. Someone shouted "Shoot!" When Vaculik was fifty metres away I started firing. I did not aim at him. It was impossible as I had previously talked with him . . . I took the handcuffs off the dead bodies. I felt pity for them.'

SS *Hauptsturmführer* Schmidt – killed on the Eastern Front, so unable to stand trial – was the target of Haug's greatest ire. Schmidt had blamed Haug for letting the prisoners escape and now was payback time. 'I saw Schmidt with a pistol in the firing position,' Haug told the court. 'As a human being, I could not have fired at any of the prisoners.' In other words, SS *Hauptsturmführer* Schmidt – the commander of the execution squad – had clearly opened fire, and was sub-human for what he had done that day.

Of all the accused, Haug's testimony had the ring of truth to it. A veteran of the First World War, he was a long-serving soldier and no die-hard SS, that was for sure. It was understandable why he would have felt such compassion for the captives – fellow soldiers whom he had seen captured in uniform while undertaking a daring mission behind the lines. His cross-examination was perfunctory, but whether Haug had done enough to win a suitable reprieve remained to be seen.

Hildemann, the truck driver, was last. Again, he chose to rely on his statement to Barkworth being read out in court. 'I am a good shot,' he explained, but 'was too excited to hit an escaping prisoner, even if I had wanted to. Somebody shouted, "Shoot! Shoot!" I therefore opened fire involuntarily. I aimed too high at the escaping prisoner, who was stooping. At the interrogation by Major Barkworth . . . I first learned of the full facts of the investigation.'

With that, the evidence of the six accused had been heard. No one, it seemed – apart from the dead SS *Hauptsturmführer* Schmidt – had actually gunned down the condemned men, apart from Ilgenfritz, who had admitted to shooting the one escapee. Apart from that, all had either shot high or had lost their magazines of ammo. Nevertheless, five men had died in that clearing on 9 August 1944, and amongst those arraigned in that court there had to be the killers. Their defence, that they had been acting on the specific order of the highest authority in the land – the Führer – on pain of death, seemed like a sound one. But it was about to be dealt a knockout blow, and from the most unexpected of quarters.

Towards the end of the afternoon, the prosecution called to the stand *Sturmbannführer Kriminaldirektor* Horst Kopkow, the Berlin commander of all *Funkspiel*, anti-sabotage and anti-SOE/SAS operations across the length and breadth of the Reich. Having overseen the executions of the last Allied agents, and having burned his files and dressed himself in civilian clothes, Kopkow had fled into hiding at war's end. But in due course he'd been tracked down. He'd been in British custody for several months, pending his own trial for war crimes. In the interim, he'd decided to turn evidence against his former SS and Gestapo colleagues. It would prove devastating.

Having outlined his role at RSHA Berlin and his relations to the Avenue Foch Gestapo, Kopkow turned to the case at hand: 'I knew men, and not containers, had been dropped. I know of no case where refusal to carry out the *Führerbefehl* [Führer Order; his term for the *Kommandobefehl*] resulted in a death sentence being carried out on those who had refused to obey it.' Kopkow's words fell like a bombshell into the courtroom. In one fell swoop he had demolished the mainstay of the defence team's argument. No one had been killed for refusing to act on the Commando Order, and so said the RSHA's Berlin supremo.

Kopkow's testimony was short and sweet, at least for the prosecution. It was 4.45 p.m. and the court adjourned. The following morning, 11 March, the court was back in session for the prosecutor to give his summing up. It proved gripping and condemnatory. It was common ground that the *Kommandobefehl* was illegal, and Knochen and Kieffer at least must have known this. Under the Hague Convention, even a spy was entitled to a proper trial. These SAS men were no spies. They were British soldiers in uniform. The argument that 'terrorists' could be shot without trial was all too convenient. 'By calling anyone inconvenient a terrorist, it is easy to find this excuse for killing without trial.'

The lack of coercion on the six accused had been proved by their getting away with not executing the wounded SAS man, Lieutenant Wiehe. If Wiehe had been saved, all could have been saved. Haug had known from the point of capture that the condemned men were British soldiers. Ilgenfritz had known this as soon as the 'sentence' was read out in English, although Hildemann quite possibly did not know. Even so, 'why were the four accused who were present at the shooting so reluctant to admit they took part in the shooting[?] . . . Each one pleads some excuse: the loss of a magazine; the jamming of a pistol; the firing deliberately into the air.' Each had tried to duck responsibility, for they knew what they had done was illegal and wrong.

The lead counsel for the defence did his best to counter these points so brilliantly made, but his arguments proved unconvincing and perfunctory: the 'military situation was so bad for Germany that everyone was afraid to disobey in any way. The atmosphere then was very different to the sober atmosphere of this court today. Can a man be guilty if he refused to choose his own death? I ask for an acquittal.' The sense in that courtroom, especially after Kopkow's testimony, was that the accused were fighting a losing battle.

But then, unexpectedly, the defence requested an adjournment, and for a reason that would prove utterly astonishing. It was agreed that the court would not reassemble until the following afternoon, for a surprise witness was willing to give evidence, one who had 'just arrived from England'. SOE agent Captain John Ashford Renshaw Starr was to be called as a 'character witness' for former Gestapo chief Hans Kieffer. So it was that at 2.00 p.m. on 12 March 1947, the former captive of the Avenue Foch Gestapo took the stand, as a witness in defence of his captors.

'I knew the accused Kieffer and I identify him,' Starr began, having been sworn in. 'I knew him at 84 Avenue Foch. I was his prisoner. He treated me very well indeed. The food I received was the same as that of my guards. Other prisoners at Avenue Foch were treated in the same way. My treatment did not change after I had tried to escape . . . From his behaviour, I do not think he would take part in the deliberate murder of British prisoners. I was at the Avenue Foch from September 1943 to July or August 1944.'

Having heard Vaculik and Jones give powerful testimony as to their own, terrible incarceration, and to the way in which even the badly wounded Captain Garstin had been treated, Starr's testimony sounded preposterous and absurd. Worse still, the very fact of his giving it appeared like an insult to those two survivors, not to mention those who had died. And it begged the question – why was Starr offering evidence in defence of a man who had sent dozens of his fellow SOE agents to unspeakable torture and death in the concentration camps, not to mention their treatment in Paris beforehand?

In some cases, Starr would have known those SOE agents personally. In the case of Madeleine (Noor Inayat Khan) he had even tried to execute an escape attempt with her, from their cells in the Avenue Foch building. After Kieffer had dispatched her to Germany, Khan had been shackled at the hands and feet, as a *Nacht und Nebel* prisoner, before being forced to kneel by her

SS and Gestapo killers and shot in the back of the head, together with three fellow female SOE agents. They had even been denied the final request of seeing a priest. The last word on Khan's lips had been *liberté* – freedom.

By now, spring 1947, the fate of numerous captured SOE agents, Noor Inayat Khan amongst them, was well known. In October 1946 Khan had been Mentioned in Dispatches for her heroism and gallantry in the face of the enemy. The case of the four SOE agents killed at Natzweiler – one of whom was still alive when shoved into the crematorium; some of whom had been processed via Kieffer's Paris Gestapo – had made headline news. It could be argued that Horst Kopkow had a motive to turn evidence against his former comrades. Held by the British as a war crimes suspect, he might be trying to curry favour with his captors. But John Starr was under no such compunction.

'I identify accused Schnur,' Starr ploughed on, as he proceeded to give evidence on behalf of Kieffer's former comrades as well. 'I do not know much about him. I never heard any complaints about his treatment of the prisoners.' Was this man's testimony somehow to be viewed as more credible than that of Vaculik and Jones? Still he wasn't done. 'I identify accused Haug. As far as I know he treated the prisoners very well. He often brought me cigarettes and had a chat. I do not think he would have enjoyed killing British prisoners.' The issue at stake wasn't whether anyone had *enjoyed* killing the SABU-70 captives. It was whether they were guilty as charged of the crime of murder.

Starr rounded off his evidence with this: 'I was not always in touch with other prisoners at the Avenue Foch, though I tried to contact them.' Which simply left the question hanging – so what exactly *were* you doing there all that time? Kieffer had had high hopes for Starr's appearance. He'd personally sought out the former SOE agent as a character witness. In truth, it had back-fired spectacularly. There was no cross-examination, for obvious reasons. Starr's testimony had proved more of a benefit to the prosecution.

In the deepest of ironies, Captain John Starr's was to be the last evidence heard in that courtroom, before the verdicts were reached. At 2.15 p.m. the court adjourned while the judges considered their ruling. 'This time, none of the accused smiled, as they passed me in the corridor,' Vaculik remarked of the adjournment. 'As the end came near, they were on edge and ill at ease.'

The court reopened thirty minutes later, although the accused had been held back in an adjoining room. 'Call the first prisoner, Colonel Knochen,' the presiding judge announced.

'Attention! Quick march,' came a sharp cry, as SS *Standartenführer* Dr Knochen was led in, pale and erect, a guard to either side. 'Halt! Right turn.'

The accused turned to face the dock. 'The court martial at Wuppertal has found you guilty of wilful murder against the persons of five British soldiers and condemns you to death by hanging.'

With that, Knochen was ordered out again, leaving as he had entered, his face set like stone. 'I remembered what we had felt in that clearing,' Vaculik would recall of the moment, 'and I could well imagine what the German was feeling as he listened to the sentence.'

'Call the second prisoner, Kieffer,' announced the presiding judge.

Sturmbannführer Hans Kieffer was marched into the court. He turned to face the panel, his face as impassive as his predecessor's. The ruling and the verdict were the same: 'Death by hanging.' On hearing it Kieffer blinked, almost in disbelief, but he did not visibly falter before he too was marched away from the courtroom.

For Vaculik, seeing Kieffer face justice was the greatest moment of all: 'the one-time commandant of the Gestapo at the Avenue Foch was marched out by the military police, under sentence of death, his head held high and his face and neck as red as ever.' Justice against the Avenue Foch's ringmaster had finally been served. But before exiting the courtroom, Kieffer paused and did the most extraordinary thing. He turned and gave a salute to John Starr, who was in the gallery.

In his written evidence, Kieffer had showed little loyalty to his former captive. Indeed, he'd testified that Starr's cooperation with the Gestapo had been extensive. Apart from making use of his draughtsmanship, Starr was used for 'wireless plays' – *Funkspiel* – checking messages to ensure they were rendered in faultless English. 'It was by means of this activity that Bob [Starr] gained a great insight into our counter-espionage work and got to know numerous arrested agents,' Kieffer averred. 'It was precisely at this time that the capture of the woman W/T [wireless] operator Madeleine took place . . . She told us nothing. We could not rely on anything she said.'

There were even reports that Starr had taken one of Kieffer's secretaries, Ottile Scherrer, as his lover while residing at Avenue Foch – accusations that were treated pretty much as fact by SOE. Whatever the truth of the matter, the two men – Kieffer and Starr – had shared some inexplicable bond that endured to the very moment of Kieffer learning of his own death sentence.

Next to be led in was Schnur. On some level, the SS

Hauptsturmführer seemed to have missed how badly the trial had gone for the accused. He glanced around at the gallery, grinning inanely, as if a guilty verdict just could not be possible. When it was read out – death by hanging – all that changed. As Schnur did not speak English, he had to wait for the translation to learn the worst, at which point he gave a despairing cry and collapsed into a faint. He had to be half-carried and half-dragged from the court.

There was little noticeable change on the presiding judge's impassive features, but was there just a hint of emotion now; of disgust even? Vaculik fancied there was. It had to be repugnance at the behaviour of a man like SS *Hauptsturmführer* Schnur, the commander of the Noailles Wood execution squad. Ilgenfritz was next up. While he too was found guilty of murder, the SS *Obersturmführer* was seen as having extenuating circumstances, in that he hadn't known the real identity of the prisoners until the moment of the shooting. He was given fifteen years' hard labour.

'Call the fifth prisoner, Haug!'

Of anyone, Jones and Vaculik felt that Haug should get away with a custodial sentence, for he was the most genuine on all counts. But when the verdict came it was the same as the first three: 'Death by hanging.' The Gestapo sergeant, who had always endeavoured to act as fairly as he could, was led away 'as pale as death'. Haug wouldn't yet know it, but his verdict was the only one that had split the judges. The rest had been unanimous, but it was four to two in favour that Haug should be hanged.

Finally Hildemann, the truck driver, was brought in. While he was also found guilty as charged, the fact that he knew even less than Ilgenfritz meant he got just five years' imprisonment.

The broad smile of relief upon hearing the verdict revealed how Hildemann figured himself fortunate to have got off so lightly.

With that, the last of the accused was hustled out of the court . . . and the ghosts of the SABU-70 victims – plus all those consigned to the *Nacht und Nebel* by the Avenue Foch Gestapo – should finally have been able to rest a little easier. But in fact, the Wuppertal proceedings weren't yet done. One by one the counsel for the accused entered immediate pleas for clemency – which would be expanded into written arguments in due course – which sought to be as emotional and persuasive as possible, especially in the case of Haug.

Lawyer Sabine for Knochen: 'His part in the affair was not big or important. He ordered that the wounded should be spared. Accused lost his wife during the war and he suffered materially from air raids. His family are faced with ruin. His age is thirty-seven.'

Lawyer Lauterjung for Kieffer: 'Kieffer was acting under duress. He treated his prisoners very well. He has three children. He lost his wife during the war. He meant no evil. His age is forty-six.' Kieffer leaned heavily on Starr, especially in his written appeal for mercy. 'My section was holding numerous prisoners, including several British officers . . . Not even these prisoners were shot. That is confirmed by the presence of witness Capt. Starr . . . According to him, the prisoners were treated very well and humanely by me. I have often granted them privileges.'

Lawyer von Bruch for Schnur: 'Schnur is not the criminal type. The war is over. Events have a different aspect now. Accused has a clean record. He is married and has two children. He has made no attempt to escape, though he has had some freedom. I ask for a humane sentence. His age is thirty-seven.'

Lawyer Ludecke for Ilgenfritz: 'He has been in prison for sixteen months already for this act. During that time he has not seen his wife or two children.' Fifteen years' hard labour was too severe a sentence for the crime.

Lawyer Kreib, for Haug: 'He had given cigarettes to the prisoners before the shooting and had talked to them. He could not have killed them intentionally ... Moreover, it is more than probable that Vaculik and Jones owe their lives to a great extent to Haug's behaviour. Haug could have shot the witnesses who fled past him, if he had wished to do so ... He has six children of minor age. His age is fifty-two ... Should the sentence be carried out, the children ... will not be able to understand that he who is such a good father should leave this world as a murderer.'

Finally, lawyer Somneer, for Hildemann: 'Accused had only a few minutes for reflection at the execution point. He participated in the events only to a very small degree. He is only a driver ... His age is forty-four.' As a simple driver, five years was far too harsh a sentence.

In the rush to seek clemency, a cast of apologists stepped forward, including the priest allocated to the accused, plus the Evangelical Church of Germany, which argued – with some justification – that for years the German people had been taught absolute obedience to Nazi authority without question. Under Hitler, those in power had wielded absolute power, without precedent in history. In the SS in particular, renouncing religion – a belief in God – had been part of the cult: it was something to be lauded. A true convert could have no other allegiance but to the SS itself.

But the most extraordinary plea for clemency would come from the chief Secret Hunter himself. On 1 April 1947 Major

Barkworth penned a five-page report, arguing for a reduction in the sentencing of those he had personally tracked and brought to trial. The main thrust of Barkworth's argument was that death by hanging was too severe: 'all gave their evidence with frankness, possibly in the mistaken belief that they had done what in their eyes seemed right.' While Knochen, Kieffer and Schnur should still face death, it should be by firing squad, Barkworth argued, not 'the most dishonourable form of death'.

Once and once only had Barkworth and Rhodes gone to see one of those that they had hunted down face his end. A few weeks prior to the Noailles Wood trial they'd watched SS *Oberwachmeister* 'Stuka' Neuschwanger hang. Though the Vosges torturer and killer went to the gallows without the slightest hint of remorse or regret, the two foremost Nazi-hunters vowed never again. 'It was something one doesn't want to do more than once,' Rhodes recalled. 'I believe we were both of the opinion that it's not nice to see somebody die.'

Very possibly, it was seeing Neuschwanger hang that inspired Barkworth's plea for clemency now – that there was a better way for those like Schnur, Kieffer and Knochen to die, especially as the latter two had expressed a certain degree of contrition and regret. But he reserved the strongest plea of all for Haug, for whom 'the death sentence . . . [should] be commuted to one of imprisonment', or the trial would risk 'smacking of the trappings of SS justice' and not of British fair play.

On 22 April 1947 the decision on all the clemency appeals was reached: all had failed. On 2 June Kieffer, Schnur and Haug were duly executed by hanging, by which time Ilgenfritz and Hildemann were already serving their custodial sentences. As for Knochen, he had been returned to the French, to be tried in a French court of law, just as Barkworth had promised he would be. (A year later, Knochen's death sentence would be commuted to life in prison).

True to their word, having watched Neuschwanger put to death Barkworth and Rhodes declined to see the Noailles Wood guilty hang. As for Jones and Vaculik, as they strolled through the war-blasted streets of Wuppertal following the verdicts, they were gripped only by a strange feeling of desolation. Where was the elation – the sense of release – that they had sought for so long?

'I felt like running,' Vaculik recalled, 'running away from this cold, acrid smell of burned debris, running away from the eyes of those fellow men who had just been condemned to death by hanging. But I knew it would be useless.' There was no running from the ghosts of the past. The 'proud and bitter memories' would remain with them for all of their lives.

By the time they were disbanded in the summer of 1948, the Secret Hunters had brought well over a hundred Nazi war criminals to justice, as described in the citation for Barkworth's MBE. 'In spite of the fact that there were initially no clues to follow up Major Barkworth . . . brought to notice over one hundred and twenty Germans who are now held as War Criminals for the perpetration of crimes . . . This officer's energy, unflagging determination and ability in carrying out his task is beyond all praise.'

Even then, with the Noailles Wood casebook closed and the work of the Secret Hunters done, there would be one last twist of the knife, one last sting in the tail. Shortly after the trial at which he had appeared as a star prosecution witness, SS *Sturmbannführer Kriminaldirektor* Horst Kopkow was brought to Britain, and incarcerated in the London Cage. Some weeks later the war crimes investigator Alexander Nicolson was tying up the last of such activities in the British zone of occupation, and he made an inquiry about Kopkow's whereabouts and his – presumably – forthcoming trial.

In August 1944 Kopkow had been put forward to receive the *Deutsches Kreuz in Silber* – the German Cross in Silver, an award instituted by Hitler in 1941 for distinguished war service. The citation would make abundantly clear the pivotal role Kopkow had played in combatting Allied parachute missions and in furthering *Funkspiel* plays: 'The successful control of the parachute agents, the recording of the radio games and their extraordinary skilful continuation is due to his quite extraordinary achievements.' Of course, Kopkow had dedicated similar energies to ensuring that captured agents – once their usefulness was exhausted – would be consigned to the *Nacht und Nebel*.

The response Nicolson received from a Lieutenant Colonel R. Paterson, of the London District Cage, was perhaps not what he had been hoping for. 'The above as you know was sent to England about ten days ago for special interrogation and when he arrived here he was found to be running a temperature and after two days was sent to hospital, where we regret to say he died of bronchopneumonia before any information was obtained from him. We enclose a certificate of death issued by the hospital authorities, and would request that you duly advise his relations.' Kopkow, it was stated, had been buried in a military cemetery along with other deceased German POWs.

Death, it seemed, had robbed the Allies of justice over the Berlin-based SS and Gestapo dark lord, a man who had sent some 300 British agents to the most horrible deaths imaginable, and who was also wanted by the Americans and the Soviets for similarly consigning hundreds of their agents to the *Nacht und*

Nebel. That was deeply unfortunate – if it was true. Sadly, it wasn't. In truth, Kopkow had so skilfully and convincingly sold his unique talents and expertise to the British Secret Intelligence Service (SIS) that his death had been entirely faked.

During his many interrogations Kopkow had deliberately and artfully played down his role in liquidating captured Allied agents, while playing up his role in tracking down agents from the east – from Soviet territories. In particular, he had stressed how prior to the war's end, scores of Russian stay-behind agents had been inserted into Germany, and were now ideally placed to spy on the Western Allies. In the new war, the Cold War, this had seemingly made Kopkow far too valuable to hand over to any pesky war crimes tribunals and to a wholly inconvenient sentence of 'death by hanging'. Instead, Kopkow was quietly disappeared, so he could be recruited into SIS 'for special employment'.

Kopkow's death certificate was faked and he was given a whole new identity. Henceforth he was to be known as 'Peter Cordes', although in later years he would feel safe enough – and apparently self-satisfied enough – to change that to Horst Cordes-Kopkow. Kopkow's specialism for SIS would become the *Rote Kapelle* (Red Orchestra) – the network of agents the Soviets established in Nazi territories throughout the war, many of whom were now said to be spying on the Western powers. In 1948 a 344-page dossier was issued by British intelligence on 'The Case of the *Rote Kapelle*', whole tracts of which were taken almost verbatim from Kopkow's own reports on the Soviet espionage network.

While much of the Kopkow story remains top secret even today – the files are either closed or have been conveniently destroyed – this much is known. By 1949 Kopkow was back in Germany, ostensibly working for a textile company in Gelsenkirchen, a city in the northwest of the country, taking up a position provided by British intelligence and still very much working for them. Gelsenkirchen was the city in which the Kopkow – or 'Cordes' – family had made their home: Horst, his wife Gerda and their children. When he returned in 1949, he was to be known as 'Uncle Peter' by all, even his own children. He and his wife reportedly slept in separate beds, to maintain their cover.

Kopkow's dealings with MI5 and MI6 stretched through to the 1960s, when he became the CEO of the textile company, a position he retained until his retirement in the 1970s. In 1986 the BBC journalist Robert Marshall went to interview Kopkow for a documentary he was making about the SOE's French section. When speaking to Marshall, Kopkow 'ranted and ranted', claiming of SOE agents that 'the British had scoured their prisons for low life and forced them to parachute into France and so killing them off was basically doing the British a service'. Unrepentant and arrogant to the last, Kopkow died in October 1990 in a Gelsenkirchen hospital, aged eighty-five, surrounded by his family.

By faking his death, shielding him from justice and protecting him for the rest of his life, SIS would ensure that Kopkow only ever ended up in the one courtroom – giving evidence in the Noailles Wood trial. For some, the widespread and horrific crimes of the war years really did set them up for life. For some, heinous war crimes really did pay handsome dividends. But for others, thankfully, there was no running from justice nor anyone to hide them. In the case of the Noailles Wood massacre, the SS and Gestapo killers had paid the proper price for their odious acts.

Captain Patrick Garstin, MC and his men had been avenged, as had the wider victims consigned by Kieffer and his cronies to the *Nacht und Nebel*.

Epilogue

Shortly after the Noailles Wood trial ended and the verdicts were enacted, Barkworth began working on his definitive study of the *Kommandobefehl*, running to seventy-one pages and with twenty-six supporting statements. Issued in June 1948, his 'Report on the Commando Orders of 18.10.42 and 25.6.44 with Reference to Certain of the War Crimes Caused by Them' is an exhaustive study of the German Supreme Command, establishing who was responsible for drawing up the *Kommandobefehl* and for its prosecution. Barkworth included six names of senior members of the Nazi regime who in his view should stand trial, making the point that significant publicity should be given to their cases, so as to demonstrate that 'the prosecution of war crimes has been moved by considerations of impartial justice, rather than those of keeping a mosaic tally'.

Above all, Barkworth made it absolutely clear in his report that the ultimate responsibility for the *Kommandobefehl* lay squarely at Adolf Hitler's door. 'Hitler's actions were not merely petulant and vindictive,' Barkworth wrote, concerning the *Kommandobefehl*, but his 'aims were clearly thought out and often based upon sound reasoning . . . to which his violence and pettiness did not always do full justice. As is known, the Führer's logic was simple: whoever was not on his side was a criminal or an imbecile.' By branding all Allied agents and Commandos in that manner, they could be condemned as 'terrorists' and 'saboteurs' and consigned to the slaughter.

Barkworth concluded that Hitler, plus a coterie of his senior military officers and legal advisors, 'were party to a conspiracy 1) to produce an order for the murder of certain categories of legal combatants of the Allied Armed Forces, who had been captured . . . 2) to cloak this bare intention with a semblance of legality . . . 3) to enforce the implementation of this order by means of a system of reports . . . 4) to hide the true facts from representatives of the Protecting Powers and the International Red Cross'.

Sadly, by the time Barkworth's report was ready, the Secret Hunters were scheduled to be disbanded: with the British war crimes tribunals coming to an abrupt end, there were no further means for suspected war criminals to be brought to trial, at least at that time. By the summer of 1948 the West had turned its attention away from its former enemy, Nazi Germany, and towards its former ally, the Soviet bloc, and the coming Cold War. No further action would be taken as a result of the recommendations of Barkworth's report, which was basically his final act as the commander of the SAS War Crimes Investigation Team, one of the most successful such outfits ever to have operated.

After the first clemency pleas had been heard on behalf of the Noailles Wood killers, further appeals were made for those who had not yet been put to death. On 1 December 1948 Knochen's sentence was reduced to life in prison. On 22 December 1950 fresh arguments for clemency were mounted, based upon newly emerged evidence of Horst Kopkow's role in the murder of the SABU-70 captives. Of course, by then Kopkow was officially dead, but secretly working for the SIS under the cover name

Peter Cordes, and was nicely ensconced with his family back in Germany. Shortly after his clemency plea had been entered, Knochen's sentence was reduced to twenty-one years. Dr Goetz, the Avenue Foch *Funkspiel* genius, would never be charged with any crime: he forged a new career for himself in Germany as a schools inspector.

On 11 July 1950 Hildemann, the death truck driver, was released from prison. After several pleas for clemency on behalf of Ilgenfritz, including one from his father concerning the penurious state of his son's family, and one from the prison governor concerning his good behaviour, Ilgenfritz was released from custody early, on 28 September 1954. Dr Knochen's lawyers continued to plead for his early release, arguing that he had saved the life of the one hospitalised SAS captive, Lieutenant Wiehe. On 28 November 1962 Knochen was released early, as an act of clemency by the French (he had been held in French custody). He retired to Baden-Baden, a spa town in southwest Germany, and died in 2003.

At that moment, all of those accused of the Noailles Wood murders had either been killed in the war, executed as a result of the Wuppertal war crimes trials or released after serving their terms in jail. Arguably, the one great exception – and the greatest stain on the consciences of the British authorities – was Horst Kopkow.

No amount of realpolitik or pragmatism in light of the onset of the Cold War could justify the shielding from justice of such a man. The fact that Kopkow's safeguarding was achieved only via high-level deception and intrigue – Kopkow was cosseted by a veritable bodyguard of lies – reflects the fact that had the British, American and French public become aware of how he was being protected, there would have been an unholy outcry. If nothing else, the families of the many hundreds of disappeared – the victims of the *Nacht und Nebel* – were seeking to discover what exactly had happened to their loved ones, and to see some form of justice being done.

In Horst Kopkow's case, due to the moral bankruptcy of (some of) those in power in Britain, justice was forever denied. In the process, the memories of those incredibly brave and spirited SOE, OSS and Russian agents, plus the special forces who served at their side, were besmirched by a few who judged that it was somehow right and proper to shield Kopkow from any kind of a reckoning, which begs the question, on what and whose authority was this done? Did the British SIS have the right to spirit away whoever it chose to be shielded from justice, no matter the depth and breadth of their crimes, and at their sole discretion? Does it still have that right today?

Either way, immediately after the Second World War the Western powers geared up for the Cold War, and in the process amoral pragmatism often triumphed, but it did so deep in the shadows. Had there been a poll at war's end of the British and Allied public, to assess if they supported the shielding of war criminals like Kopkow, the overwhelming response would have been 'no'. After all, it was largely as a result of public outcries over the Nazi concentration camps, and the mass of related atrocities coming to light, that the British government had been forced to act and institute war crimes trials in the first place. The powers that be were only ever sceptical and reluctant participants.

Kopkow's case is sadly not an isolated one. In 1945 the US authorities had issued guidance to their military commanders that they must arrest and hold all suspected Nazi war criminals. However, there was one caveat: 'In your discretion you may make such exceptions as you deem advisable for intelligence and other military reasons.' In other words, if senior US commanders believed a Nazi war crimes suspect might furnish more assistance to the Allied cause by not being put on trial, so be it. In due course Brigadier General Reinhard Gehlen, Nazi Germany's former intelligence supremo for the Eastern Front, was brought into the Allied fold, along with his extensive files on the Soviets, and he duly recruited many of his former associates to work for the Allies.

What became known as the 'Gehlen Organisation' made extensive use of former SS and Gestapo men, especially those with widespread experience on the Eastern Front. In 1949 the Central Intelligence Agency (CIA) – formed out of the OSS – took full control of the Gehlen Organisation and would run it as an adjunct of the CIA and with Gehlen at the helm for the next several years. In 1950 Gehlen was formally appointed as the head of the West German intelligence service, what would become the *Bundesnachrichtendienst* or BND.

In 1972 Gehlen would publish his memoirs, called simply *The Service*. The title of the book's prologue gives a sense of the contents: 'From Hitler's Bunker to the Pentagon'. The book was trumpeted as 'the . . . memoir of General Reinhard Gehlen, legendary spymaster-in-chief, Hitler's head of military espionage in Russia, who, as war ended, transferred his mammoth files and network of spies to the United States'. But mostly, the recruitment by the CIA and other US agencies of war crimes suspects would be revealed under the 1988 Nazi War Crimes Disclosure Act, which compelled the CIA, OSS and other US agencies to release millions of pages from files that pertained to the recruitment of Nazi war criminals.

And that is the key point: this is an American act of law. Under it, some eight million pages have been declassified and the work is ongoing. As a result Nazi war criminals and SS commanders including Walter Rauff, Willi Krichbaum, Dr Franz Six, Alois Brunner, Klaus Barbie and many others have been shown to have been shielded by the US intelligence community. Nazis who served at Auschwitz, Treblinka, Buchenwald, Dachau and other concentration camps were also recruited. But there is no equivalent act in Britain and neither is there any sense that one is even being mooted.

We know most of what we know about the Nazi war criminals who worked for the CIA due to the Nazi War Crimes Disclosure Act. We know precious little about the equivalent programme in Britain, a part of which was codenamed Operation Darwin. The fate of Kopkow has only been revealed as the result of a clutch of MI5 files being made available. Even those indicate that heavy redactions of the most sensitive information have been made. There are seven files, containing dozens of documents, that are all marked in handwritten scrawl: 'Destroyed 9/1/62'. Clearly somebody went through the Kopkow files in 1962 and removed those documents deemed too sensitive, decades before there was even any hint of these files being opened to the public.

Without a release of the relevant wartime and immediate post-war files held by SIS, we will never know how extensive was the British programme to recruit and shelter Nazi war criminals. In this sense, the American government is to be commended for legislating in favour of transparency and a proper reckoning. The British government, by contrast, appears wedded to a diet of blanket secrecy, despite the passage of time. It is seventy-five years since the end of the Second World War. This policy is well past its use-by date, especially because in many cases the living descendants of those who perished in the *Nacht und Nebel* are still hungry to learn the full facts of what happened to those who paid the ultimate price, in freedom's cause.

There were so many. Some 300 British agents went to their deaths at Kopkow's hands. Then there were the American, Russian and numerous other Allied nationals – Norwegians, Belgians, Poles and Czechs, to name but a few – who fell victim to the *Nacht und Nebel* policy, especially as Britain was largely the headquarters for the formation and training of agents of all free nations who stood against Nazi Germany, and for dispatching those agents into enemy-occupied lands. For long months, the majority of agents of all nationalities sent behind the lines were dispatched from British shores. Then there were the special forces victims – SAS, Commandos, Jedburghs and others.

The overall achievements of the SAS in France have been dealt with in the main body of this book, but the high costs they paid deserve fuller mention. Of the hundred or so SAS captured after D-Day, only six survived the war. By Barkworth's own reckoning, only fifteen captured 2 SAS men returned from enemy captivity throughout the entirety of the conflict. The vast majority were consigned to the night and the fog. Thankfully, the SAS itself did not fall victim to a similar termination, as those in high places had been so adamant should be the case at war's end.

For Winston Churchill, David Stirling, Blair Mayne, Brian Franks, Yurka Galitzine and others, the work of the Secret Hunters had achieved an associated, yet deeply cherished aim: their very existence until summer 1948, operating across Europe and wearing the winged-dagger cap badge and regimental insignia, had kept the spirit and essence of the SAS alive long enough for its resurrection to get underway. In July 1947 the storied Artists Rifles regiment – a volunteer light infantry unit formed in 1859 – merged with the supposedly 'defunct' SAS to form the 21 Special Air Service Regiment (Artists) (Reserves). Although this was a reservist, territorial unit, nevertheless it represented the much-strategised partial resurrection of the SAS.

It was only right and proper that the first commanding officer of the newly constituted regiment should be Lieutenant Colonel Brian Morton Forster Franks, MC, DSO, Croix de Guerre and Légion d'Honneur, the one man who had schemed, plotted and striven most tirelessly to ensure that the supposed demise of the SAS in October 1945 would prove far from permanent. Appointed as an honorary colonel in that role, he would remain in command of '21 SAS', as it would become known, until the refounding of the Special Air Service in the 1950s, when it became clear that the new kind of warfare Britain faced – chiefly the Malayan Emergency – called for the unique skillsets of the SAS.

Brian Franks would be appointed as colonel commandant of the newly reformed regiment, and fittingly, many of those who refounded the SAS were veterans of its Second World War operations. And the rest, as they say, is history. Colonel Franks would go on to marry and have two children, and he would pass away in 1982, in Suffolk, of natural causes.

Once the Secret Hunters had been disbanded, in summer 1948, Bill Barkworth struck out for new shores. After emigrating to Australia, he would end up building a business there and marrying his German secretary from the days of the Villa Degler operations. They would have three children, all of whom were girls – Catherine, Amy and Camilla. Barkworth's wife had been living in England prior to the war, working as a governess, and had been interned as an 'enemy alien' at the outbreak of hostilities. In 1944 she had been returned to Germany and served in an administrative role, providing provisions to frontline troops.

Amy Crossland, the middle of their three children, would write to me about her mother, saying: 'These were difficult times for her, but she had the brightest, sunniest, optimistic personality which must have helped get her through.' Of her father's work on the Commando Order, and of the sidelining of escapee Lieutenant James Hughes's earliest warnings about it, she would remark: 'I think Pa was annoyed the matter was not taken more seriously at these high levels.' One of her father's greatest qualities was that he was extremely loyal to the men of the SAS, so their safety would have been foremost in his mind. Denying the Commando Order went against all that, of course.

On her father's life in Australia, she would write: 'Pa was the director of the Good Neighbour Council, a government-funded body set up to assist post-war migrants settle into the community. Pa's language skills helped him greatly here. He would often be called in the middle of the night to interpret at a hospital for migrants with sick children . . . he always wanted to ensure no one was disadvantaged through lack of English . . . I remember being in the office once and a Frenchman came in, saying he needed to speak again to "the Frenchman" (Pa)!' Barkworth would die on 18 July 1985.

Sergeant Fred 'Dusty' Rhodes returned to his native Barnsley after the work of the Secret Hunters was done, taking up work again with the local parks department as a gardener. Rhodes would return to France and Germany often, to commemorate those brave SAS who had lost their lives, and also the villagers of the Vosges who had paid such a heavy price for sheltering, feeding and aiding the SAS during Operation Loyton. In particular, the village of Moussey, which above all paid the heaviest price, has become something of a living memorial to those who died in the Vosges – French villagers, French Resistance and SAS alike. Several of the Operation Loyton *Nacht und Nebel* victims are buried in the Moussey church graveyard, which likewise has become a regular place for the commemoration of such wartime courage and valour.

Some years after the war, Rhodes granted a series of interviews, some of which are held by the Imperial War Museum, regarding his service on Operation Loyton and thereafter as a Nazi-hunter. In them he made clear the level of dissatisfaction and frustration he felt that the official files concerning their war crimes work had been closed by the British Government for such an inordinately long time. 'Why they put a seventy-five-year restriction on that I really don't know,' Rhodes remarked.

The files of the Secret Hunters had been closed for seventy-five years. They were not to be opened during Rhodes's lifetime, and the very existence of the SAS War Crimes Investigation Team remains something of a closely guarded secret until today. The SAS's official diary for the war years, published in the last few years, contains just a brief entry concerning their extraordinary work. 'In October 1945, the SAS was disbanded. Franks came to an unofficial arrangement with one individual from the War Office and the [war crimes] unit continued. It operated totally openly, as if it was official. The unit ended its hunt in 1948, three years after the SAS was disbanded.'

If Barkworth, Rhodes and the rest of the Secret Hunters had not endured until summer 1948, it is without doubt that the Noailles Wood killers would never have been tracked down or brought to trial. Rhodes was able to attend his last Vosges reunion in 1988, and he was to die two years later. As his son, Phil Rhodes, was able to tell me, he was in the process of writing a book about his war years when sadly he passed away. It was never finished, but thankfully Phil was able to share with me his father's handwritten notes of his wartime and post-war work, which had been a key source for his own book.

Of the SABU-70 patrol, six men survived the war: Lieutenant Wiehe, Corporals Vaculik and Jones, and Troopers Morrison, Norman and Castelow. Of those who perished, the graves of the five murdered men are ranged in line in the Marissel French National Cemetery in Beauvais, 40 miles north of Paris. Along with graves from the First World War there are 158 burials from the Second World War, four of which are unidentified. Under Commonwealth War Graves Commission headstones lie Patrick Garstin, Paddy Barker, Thomas Varey, Joseph Walker and William Young, in that order. The cemetery is situated on the east side of the Rue d'Amiens (D1001), just to the north of Beauvais city centre.

There is also a memorial plaque in Randalstown, Northern Ireland, which, beneath a winged dagger motif, reads: 'Trooper William Pearson Young (Billy), 14 Kemmilhill Park, Randalstown. 9.8.1944 Aged 22 Years. Posthumously awarded the Croix De Guerre.'

In 1960 the French government proposed giving the Croix de Guerre to all five of the Noailles Wood murder victims, in recognition of their valorous acts. Inexplicably, the British government refused the offer, stating that it was not their policy to accept foreign decorations more than five years after the acts being honoured. In the case of Trooper Young at least, it appears that the high-valour medal was subsequently secured, and according to newspaper reports, Trooper Walker's parents went to France in person, both to visit the place of his death and to 'receive the Croix de Guerre which the French government has posthumously awarded their son'.

It remains unclear whether the families of Garstin, Barker or Varey got to receive the posthumous Croix de Guerre on behalf of those who had perished. What is very clear is the way in which the memory of their sacrifice is remembered and cherished on the ground in France. A number of memorials stand at the key sites – at the La Ferté-Alais drop-zone and at the location of their deaths. Many are in French, but one that is (mostly) in English reads: 'Here, on August 9th 1944 British Paratroopers of the 1st SAS Regiment . . . Captain P. B. Garstin MC 26 Ans, Sergeant T. Varey 30 Ans, Private T. J. Barker 21 Ans, Private J. Walker 22 Ans, Private W. P. Young 22 Ans were brutally murdered by the enemy.'

In October 1965 Captain Patrick Garstin's widow, Susan, would write to the Foreign Office, from the family's Canterbury home, which she had shared with their son, who was by then around twenty-one years old, but of course had never got to know his father. 'My husband was imprisoned at Gestapo headquarters Avenue Foch Paris. He was in the 1 SAS and captured on the night of 4/5 July. He had three wounds in his back and two in his neck. I believe he was first taken to hospital, where the Germans refused him any sort of medical attention. I understand he was made to change into civilian clothes and on 9 Aug. 1944 was taken with the rest of his troops . . . to the grounds of a chateau near Noailles and shot.'

In June 1964 the British and German governments had reached

384

an agreement over compensation to be paid to UK nationals who had fallen victim to Nazi war crimes. Garstin's widow's letter was in connection with that. In December 1965 she was given a 'death grant' for the loss of her husband – 'one of the Noailles cases' – of £2,293, around £40,000 at today's values.

Of those from Captain Garstin's patrol who survived, Lieutenant Wiehe would be paralysed for life and would neither marry nor have any children. Taking solace in a religious life, plus the companionship of his dog, Titch, he was able to forgive those who had injured and mistreated him, and for a time he was reasonably independent, driving a Morris Minor motor car specially adapted for a wheelchair user.

On 11 June 1960 Wiehe gave his precious rosary – the one that had sustained him through his darkest times in the war – to his godson, having already drawn up a will in which he left much of his worldly possessions to Sister Ruscoe, the English nurse who had accompanied him to Mauritius, and had stayed there to become his lifelong nurse. Having been on morphine medication ever since sustaining his injuries, on 9 September 1965 Wiehe would pass away in Mauritius, aged forty-nine, and would be buried in the family graveyard. He is commemorated to this day not only as a courageous soldier, but also as a man of faith who gave his all in freedom's cause, and as one who bore his injuries with extraordinary forbearance and good grace until the very end of his days.

In the lush gardens of the Labourdonnais Estate, the Wiehe family home in Mauritius, there is a memorial to Wiehe's life. It reads: 'In homage to Uncle Hyacinthe, who lived in the gardens of Labourdonnais, war-wounded in 1944. Through his bravery and his heroism, he was an example to his family and friends. His suffering, his fervent faith, his courage and his holiness, his sweetness and his humility, mark him as one of a select few worthy of praise and admiration. He liked to be surrounded by trees and birds, in his quest for the absolute. Father J. J. Adrien Wiehe, Priest of the Diocese of Port-Louis, Mauritius.' The Wiehe family shared with me Lieutenant Wiehe's wartime diaries and other family archival materials, which were hugely useful in fleshing out his story.

Of the two survivors of the massacre at Noailles, having first been threatened with prosecution by the French authorities, Serge Vaculik would eventually be awarded the Croix de Guerre by them. However, he too would be dogged by his wartime injuries. He was also discomfited at winning his own decoration for valour, for he pointed out that most of the 'Commandos and parachutists were lucky if after desperate missions and hair's-breadth escapes they managed to get a bronze star – they were more likely to get a wooden cross.' In 1954 Vaculik published his life story, in French, which would subsequently be translated into English, and published under the title *Air Commando*. That text has proven a primary source of inspiration and information for this book.

After giving evidence at the Noailles Wood trial, Jones and Vaculik would meet just once more, at a Resistance reunion in France, in 1980. They would die within twenty-four hours of each other – Jones on 6 December 1990, and Vaculik the following day. The life thread that had united the two of them and had enabled their remarkable survival was clearly an immensely powerful – and seemingly inseverable – bond, until the very end. Vaculik had attended many such reunions in France, and in 1954 he met up with Captain Patrick Garstin's widow and his son, to mark the tenth anniversary of the mission.

Lieutenant Colonel Mayne – 1 SAS's commanding officer and

source of inspiration for the SABU-70 patrol members – would be awarded four Distinguished Service Orders (DSOs) during the war, the last of which, in October 1945, was controversially downgraded from a Victoria Cross. The original citation for the VC was signed off by no less a figure than Field Marshal Bernard Montgomery, and the subsequent downgrading led the king to enquire why Mayne had been denied the honour of the VC, which 'so strangely eluded him'. David Stirling also objected, noting the considerable prejudice that had extended from elements of the British establishment to the outspoken, uncompromising and peerless SAS commander.

In May 1945 Mayne had been able to host two very special visitors at the SAS's Scottish training base. Captain Patrick Garstin's widow, Susan, had travelled up to Darvel from Canterbury, along with her infant son. Once Patrick Garstin junior had succeeded in executing eight 'parachute jumps' off the bar, with a little help from several SAS old hands, Mayne presented the youngster with his SAS wings. They were pinned proudly to the boy's pram, to his mother's joy.

Mayne died on 13 December 1955, aged forty, in a late-night car accident in his hometown of Newtownards, Northern Ireland. He had also been awarded the Croix de Guerre with Palm, and the Légion d'Honneur, by the French. The latter decoration is that nation's highest gallantry medal, instituted by Napoleon Bonaparte in 1802, making it the nearest French equivalent to the honour that had been denied him by his own country – the VC. But as Mayne's nearest surviving relative, Fiona Ferguson (née Mayne), told me about her uncle, he would not have cared greatly for honours and distinctions: he cared only to stand tall amongst the men of his command.

Fiona gave me access to her uncle's wartime trunks, stuffed full of reports, letters, photos, film and mementos, which proved an invaluable source of inspiration for this book. Her priority in doing so was to ensure that her uncle's memory be suitably preserved, and that his multifaceted character be more fully appreciated. It was of course a privilege to view and read such original wartime materials.

Not long after the disbandment of the SAS, the SOE would also be disbanded, and in the latter's case, sadly it would be for good. I say 'sadly' because, despite SOE headquarters falling victim to the *Funkspiel* and letting down many of their agents, the SOE did an enormous amount of highly valuable work during the war, which was so often distinguished by the unorthodox, the unthinkable and the outright daring. Many of SOE's stories of courage and fortitude in the face of the enemy remain untold to this day.

Acknowledgements

I could not have written this book without the help of the following people, and please forgive me for any individuals I may have inadvertently forgotten. I extend my immense gratitude to you all (notwithstanding the fact that some of the research has had to be carried out in the midst of the Covid-19 pandemic, so has been conducted remotely):

The Wiehe family, and in particular Jacques Wiehe, Father Alexis Wiehe, Dominique Gibson and Olivier Lalouette. Thank you for giving me access to family records and to Lieutenant Wiehe's diaries and letters from the war years, such as you were able to.

The Garstin family, and in particular Sean Garstin, Captain Patrick Garstin's son, for your correspondence and for sharing with me family papers, archival documents and photos regarding Captain Garstin's wartime career, such as you were able to.

James Irvine, for sharing with me your archival research and family records regarding SAS Trooper Leslie Herbert William Packman, and of the efforts of the Operation Gain 2015 memorial team – fabulous work.

Phil Rhodes, for sharing with me the private family papers of Fred 'Dusty' Rhodes, and much of the Rhodes family memorabilia, photos and other materials from the war years.

Joanne Turner, of the Dumfries Museum, and the family of C.

Riding for kindly granting me access to the wonderful Captain Cecil Riding, MC collection, including his diary from the war years and rich archive of related photographs and documents.

Fiona Ferguson, niece of Colonel Blair Mayne, for allowing me to access your late uncle's war chests and the letters, reports, documents, photos and memorabilia that they contain, and for the endless insight you have been able to provide into your uncle's wartime career and his wider achievements. To you and your husband, Norman, enormous thanks, and especially for so warmly inviting me into your family home.

Many thanks to Chris Drakes, whose father, Sergeant Peter Drakes, served in the SAS War Crimes Investigation Team, for the help with research and provision of photographs.

Peter Forbes and all of The Keepers, including Gary Hull, Roy Magowan and David McCallion, for allowing me to access the extraordinary records and memorabilia you have safeguarded from the war years, especially those concerning Colonel Mayne and his fellow SAS raiders, and for generously showing me the key sites in and around Newtownards that reflect upon this story. Sally Forbes, the good wife of Peter Forbes, for the enormous hospitality I was treated to in your family home.

Michael de Burgh, at ninety-six the last Second World War survivor of the 9/12 Lancers, for corresponding with me about your war years and about Ralph 'Karl' Marx, one of the Operation Loyton commanders. Robin Collins, Mr de Burgh's grandson, for corresponding with me about the same and for introducing me to your grandfather.

Eoin McGonigal and Patric McGonigal, for corresponding with me over your late uncle Eoin McGonigal's war years and his relations to Robert Blair 'Paddy' Mayne.

Jack Mann, Second World War LRDG, SAS and SBS veteran, for reading the entire manuscript of this book and for giving me your perceptive and enlightening comments. I am hugely grateful, once again, for the insight and inspiration so provided. Alec Borrie, Second World War SAS veteran, for your insight into the SAS terms 'SABU' and its origins and what it signified during operations behind the lines in France. I am immensely grateful.

Gregory Lunt, whose father, John 'Jack' Frederick Lunt, was a wireless operator with 196 Squadron, flying Short Stirlings, for sharing some of your father's fascinating stories of the war with me.

Huge thanks to Simon Kinder, whose grandfather, Harry Kinder, was one of Major Barkworth's Secret Hunters, and who provided fascinating documents and photos regarding their work.

Terry Lowe, for corresponding with me on the fate of the Operation Gain disappeared and their remembrance today in the French villages where they operated. Mr Alan Lockey, for the correspondence and the details you provided on the wartime career of Major Ian Fenwick. Patrick Baty, for correspondence over Major Ian Fenwick and alerting me to his Bruton parish church burial plot. Alain Lavigne, for correspondence over Serge Vaculik's war record and the archives held on Vaculik at Minstère Des Armees, Mémoire des Hommes. James Harris, for your help and advice on explaining how exactly parachutists exited from a Short Stirling.

Dr Phil Judkins, for expert insight into all things Luftwaffe and Second World War, and in particular operations at the Étampes airbases. Mike Holmes, for permission to quote from Mediterranean Odyssey, the life story of his father, Mike Holmes,

MM, and for the meetings, chats and insight. Author Asher Pirt, for lengthy communications on all things Phantom, SAS and 'SABU'-related in particular: a font of knowledge and information as always. Julian Barnes, at Chicksands Military Intelligence Museum, for corresponding with me over this story.

The staff at various archives and museums also deserve special mention, including those at the British National Archives, the Imperial War Museum and the Churchill Archive Centre at Churchill College, Cambridge. Some files from the National Archives were made available to me as a result of Freedom of Information requests, and I am grateful to the individuals at the Archives who made the decision that those files should be opened.

My gratitude is also extended to my literary agent, Gordon Wise, of Curtis Brown, for helping bring this project to fruition, and to all at my fantastic publisher, Quercus, for same, including, but not limited to: Charlotte Fry, Hannah Robinson, Bethan Ferguson, Ben Brock, Fiona Murphy and Jon Butler. My editor, Richard Milner, deserves very special mention, as always. Many thanks also to Wendy McCurdy at my American publisher, Kensington, and to all of her team, and to George Lucas, the agent who represented this book in the USA, and to Luke Speed, my film agent at Curtis Brown.

I am also indebted to those authors who have previously written about some of the topics dealt with in this book and whose work has helped inform my writing; I have included a full bibliography.

I am also indebted to Marilyn de Langladure, retired commercial lawyer and sailor, a dedicated supporter of Diverse Abilities, a wonderful charity for children and adults with physical or learning disabilities and a founder member of the Dorset National Park Project.

Finally, of course, thanks are due also to Eva and the ever-patient David, Damien Jr and Sianna, for not resenting Dad spending too much of his time locked away . . . again . . . writing . . . again.

Bibliography

Note: this book contains public-sector information licensed under the Open Government License v3.0.

Archives, Museums, Research Organisations

The National Archives at Kew are a rich repository of documents underlying the stories depicted in these pages, including files related to the Special Operations Executive, the Army, Royal Navy and Royal Air Force, plus official War Office and Cabinet papers, records of the Chiefs of Staff meetings and Churchill's correspondence concerning same.

The National Army Museum's Special Forces Collection constitutes a rich resource of images, records and memorabilia from the war years, including from the operations depicted in these pages.

The Imperial War Museum (IWM) is also rich in records, including those held at the IWM's London site, namely unpublished records and reports from those who are depicted in these pages, and photographs and film footage related to the operations portrayed. At the IWM Duxford, the Airborne Assault Archive also contains key documents and images.

The Churchill Archives Centre at Churchill College, Cambridge, contains useful papers pertaining to Winston Churchill's role within the stories depicted in these pages.

Unpublished Sources

Bien-aimé Tonton Hyacinthe, Père Alexis Wiehe, English translation (unpublished), part of the Wiehe family collection.

A Personal Memoir Written by Captain Cecil Leyland Riding MC, 'D' Squadron, 1st SAS Regiment, part of the Dumfries Museum Captain Cecil Riding MC collection.

Report on the Commando Orders of 18.10.42 and 25.6.44 with Reference to Certain of the War Crimes Caused by Them, Major Barkworth, June 1948, part of the Barkworth family collection.

Fred Rhodes, handwritten notes on the war years, provided by Phil Rhodes, as part of the Fred Rhodes family collection.

National Archives, TS 26/855 SHAEF Court
National Archives, FO 950/4873 Mrs S. N. Twyman
National Archives, WO 218/192 Gain Reports
National Archives, WO 219/2389 July Reports
National Archives, WO 205/208 June–Aug 44 Reports
National Archives, WO 205/651 June Reports
National Archives, WO 311/7 Hitler KO
National Archives, WO 208/6856 Hughes Report
National Archives, WO 26/855 SHAEF Court
National Archives, WO 218/193 Key Reports
National Archives, HS 9/1406/8 Starr
National Archives, WO 235/560 Noailles Trial
National Archives, WO 311/76 Papers
National Archives, AIR 20/8937 Report SAS Operations
National Archives, WO 309/1405 Early Papers
National Archives, WO 208/4669 Pre-Trial Papers

National Archives, WO 208/3322/100–101 Vaculik/Jones Escape Reports
National Archives, WO 309/659 More Statements
National Archives, WO 309/660 Noailles Witnesses
National Archives, WO 218/212 2 SAS Missing Parachutists
National Archives, WO 311/724 SAS
National Archives, WO 311/78 Pre-Trial
National Archives, WO 373/86 Decorations
National Archives, KV-2-1500-1 Kopkow
National Archives, KV-2-1500-2 Kopkow
National Archives, KV-2-1501-1 Kopkow
National Archives, KV-2-1501-2 Kopkow
National Archives, KV-2-1501-3 Kopkow

Published Books

Lorna Almonds-Windmill, *Gentleman Jim*, Constable & Robinson, 2001

W. V. Brelsford (ed.), *The Story Of The Northern Rhodesia Regiment*, Government Printer Lusaka, 1954

Anthony Cotterell, *Apple for the Sergeant*, Hutchinson, 1944

Virginia Cowles, *The Phantom Major*, William Collins, 1958

Martin Dillon with the late Roy Bradford, *Rogue Warrior of the SAS*, John Murray, 1987

Ian Fenwick, *Enter Trubshaw*, Collins, 1944

Roger Ford, *Fire from the Forest*, Cassell, 2003

Helen Fry, *The London Cage*, Yale University Press, 2018

Jean Overton Fuller, *The Starr Affair*, Victor Gollancz, 1954

Charles Glass, *They Fought Alone*, 2018, Penguin Random House

Alex Kershaw, *Avenue of Spies*, Crown, 2015

Derrick Harrison, *These Men Are Dangerous*, Bladford Press, 1988

Sarah Helm, *A Life in Secrets*, Little, Brown, 2005

Alan Hoe, *David Stirling*, Sphere, 1994

Richard Holmes, MM, *Mediterranean Odyssey*, 2016

Anthony Kemp, *The Secret Hunters*, Michael O'Mara, 1986

Damien Lewis, *The Nazi Hunters*, Quercus, 2015

Damien Lewis, *Hunting the Nazi Bomb*, Quercus, 2016

Paul McCue, *SAS Operation Bulbasket*, Leo Cooper, 1996

Mike Morgan, *Daggers Drawn*, Sutton, 2000

Gavin Mortimer, *Stirling's Men*, Weidenfeld and Nicolson, 2004

Jeremy Murland, *Dunkirk 1940*, Pen & Sword, 2016

Christopher J. Murphy, *Security and Special Operations*, Palgrave
    Macmillan, 2006

E. C. W. Myers, *Greek Entanglement*, Rupert Hart-Davis, 1955

T. B. H. Otway, *Airborne Forces*, Imperial War Museum, 1990

John Randall and M. J. Trow, *The Last Gentleman Of The SAS*,
    Mainstream, 2014

Dean Reuter, Colm Lowery and Keith Chester, *The Hidden Nazi*,
    Regnery History, 2019

Hamish Ross, *Paddy Mayne*, Sutton, 2004

Streak Designs Ltd and Coretra Ltee, *Lieutenant John H. Wiehe
    [1916-1965]*, Streak Designs (Ed), 2016

Stephen Tyas, *SS-Major Horst Kopkow*, Fonthill Media, 2017

Nicola Tyrer, *Sisters in Arms*, Weidenfeld and Nicolson, 2008

Serge Vaculik, *Air Commando*, Jarrolds, 1954

Guy Walters, *Hunting Evil*, Bantam, 2009

A. P. Wavell, *Other Men's Flowers*, Jonathan Cape, 1944

Charles Whiting, *Death on a Distant Frontier*, Leo Cooper, 1996

Père Alexis Wiehe, *Bien-aimé Tonton Hyacinthe*, Éditions Du
    Lau, 2016

Dennis Williams, *Stirlings in Action with the Airborne Forces*, Pen & Sword, 2008

Ex-Lance-Corporal X QGM, *The SAS and LRDG Roll of Honour 1941–47*, SAS-LRDG-RoH, 2016

Index